Counseling Youth
Foucault, Power, and the Ethics of Subjectivity

Tina Besley

University of Illinois at Urbana-Champaign, USA

Foreword by

James Marshall

SENSE PUBLISHERS
ROTTERDAM / TAIPEI

A C.I.P. record for this book is available from the Library of Congress.

ISBN 90-77874-11-9

Published by: Sense Publishers,
P.O. Box 21858, 3001 AW
Rotterdam, The Netherlands
http://www.sensepublishers.com

Printed on acid-free paper

Counseling Youth

CONTENTS

CULTIVATING A CULTURE OF THE SELF

The appeal of Michel Foucault has not diminished over time. If anything, the power of his analyses, his elucidation of classical texts, the attraction of his style and the fruitfulness of his approaches have grown and further increased his stature as one of the most original thinkers of the post-war years. In part, this increased appeal is due to Foucault's growing influence across the disciplines, and even if in aspects of his work such as the history of sexuality, scholars have improved upon his scholarship and readings of the texts of Antiquity, Foucault remains the philosopher-historian who drew us to look closely and in particular ways at the social archaeology of practices of the self that inaugurates and constitutes what he called "the culture of the self" that characterizes the Western tradition.

When I wrote *Counseling Youth* I was in a sense overpowered by Foucault, by his stunning historical insights, by the peculiar angles he addressed that enabled us to see the familiar in a fresh light, and by the unequalled philosophical comprehensiveness of his approach. I was enthralled by the usefulness of his work and the ways in which it could throw counselling both as a discipline and as a practice into new light, exposing its power relations, its subjugated knowledges, and its contribution to shaping the moral constitution of youth in the postmodern world. Foucault, I thought, not only provided us with a story of therapeutic culture but he detailed in overlapping narratives the significance of relations between subjectivity and truth that have taken a myriad of complex forms in the present. He also helped to reinsert ethics into political and social theory and demonstrated the range of analysis that might rejuvenate the study of the self. Perhaps, even more than this, for counsellors and for educators, he pioneered a set of new concepts and approaches that have enabled us to question the new dogma that has grown up around the 'reflective practitioner'.

In this book I was concerned to bring the originality and power of Foucault's analysis to counsellors and to provide an introduction to Foucault based on an historical acquaintance with the self as an institution, as a set of practices, that is, as a culture. I was also concerned to use Foucault to understand what I called the "psychologizing of adolescence" and the "sociologizing of youth" as a preparation for talking about the moral constitution of youth, the ethics of school counseling, and the promise of narrative therapy. I still hold to these ideas and their progression in the overall structure of the book. The ideas seem to me to be not only still valid but the basis of an overall problematic that will only grow in importance.

"Youth" is the group of our society that is the most radical politically speaking; that supports the seemingly unsupportable causes; that is the most experimental in all phases of living; that, to utter the biblical truism, have the power to transform the future. At the same time they are also, along with "children" in general, the most expendable; the most harmed and mistreated of any group, systematically denied their rights, especially in the Third World but also at home. Counseling youth, therefore, has special responsibilities. Let me mention one in particular: let us not *speak* for youth. Part of the special responsibility of the counselor is to let youth speak for themselves. Indeed, to encourage it, to create opportunities for it to happen, to reward it and to guard this healing power of self-thought, self-expression, and self-narrative as part of the culture of the self.

Since writing this book now over five years ago more of the Foucault archive has come to light and I am particularly thinking of his lectures at the Collège de France, a course of twelve, two hour lectures a year that he gave as part of the responsibility of his Chair in the History of Systems of Thought. Beginning in 1970 Foucault gave these courses every year. The early ones are clearly recognizable in his published work: "La Volonté de savoir" (1970-71), "Théories et Institutions pénales" (1971-72), "La Société punitive" (1972-73), "Le Pouvoir psychiatrique" (1973-74), "Les Anormaux" (1974-75). The remaining eight courses focussed squarely on the problematic of the subject and the relation between subjectivity and truth: "It faut défender la société" (1975-76), "Securité, Territoire, Population" (1977-78), "Naissance de la biopolitique" (1978-79), "Du gouvernement des vivants" (1979-80), "Subjectivité et Vérité" (1980-81), "L'Herméneutique du subjet" (1981-82), "Le Gouvernement de soi et des autres" (1982-83), "Le Gouvernement de soi et des autres: le courage de la verite" (1983-84). Many of the courses have been published, (some as yet only in French) and a few remain to be edited and published. We are fortunate that the course described as *The Hermeneutics of the Subject* (1981-82) has been translated into English recently (see Foucault, 2005). Some of the themes addressed by this material will be already familiar to Foucault scholars particularly from the third volume of *Historie de la sexualitié*, *Le Souci de soi* (*The Care of the Self*). But as Foucault himself says in the very first lecture:

> I tried to get a historical reflection underway on the theme of the relations between subjectivity and truth. To study this problem I took as a privileged example .... the question of the regimen of sexual behaviour and pleasures in Antiquity. ...This year I would like to step back a bit from this precise example ...and extract from it the more general terms of the problem of "the subject and truth" (Foucault, 2005, p.2).

He goes on the expound the hermeneutics of the self, analysing its theoretical formulations and studying it in relation to a set of practices significant in classical and late Antiquity. Foucault uncovers and reconstructs "care of the self" both as a philosophical principle and a practice, and its connection with the better known theme of self-knowledge expressed in the Delphic invocation "know your self". "Care of the self" became for Socrates an entrusted mission to teach youth how to take care of themselves (rather than their possessions) and to take care of their city-state (as an aspect of their citizenship). It was, Foucault says, a mission that Socrates performed without payment and out of "pure benevolence". In this regard we cannot forget that Socrates at seventy years old, perhaps the most famous teacher of all teachers, stood before a jury of his fellow Athenians excused of "corrupting youth" (and of "refusing to recognize the State gods") and is condemned to death by being forced to drink hemlock. Socrates, the philosopher of the care of the self and the originator of a critical philosophy aimed at "the improvement of the soul", is put to death by a majority of fellow Athenians administered by the city fathers. As Foucault indicates Socrates berates his accusers by telling them that they have devoted too much care to increasing their wealth, reputation and honor and not enough to caring for themselves, for their reason, truth, and constant improvement. What becomes of a city or society where citizens no longer care for themselves--a spiritual and philosophical activity--or no longer are concerned to teach youth to care for themselves? This question is painfully relevant in age of renewed fundamentalisms where even those who hold positions of authority over youth do not theorize their own power, have given up on their traditional responsibilities and either abuse their position or simply indoctrinate.

Care of the self becomes a therapeutic pedagogy that performs a critical function enabling one to get rid of (*un*learn) bad habits and false opinions. It is a matter of instilling and developing courage so that the individual is equipped to struggle for themselves for the rest of their life. But most of all, as Foucault emphasizes in his Course Summary (p. 496) "this culture of the self has a curative and therapeutic function". He goes on:

> It is much closer to the medical model than to the pedagogical model. Of course, we should remember certain very ancients facts of Greek culture: the existence of a notion like pathos, which signifies the soul's passion as well as the body's illness; the extent of a metaphorical field that allows expressions like nursing, curing, amputating, scarifying, and purging to be applied to both the body and the soul. We should also remember the principle, familiar to the Epicureans, Cynics, and Stoics, that the role of philosophy is to cure diseases of the soul (Foucault, 2005. p. 496).

As Foucault also remarks the relation to the self, in Antiquity and after, relies on a relationship with a master, guide or mentor and that this relationship becomes increasingly independent of the love relationship. Care of the self increasingly becomes comprised of a set of practices and exercise designated by *askesis* (likened to the training of an athlete) and support by a multiplicity of social relations including schools, private counselors (especially in Rome), family, friendship and other kinds of relationships. In classical Greece, Foucault reminds us, one also sees the emergence of discourses concerning philosophical *askesis* that come to fruition at the intersection of relations between subjectivity and truth; that emanate in a series of techniques and method for getting to soul to turn on itself to discover its true nature. These techniques included the importance of different kinds of listening and writing, ways of taking stock of oneself and for memorizing what one has learned. This culture of the self then comprised a host of techniques that enabled systematic self-reflection and self-action that constitutes a true hermeneutics of the self.

It is to these practices of the self that counseling owes its existence and it is through the examination of this critical ethos that youth counselors today might discover something about themselves.

I would like to take this opportunity briefly to thank Peter de Liefde of Sense Publishing for undertaking the publication of a paperback version of this book, and to my husband, Michael Peters, for his constant encouragement and support.

REFERENCE

Foucault, M. (2005) *The Hermeneutics of the Subject: Lectures at the Collège de France 1981-1982*. Edited by Frederic Gros, translated by Graham Burchell. New York, Palgrave Macmillan.

Tina (A.C.) Besley
University of Illinois at Urbana-Champaign
September, 2005

FOREWORD

Tina Besley's *Counseling Youth: Foucault, Power, and the Ethics of Subjectivity,* developed from her Ph.D. thesis (2000) at the University of Auckland, is an important book and for two main reasons. First, it is an original application of a Foucauldian perspective to counseling and education in particular, and how the notion of "youth"—the client of school counseling—was constituted. Second, it discusses how counseling constituted itself as a profession, as a disciplinary body. Besley discusses these two themes through a number of interrelated subthemes or aims. First, she considers philosophically from a Foucauldian perspective, the notion of the self, or identity, as it is to be found in counseling theories and practice. Second, she writes a critical and Foucauldian-enhanced, history of counseling in New Zealand, though she does relate this to other international developments, especially in the United States. Third, she discusses recent moves in counseling toward narrative therapy, based as it is, in part, upon a reading of Foucault. This is a book, therefore, that is rich in ideas and critical themes and will be invaluable to counselors everywhere, and more generally those interested in Foucault and his critiques of the human sciences.

I will elaborate on these two main themes only. A Foucauldian perspective enables Besley to problematize if not challenge a number of school counseling practices by placing them within the notion of the "psy-sciences" (Nikolas Rose's term), and the practices of school counseling within educational institutions or disciplinary blocks, as Foucault called them. After an introductory chapter on Foucault, Besley looks at the self and the counseling of the self and problematizes the notion of youth in chapters 3 to 5 by examining psychological notions of adolescence and sociological and moral notions of the proper constitution of the self, if such moral panics as occurred in New Zealand, and internationally, in the 1950s are to be avoided. There are interesting case studies in chapter 5 of the mental hygiene films that were developed in the United States and on the "Mazengarb Report" (an outcome of an undoubted moral panic) in New Zealand.

Besley looks at the development of counseling in New Zealand in chapter 6. This is well documented and is an important and original critical history in its own right. Her particular concern is, however, how counseling professionalized itself as a disciplinary body and the roles it plays in governing youth. She continues the Foucauldian theme into the final main chapter, where she looks at narrative therapy, as initially developed in the work of Michael White and David Epston. Narrative theory is poststructuralist-inspired and challenges liberal humanist notions of the self that are embedded in the psy-sciences. Essentially, White and Epston challenge the assumptions of the psy-sciences that therapy is a neutral activity. Their position is that therapy is inherently a political activity, and that it is inscribed by power relations. According to Besley, narrative theory in school counseling holds a substantial promise for the practice of school counseling. This takes her full circle, as a very experienced school counselor, to the inherent theme of improving such practices.

This is a book, then, rich in ideas, and it will be rewarding reading for counselors, social scientists, and students of the social sciences, education, and counseling.

James Marshall
University of Auckland Glasgow, November 2001

ACKNOWLEDGEMENTS

My first debt is to my parents, Athlone and Malcolm Besley, who supported me unfailingly throughout various ventures and adventures in my lifetime.

This book is a much revised version of my Ph.D. thesis that began with my disappointment that most counseling literature focuses on skills and techniques. Much of this work is immensely valuable, but I was curious about the "big picture"—about young people, about why the "techne" of school counseling had emerged and where it was going.

I wish to acknowledge my Ph.D. supervisors, Professor James Marshall and Dr. Hans Everts from the School of Education, University of Auckland, for their support and encouragement. Their questions, comments, and combined expertise in different areas offered an important source of ideas and encouragement. James Marshall's scholarship on Foucault, philosophy, and education and his reading of draft chapters of this book has been invaluable. Hans Everts offered his detailed knowledge of school counseling in New Zealand and his expertise and skills in counseling. Both men helped me to clarify my thoughts and to explore certain themes concerning power and knowledge that radically called into question school counseling and my own practice.

This book was built on my further reading, especially of Foucault and of recent writings in narrative therapy. It has been completed in my first year as a postdoctoral fellow at the University of Glasgow, and in this respect I would like to thank Dr. Christine Forde, Head of Educational Studies, and Dr. Doret de Ruyter for their support. I also wish to thank the school counselors, principals, counselor educators, and those who have formerly held such positions, as well as members of the New Zealand Association of Counsellors (NZAC), who have freely given their time, friendship, assistance, advice, comments, information, and collegial support. My thanks go to Cliff Edmeades, Principal of Rutherford College, the Rutherford College Board of Trustees, and my counseling colleague, Sue Tai-Luamanuvae, for their support when I was completing my Ph.D. while working full-time as a school counselor and Head of the Guidance Department at Rutherford College, Te Atatu Peninsula, Auckland.

Lastly, I wish to acknowledge my husband, Michael Peters, Professor of Education at the University of Auckland and Research Professor at the University of Glasgow, for his wisdom, intellect, professionalism, encouragement, and sense of humor while I completed this book. He put up with my questions and with reviewing sections, and he offered advice that was invaluable. Without his support, I may have settled for an easier life.

MY IDENTITY AS A SCHOOL COUNCELOR: A PROFESSIONAL NARRATIVE

The introduction to this book opens with my own "insertion into the text" in a narrative account of my own changing personal identity, which in adulthood became closely tied to my profession as a school counselor. But that professional identity has been only one of several different professional identities in my checkered career and is, to a certain extent, an expression of multiple facets of my "self" and identity that has developed or been constructed over the years. My narrative, therefore, involves some of the themes of the book. In part, it is a form of "confession" (as discussed in chapter 1)—that is, a *self-reflexive turn*, which I think is important and necessary for all school counselors—a process of professional self-reflection on how one becomes constituted as a counselor. This helps us to understand the nature of our own biases and the influences and effects of *power-knowledge* and how we construct our world view. I adopt the first-person mode as a narrative that provides a personal link to this author-as-child, growing up and experiencing adolescence in the 1950s and 1960s—the social context of mental hygiene films and the period crucial for the setting up of guidance counseling in New Zealand secondary schools (as elaborated in chapter 5). The intent is to provide something of a *counterpoint* that interweaves the themes of the book, where the personal narrative is a view from the bottom up, while the notions of the late French philosopher, Michel Foucault, provide an overarching perspective from the top.

My personal narrative or journey toward becoming a professional counselor dealing with youth in New Zealand secondary schools has forced me to reflect on my "self" and identity at a number of critical points in my life, hence my focus on the wider issues of counseling, self, and identity in chapter 2. Issues of self-disclosure, "confession," subjectivity, power-knowledge, and truth-telling are central to counseling. A school counselor needs to be able to establish positive relationships with young people. Hence it became important for me to reflect upon my own family relationships and experiences of growing up in Christchurch, New Zealand, in the 1950s and 1960s. Unlike many of the young people I counseled, I was fortunate to grow up in a stable, nonviolent, two-parent family, where both parents worked. In an era when most women were homemakers, my mother worked not only because they needed the money, but also because both parents believed firmly in the notion of equality. Although I had a cousin eight years older than I who stayed with us a great deal and was like a big sister to me, I didn't have to deal with a “real” sibling until my sister (whom I treated as my baby) was born when I was six years old. So I grew up largely as an “only child,” and like most people, I experienced various difficulties in growing up. I can remember feeling somewhat lonely, different, and alienated from my peers. I vividly recall—and barely forgave—the painful experiences from the nasty little girls who ridiculed and bullied me and left me out of games and friendship groups at primary school. They picked on me because mum, who was an expert seamstress, made pretty dresses for me in the latest nylon fabric. School uniform was optional, and to avoid being picked on, I begged to wear it. But “catch-22” struck. Because I was “correctly” dressed in uniform, I was often asked to run messages, and so many of my classmates had further reason to tease me. It didn’t entirely cower me, and I learned to negotiate around those girls, to be pleasant and friendly when they were all right and to ignore or avoid them when they were at their worst. The “sticks and stones will break my bones, but names will never hurt me” maxim, which I thought was untrue, nevertheless came to the fore a few times. I learned to be tough (i.e., not cry), to hide my feelings, and to be strong in my sense of self, and that it was OK to be different, to be an individual and not just to follow the crowd.

From when I was two years old, mum worked at the ice rink, so it became my other “home,” and I became a national ice-skating champion. As a teenager I was seen as a bit of a “goodie goodie” and didn’t quite fit in. I was dismayed that the boys at the rink liked the faster, louder girls who wore lipstick and tighter and more fashionable clothes than I was allowed and that they wouldn’t skate with me because I was too good. They seemed to like the more helpless girls, and although I wasn’t going to play that game, once or twice I deliberately used hired skates instead of my own to pretend that I couldn’t skate very well. Although I tried to keep any sporting or academic success largely hidden, I began to learn the hidden curriculum about gender relations in terms of male egos and female success, the place of women, desirability and sexual bargaining, and the pain of being different and standing out from the crowd. This personal experience has shaped my work and understanding of youth and of the ways they negotiate their place and space in relationships and the world around them.

I attended a large newly established coeducational state high school of approximately 1,200 students, where I was shocked to be placed in the top class. My high school had no guidance counselor. There was one career advisor for the boys and another for the girls. My only contact with the career advisor was in my second-to-last year, when I was told that because I was in one of the top classes, I should go to the university and probably go into teaching. There was certainly no testing, nor discussion of career options. To be thus dismissed so readily provided an important lesson for me when I became a counselor. It made me keenly aware of a common assumption that needs challenging: that students in top classes don’t really need counselors, life skills, or guidance programs as much as other students do because they are smart enough to work things out for themselves. To a certain extent, such cursory treatment also reflects the attitude that it is “weak” to ask for help, that considerable stigma is still attached to asking for help for emotional problems or mental illness.

The impact of social changes of the 1960s and 1970s, a traumatic marriage break-up, and the onset of rheumatoid arthritis threw all my values and principles into question once again. I was forced to reconsider my own identity, to face up to why certain things were happening, who I was, where I was I going, and what I wanted to do (or become)— all questions about my self and my identity. I spent four years as a secondary-school teacher but became totally disillusioned with the way schools dealt with students in the early 1970s. I left teaching to see the world—the big OE (overseas experience) that so many New Zealanders feel compelled to undertake because of the tyranny of distance. New Zealand seemed so far away from where it was all "happening," and I desperately wanted to experience other places and cultures. I traveled the world when I worked for Air New Zealand for the next nine years, with over six as an international cabin attendant. Long night flights across the Pacific Ocean and our crew-drinks times (an unofficial debrief on arrival in a foreign location) all involved conversations where we "solved" the world's and people's relationship problems. On reflection it seems that there was as much learning about the self as there was learning about others. When Air New Zealand flight 901 crashed into Mount Erebus, Antarctica, in 1979, killing all 257 people on board, I was very affected. I had crewed on the previous week's Antarctic flight and knew all of the crew who perished, including my cousin's husband. The night after the crash I had to leave on a week-long trip—one of the hardest ever. We had to maintain an air of professional calm and dignity, reassuring passengers, welcoming them and smiling at them amidst our enormous sorrow. It took almost a week to cry, the shock had been so great, the questions so wanting, the "what ifs" when I, like other staff, had been so proud of our national airline, its safety and service. This was first-hand learning about trauma, loss, and grief, something that as a school counselor one deals with all too frequently. I learned how to put on a calm professional face and subsume my own feelings in serving the needs and fears of others, something that I would need as a counselor helping others through crises such as the suicide of students.

It took quite some time to establish my professional identity as a school counselor. In 1985 there was a suicidal crisis for a member of my extended family. A call-out was made to LifeLine (a voluntary counseling agency). The LifeLine crisis team showed that with support and counseling it was possible to have some breathing space so the crisis could pass and for life to continue, even if relationships and businesses failed. I was so grateful that my loved ones had been spared that I became a volunteer telephone counselor with LifeLine, Auckland, which used a person-centered counseling approach. This foray into counseling challenged and changed me personally, emotionally and intellectually. After a couple of years I left the business world and returned to secondary teaching and to my home city of Christchurch, where I joined the local branch of LifeLine and was trained in transactional analysis and Jungian approaches.

Although I loved teaching geography, social studies, and English, I knew that I didn't want to be a classroom teacher. I much preferred to deal with students individually and in small groups and always put them into groups in class. As a result, I decided to become a school counselor, and in 1988 I started a Master of Education course in counseling at Canterbury University, Christchurch, New Zealand. This demanded another reexamination of "self" in T-group activities as part of the counseling course. I was rather shocked by this experience; I had never thought of myself as others in the group described me—Joan of Arc was going a bit too far—I'm certainly no sort of martyr! However, their perceptions and feedback brought me up short and made me a lot more self-reflective. The experience taught me to acknowledge my fears and not to be so closed off and self-contained. The person who suggested the U2 song, "I still don't know what I'm looking for," as a personal description was probably closest to the mark. I had come to understand that that the self changes constantly and is shaped sometimes by deliberate work and sometimes unintentionally through a time of crisis.

The university counseling course emphasized brief solution-oriented therapy and so added to the Rogerian, transactional analysis, and Jungian approaches from my LifeLine training. In 1989 I attended a brief course in psychodrama, and I had my first brush with narrative therapy when I attended an evening course over six weeks at the Durham Centre, Christchurch, run by people who had been trained by Michael White at the Dulwich Centre in Adelaide. This was my introduction not only to Michael White and David Epston's narrative therapy (as discussed in chapter 7), but also to Foucault and to his concepts of the Panoptican and power-knowledge (see chapter 1). All these courses contributed to the development of my professional identity as a counselor at school and in the community, and ultimately to the transformation of my personal identity.

While attending university counselor education I was employed for four years as a guidance teacher—a position that consisted of 50 percent teaching and 50 percent counseling—which involved considerable role difficulties. When I shifted to Auckland in 1992, I became a full-time guidance counselor, and in 1993 I was appointed as head of the Guidance Department at Rutherford College, a coeducational, multiethnic high school with over 1,100 students. There I was in charge of two guidance teachers who counseled part-time. I held this position until mid-2000, when, following the completion of my Ph.D., I was appointed as a Research Fellow in the Faculty of Education at the University of Glasgow, Scotland.

The job description for a school guidance counselor is usually very extensive (see Besley, 2000), so to make it more manageable and to use our specialist counseling education, counselors at our school work primarily in personal counseling for students. Educational guidance and advice on option choices are assigned to deans at each year level. The transition department provides career advice and health education, which now includes many guidance programs in the new, compulsory Health and Physical Education Curriculum (Ministry of

Education, 1999b). Counseling has a largely hidden role in schools due to its private and confidential nature. I really don't know how students would even think of approaching a counselor they didn't vaguely know or had seen around the school. So, to become visible and known by the students and staff, I would frequently talk at assemblies, visit form times, do grounds duty, become involved in extracurricular activities, and sometimes teach health education (especially on sensitive topics like sexuality, abuse, and mental health). The strategy seems to have worked, because almost all of our work was from self-referrals.

I don't think a school counselor's job finishes at the school gates. I continued my personal commitment to our young people and to social justice beyond the school by involvement on several different committees in the local West Auckland (Waitakere) community, including the steering and then management committee for "at-risk" teenagers, truancy, and "Strengthening Families." I also believe that this forms an important part of the professional role of a school counselor in today's world. Committee work did not stop there. I joined the New Zealand Association of Counsellors (NZAC) in 1990 and became actively involved in the Auckland branch of the committee, as secretary, coordinating the local school counselor network. I was also on the nationwide membership committee. My personal experiences and the knowledge gained through my involvement in NZAC not only helped to constitute my professional identity, but also contributed to my understanding of ethical practice, counselor effectiveness, accountability and professionalization. This experience underlies the discussion in chapter 6.

I undertook a Ph.D. thesis in my late forties. This certainly involved my professional interests, but it was also very much to do with my "self" and my "identity." I wanted to prove to myself that I had the ability to achieve the highest academic qualification possible, so this was done not as a specific career move, but mostly for personal satisfaction. It was an interaction of personal and professional identity, self, and subjectivities. It was from that thesis that this book has emerged. This "petit" narrative of my development as a school counselor may have finished with my move into academia, but as I now proceed to outline, this book involves different narratives throughout and deliberately starts and ends with "narrative."

OUTLINE OF THE BOOK

This book provides a set of historical narratives in the form of a "critical history" that reveals the layers that help to constitute the subject and shape identity, to look at what constitutes adolescence/youth and the conditions that have established the nature, limits, and realities of the school counseling profession. The story traces changes that have occurred over time, not in a linear fashion, but more in a Foucauldian manner, as elucidated in chapter 1. This book provides a critical account of school counseling through a Foucauldian-inspired investigation of the twin notions of "identity" and the "self," as these concepts apply to adolescence and youth—the subjects/clients of school counseling, on the one hand—and the counselor and his/her professional identity, on the other. The book is not an attack on counseling but a critique that serves to do what we expect our clients to do—to be self-reflective about our "self," our relationships, our profession, and our practices. If we expect this of clients, then the very least that we can do is to apply it to ourselves as professionals and to our profession.

In the broadest terms, the book is a critical history of the human sciences and their constitution of the subject of school counseling: adolescence and youth. I see this work as necessary for developing a more self-reflexive form of counseling, aware of its own power/knowledge and the ways in which the human sciences, despite their sincere intent of helping and liberating, often inadvertently end by imposing one form of domination for another. A critical history "enables us to think against the present, in the sense of exploring its horizons and its conditions of possibility. Its aim is not to predetermine judgement, but to make judgement possible" (Rose, 1998: 18). It enables me to problematize what is thinkable, to contest assumptions, to examine, challenge, and disturb the status quo, revealing "the fragility of that which seems solid, the contingency of that which seems necessary, the mundane and quotidian roots of that which claims lofty nobility and disinterest" (Rose, 1998: 18). Without critical reflection and attention to power relations, school counseling could easily become smug, self-serving, and inward-looking, ultimately bypassing or suppressing the interests of clients. I have used a variety of different forms of analysis, including philosophical critique, critical history, a chronicle of events, the analysis of policies and processes, and forms of textual and narrative analysis. Therefore notions about youth and forms of professionalization and ethical self-regulation are scrutinized in the book. Foucault's notions underpin the whole volume. Some of the more general notions—confession, problematizing, archaeology, genealogy, power, power-knowledge, Panoptican, gaze, and governmentality—are outlined in chapter 1. Others, such as technologies of domination and of the self, political rationality and morality, subjectivity, power, and ethics, are discussed within particular chapters.

In chapter 2, I discuss the relations between the concepts of "self" and "identity" in relation to counseling, and I provide a Foucauldian analysis of the self. Rather than any specific notion of identity or the self, I focus on a shift in meaning from the notion of self to the notion of identity in contemporary discourse. "Identity" enables me to talk in general terms about the identity of the profession of school counseling and of the identity of its clientele—"adolescence" or "youth," as it has been variously defined. Moreover, identity is a complex notion with various formulations and is one of the guiding and most important concepts for contemporary accounts of counseling. It has been closely and intimately connected with the notion of "self" and of related notions of self-knowledge, self-direction, and self-development, including traditional liberal and humanist ideas of autonomy and responsibility for the self. Therefore, the notion of identity is caught up in the changing history of Western philosophy concerning the self and of what it means to be a human being. Our modern Western sense of identity, in turn, shapes our philosophy, our language, and our relationships, often in ways that are not readily apparent. Under the influence of postmodernism, Western understandings of identity and self have shifted from metaphysical (or philosophical) views that seek to identify logically the self—attempts of self-definition (and possibly self-assertion)—as an essence or form, to notions of identity that are contingent or that rest upon descriptive criteria springing from a specific culture or an age. Foucault's work and that of a number of theorists who have developed his work, especially in relation to the critique of humanism and the autonomous, rational subject that is at the center of liberal education, is discussed.

Humanism is a general world view that positions mankind in terms of the underlying philosophical assumptions about what constitutes human nature, human inquiry, and the relationships of human beings to the natural world. Rather than being dependent on divine order on the one hand or simply part of the natural order on the other, under humanism, mankind is seen to have unique capacities and abilities that lead to studies of the individual in all forms and under all conditions. Humanism developed during the Renaissance and under Enlightenment thinkers and continues to dominate as the West's commonsense world view. Values often associated with liberal humanism include freedom, equality, tolerance, secularism, social and political reform, progress, pragmatism, scientism, and the perfectibility of human nature (see Audi, 1995).

Foucault's project concerned the mode by which human beings become subjects, and he indicated the ways in which this process takes place. He was, above all, concerned to *historicize questions of ontology*, treating the self as a contingent historical construction rather than an unchanging eternal essence or human nature, fixed once and for all. Foucault thought that self is a contingent matter shaped differently in different historical periods. Selves are "constructions" in this sense. My reading of the self and identity is based upon insights from Foucault's "care for the self," "technologies of the self," and the "ethics of self-formation." I also raise some criticisms against him. Notions of critical method, critical history or historical narratives, and narratology (i.e., structuralist approaches to narrative) are closely related to Foucault's *genealogy*, a form of critical history that he bases on Nietzsche.

In chapters 3 and 4, Foucault provides the inspiration for me to provide a *genealogy* of *how* the discourses of the human sciences of both psychology and sociology conceptualize and, respectively, "psychologize" adolescence and "sociologize" youth. Foucauldian approaches collapse the old binaries and provide "a new construct for comprehending the stubbornly different levels of explanation usually known as the "sociological" and the "psychological," and with a clue to . . . the secret of its operation" (Henriques et al., 1984: 52, cited in Middleton, 1998: 120). Following this line of thinking, I draw explicitly upon the work of the Foucauldian theorist Nikolas Rose. These critical genealogies then permit me, following Foucault, to critique the notions of the *humanistic subject* that underlie humanistic counseling, the *biomedical-genetic* model of the subject, and the *psychiatric* subject, based on drives and the repression of those drives.

Chapter 5, entitled "The Moral Constitution of Adolescence/Youth," while not explicitly adopting a Foucauldian form of analysis, is inspired by him. It investigates how youth were morally constituted in the historical context when youth culture began to emerge—the time that saw the birth of guidance counseling in the U.S., British, and New Zealand secondary schools. This chapter aims to expose the power-knowledge constitution of adolescents and youth, especially through the historical study of notions of "mental hygiene" and the moral panics in 1950s New Zealand, with particular reference to a case study of the Mazengarb Report. The report sets out the dominant historical view (discourse/ narrative/story) of youth and its moral constitution, indicating the prevailing attitudes of adolescence as being a dangerous time. This was implicitly theorized at the time by reference to the moral category of "delinquency" and to sexual practices defined and influenced by the Church and focused particularly on female sexuality. The Mazengarb Report displayed the power relations involved in the control of the sexuality of adolescent behavior by the state and other national organizations, including, most noticeably, representatives of various religious denominations.

The next two chapters concern the other half of the counseling relationship—the counselor. Here I provide not only a history of the present but also a critical lens that focuses on ways of using Foucault's work on *governmentality* in relation to the professionalization and ethical self-regulation of counseling in chapter 6 and a new form of counseling— narrative therapy—in chapter 7.

While it might be argued that there is no singular or one "identity" of school counseling but, rather, multiple identities, reflecting different approaches and different organizations, there have been historical transformations to school counseling bought about by deliberate policy changes. Neoliberal policies set out new demands for professional accountability and performance management that spring from the new managerialism. Partly in response to these, there has been an increased emphasis on the professionalization and accountability of counseling, interpreted in detailed ways by professional associations—for example, changes in membership criteria and in ethical practice that are at the heart of counselor professionalization. Chapter 6 picks up the Foucauldian theme of governmentality as a means of critically examining the professional counseling organization. The hegemony of the conservative and technocratic neoliberal environment, despite being powerful, has not been entirely crushing or monolithic, for, as Foucault points out, where there is power, there are the possibilities for resistance, struggle, alternatives, opposition, and creative ways of dealing with power relations (Foucault, 1977, 1980a,b, 1982).

The notion of "narrative" forms an underlying subtext and a major organizing concept throughout the book, not just in specific terms as a beginning and end that includes a number of elements. First, a personal or self-narrative of my own constitution as a counselor starts the book and also colors the other chapters. Second, there are narratives of self and identity. Narrative is linked to the concept of identity, for it is through the imposition of meaning on our individual life histories that we constitute and shape our own multiple identities. Third, there are narratives of how the human sciences—psychology and sociology— have constituted young people: the social subjects, differently defined as "adolescents" and "youth," who are the subjects of school counseling. Fourth, there is a historical narrative in relation to notions of the development of the personal and professional ethics of the school counselor. Finally, there is a study of narrative therapy with its Foucauldian basis as applied in school counseling and in general in schools.

The analysis of the concept of narrative reveals that it is an activity based on hindsight through which we construct and give meaning to the past. Historical narratives provide us with ways of structuring the past, a means by which we the *emplot* facts and events that form a chronicle in order to tell a story. One might argue that there is a reciprocal relation between narrative and facts in the sense that the "facts" constrain the historical narrative in some sense insofar as it purports to be a "truthful" story, but the narrative, once established in outline, also helps us to select the facts we consider relevant. Language affects not only how we frame our notions of the "self" and "identity," but also how counselors deal with a client and their sense of meaning of the world in which they live.

Chapter 7, the last chapter of the book, outlines narrative therapy, a poststructuralist counseling modality that developed in Australasia in 1989. The chapter investigates Foucault in relation to the turn to narrative therapy, the philosophical foundations of narrative therapy, its critique of humanistic psychology, and the application of narrative therapy in school counseling in New Zealand. By highlighting a new counseling modality of the 1990s, this chapter links both backward and forward: back to chapter 2, with its overview of humanist–existential psychology and counseling theories, and forward to the future. So the book involves different narratives throughout and deliberately starts and ends with narrative.

CHAPTER 1

AN INTRODUCTION TO FOUCAULDIAN ANALYSIS

WHY USE FOUCAULT?

The first question that needs to be addressed in this book is: why use Foucault?

There are two reasons: one is personal, the other is academic, because Foucault sets up a framework of critique that enables me to challenge some taken-for-granted practices in school counseling, in how we see or think of the young people who are the clients of school counseling, and in how we are constituted as school counseling professionals. The personal reason is, of course, linked with professional and academic ones. As I point out in the Introduction, the first course in narrative therapy that I attended was in 1989. It provided my first contact with the name of Michel Foucault and a brief introduction to Foucault's use of the Panoptican and his understanding of power-knowledge. In time and with undertaking further study, my reading and understanding of Foucault was to expand considerably. Part of the difficulty was because, as Smart (1985: 18) points out, Foucault's work "is not easily assimilated into the concepts and fields of inquiry defined and delimited by the human sciences" and certainly not in areas with which I was familiar. The first of his books that I read was *Discipline and Punish* (Foucault, 1977). For some time, I found it easier to gain an overview of what Foucault was talking about by reading the work of some commentators on him and his interviews before returning to his texts and back again (see Foucault, 1989a,b,c,d,e,f; Nilson, 1998; Smart, 1985). Many of my fellow counselors have admitted to me that they, too, have found it hard to read Foucault; therefore, I thought that I would try to help people who are not familiar with his ideas by providing my own brief overview: hence this introductory chapter.

This book is not simply a citation that uses Foucauldian terms without explanation. It is not an explication or analysis of Foucault's philosophy, writings, or methodologies, nor an adaptation that applies his ideas to topics not investigated by him (Stone, 2001). Rather, it is a conceptualization, "a transfer of central ideas from Foucault separate from his historical methodologies to new arenas" (Stone, 2001: 2). It uses some of Foucault's ideas in relation to the history and formation of school counseling, counselors, and youth as their subjects, particularly as they pertain to notions of "self," "identity," and "subjectivity."

Michel Foucault was born in Poitiers, France, in 1926, into a petit-bourgeois family; he died from an AIDS-related illness in 1984. During his short lifetime Foucault's work became an emblem for his generation of postwar intellectuals for his creative, controversial, and original thinking on philosophical–historical–social ideas. Yet he did not propose any grand, global, utopian, or systematic solution to societal ills. His critique, however, opens up possibilities for us to sort out how we might see, understand, and in turn negotiate our subjectivity and the power relations in our world. He passed the entrance exam for the Sorbonne and attended the prestigious École Normale Supérieure, where he studied philosophy, taking his *licence de philosophie* in 1948. He changed direction, abandoning formal philosophical studies in favor of psychology, obtaining his *licence de psychologie* in 1951 and a diploma in psychopathology in 1952. During the 1950s he worked in a psychiatric hospital and overseas in French departments in Swedish, Polish, and German universities. Foucault decided to obtain a tenured position in a French university, but he required a doctorate. To obtain a doctorate at the Sorbonne required a principal thesis and a complementary thesis, as well as a report from an academic patron who also sat on his thesis jury, following which the thesis had to be published. For his doctorate, Foucault's complementary thesis was a translation of and introduction to Kant's (1798) *Anthropologie in pragmatischer Hinsicht* [*Anthropology from a Pragmatic Point of View*]; his studies on a history of madness, *Folie et déraison: Histoire de la folie à l'âge classique* [translated as *Madness and Civilization: A History of Insanity in the Age of Reason*, 1965] formed his major thesis (Macey, 1993). Foucault's doctorate was finally achieved in 1961. His first chair was in 1964 as professor of philosophy at the University of Clemont-Ferrand. Then he moved to the University of Vincennes and in 1970 to the prestigious Collège de France, where he chose the title "Professor of the History of Systems of Thought" to make it clear that his work differed from the history of ideas, philosophy, or social history (Marshall, 1996; Smart, 1985). This potted biography is presented because Foucault states: "In a sense, I have always wanted my books to be fragments from an autobiography. My books have always been my personal problems with madness, with prisons, with sexuality," and "each of my works is a part of my own biography" (Foucault, 1981, cited in Macey, 1993: xii). In other words, the personal and the philosophical ideas of Foucault are inextricably entwined.

Little of Foucault's work was written explicitly about education or schools and none about school counseling, and he certainly does not offer "solutions" for issues in education or for school counseling. But, Foucault provides a devastating critique of the subtle and complex power relations that pervade educational institutions, which shape our identity, and which make us governable by masking the reality that our identities are being constituted. What he does provide is an alternative approach to social institutions and their accompanying practices which are themselves informed by the social sciences. (Marshall, 1996: 216)

By suggesting that the real "political" task facing our society is to criticize the working of institutions, especially those institutions that appear to be both neutral and independent, Foucault (1984a) highlights ways in which one can question the discourse of disciplines and institutions and their practices. It is this remark that helps to set the tone for this book. But, as is so often the case with Foucault, what makes him hard for many people to follow at first is his assigning wider and somewhat different meanings to familiar words. He did not provide definitive concepts but presented his notions both in texts and in interviews, which were often used to clarify ideas he had already presented in his texts (Nilson, 1998). When speaking of the "political," Foucault meant "political" not in the sense of party politics, but in the vastly wider sense of power relations—a notion that at one point in his development meant "power-knowledge" and pointed to the twin set of relations between government and self-government on the one hand, and government and the development of certain kinds of expert knowledge that permitted "government at a distance" through expert systems on the other.

This chapter introduces the Foucauldian notions that inform the various themes and analyses of this book: confession, problematizing of the present, archaeology, genealogy, power and power-knowledge, the Panoptican and the gaze, and governmentality. Other Foucauldian notions, such as his ideas on political rationality, morality, subjectivity, and ethics, are interwoven within sections of relevant chapters of the book (chapters 5 and 6). All of these have applications in understanding and analyzing youth and school counseling. Finally, chapter 7 points out how his ideas and poststructuralist challenge have been brought into the world of counseling via narrative therapy and can critique the dominance of structuralism/humanism that has pervaded counseling theories and practices.

Foucault's ideas and work changed direction and emphasis during his lifetime, and his work does "not appear to fit into recognizable categories and does not employ reputable or even recognizable methodologies" (Marshall, 1996: 4). As a result many academics—historians, philosophers, and Marxists—find his work problematic and challenging. To a large extent, Foucault resists being pigeonholed into a particular academic discipline and being categorized and labeled. As Foucault himself says:

> I think I have been situated in most of the squares on the political checkerboard, one after another and sometime simultaneously: as anarchist, leftist, ostentatious or disguised Marxist, nihilist, explicit or secret anti-Marxist, technocrat in the service of Gaullism, new liberal etc. . . . None of these descriptions is important by itself; taken together, on the other hand, they mean something. And I must admit that I rather like what they mean. (Foucault, 1984a: 383–389)

Despite his rejection of the notion of "general intellectual" (in favor of the "specific intellectual") and of familiar political or disciplinary classifications, Foucault is generally considered to be a philosopher and social historian. Yet he did not write only for an academic audience; he also gave many interviews (Foucault, 1989a,b,c,d,e,f; Marshall, 1996; Smart, 1985). He was influenced by broad range of thinkers, most importantly philosophers in the German tradition, including the three "masters of suspicion"—Nietzsche, Marx, and Freud—together with Kant and Heidegger: Kant, to whom he returned at the end of his life, and Heidegger, who provided an important critique of humanism and phenomenology.

In the French tradition he was influenced by philosophers who were his teachers, including Althusser, Bachelard, Canguilhem, and Cavaillès on the philosophy and history of science. Hyppolite, Koyré, and Kojève provided readings on Hegel that formed an important aspect of Foucault's philosophical background. In addition, he was strongly influenced, perhaps negatively, by French thinkers in the phenomenological and existentialist traditions, including Bergson, Sartre, Merleau-Ponty, and de Beauvoir, especially on the temporality and finitude of existence of the subject and also the notion of embodied consciousness, although Foucault reacted strongly against the phenomenological subject. It should not be forgotten that Foucault also had important links with members of the avant-garde, including Bataille, who had links with surrealism and other art movements, and Blanchot. One can trace also, especially in the writing of history, the influence of Braudel and the Annales School, along with Veyne and Hadot. Finally, we cannot ignore the influence on Foucault of his contemporaries, above all Deleuze, but also Derrida, Serres, Lacan, Dumezil, and many others (Marshall, 1996; Olssen, 1999; Peters, 1996; Smart, 1985).

Foucault acknowledges Nietzsche's influence on his work in several interviews and in his essay "Nietzsche, Genealogy, History" (1984c). But it was through the writings of Heidegger rather than of Nietzsche himself that he approached the latter, and Heidegger influenced his philosophical development (Olssen, 1999). The combination of Nietzsche's and Heidegger's thoughts helped Foucault to shape his work as a history by which human beings become subjects and to change from his early emphasis on the political subjugation of "docile bodies" to his later emphasis on individuals as self-determining beings who are continually in the process of constituting themselves as ethical subjects. He clarifies his aims thus:

> My objective . . . has been to create a history of the different modes by which, in our culture, human beings are made subjects. My work has dealt with three modes of objectification which transform human beings into subjects. . . . The first is the modes of inquiry which try to give themselves the status of the sciences. . . . In the second part of my work, I have studied the objectivizing of the subject in what I shall call "dividing practices." . . . Finally, I have sought to study—it is my current work—the way a human being turns him- or herself into a subject. For example, I have chosen the domain of sexuality. . . . Thus it is not power, but the subject, that is the general theme of my research.
>
> It is true that I became quite involved with the question of power. It soon appeared to me that, while the human subject is placed in relations of production and of signification, he is equally placed in power relations that are very complex. (Foucault, 1982: 209)

However, apart from talking in interviews and in making general references to the people who influenced him within his writings, he almost invariably avoids following traditional academic citation and referencing practices. While some commentators are highly critical of this practice, it has the effect of freeing

Foucault up to range far and wide in his writings.

Various writers have divided up Foucault's work into different parts. Dreyfus and Rabinow (1982) point to four chronological stages: one influenced by Heidegger (e.g., *Madness and Civilization*), then an archaeological stage where Foucault flirts with structuralism (e.g., *The Archaeology of Knowledge* and *The Order of Things*), but, finding the archaeological notion to be limited, he moves to a Nietzschean-influenced genealogical stage (e.g., *Discipline and Punish*), and finally to ethical self-constitution and governmentality (e.g., *History of Sexuality,* Vols. II, III).

In his early work, Foucault displayed his professional interest in psychology and psychopathology in his writing about madness and psychiatry. Foucault's doctorate became the basis for *Madness and Civilization: A History of Insanity in the Age of Reaso*n (1965). Foucault used approaches to phenomenology and existential psychiatry in this early work and an introduction entitled "Dream, Imagination and Existence" to the work of the Heideggerian psychotherapist, Ludwig Binswanger. In studying madness, Foucault maps the way the mad were not confined in any institution before 1600 but were wanderers; they became excluded persons by the middle of the seventeenth century, the position previously occupied by lepers. Prior to the eighteenth century madness was a legal issue, not a medical one. The figure of madness changes between the Renaissance and the seventeenth and eighteenth centuries (the *epistème* that Foucault calls the Classical Age), to become silent and to exist in antisocial figures (e.g., the debauched, dissipated, libertine, or the homosexual, or the magician). Strategies then change, from the beginning of the seventeenth century, with these people being confined in hospitals, workhouses, and prisons (the *Hôpital Général* was formed in 1656). The sorts of "dividing practices"—separating the normal and the pathological—foreshadowed themes that Foucault pursued in *The Birth of the Clinic: An Archaeology of Medical Perception* (1973).

Until the nineteenth century, madness was a juridical matter rather than a medical matter, and the mad or insane were not judged to be ill. Therefore, Foucault argues that there is no basis for researching the antecedents of the treatment of the mentally ill in the either the history of psychiatry or the history of medicine. Historical discontinuities are revealed in how madness has been thought of at different times. In the Renaissance, madness emerged as a theme in literature and iconography because the mad person was seen as a source of truth, wisdom, and criticism of the existing political situation. Madness has its own form of reason was seen as a general characteristic of human beings where it was possible to hold both unreasonable reason and reasonable unreason. In the seventeenth and eighteenth centuries the madness was reduced to "unreason," something shameful and to be hidden, and so it became silenced. *Folie* in French encompasses both the English "folly" and "madness," to include both criminal and insane behavior or "unreason." In the nineteenth century there was no great medical discovery that caused the alignment of psychiatry and asylums. Rather, a greater concern for individual rights had arisen in the wake of the French Revolution, and redefining madness as mental illness meant that medicine and psychiatry gradually moved into the asylum to treat the mentally ill. The asylum emerged in the eighteenth century as a specific site or institution for dealing with madness and became transformed into a space of therapeutic practices rather than a solely punitive institution. Medical knowledge and power replaced juridical power, so that madness became medicalized in the nineteenth and twentieth centuries. Therefore, for Foucault, discontinuity between eras, or *epistèmes*, predominates in the history of madness.

Schools appear only indirectly in Foucault's work, being used to illustrate the notions of power-knowledge, techniques of domination, and disciplinary blocks and practices in his work on prisons in *Discipline and Punish* (1977). He comments more explicitly about schools in some of his interviews (e.g., Foucault, 1980a). Marshall (1996) suggests that because Foucault's critique of education was very limited and largely indirect, it needs to be constructed from what is implicit in his work. The critique that this book develops regarding education and school counseling involves the assumed neutrality of these institutions—institutions that seem unaware of their power-knowledge relationships.

Foucault's ideas and forms of analysis have inspired a significant body of work by many subsequent writers. Marshall (1996) and Peters and Marshall (1996) use his notions to examine the neoliberal environment's impact on education, as is discussed in chapter 5. In relation to psychology, counseling, and schools, Valerie Walkerdine's (1984, 1986) and Nikolas Rose's work are important for this book, because both have been inspired by the work of Michel Foucault and are particularly challenging of accepted notions (see chapter 2). Walkerdine uses Foucault as "archaeologist" to analyze ways in which Piagetian developmental psychological discourse has produced particular sets of parameters that have normalized the subject of the developing child as the object of scientific investigation. She argues that despite being inserted into a child-centered pedagogy, Piagetian notions have not had any liberating effect because they have prevented other objects from being the focus of scientific investigations. Piaget prevented alternative formulations of the individual from being made and created instead a hegemonic discourse. The object of the gaze has been on the "developing child," on how it "acquires" or "develops" certain traits. This has set up a circularity of argument where the structure sets up stages that are then represented as truth (Walkerdine, 1984, 1986).

Nikolas Rose (1989, 1998) provides a critical history of the relationship between psychology, what he called the "psy" sciences, and notions of the self and society. Counseling, evolving out of various strands of psychology, in his view would be considered a "psy" science. How the "psy" sciences of the twentieth century have conceived of and positioned youth displays complex notions of self, the other and issues of governance (chapter 2). Rose said that he used Foucault's work because his writings are attempts to explore the "games of truth and error through which being is historically constituted as experience; that is as something that can and must be thought" (Foucault, 1985: 6–7). By experience here, Foucault does not refer to something primordial that precedes thought, but to "the correlation between fields of knowledge, types of normativity, and forms of subjectivity in a particular culture" (p. 3), and it is in something like this sense that I use the term in this book. I explore aspects of regimes of knowledge through which human beings have come to recognize themselves as certain kinds of creature, the strategies of regulation and tactics of action to which these regimes of knowledge have been connected, and the correlative relations that human beings have established with themselves, in taking themselves as subjects. In doing so, I hope to contribute to the type of work that Foucault described as an analysis of "the problematizations through which being offers itself to be, necessarily, thought-and the practices on the basis of which these problematizations are formed." (Rose, 1998: 11, citing Foucault, 1985: 11)

From this perspective the history of the "psy" disciplines is "intrinsically linked to the history of government." This is not "politics," but the Foucauldian sense of government, which "is part of the history of the ways in which human beings have regulated others and have regulated themselves in the light of certain games of truth. But on the other hand, this regulatory role of psy is linked, I suggest, to questions of the organization and reorganization of political power that have been quite central to shaping our contemporary experience" (Rose, 1998: 11).

CONFESSION

Foucault criticizes psychoanalysis as "the aggravated Christian compulsion to confess" (Nilson, 1998: 7), in turn supporting Thomas Szasz's claims in *The Manufacture of Madness* (1973) that the therapeutic state has replaced the theological state (Foucault, 1989e). From such a viewpoint, the psychotherapist or counselor could be considered akin to the priest in a secular society. Certainly, in the use of listening techniques and in the uncovering of self, there is an element of similarity, but there is considerable difference in the elements of advice, admonition, and punishment that are involved in the religious forms of confession that are certainly no part of counseling.

Contemporary notions of "confession" are derived not simply from the influence of the Catholic Church and its use of strategies for confessing one's sins, but from ancient, pre-Christian philosophical notions. While "confession" means "acknowledging," it involves a declaration and disclosure, acknowledgment, or admission of a crime, fault, or weakness. The acknowledgment is partly about making oneself known by disclosing the private feelings or opinions that form part of one's identity. In its religious form, confession involves the verbal acknowledgment of one's sins to another. One is duty-bound to perform this confession as repentance in the hope of absolution.

In the literary sense, confession also contains elements of identifying the self in a deliberate self-conscious attempt to explain and express oneself to an audience within which the individual exists and seeks confirmation. Confession, then, is both a communicative and an expressive act, a narrative in which we (re)create ourselves by creating our own narrative, reworking the past, in public, or at least in dialogue with another. Foucault in *The Use of Pleasure* (1985: 29) talks of technologies of the self as "models proposed for setting up and developing relationships with the self, for self-reflection, self-knowledge, self-examination, for deciphering the self by oneself, for the transformation one seeks to accomplish with oneself as object." It seems that when the subject is confessing and creating its "self," it feels compelled to tell the truth about itself. Counseling is a practice predicated on the assumption that the client is telling the truth about his/her self.

In the religious milieu, Foucault (1980a,b) points out that the concept of confession originated in Catholicism as the principal technology for managing the sexual lives of believers. Notions of a wide range of sins mostly equated with sexual morality. But the procedures of confession have altered considerably over time. Until the Council of Trent in the mid-sixteenth century, when a new series of procedures for the training and purifying of Church personnel emerged, confession in the Church was an annual event, so the confession and surveillance of sexuality was quite limited (Foucault, 1980b). After the Reformation, confession changed profoundly to involve not just one's acts but also one's thoughts. Then in the eighteenth century Foucault suggested that there was "a very sharp falling away, not in pressure and injunctions to confess, but in the refinement of techniques of confession" (Foucault, 1980b: 215). This point in time saw "brutal medical techniques emerging, which consist in simply demanding that the subject tells his or her story, or narrate it in writing" (p. 215).

Foucault defined his sense of confession [*aveu*] as "all those procedures by which the subject is incited to produce a discourse of truth about his sexuality which is capable of having effects on the subject himself" (pp. 215–216). As confession became secularized, a range of techniques emerged in pedagogy, medicine, psychiatry, and literature, with a high point being psychoanalysis or Freud's "talking cure." Since Freud, the secular form of confession could be argued as having been "scientized" through new techniques of normalization and individualization that include clinical codifications, personal examinations, case-study techniques, the general documentation and collection of personal data, the proliferation of interpretive schemas, and the development of a whole host of therapeutic techniques for "normalization." In turn, these "oblige" us to be free as self-inspection and new forms of self-regulation replace the confessional. As Rose (1989: 240) commented, this new form of confession was an affirmation of our self and our identity:

Western man, Michel Foucault argued, has become a confessing animal. The truthful rendering into speech of who one is, to one's parents, one's teachers, one's doctor, one's lover, and oneself, is installed at the heart of contemporary procedures of individualization. In confessing, one is subjectified by another, for one confesses in the actual or imagined presence of a figure who prescribes the form of the confession, the words and rituals through which it should be made, who appreciates, judges, consoles, or understands. But in confessing, one also constitutes oneself. In the act of speaking, through the obligation to produce words that are true to an inner reality, through the self-examination that precedes and accompanies speech, one becomes a subject for oneself. Confession, then, is the diagram of a certain form of subjectification that binds us to others at the very moment we affirm our identity. (Rose, 1989: 240)

This confession involves a type of "discipline" that "entails training in the minute arts of self-scrutiny, self-evaluation, and self-regulation, ranging from the control of the body, speech, and movement in school, through the mental drill inculcated in school and university, to the Puritan practices of self-inspection and obedience to divine reason" (Rose, 1989: 222). While confession is autobiographical, compelling us to narratively recreate ourselves, it is also about assigning truth-seeking meaning to our lives. One can be assisted in this through therapeutic endeavors such as counseling.

PROBLEMATIZING

Foucault's *oeuvre* examined the present by "problematizing" it—that is, by posing questions about the present, then going back to the past in a form of critical history that he first describes as an "archaeology" and later, somewhat differently, as a "genealogy." In commenting on perceived changes in his work over time, Foucault said:

> One has perhaps changed perspectives, one has turned the problem around, but it's always the same problem: that is, the relations between the subject, the truth and the constitution of experience. I have sought to analyze how fields like madness, sexuality and delinquency could enter into a certain play of the truth, and how on the other hand, through this insertion of human practice and behavior into the play of truth, the subject is himself effected. That was the problem of the history of madness, and of sexuality. (Foucault, 1989c: 310)

By "production of truth," Foucault states, "I mean not the production of true utterances, but the establishment of domains in which the practice of true and false can be made at once ordered and pertinent" (Foucault, 1991: 79). He uses *"problematization"* as a form of methodology to pose questions about the where, how, and by whom of social life and its institutions. For example, the ways in which behavior was constituted was characterized by the language of adjustment and maladjustment in the mid-twentieth century, with youth culture being initially described in terms of deviance and delinquency. The notion of adjustment had become normalized and was largely unchallenged at this point, until various researchers problematized youth discourse differently (see chapters 3, 4, and 5). In one of his last essays, Foucault acknowledges that despite the "truth" taking a very different form in his last two books, *The History of Sexuality* (Vol. II, 1985; Vol. III, 1990) that all his works since *Madness and Civilization* (1965) have the notion of problematization in common (Foucault, 1989a). Foucault elaborates:

Problematization doesn't mean the representation of a preexistent object, nor

> the creation through discourse of an object that doesn't exist. It's the set of discursive or nondiscursive practices that makes something enter into the play of the true and false, and constitutes it as an object for thought (whether under the form of moral reflection, scientific knowledge, political analysis, etc.). (Foucault, 1989b: 296)

ARCHAEOLOGY

In his earlier works on madness and the human sciences, especially *The Order of Things* (1970) and *The Archaeology of Knowledge* (1972), Foucault uses the term *"archaeology."* This is a form of historical analysis of discourse or systems of thought that describes the *archive* in terms of "expressibility, conservation, memory, reactivation and appropriation"—in other words:

> what may be spoken of in discourse; what statements survive, disappear, get reused, repressed or censured; which terms are recognized as valid, questionable, invalid; what relations exist between "the system of present statements" and those off the past, or between the discourses of "native" and foreign cultures; and what individuals, groups, or classes have access to particular kinds of discourse. (Smart, 1985: 48)

In *The Order of Things* Foucault proposes an archaeology of the human sciences based upon discovering the laws, regularities, and rules of the formation of systems of thought that emerged in the nineteenth century. Foucault's "archaeological" method focuses on the conditions under which a subject is constituted as a possible object of knowledge, and he provides the following rationale:

> I do not wish to deny the validity of intellectual biographies, or the possibility of a history of theories, concepts, or themes. It is simply that I wonder whether such descriptions are themselves enough, whether they do justice to the immense density of discourse, whether there do not exist, outside their customary boundaries, systems of regularities that have a decisive role in the history of the sciences. (Foucault, 1970: 385).

This reflects a "concern to establish thresholds, ruptures, and transformations" in order to confront them "with the true work of historians, which is to reveal continuities" (Foucault, 1972: 204). Later on, in an interview with J. J. Brochier, Foucault reflects on and discusses his use of the term "archaeology":

> I first used the word somewhat blindly, in order to designate a form of analysis that wouldn't at all be a history (in the sense that one recounts the history of inventions or of ideas) and that wouldn't be an epistemology either, that is to say, the internal analysis of the structure of a science. This other thing I have

> called therefore, "archaeology." And then retrospectively, it seemed to me that chance has not been too bad a guide: after all, this word " archaeology" can almost mean—and I hope I will be forgiven for this— description of the *archive*. I mean by archive the set (*l'ensemble*) of discourses actually pronounced; and this set of discourses is envisaged not only as a set of events which would have taken place once and for all and which would remain in abeyance, in the limbo or purgatory of history, but also as a set that continues to function, to be transformed through history, and to provide the possibility of appearing in other discourses. (Foucault, 1989g: 45)

In this interview, Foucault further elaborates about archaeology as not studying the beginning in the sense of the first origin, of a foundation starting from which the rest would be possible. . . . It's always the relative beginnings that I'm searching for, more the institutionalizations or the transformations than the foundings or foundations. And then I'm equally bothered by the idea of excavations. What I'm looking for are not relations that are secret, hidden, more silent or deeper than the consciousness of men. I try on the contrary to define the relations on the very surface of the discourse; I attempt to make visible what is invisible only because it's too much on the surface of things. (Foucault, 1989g: 46) Archaeology is about a type of digging down empirically through layers to uncover structures. Foucault provides a lengthy definition of *epistème* (1972: 190), which, he says, is not "a form of knowledge," but "the totality of relations . . . between the sciences when one analyzes them at the level of discursive regularities." An *epistème* is "a world view," "a slice of history common to all branches of knowledge," "a general stage of reason," "a structure of thought," "the total set of relations that unite the discursive practices that give rise to epistemological figures, sciences and formalized systems," and the way the transitions between the various stages in the progress of a science operate. Foucault identifies the Renaissance, the classical age (seventeenth and eighteenth centuries), and the modern age as three *epistèmes* or systems of thought each with its distinctive structure.

Foucault's archaeology aims to show that both continuities and discontinuities are formed from the same set of discursive practices. It differs from the type of history of ideas that uses models of consciousness, creation, or evolution to explain changes and differences; and instead, it attempts to establish what the system of transformations is that shapes change in the human sciences.

Although archaeology was supplanted by "genealogy" in Foucault's later work, it retained a presence, especially as a method of analyzing local discourses. In fact in his essay, "What is Enlightenment?" he states that his historical work combines archaeology as a "method" and genealogy as a "design" (Foucault, 1984d).

GENEALOGY

In the 1970s Foucault moved away from archaeology and *epistèmes* to notions of genealogy, bio-power, and how this produces certain kinds of "subjects," and also to notions of governmentality in his later work (e.g., *Discipline and Punish*, 1977;

The History of Sexuality, 1980a, 1985, 1990). Rather than a break, this change constitutes a shift in emphasis to social practices, institutions, regimes of power, and technologies of the self rather than the more quasistructuralist orientation that emphasized discourses and discontinuity and the rules that govern the formation of discourses. Foucault's essays "Two Lectures" (1980c), "Nietzsche, Genealogy, History" (1984c), and "What Is Enlightenment?" (1984d) provide some understanding about his notion of genealogy, but no pat definition.

"Genealogy" was a term introduced and used in a particular philosophical way by Friedrich Nietzsche in *The Genealogy of Morals* ([1887] 1956). Foucault was clearly influenced by this and other works by Nietzsche (Macey, 1993; Nilson, 1998; Smart, 1985). In a Foucauldian sense, genealogy is a history of the present. A genealogical analysis begins by posing a question in the present—problematizing the present—and how a problem is expressed in the current situation. Then its genealogy is worked out by moving backward in a process of descent.

In analyzing history, Foucault uses the Nietzschean notions of "descent" and "emergence" rather than evolution or a process of development. The analysis of descent involves a move backward in time to reveal the many events, struggles, complexity, fragility, contingency, and discontinuities that exist behind historical beginnings. Emergence is not seen as "a culmination of events, or as the end of a process of development but rather as a particular momentary manifestation of the 'hazardous play of dominations' . . . as transitory 'episodes in a series of subjugations,' or embodiments of dynamic relationships of struggle" (Smart, 1985: 57). Genealogy is about problematizing the present and historicizing or reevaluating the past in the light of current concerns. As a history that is concerned with the present moment, genealogy intervenes in the present moment.

What genealogy provides is the "history of an answer—the original, specific, and singular answer of thought—to a certain situation" (Foucault, 1985: 116). In other words, genealogy seeks to explain present-day cultural phenomena and problems by looking to the past and analyzing how it was derived and constituted historically. It not only looks at who we are at present but also opens up possibilities of what might be and from where we might start to be different in the present. It forms a critical ontology of our selves. For Foucault, living in one's own time involved the ethical constitution of self through a critical reflexiveness about the culture and forces that operated to constitute it.

Foucault's genealogy is radically different from traditional historical analysis. First, genealogy does not seek points of origin, timeless and taken-for-granted universal "truths" about life, evidence of human progress, or constants in order to find a stable understanding of events. Genealogy challenges the humanist model of consciousness as one that is unified and fully transparent to itself and linear in the sense that it stores memories in the same way as a novel progresses a plot. It also challenges the progressivist agendas of the Enlightenment by emphasizing dispersion, disparity, and difference.

Genealogy shifts "to the interface between nondiscursive and discursive practices" and "uncovers the eternal play of dominations, the domain of violence, subjugations and struggle" (Smart, 1985: 47, 59). Furthermore, the focus is on events, on their distinctive characteristics and manifestations, not as a product of destiny, regulative mechanisms or the intention of a constitutive subject, but as the effect of haphazard conflicts, chance and error, of relations of power and their unintended consequences struggle. Third, the objects of genealogical analysis are not, as in the case of traditional history, "the noblest periods, the highest forms, the most abstract ideas, the purest individualities" but neglected, "lower" or more common forms of existence and knowledge (e.g. of the body, sexuality). Finally genealogy introduces a mode of historical analysis which affirms the perspectivity of knowledge, a conception of which is in good part already implicit in Foucault's identification of the limits of archaeological knowledge. (Smart, 1985: 59)

Foucault developed a Nietzschean viewpoint, considering genealogy as an "antiscience" in that "it does not produce truths and certainties, but is a strategy of resistance" with results that do not confer identity nor a uniform theory (Nilson, 1998: 73); instead, they disturb and alert us to the dangers of science. If what was thought to be evident or obvious is shown to not be so, then genealogy challenges what we have assumed to be the natural and necessary in understanding ourselves. By examining discontinuities, breaches, contradictions, errors, and incongruencies in accepted forms of historical meaning, genealogy challenges the form of history that promotes notions of continuity and progress. In this way genealogy is "a diagnostic method that is not seeking history's inherent soul, but studying its body of development" (Nilson, 1998: 114). It does not look at history as a means of glorifying or being horrified by the past, but as a means of shedding light on the here and now. It develops generalizations by delving into and comparing different aspects of the past.

Foucault's shift from archaeology to genealogy is exemplified in *Discipline and Punish* (1977). This text focuses on the *will to knowledge* that reflects both discursive and nondiscursive (i.e., institutional) practices and the complex relations among power, knowledge, and the body. Foucault points out that the body is an object or site of certain disciplinary technologies of power. He provides a genealogy of forms that range from torture in the opening account of Damien to other forms of punishment that echo Nietzsche's list in the *Genealogy of Morals* (1956), to discipline, the prison, and the development of the modern penal institution.

Foucault sets out three areas in his discussion of discipline: "docile bodies," "the means of correct training," and "panopticism." He argues that the disciplines became general formulas of domination in the seventeenth and eighteenth centuries, as evidenced in a multiplicity of often minor processes at different locations that eventually coalesced into a general method. Disciplinary techniques "were at work in secondary education at a very early date, later in primary schools; they slowly invested the space of the hospital; and, in a few decades, they restructured the military organization" (Foucault, 1977: 138). One form of disciplinary techniques involves spatial distributions. The monastic model of enclosure and partitioning becoming an educational model, a form of "machine" that enabled supervision at the same time as it prevented dangerous communication between inmates.

> The organization of a serial space was one of the great technical mutations of elementary education that made it possible to supersede the traditional apprenticeship system where the student spends a few minutes with the master while the rest of the group remains idle. By assigning individual places it made possible the supervision of each individual and the simultaneous work of all. It organized a new economy of the time of apprenticeship. It made the education space function like a learning machine, but also as a machine for supervising, hierarchizing, rewarding. (Foucault, 1977: 147)

Other disciplinary technologies involve "the control of activities" of bodies by means such as the timetable and exercises and that discipline creates out of the bodies it controls four types of individuality, or rather an individuality that is endowed with four characteristics; it is cellular (by play of spatial distribution), it is organic (by the coding of activities), it is genetic (by the accumulation of time), it combinatory (by the composition of forces). And, in doing so, it operates four great techniques; it draws up tables; it prescribes movements; it imposes exercises; lastly, in order to obtain the combination of forces, it arranges "tactics." (Foucault, 1977: 167)

The means of correct training is discussed in terms of "hierarchical observation," normalizing judgment, and the examination where "the school building was to be a mechanism for training . . . a 'pedagogical machine'" (Foucault, 1977: 172). The examination "transformed the economy of visibility into the exercise of power," introduced "individuality into the field of documentation," and "surrounded by all its documentary techniques, . . . [made] each individual a 'case'" (Foucault, 1977: 187 ff.).

Foucault, therefore, provides an account of "disciplinary pedagogies" and discusses the way in which discipline proceeds from the distribution of individuals in space, involving several techniques such as enclosure, partitioning, functional sites, and ranking (see Foucault, 1977: 141–149). In talking about "distribution," "economy," "architecture," "archaeology," the "machine," and the Panoptican (which is outlined later in this chapter), Foucault is, in effect, discussing a spatializing of power (Peters, 2001a). So, in Foucault's genealogy, the body becomes both an object of knowledge and a site where power is exercised.

In being a history of the present, Foucault's genealogy acknowledges Nietzsche's perspectival notion of knowledge. A writer's own perspective on an issue at hand needs to be acknowledged, so history is "a deliberate appraisal, affirmation, or negation" that examines the past in order to intervene in the present and "prescribe the best antidote" (Foucault, 1984c: 90). Foucault's genealogy enables him to critique the human sciences more explicitly, especially in their hierarchies of knowledge based on scientificity. Foucault calls on "the insurrection of subjugated knowledges" that oppose "the tyranny of globalising discourses" to "establish a historical knowledge of struggles and to make use of this knowledge tactically today" (Foucault, 1980c: 81, 83). He suggests that there are two classes of "subjugated knowledges": one constitutes previously established, erudite knowledges that have been buried, hidden, disguised, masked, removed, or written out by revisionist histories; another involves local, popular, or indigenous knowledges that are marginalized or denied space to perform adequately. These knowledges are lowly ranked, being considered inadequate for the accepted standards of knowledge and science. In recovering these knowledges, we can rediscover the history of struggle and conflict and challenge the "effects of the centralizing powers which are linked to the institution and functioning of an organized scientific discourse within a society such as ours" (Foucault, 1980c: 84). These subjugated knowledges might be disciplinary networks of power or the arts of existence or the practices of sexuality in the ancient world. It is these subjugated knowledges that narrative therapy seeks to harness in developing alternative narratives that challenge the dominant stories in peoples lives (see chapter 7).

POWER AND POWER-KNOWLEDGE

Discipline and Punish (Foucault, 1977) is concerned with the operation of technologies of power and their relations to the emergence of knowledge in the form of new discourses, based around modes of objectification through which human beings become subjects. It is a theme that Foucault develops further in his work on the history of sexuality. Foucault asks:

> Why has sexuality been so widely discussed and what has been said about it? What were the effects of power generated by what was said? What are the links between these discourses, these effects of power, and the pleasures that were invested by them? What knowledge was formed as a result of this linkage? (Foucault, 1980a: 11)

It is in the course of his inquiries into sexuality and the proliferation of associated discourses that Foucault coins the term "bio-power," considered as a kind of anatomo-politics of the human body and control of the population at large.

For Foucault, "power" as a concept is quite different from the liberal or Marxist sense of coercion, domination, and oppression. As he says: "power must be understood in the first instance as the multiplicity of force relations immanent in the sphere in which they operate and which constitute their own organization" (Foucault, 1980a: 92). For him, the notion of power is productive, positive, and strategic. It is not a possession or property of a person or class, state or ruler; it is not conceptualized as a structure or institution but, rather, as a strategy or a complex strategic situation that is dispersed in a "multiplicity of force relations" (Foucault, 1980a: 97). Where there is power, Foucault maintains, there is also resistance, and often it is the case that these resistances are plural— that is, they cannot be reduced to a single point of rebellion.

Foucault is interested in the question, "How is power exercised?" In answering,

Foucault tried to move beyond the discourse of right and truth that had dominated and legitimated the notion of sovereign power since the Middle Ages. Once Foucault's notion of power is understood, it readily becomes clear that it has huge application to analyzing the "psy" sciences in the way that Rose (1989, 1998) develops in his project. It also points to an appropriate—methodologically speaking—way of analyzing counseling. One could argue that counseling is a paradigm example of the "analytics of power" in Foucault's sense, as we can clearly tell from the description of Foucault's methodology for analyzing power.

Smart (1985) suggests that in a methodological sense, Foucault's analysis provides five "precautions" concerning the form, level, effect, direction, and knowledge "effect" of power:

First, analysis is to address not centralized and legitimate forms of power but techniques which have become embodied in local, regional, material institutions. Second, analysis should concern itself with the exercise or practice of power, its field of application and its effects, and not with questions of possession or conscious intention. Analysis needs to be focused upon the way in which things "work at the level of ongoing subjugation, at the level of those continuous and uninterrupted processes which subject our bodies, govern our gestures, dictate our behaviours, etc.". . . Instead of concentrating attention on the motivation or interests of groups, classes or individuals in the exercise of domination analysis is to be directed at the various complex processes through which subjects are constituted as effects of objectifying powers. Third, power is a not a commodity or a possession of an individual, a group or a class, rather it circulated through the social body, "functions in the form of a chain," and is exercised through a net-like organization in which all are caught. (Smart, 1985: 78–79) Fourth, Smart argues that Foucault analyzes power not at the conventional macroinstitutional level but, rather, at the microlevel exhibited in the particular histories, techniques and tactics of power. Smart (1985: 79) remarks that only by paying close attention to the "microphysics of power . . . literally to how power functions, only then will it be possible to see how at a precise conjunctural moment particular mechanisms of power become economically advantageous and politically useful." The final methodological element focuses on the relations between knowledge and power. As Smart comments, for Foucault, historically, mechanisms of power developed through the formation and accumulation of knowledge, including its methods of observation, its techniques of registration and report, its procedures for investigation and research, its apparatuses of control and reform, and, more recently, its ethics. Thus, the analysis of power in Foucault's hands is directed away "from the juridical-political theory of sovereign power and analysis of the state, to a consideration of the material techniques of power and domination which began to emerge in the seventeenth and eighteenth centuries" (Smart, 1985: 80). This new form of power—disciplinary power—used through systems of surveillance in the prison, the factory, and the school, operated materially on the body of the subject to minimize expenditure and maximize returns. As Smart (1985) argues, disciplinary power is intimately tied up with the emergence of the human sciences in industrial capitalist societies.

The French words *savoir* and *connaisance* are both translated into English as "knowledge," but in the French *connaisance* refers to the body of knowledge of a particular discipline, whereas *savoir* refers to the totality of knowledge existing at any one time (Foucault, 1972: 15, 185). For Foucault, "knowledge," in terms of its two meanings as expressed in the French *savoir* and *connaisance*, is about how uncovering depth knowledge [*savoir*] enables the surface knowledge [*connaisance*] of a particular discourse to emerge (Hacking, 1981). On the Foucauldian view, knowledge in the human sciences is not a disinterested, neutral, objective, or value-free phenomenon; it is "inextricably entwined with relations of power" and "advances in knowledge are associated with advances and developments in the exercise of power" (Smart, 1985: 64). As Foucault states: "power produces knowledge (and not simply by encouraging it because it serves power or by applying it because it is useful); that power and knowledge directly imply one another: that there is no power relation without the correlative constitution of a field of knowledge, nor any knowledge that does not presuppose and constitute at the same time power relations" (Foucault, 1977: 27).

In other words, "a site where power is exercised is also a place at which knowledge is produced" (Smart, 1985: 64); hence in a Foucauldian sense, power has tended to become known as *power-knowledge*:

These "power-knowledge relations" are to be analysed, therefore, not on the basis of a subject of knowledge who is or is not free in relation to the power system, but, on the contrary, the subject who knows, the objects to be known and the modalities of knowledge must be regarded as so many effects of these fundamental implications of power-knowledge and their historical transformations. In short it is not the activity of the subject of knowledge that produces a corpus of knowledge, useful or resistant to power, but power-knowledge, the processes and struggles that traverse it and of which it is made up, that determines the forms and possible domains of knowledge. (Foucault, 1977: 27–28)

In one of his last essays, "The Subject and Power" (1982), Foucault outlines the five points involved in the analysis of power relations:

1. The system of differentiations which permits one to act upon the actions of others
2. The types of objectives
3. The means of bringing power relations into being
4. Forms of institutionalisation
5. The degrees of rationalisation. (Foucault, 1982: 223)

THE PANOPTICAN AND THE GAZE

It was in relation to power and discipline in *Discipline and Punish* (1977) that Foucault used the notion of the *gaze* and the *Panoptican*. The Panoptican was an architectural form proposed by Jeremy Bentham in the eighteenth century as an efficient form of surveillance for use in military camps, schools, monasteries, or prisons. The Panoptican operates by permitting the relentless and continual observation of inmates at the periphery by officials at the center, without them ever being seen. The model features a circular building (that could be of several levels), divided into rooms, with a courtyard in the center (or buildings around a courtyard). The rooms were to be only one room wide, with only a small rear window to allow back-lighting, but large openings onto the courtyard, which included an observation tower to house the guards or those in control. To prevent contact between the occupants, there was to be no connection or window between the rooms. The structure enabled the guards to have an uninterrupted view and perpetual observation or gaze of the activities in each space. The design made the guards invisible to the occupants, who were never sure when the gaze was upon them and so had to assume that they were subject to it at any time. The spaces or cells of the occupant were: "like so many cages, so many small theatres, in which each actor is alone, perfectly individualized and constantly visible. The panoptic mechanism arranges spatial unities that make it possible to see constantly and to recognize immediately. In short, it reverses the principle of the dungeon" (Foucault, 1977: 200).

But the guards in the Panoptican are not immune from the gaze. They are subject to visits by many people who may be supervisors, or may report what they find, and who may arrive at any time. This has the effect of putting the guards under ongoing evaluation by persons who are invisible or unknown to them.

The Panoptican was designed not only to be a very efficient system of surveillance, but also to be a very economic one that minimized the amount and hence the cost of supervision. The major effect of the Panoptican is "to induce in the inmate a state of conscious and permanent visibility that assures the automatic functioning of power" (Foucault, 1977: 201). But the panoptic arrangement also provides the opportunity for classifying, measuring, comparing, differentiating, qualifying, and judging the occupants according to norms set by the organization, and it enables the occupants to be thought of as individual cases. According to the norms, individuals could become subject to training or correction. In this manner the ever-present objectifying gaze has a normalizing effect. The file that was set up to write down the details about the individual "enabled individuals to be 'captured and fixed in writing' and facilitated the gathering of statistics and the setting of norms—that is, the construction of unitary and global knowledges about persons" (White and Epston, 1990: 70) and became a further mechanism of social control.

The Panoptican presents a *space* that is transparent, exemplary, and utopian. It is where, on the one hand, social control is achieved through the operation of an automatic and anonymous form of power and, on the other, where the disciplinary technologies of power, domination, and the objectification of the human subject produce new knowledges that enable the human sciences to develop. Foucault argues that the idea and techniques of the Panoptican became central to the rise both of capitalism and of the human science disciplines.

If the economic take-off of the West began with the techniques that made possible the accumulation of capital, it might perhaps be said that the methods for administering the accumulation of men made possible a political take-off in relation to the traditional, ritual, costly, violent forms of power, which soon fell into disuse and were superseded by a subtle, calculated technology of subjection In fact the two processes—the accumulation of men and the accumulation of capital—cannot be separated. (Foucault, 1977: 220– 221)

Disciplinary technologies were applied in institutions outside the penal system. In schools their application permitted the creation forms of control that could be exercised upon children and youth in order to render their bodies both docile and productive. Foucault's thought is significant in providing theoretical and methodological means to study education and school counseling as fields of the emergent human sciences, focusing on power–knowledge relations and conditions under which subjects are constituted objects of knowledge.

GOVERNMENTALITY

Rose (1998) argues that the development of "psy" disciplines was intrinsically linked to the history of government, not just politics, but in the broader sense of what Foucault termed "governmentality," a neologism for "governmental rationality" (Foucault, 1991). Governmentality became a focal theme in a series of lectures as part of Foucault's later philosophy, where he problematized notions of security, population, and government (Gordon, 1991).

Foucault's "disciplinary power" gave way, in his later work, especially in *The History of Sexuality* Vol. III (1990), to forms of power implicit in the formation of the subject and its relations to the will to truth. Such a view was part of Foucault's notion of governmentality which, he suggested, implied: "The relationship of the self to itself, and . . . [covers] the range of practices that constitute, define, organize and instrumentalize the strategies which individuals in their freedom can use in dealing with each other. I believe that the concept of governmentality makes it possible to bring out the freedom of the subject and its relationship to others—which constitutes the very stuff [*matière*] of ethics" (cited in Rabinow, 1997: xvii).

From this point onwards, Foucault addresses the issue of power in terms of ethics, and he returns to the Stoics to entertain the notion of the "care of the self," which has priority over and develops earlier than "care for others" and is discussed in chapter 2. Foucault moves "back to the subject," to the ethics of self-formation considered as an ascetic practice. He argues that "work" done on the self is not to be understood in terms of traditional left-wing models of liberation but, rather, as (Kantian) *practices of freedom*, for there is no essential, hidden, or true self, that is "concealed, alienated, or imprisoned in and by mechanisms of repression" that is in need of liberation (Foucault, 1997: 283). Instead there is only a *hermeneutics of the self*, a set of practices of self-interpretation. Foucault emphasizes that freedom is the ontological condition for ethics.

These twin conceptions of power—the early disciplinary account and the later form of ethical self-constitution—provide exemplary, if unusual, modes of analysis that are relevant and suitable for analyzing counseling. The first, disciplinary form is applicable to the history of the emergence of counseling in New Zealand schools, as a set of techniques and, therefore, a form of disciplinary power that developed in association with psychology. Perhaps, more interestingly, the second form of governmentality allows us to understand counseling both in its recent developments under neoliberalism (with demands for accountability and professionalization) and as part of the Western tradition—a set of practices and techniques inserted into schools—devoted to assisting students to "take care of the self," requiring both knowledge of oneself and freedom as an ontological condition of ethics (chapter 6).

Foucault's early work, *Discipline and Punish* (1977), suggests that understanding the operation of a range of social and economic institutions in society—the prison, the factory, and the school—could be understood by techniques of power that were a form of "power-knowledge" that observed, monitored, shaped, and controlled the behavior of individuals within these institutions. In discussing his research, Foucault states clearly that he was not aiming to analyze "institutions," "theories," or "ideology" per se, regardless of the part that these may play. Instead, he aimed to analyze a regime of "practices"—that is, the "places where what is said and what is done, rules imposed and reasons given, the planned and the taken for granted meet and interconnect," and which have "their own specific regularities, logic, strategy, self-evidence, and reason" (Foucault, 1991: 75). He wanted to find out the conditions that made practices acceptable at a given moment.

While Foucault's work resulted in considerable acclaim, according to Gordon (1991), it also attracted much criticism. Gordon summarized three points of objection to Foucault's work: First, Marxists contended that Foucault's "attentiveness to the specifics of power relations and the detailed texture of the particular techniques and practices failed to address or shed light on the global issues of politics, namely the relation between society and the state" (Gordon, 1991: 4). Second, by challenging current notions of the self, of autonomy, and of agency, Foucault represented "society as a network of omnipresent relations of subjugating power that seemed to preclude the possibility of meaningful individual freedom" (Gordon, 1991: 4). Foucault's notion of freedom is discussed in chapter 2 of this book, using the points he makes in later essays and interviews on the self, ethics, and power. Third, Foucault was criticized for presenting a "'political philosophy of nihilistic despair' that was exemplified in his bleak account of the effects of humanitarian penal reformism" (Gordon, 1991: 4). Foucault discusses a change in the tenor and focus of his work in various interviews, such as those published in *Foucault Live* (1989) and *The Foucault Effect: Studies in Governmentality* (1991); he eventually poses his work on "governmentality" in answer to some of the criticism.

Although he pays particular attention to the historical political domain of government, especially to ancient Greek and early Christian times, to early modern European states, to liberalism and neoliberalism, Foucault defines the term "government" in a broad manner. In Foucault's broad sense, "government" means "the conduct of conduct" or "a form of activity aiming to shape, guide or affect the conduct of some person or persons": "Government as an activity could concern the relation between self and self, private interpersonal relations involving some form of control or guidance, relations within social institutions and communities and, finally, relations concerned with the exercise of political sovereignty" (Gordon, 1991: 2–3).

In outlining three aspects of "governmentality," Foucault implicitly criticizes the contemporary tendency to overvalue the problem of the state, its history, development, power, and abuses, and to reduce it to a unity or singularity based upon functionality, such as its productive forces. He was interested in the question of *how* power was exercised, and so by a history of "governmentality" Foucault means three things:

1. The ensemble formed by the institutions, procedures, analyses and reflections, the calculations and tactics that allow the exercise of this very specific albeit complex form of power, which has as its target population, as its principal form of knowledge political economy, and as its essential technical means apparatuses of security.
2. The tendency which over a long period and throughout the West, has steadily led towards the pre-eminence over all forms (sovereignty, discipline, etc.) of this type of power which may be termed government, resulting, on the one hand, in the formation of a whole series of specific governmental apparatuses, and, on the other, in the development of a whole complex of *savoirs*.
3. The process, or rather the result of the process, through which the state of justice of the Middle Ages, transformed into the administrative state during the fifteenth and sixteenth centuries, gradually becomes "governmentalized." (Foucault, 1991: 102–103)

In Foucault's view, "governmentality" means the complex of calculations, programs, policies, strategies, reflections, and tactics that shape the conduct of individuals, "the conduct of conduct" for acting upon the actions of others in order to achieve certain ends. Those ends are "not just to control, subdue, discipline, normalize, or reform them, but also to make them more intelligent, wise, happy, virtuous, healthy, productive, docile, enterprising, fulfilled, self-esteeming, empowered, or whatever" (Rose, 1998: 12). Governmentality is about control not simply in its negative sense but also in its positive sense, in its contribution to the security of society. The governing of others is conducted by a large array of authorities, be they political, economic, military, police, educational, theological, medical, welfare, and so on, with the general purpose of avoiding negatives and ills such as crime, mental illness, ignorance, and poverty while promoting what was considered desirable by society— health, wealth, and happiness. Thus modern Western societies are characterized by a form of security that is an interdependence of the political, the governmental, and the social.

Foucault develops his notion of governmentality from a historical analysis of the "art of government" in Europe. He considers that an explosion of interest in the "art of government" in the sixteenth century was motivated by four diverse questions. These were about the government of oneself or one's personal conduct; the government of souls and lives or pastoral conduct; the government of children, which subsequently involved pedagogy and their education; and the government of the state by its prince or ruler. Foucault poses questions about the *how* of government: "how to govern oneself, how to be governed, how to govern others, by whom the people will accept being governed, how to become the best possible governor" (Foucault, 1991: 87). Self-government is connected with morality, governing the family is related to economy, and ruling the state to politics. In the sixteenth-century context, Foucault suggests that such questions highlighted the general problematic of government as the intersection of two competing movements: a tendency toward state centralization and a logic of dispersion and religious dissidence.

Foucault believes that the introduction of economy into political practice was the essential issue in establishing the art of government. The introduction of economy and governing the family became imperative to the state as the art of government became established in sixteenth-century Europe. Foucault espouses Rousseau's notions of "political economy," pointing out that economy involved "the correct manner of managing goods and wealth within the family," and, in turn, "wise government of the family [was] for the common welfare of all" (Foucault, 1991: 92). But since this required a form of control and surveillance over the subjects, over the wealth and behavior of all, good government also came to involve notions of "policing" and "policy." Added to this was the "knowledge of the state . . . its different elements, dimensions and factors of power, questions which were termed precisely 'statistics'" (p. 96), meaning the science of the state. Foucault maintains that the art of government crystallized for the first time in the late sixteenth and early seventeenth centuries around the notion of "reason of state" [*raison d'état*] that in effect challenged the "divine right of kings" to rule: "the state is governed according to rational principles which are intrinsic to it and which cannot be derived solely from natural or divine laws or the principles of wisdom and prudence; the state, like nature, has its own proper form of government, albeit of a different sort" (Foucault, 1991: 97).

Therefore, according to Foucault, from the sixteenth century on, the art of government came to involve administration, policing, statistics, and sovereignty. Once however, the notion of "population" emerged in the eighteenth century, Foucault argues that it displaced the family as central to the art of government, and recentered the notion of economy. Statistics reveal details about the domain of population—rates of birth, disease, death, labor, wealth—that show and quantify how "population has specific economic effects" (p. 99). Family "disappears as a model of government, except for a certain number of residual themes of a religious or moral nature" and becomes simply an element or segment internal to population, albeit "a fundamental instrument of its government" (p. 99). Foucault believes that this fundamental shift of the mid-eighteenth century, where "the family becomes an instrument rather than a model: the privileged instrument for the government of the population and not the chimerical model of good government" (p. 100), enabled population to become the ultimate end of government. It was this that enabled the purpose of government to be concentrated no longer on enhancing the power and wealth of the sovereign, but on the welfare of its population, to embark overtly or indirectly on large-scale campaigns involving vaccinations, marriage, and employment, and improving the population's health, wealth, and mortality rate. It was this context that enabled the psy sciences to evolve.

In elaborating the notion of governmentality, Foucault concentrates on understanding government in its pluralized forms, its complexity, and its techniques in the question of *how* power is exercised. Our present is characterized by the "governmentalization" of the state. Using Foucault's theories, we come to understand the rationality of government in both permitting and requiring the practice of freedom of its subjects. This is where the relations between government and self-government, public and private domains, coincide and coalesce, which only becomes possible at the point where "policing" and "administration" stops and the freedom of the subject becomes a resource for, rather than a hindrance to, government.

Rose (1998) contends that in liberal democracies, governing others has always been linked to subjects who are constituted as being "free" to practice liberty and responsibility simultaneously in governing the self. Analyses in terms of governmentality then involve problematization, critique, and contestability about these practices of governance of the self and of others. The issue of governmentality in relation to school counseling, its clients and institutional policy, therefore forms one of the themes for this book that is discussed in chapter 6.

CHAPTER 2

COUNSELING AND FOUCAULT: IDENTIFYING THE SELF

INTRODUCTION: PHILOSOPHICAL PERSPECTIVES

> I know that I exist; the question is, what is this "I" that I know? (Descartes, [1642] 1986)

> The soul, so far as we can conceive it, is nothing but a system or train of different perceptions. (Hume, [1739] 1977)

> The crtical function of philosophy derives from the Socratic injunction "Take care of yourself, " in other words, "Make freedom your foundation, through mastery of yourself." (Foucault, 1997a: 301)

> A self . . . is . . . an abstraction . . . [a] Center of Narrative Gravity. (Dennett, 1991)

While not attempting to be a complete philosophical treatise on the "self" and "identity," this chapter summarizes some important historical philosophical notions in taking up Taylor's (1985) suggestion that we cannot "see the full complexity and richness of modern identity . . . unless we see how the modern understanding of the self developed out of earlier pictures of human identity" (Taylor, 1985: x). Questions about the self and identity and changes in how they have been theorized are by no means a twentieth-century phenomenon. There are two main ways in which Western philosophy has conceived of the self. One is derived from Plato and was subsequently adopted by forms of Christianity; the other arose out of Rousseau and a contemporary form of philosophy, phenomenology, existentialism, and pragmatism in the nineteenth and twentieth centuries. This is clearly evident in the writings of Nietzsche, Husserl, Heidegger, and contemporary French philosophy—e.g., Sartre, de Beauvoir, Merleau-Ponty, Foucault, and Derrida—on the one hand, and in the pragmatist writings of William James, Dewey, Mead, and Rorty, on the other.

The Platonic view based on the implacable distinction between the world of appearances and the world of reality holds that the self is a fixed essence—the "psyche" or "soul"—a form that temporarily locates itself in the body. According to this view the soul is the eternal form of the self that on the death and decay of the body returns to the fixed circle of souls. This self, once born, is "dis"-covered or uncovered as one learns through life. Plato, wedded to the doctrine of *anamnesis,* suggests that all learning is simply a form of recollection. Education, then, becomes the means by which, through a judicious series of questions, the learner is taught to remember or recollect what (s)he already knows. Descartes's mind/body split might also be said to follow a similar line of thinking in that the *cogito* or the "thinking self" is privileged with regard to the body: it is that which can guarantee us certainty in knowledge and, indeed, makes knowledge possible (Descartes, [1642] 1986). Descartes's notion is briefly examined in the second section.

In general, this privileging of the mind or intellect over the body, which dominated the Western tradition and has been sustained and reiterated in modern philosophy beginning with Descartes, has also been responsible for shaping approaches to education. In the liberal tradition, education meant an education of the mind rather than an education of the body. In line with this overall approach to education, many theories informing counseling have tended to embrace similar ideas.

Many counseling therapies are conducted through the "rational" means of language or conversation. Clients are assisted to produce a "talking cure" (in Freud's sense), to reveal the truth about their self and their identity in what might be seen as a confessional mode in a modern secular society (see Foucault, 1980a,b). This form of confession has already been outlined in chapter 1. Most forms of counseling that draw upon the model of the "dialogue," the "autobiography," the "confession," the "structured conversation," and even the "argument" tend to accept the mind/body split and to privilege the mind over the body. Rational emotive therapy is a particularly clear exemplar of this. Even modalities such as gestalt, existential counseling, psychodrama, some pastoral counseling, transactional analysis, and body therapies, while they may use body-oriented and physical techniques, still involve some processing of what has occurred through forms of dialogue, conversation, and confession in enabling the individual to gain an understanding of the self and one's relationship to the problem or issue of concern. Hence the mind or intellect gains a sense of knowing or understanding and makes meaning for the person. These forms of counseling attempt to take seriously the way in which the *cogito* or the cognitive has been privileged. The extent to which the counteremphasis on the body or "passions" is opposed to the intellect as a conscious product of philosophical understanding is questionable.

The phenomenological view of self starts from the premise that the world of appearance is all that is. There is no other reality, and, given this fleeting and temporal existence, the self is viewed as something that *becomes*—that is, it comes into existence and goes out of existence: existence is fundamentally temporal. Martin Heidegger makes this his thesis in the now famous *Being and Time* (1993). The same point is given a different expression by Jean-Paul Sartre (1948: 26), who, in his *Existentialism and Humanism,* suggests that what all existentialisms have in common is the fact that "they believe *existence* comes before *essence.*" As he says,

"Man is nothing else but that which he makes of himself" (Sartre, 1948: 28). That simple statement emphasizing the temporality of humankind—its *becoming*—is a powerful thought that has motivated postwar philosophy, be it in its pragmatic guise, focusing upon the pure contingency of existence, or be it in its existentialist or phenomenological guise. What follows from this is a reevaluation of the mind/body, appearance/reality dualisms and a reconsideration of both the body and our freedom. In his later work, Sartre (1966) points out that, if existence is prior to essence, the first moral effect of existentialism means that "man" is responsible for what he is, both individually and collectively. Existentialist and phenomenological theories informing counseling (as mentioned below) accordingly place great emphasis on the idea of freedom to choose and individual autonomy and responsibility: in particular, the way we become who we are through the choices that we make.

The notion of identity is one that has been challenged in the latter part of the twentieth century by postmodern and poststructuralist theorists. While there are many postmodern positions, a central theme, with different inflections, is that *the self is fundamentally social*. This notion has been adopted by many people; it has antecedents in Christian notions expressed in the words of the metaphysical poet John Donne that "no man is an island unto himself." Both sociology and Marxist thought have made the notion of the social self fundamental. Discourses of the "postmodern self" tend to revolve around a cluster of questions: what is the extent or the limits of the self; what is the relationship between the inner and the outer, between the mind and the body, or between the public and the private self? Is such a differentiation even possible? Is the self unified or fragmented, singular or plural? What is the relationship between the concepts of self and of identity? These questions are, in large measure, the subject matter for this chapter, where I provide some account of the self and of identity and attempt to sort out the conceptual relations between them. I provide an introduction to the notion of self that has proved popular with counselors and has, implicitly, underwritten counseling theory and practice. I also provide an argument and brief review of the shift from the notion of the self to that of identity that characterizes much contemporary theorizing, and I investigate Michel Foucault's influential work, in particular his notion of "care of the self."

"SELF," "IDENTITY," AND COUNSELING

In recent times, particularly since the 1980s, there has been a shift in how some theorists—philosophers, anthropologists, sociologists, therapists, and counselors—have conceived the self. In the early part of the twentieth century—as, for example, reflected in Freudian tripartite notions of id, ego, superego and similar variants by neo-Freudian theorists—the self had been seen as having different components: an inner and an outer self, with the latter two concepts of ego and superego incorporating elements of the social dimension. With an emphasis being placed on the inner as being the "real" or "true" self, it became important to discover this inner being or unconscious part—a task that often created deep ontological anxiety. Such anxiety might be seen as culminating in the postwar baby-boomers, who are sometimes portrayed negatively in the popular media as overly a self-centered "me-generation," "navel-gazers" forming what Christopher Lasch (1979) calls in the book of the same name, a "culture of narcissism." Furthermore, neo-liberal political environments at the end of the twentieth century focus on self responsibility rather than state responsibility in managing one's life.

Contemporary philosophers, such as Ludwig Wittgenstein (1953), have challenged earlier ideas about the self and emphasized how our thinking depends on language. When the self is seen as part of a public language game and language is formed in our interactions with our everyday world, then, as Schopenhauer and Wittgenstein both argue, the idea of self as a inner sanctum or a set of inner processes that are private to the individual becomes unintelligible or meaningless. A consequence of this line of thinking might be to believe that human beings are much "lighter," so to speak, as portrayed, for example, by Milan Kundera (1984) in *The Unbearable Lightness of Being*. Under this description, people no longer have the "heavy" load of "finding themselves," or of revealing their true inner core. Rose (1989) argues that it has been psychological discourse that has enabled and taught people ways of constituting or "inventing" themselves. I would argue that there has been a distinct move away from forms of counseling and therapy that investigate the self and its inner being for the sake of itself, to forms of counseling that focus more on the everyday realities and problems that people present (such as sexual abuse, violence, anger, drug and alcohol abuse, family relationships, depression, suicidality, and phobias), aiming to help them cope with these. This is not to say that the "deep work" on finding the self is necessarily any better or more workable than other forms, but that as times have changed and as people's needs have changed, so the forms of therapy have tended to change. There has been a refocus on the importance of the language used in counseling, so that it is seen not just as a form of "talking cure" (in the Freudian sense) but as having become "technologies of language"—talking, writing, and reading the self, as used in narrative therapy.

In the counseling literature in the English-speaking world, the two notions self and identity are central to theory and practice, yet the conceptual relationships between these two terms have not always been carefully mapped or explored. As elsewhere, they are often used interchangeably without explanation or due regard to their conceptual differences. The two terms also seem to exist in quite separate literatures and in different social science disciplines. The notion of self figures strongly in key psychological discourses—both measurement-oriented and humanistic—focusing on the related family of terms that include "self-determination," "self-disclosure," "self-concept," "self-esteem," "self-assertion" and "self-reporting." Identity seems to figure alternatively and more recently in sociologically oriented literatures focusing upon identity formation and "identity politics" related particularly to race, gender, and sexuality. Furthermore, in recent innovations in counseling based on narrative therapy, the notion of identity becomes "subjectivities" as the preferred terminology (Drewery and Winslade, 1997: 39).

These separate discourses—self and identity—which are still prevalent and indicate major lines of practice and research both in psychological and in counseling theory, also point to contemporary shifts in meanings of these terms. In particular, one might argue that the notion of self underlying early counseling practice was more of an essentialist one that allowed for stages of growth or development and assumed a stable core personality or essence of being, whereas the recent sociologically inflected discourses, drawing on structuralist and poststructuralist innovations, tend to adopt constructionist approaches to render identity and even self as social constructions. These have been reflected in counseling in two different therapies (Drewery and Monk, 1994): "constructivist therapy" (Niemeyer, 1993) and the "constructionist"-influenced "narrative therapy" that is discussed in chapter 7.

In Western philosophy, the notion of the sameness of the self stemmed from qualities described by two seventeenth-century philosophers: John Locke, in his *An Essay Concerning Human Understanding* ([1690] 1964), and René Descartes, in his treatise, *Meditations* ([1642] 1986). For Des-cartes, the self (or the ego or I) became certain of its existence through its own acts of cognition, which became the epistemological foundational reassurance against an ambiguous and deceptive world. *Cogito ergo sum*, translated as "I think, therefore I am," represents Descartes's subjectivist attempt to find an inviolable and indubitable starting point or foundation to all knowledge, on the basis that if there is not a certain class of privileged proposition immune to doubt, then knowledge is impossible. Descartes found this privileged class of propositions in the "primitive" reflection on the *subjectum*. The foundational proposition immune to doubt for Descartes was part of what has been called the *cogito* argument. But the *cogito* argument remained valid only if the self remained the same or identical. In Descartes's time, *cogito* or "thought" had a far wider meaning than it does today, and it included all mental acts and data such as will, feeling, judgment, and perception; it is often translated as "consciousness," with clear implications favoring rationality. Des-cartes brought to prominence the notion that the mind conceives, first of all, itself by itself. The self, thus, became the subject, in the dual sense of being subjected to the conditions of the world and, simultaneously, being the agent of knowing and doing in that world. The belief in this subject became an *a priori* presupposition for the possibility of knowing the world. In other words, the "knowing I"—the *cogito* reflecting on its own existence—became the basis or foundation not only for knowledge but also for acting and doing, and, hence, morality and politics. Des-cartes's mind–body dualism maintained that the mind and the body have different essences because of their different spatiality. The essence of the physical (body) involves space but because minds have no such extension in space they cannot be considered physical substances. By contrast, their essence is to think.

Descartes's model of consciousness and the mind/body split it assumed and perpetuated really represented a watershed in the history of the philosophy of the self. Descartes's conception has been enormously influential. We might even say that his view of the self—a picture of the cognitive self that epistemologically underwrote all other human activity, including morality—became established as the prevalent view for modern philosophy and the culture of modernity. The mind–body problem has resulted in different stands in modern philosophy that have considerable impact on many different psychology and counseling theories: epiphenomenalism—that physical states cause mental states; parallelism—that the mental and physical realms run in parallel; monism—the rejection of the Cartesian dualism; materialism and "central state materialism"—according to which mental states are considered to be contingently identical with brain states; and functionalism—characterized by cognitive psychology and connectionism research.

Descartes is still referred to by various contemporary philosophers, for instance Noam Chomsky (a modern Cartesian), who in his early work embraced an essentialist "universal grammar," or Ludwig Wittgenstein and Michel Foucault, who use Descartes as a point of departure or reaction to a "picture that held us captive." Michel Foucault, for example, in analyzing how a given form of knowledge was possible, rejected the way phenomenology and existentialism held *a priori* theories of the subject stemming from Descartes. He tried to show that what constituted the subject revolved around "games of truth" and practices of power and what he termed "technologies of the self," comprising disciplinarity or technologies of domination and "governmentality." Foucault's notions of the self is discussed in greater detail later in this chapter.

The notion of identity in psychological discourse has undergone a paradigm shift in the late twentieth century, especially with the advent of "social constructionism" and the development of discursive psychology (see, e.g., Nightingale and Cromby, 1999). Developed from seventeenth-century philosophical notions of John Locke (1964) about the individuated subject in terms of "sameness" through time, be it for an organism, animal, or person, identity originally meant "sameness," as in "self-sameness"—that is the sense of an identity that is continuous through time. Identity was what made a human being a person, a rational, autonomous individual, and it was understood as a set of basic personality features acquired mostly during childhood. Once integrated, particularly in adolescence, the basic personality, it was held, became largely fixed and stable. A "personality" that was inconsistent or fragmented or not integrated into a single unity was regarded as a disordered or disturbed one, or even as a psychologically or mentally ill one. It was a self that comprised nonsameness; hence it became a nonidentity, and as such it often had to be controlled, or even locked up in mental institutions. Such "disorders" of the self were often classified in terms of the paradigm notion of "schizophrenia" or the "split self," the incidence of which is considered to have increased in the "postmodern condition" (Lasch, 1979, 1984), not only in terms of the incidence of instability problems having to do with the "core" self, but also with changes in the kind of presenting problem. Lasch (1984) argues that we are no longer concerned so much with anxiety disorders or problems of an otherwise stable self, but, rather, with problems of self that reportedly involve a fragmentation of the core—the so-called "minimal self." These are considered serious clinical problems, to be dealt with in the setting of mental health institutions. In other words, the problem of the fragmentation of the "core" self has become medicalized, to be clinically treated and often hospitalized.

In Wittgenstein and Foucault the self is considered a form (or concept); it is not an individuated substance, as it is in traditional metaphysics (Descartes, Locke). A form is a logical place holder, to be filled out with detail, description, qualities, and qualifications. The self is a conceptual form that can be filled in in a number of ways: male, female, heterosexual, bisexual, Maori, Pakeha, young, old, employed, disabled, victimized, abused, happy, positive, honest, and so on. Once individuals have been individuated, one can talk about identity. "Individuation" is a concept in logic that distinguishes one individual from another. Identity and "individuation," in the philosophical discourse following Descartes and on through the twentieth century, tend to be two concepts that are run together. They have been thought to be logically necessary criteria for identifying a thing or a person. Ludwig Wittgenstein argues that this is not the case (see Peters and Marshall, 1999; Strawson, 1997), so the criteria of identity are not absolute and can be filled by various descriptions at various times. This means that these criteria, and the notion of identity itself, are historicist; they are context-dependent or contingent criteria—that is, not absolutely and necessarily binding. So identity rests upon such culturally variable criteria as gender, class, ethnicity, sexual orientation, "age group" (such as "adolescent" and "youth"), and, as Foucault suggests, corporeality.

"Corporeality" means inhabiting a body, being embodied—the self inhabits a body. This criterion of corporeality has a history, at least in French philosophy, stretching back to phenomenology, Nietzsche, and existentialism, and is strongly developed by Simone de Beauvoir, Jean-Paul Sartre, and Maurice Merleau-Ponty (see O'Loughlin, 1997). Nietzsche rehabilitates a notion of "embodied reason" by talking about the body in ways that challenge the mind/body dualism of Cartesian philosophy (see Nietzsche, *Thus Spake Zarathustra,* 1961, Part I). The body occupies a spatial–temporal location that fixes the subject in time and in the process breaks down Cartesian universalist assumptions of individuality, pure rationality, and self-interest. Peters (2002) argues that Nietzsche's embodied form of reason is deeper than a superficial rationality. For Nietzsche it is true reason because it has the power to govern our passions and to regulate ourselves. Nietzsche does not believe in biological determinism. Rather, he suggests that the passions become an instrument of a *restored* and embodied form of reason that can regulate the passions and redirect reason to focus on the self (or humankind) as a *work* that can be shaped. Postwar French philosophy calls on Nietzschean ideas to bring forward knowledges of the self that have been subjugated by emphasizing the corporeality of the enfleshed, embodied, and engendered subject (Peters, 2002). Furthermore, the metanarrative[1] of the autonomous self and the seemingly obvious assumptions of the Cartesian–Kantian subject—autonomy, rationality, and self-transparency—have been challenged by Nietzsche, Wittgenstein, and other scholars. They have sought to develop notions of embodied and engendered reason and subjectivity that disputes the mind/body dualism of the Cartesian heritage. This notion of corporeality has moved some forms of contemporary investigation, especially by poststructuralists, away from studies of the self per se to concentrate on bodies and how they are controlled, inscribed, and stylized. Poststructuralist thinkers have built on the insights of structuralist thinkers to emphasize the temporality, finitude, and corporeality of the human subject in all its sociocultural and historical complexity.

The concern for the self and the application of these descriptive criteria of identity indicate the way in which diverse and significant strands of contemporary philosophical thought on the self, including phenomenology, existentialism, and poststructuralist philosophy, might be characterized as a series of increasing historical specifications of the subject. These involve a shift from alternative formulations of the concept or logical form of the self, that attempt to define its essence, to accounts that increasingly specify the subject in terms of contingent identity criteria, focusing upon the finitude, the temporality, the corporeality of the gendered, embodied, "racialized" individual. This shift in thinking has very strong implications for the ways in which school-aged children have been specified, categorized, and theorized as the subjects of education and of counseling. If we accept the shift from *the essence of self* to *descriptive criteria of a contingent identity*, then we can see that it has important implications for definitions of the descriptions of "adolescence" and "youth" as they have operated in the counseling and psychological literatures.

In psychology, "individuation" is an important process that is linked with identity, involving the development of the personality through the separation of the baby and child from the mother and father. In this sense it is important for the establishment of identity because it bespeaks difference and uniqueness, at least in the sense that an entity or being occupies a particular time and space that cannot be taken up by another being (conjoint twins being the exception). Identity is how one recognizes and identifies that one is different from the other. It is identity that provides a nonstatic way of describing the being that is described by the self and by others. The self is an essential, conceptual, grammatical form, while identity provides the sociohistorical contingent description. In people with no clear sense of identity, as in those who develop dementia or Alzheimer's disease, so that the memory and brain function are impaired, the sense of self and identity begins to collapse, and they eventually deteriorate into what is considered a vegetative state. At this point they may be functioning physically, but they no longer have a sense of self or an identity and are usually institutionalized as no longer being able to function. So self and identity can be seen to be vital for what is considered a fully functioning human being.

In anthropological discourse, the notions of identity and self tend to be approached separately. Conceptualization of the Western self, mostly characterized as autonomous and egocentric, is generally taken as the norm, with the concepts of self of the traditional subjects of anthropology, the non-Western subjects, defined through the negation of these Western norms and characteristics. Anthropological conceptualizations of identity about non-Western selves tend to focus on elements shared with others rather than on the characteristics of individuality and so divert attention from actual individuals and selves. In addition to any culture-specific attributes, the self is held to be endowed with reflexivity and agency.

In social anthropology, identity has been used mostly in the sense of "ethnic identity," not just self-sameness, but sameness of the self with others, a consciousness of shared characteristics encompassed in a common language, history, and culture that contributes to the constitution of the group's identity. These notions tend to be complementary rather than contradictory, since the group to which a person belongs constitutes an important part of the sociocultural environment in which and through which personal identity is formed. Erik H. Erikson expanded the notion of identity to combine the two: "The term 'identity' expresses such a mutual relation in that it connotes both a persistent sameness within oneself [self-sameness] and a persistent sharing of some kind of essential characteristics with others" (Erikson, 1980: 109).

Foucault analyzed the self or "subject," not as the source and foundation of knowledge, but, rather, as itself a product or effect of networks of power and discourse (Foucault, 1977,a,b,c, 1980). Contemporary discourses of social science influenced by poststructuralist thought tend no longer to talk about identity in the singular, defined by sameness and unity; instead they refer to difference and plurality (see Derrida, 1982; Lyotard, 1988). Difference points to the contrasting aspects of identity and emphasizes the implicit condition of plurality. Identity is a combination of a number of social pluralities: family, class, ethnicity, gender, culture, nationality, and age. In addition, the plurality of intersecting lines comprising identity is now more often than not conceived as a set of life-style choices or even "political" choices that one makes at the personal level about appearance, sexuality, and group inclusiveness. The emphasis on difference has called into question conventional assumptions of both a shared homogenous cultural identity and a unified personal or individual identity. Psychology has only recently turned its attention to the contradictory notion of multiple identities (see Gergen, 1991; Melucci, 1997; Rosenberg, 1997). The self is now depicted as fragmented and minimal (Jameson, 1984; Lasch, 1984), fluid, and manysided, as in Lifton's (1993) "protean self," or comprising multiplicities, as in Gergen's (1991) "saturated self." In anthropology, discourses about the self and identity have mostly been treated separately, although an increased attention to the social and cultural contexts of plural identities may lead to a better understanding of both concepts (Sökefeld, 1999).

Many poststructuralist feminist theorists, such as Luce Irigaray and Julia Kristeva, argue that Western philosophy and culture is deeply *phallo-logocentered*. They criticize Platonism, a tradition that posits universal and gender-neutral abstractions but secretly supports the patriarchal hegemony by associating females with the sensuous, nature, emotion, and irrationality. Irigaray argues that despite claims of universality and neutrality, everything, including the subject, has always used the masculine form, "*man*" (Irigaray, 1993). Historically, in the human sciences, the body has been associated with the feminine, the female, or woman, and in turn denigrated as weak, immoral, unclean, or decaying. Kristeva was influential for bringing the body back into discourses in the human sciences, particularly the importance of the maternal body (and the preoedipal) in the constitution of subjectivity and the notion of abjection. Kristeva's notion of a subject-in-process is seen by many feminists as a useful alternative to traditional notions of an autonomous unified (masculine) subject.

In poststructuralist feminist discourse, when the self is considered, it is the corporeal self that is usually invoked. Judith Butler (1990) maintains that identity and associated questions, such as "who am I?" and "what am I like?" are an illusion. She sees the self as an unstable discursive node and sexed/gendered identity as merely a "corporeal style" that is a form of performance that imitates and repeats the enactment of ubiquitous norms. She considers that psychodynamic accounts of the self, including those of Kristeva and Nancy Chodorow, mask the performative nature of the self and collaborate in the cultural conspiracy that maintains the illusion that one has an emotionally anchored interior identity that is derived from the biology of one's genitalia. Such accounts conceal the ways in which normalizing regimes deploy power to enforce the performative routines that construct both "natural" sexed/ gendered bodies and debased, "unnatural" bodies. The arbitrariness of the constraints that are being imposed is obscured, and resistance is deflected. So Butler wants to "question the categories of biological sex, polarized gender, and determinate sexuality that serve as markers of personal identity, to treat the construction of identity as a site of political contestation, and to embrace the subversive potential of unorthodox performances and parodic identities" (Peters, 2002). Such various feminist notions of self and identity inform feminist counselors and feminist counseling theories.

POSTMODERNISM AND POSTSTRUCTURALISM: NEW APPROACHES TO THE CONCEPT OF IDENTITY

This section looks at contemporary discourses in postmodernism and poststructuralism and how these relate to approaches to the notions of the self and of identity. Although Foucault (1989a, 1989f) was very clear on several occasions that he did not consider himself a "postmodernist" nor a "structuralist," it is within the overall context of these movements, but particularly the poststructuralist movement, that one can gain an understanding of the work of both Foucault and Rose.

Douglas Kellner (1992) suggests that notions of identity have passed through three stages of transition, from premodern, to modern, to post-modern identity. These eras are not so much indicative of calendar time, but of a predominant way of thinking and style of existence, somewhat akin to Foucault's *epistèmes*. Kellner suggests that identity is considered to be a nonissue and unquestionable for premodern communities, since one's thought, behavior, and place have been restricted and largely predetermined within communities that have a world view based on traditional myths and kinship systems that ascribe roles. Identity was, therefore, seen as being stable and based on ascribed roles and clearly defined relationships to others in the premodern community. Premodern or traditional societies often have no notion that matches the Western "individual," and findings from comparative anthropology suggest that identity is status- and role-oriented and often determined by birth into hierarchical relations.

The Enlightenment (or age of reason), which began in Europe in the seventeenth century, is considered to be the beginning of modernity, and it was during this age that Kellner suggests that identity was first brought into focus as an issue. Modernity involves the rejection of the past and of traditional restrictions in favor of progress toward human emancipation and moral perfection. Traditional rural feudal or subsistence societies based on ascribed roles gave way to newly urbanized societies, where people entered into new relationships outside kith and kin, especially in relation to work. For the first time the notion of identity became fluid and more dependent on roles other than ascribed ones. Dress, manners, residence and neighborhood, education, and many other factors, including those of class, gender, and race, helped to determine one's identity.

The ideals of modernity—rationality, progress, optimism, the search for universal or absolute knowledge in science, society, politics—in an important sense was seen to rest upon gaining knowledge of the *true self*; it was considered the foundation for all other knowledge. Modern identity, in posing questions about the self, raised the possibility that perhaps there was something lying behind the public persona—a real, true, or innate self. Such questioning or skepticism also expanded the possibilities of what we might become. In questioning the self, Sigmund Freud developed his theory of psychoanalysis, which saw this "true self" being based in unconscious instincts of the bourgeois family. Sociology developed and focused on the interactions of the individual and society, with many sociologists arguing that the family and the school provide the network of social interactions that helps to form a permanent "core" identity that is developed in childhood and adolescence. The emerging notions of modern identity introduced a new self-consciousness and initiated a persistent questioning: Who am I? What can I become? What should I be doing with my life? What is my true vocation? While it became more possible to determine one's identity rather than be restricted by traditional roles imposed from birth, it also increased anxiety about personal identity.

Postmodernity is the subject of considerable debate. For some theorists it is seen as a complete epistemological, aesthetic, and ethical break with modernity, which, it is alleged, has declined or exhausted itself. Post-modern philosophy has seriously challenged notions of universality, rationality, instrumentalism, and utility that characterize modernity; it has punctured the ethnocentrism and eurocentrism that these notions engendered. Postmodern philosophy is often considered to be a negative, pessimistic, nihilistic movement, in opposition to the Enlightenment and one that supports irrationality. Other theorists see postmodernity as an extension of modernity and a form of postindustrial society. There is no one date or point of separation between the two eras, nor is there any one definition of "postmodernity" and "postmodernism," but the late twentieth century, after the Second World War, seems to be a markedly different place from what it was before this time. While postmodernism seems to have social, economic, technological, and cultural components, there is no definitive essence of the postmodern. Postmodernism provides a flexible, critical way of thinking about the world and our relationship to it, rather than the uncovering of particular "facts," "truths," and "qualities" of our world. Postmodernity, in contrast to modernity, emphasizes a flexible shifting notion of identity that is very much the product of a network of shifting relationships (see Kvale, 1992). Postmodern philosophy is, above all, a challenge to foundational accounts of the self that are anchored in God, Reason, or Truth.

Structuralism and, particularly, poststructuralism form much of the philosophical basis of postmodernism. Postmodernist thought has been strongly influenced by how language has been perceived by structuralist and poststructuralist theorists. Structuralist thought centers on the work of Ferdinand de Saussure and Claude Lévi-Strauss. Three main structuralist notions are that meaning only occurs in relation to structure, that language provides the clearest demonstration of the structural and relational aspects of meaning, and that language enables us to give meaning to the world, to organize and construct it and ourselves.

Poststructuralism developed initially in France in the 1960s, from the work of Jacques Derrida, Jean-François Lyotard, Michel Foucault, Giles Deleuze, and Jean Baudrillard (Peters, 1996). It draws from a variety of sources to provide a specific philosophical position, strongly informed by the work of Nietzsche and Heidegger, against the social scientific pretensions of structuralism in "a reappraisal of the culture of the Enlightenment and its notion of universal reason" (Peters, 1996: 1). Nietzsche is pivotal for poststructuralism in many different ways—his linguistic ability, his genealogical inquiries, wherein he cultivates a form of historical narrative, his critique of truth, his conception of "will to power," his biological emphases, and, especially, his critique of the Cartesian–Kantian subject and his substitution of genealogy for ontology.

Peters (1999) argues that the theoretical development of French structuralism during the late 1950s and 1960s led to an institutionalization of a transdisciplinary "megaparadigm" where the semiotic and linguistic analysis of society, economy, and culture became central to the scientific analysis of sociocultural life in diverse disciplines such as anthropology, literary criticism, psychoanalysis, Marxism, history, aesthetic theory, and studies of popular culture. Structuralism helped to integrate the humanities and the social sciences, but it did so in an overly optimistic and scientistic (science as an ideology) conception. While poststructuralism shares structuralism's radical questioning of the problematic of the humanist subject, it challenges the way that structuralism's scientism and totalizing assumptions had been elevated to the status of a universally valid theory for understanding language, thought, society, culture, economy, and, indeed, all aspects of the human enterprise (Peters, 1999).

Poststructuralism can be defined in terms of both its affinities and continuities on the one hand and its theoretical innovations and differences with structuralism on the other (Peters, 1999). The affinities center on the critique of the humanist (Cartesian–Kantian) subject as rational, autonomous, and self-transparent. Poststructuralism also shares with structuralism a theoretical understanding of language and culture as linguistic and symbolic systems. The two related movements share a belief in unconscious processes and in hidden structures or sociohistorical forces that constrain and govern our behavior. Finally, they share a common intellectual inheritance and tradition based upon Saussure, Jacobson, the Russian formalists, Freud, Marx, and others. Poststructuralism inherits three broad ideas from structuralism: first, that language is a system that cannot point outside itself (meaning that it is not dependent upon correspondence with "reality" or with the world); second, that language *produces* rather than reflects meaning; and third, that language is not a product of individual intentionality of individual meaning-making—that is, individuals are born into a language and a culture and does not create it for themselves. Poststructuralism opens up texts to "free up" meaning by challenging the dogma that a text's meaning is dependent upon an author's intention. In the poststructuralist view the meaning of texts is never final: they have multiple meanings and are open to the active interpretation of the reader. Structuralism, in contrast, saw language as a closed system.

The importance of language and meaning to counseling, as exemplified by structuralist and poststructuralist modes of thought, is profound and has been largely unexplored by counselors. Language not only affects how we frame our notions of the self and identity, but also how a counselor deals with a client and their sense of meaning of the world in which they live.

Poststructuralism's innovations revolve around the reintroduction of and renewed interest in history, especially as it involves the "becoming" of the subject, where genealogical narratives replace questions of ontology or essence. Poststructuralism offers a challenge to the scientism of structuralism in the human sciences, an antifoundationalism in epistemology, and a new emphasis upon "perspectivism" in interpretation (that there is no one textual "truth," texts are open, instead, to multiple interpretation). Poststructuralism challenges the rationalism and realism that underlie structuralism's faith in scientific method, in progress, and in discerning and identifying universal structures of *all* cultures and the human mind. In other words, it is suspicious of metanarratives, transcendental arguments, and final vocabularies. These views involve the rediscovery of Nietzsche's critique of truth and his emphasis upon interpretation and differential relations of power, and also Heidegger's influential interpretation of Nietzsche. More recently, poststructuralism has developed a political critique of Enlightenment values, particularly of the way modern liberal democracies construct political identity on the basis of a series of binary oppositions (e.g., we/them, citizen/noncitizen, responsible/irresponsible, legitimate/illegitimate) that exclude "others" or some groups of people. In this sense poststructuralism can be seen as a deepening of democracy. Perhaps most importantly, poststructuralism explores the notion of "difference" (from Nietzsche and Saussure, and developed by Derrida and Lyotard), which serve as a motif not only for recognizing the dynamics of self and other, but also contemporary applications in multiculturalism and immigration. Poststructuralism invokes new analyses of power, particularly Foucault's "analytics of power" and the notion of "power/knowledge," both of which differ from accounts in liberal and Marxist theory, where power is seen as only repressive (see Peters, 1996, 1999).

It is the core assumptions about an essential human nature—its uniqueness and individuality—that are challenged by both structuralism and poststructuralism. A poststructuralist critique of humanism (as in narrative therapy, as discussed in chapter 7) does not attempt to uncover some preexisting dormant knowledge in the mind or heart of the person, nor any "true," "real," "authentic" or "essential" self. It also challenges individualistic, expert-centered forms of professional knowledge that aim to liberate the "real" or "repressed" or "hidden" self. Traditional humanist assumptions about the subject in psychology and counseling usually position it as a stable, fixed, autonomous being, often characterized as fully transparent to itself and responsible for his or her actions. In contrast, the notion of identity in poststructuralism (and narrative therapy) tends to be replaced with the notion of "subjectivity," which does not assume that people's identities are primarily stable and singular, but, rather, that they change and are contradictory (Lifton, 1993; Gergen, 1990, 1991, 2001).

Postmodern identity has rejected the modernist notion of a timeless, deep, inner authentic essential self in favor of an identity that is constructed, constituted, antiessentialist, chosen, fragmented, and even disintegrated and without substance. It is, in an era of mass consumerism that has seen lifestyle choices displace authenticity, a self where image, appearance, and style are what matters. This is termed *aestheticism* or *stylization* of life. Identity is particularly influenced by the predominance of urban cultures and is established by what we buy or hanker for, so that goods become symbols or signs of individuality, difference, and solidarity. Postmodern identity, because it is constructed, is fluid and dynamic, with public expression not necessarily consistent with the private self.

Some theorists negate the idea of any inner self. Goffman (1969) examined the self in terms of how people react in social situations and suggested that different façades are presented in different settings, with the self being an effect of the façade. He suggested that the self has no specific organic location, that it is not individually owned but arises instead from interaction with other social beings. The constructed self is the product of tension between two ideas that are often reduced to the old argument of determinism versus free will. First, we are not born with substance; we become what we are through being acted on by a series of social factors—that is, we are constructed and determined by the social and the cultural. Second, we have a degree of choice and are free, to an extent, to construct our identities for ourselves. A different role, which equates with a different self, is likely to be taken in a different social situation. There is no single essential self underneath the façade that is presented to the world, because the self is scattered over and by a complex of social forces.

In terms of the modernity/postmodernity, modernism/postmodernism debate, we might say for the purposes of this book that modernity is a humanism (see chapter 1) and that postmodern philosophy involves both an attack on the theoretical foundations of this humanism and a reevaluation of it, beginning with Nietzsche and continued, in their different ways, by Heidegger, Sartre, Derrida, and Foucault. For instance, Heidegger (1993), in his famous *Letter on Humanism* first published in 1946, questions the false and naïve anthropologism that has motivated humanism since its first formulation by Roman thought. In all its subsequent formulations, Heidegger laments, humanism never really questions its own metaphysical basis. While Heidegger's strategy is to rediscover primordial being in its pure state in the culture of the early Greeks—a strategy that seeks an uncorrupted form of the self, so to speak, in our ancient past—others, like Sartre, Derrida, and Foucault, have subsequently tried to bypass "essence" or being by historicizing questions of ontology.

In broad terms, the ideology of humanism centrally involves a stable, coherent, knowable, transparent self, who is deemed to be fully conscious, rational, autonomous, and universal. Heidegger and Sartre, among others, argue that it is this notion of self as unified and universal that underlies humanism and in its more robust forms seems to preclude all cultural and historical variation. Such a view relies upon the self as a source of knowledge—indeed, the inviolable foundations of knowledge for modern epistemology, starting with the philosophy of Descartes. Thus, the self knows itself and the world through reason, and this mode of knowing produced by the rational self is "objective knowledge" considered to amount to science—a form of knowledge that can produce truths about the world. Such objective knowledge is the basis for modernity's belief in progress and perfection, which can also provide scientific principles for human institutions, including education and learning. The old notion of ethics and politics as a practical form of reason falls away, to be replaced in the modern period by a new belief in science and the science of politics.

According to this humanist view, freedom is seen to consist of obedience to the laws conforming to the knowledge discovered by reason. In modernity science is the paradigm of all knowledge; it is considered both neutral and objective, and scientists who follow scientific methodology, motivated by the concerns of pure reason, are thought to pursue the Truth. Humanism as an ideology of modernity not only promotes this error-free and uncritical view of science, but also tends to assume, especially in the later twentieth century, that all knowledge is languagebased, that language as the mode of expression is also rational and transparent to the mind that formulates statements and propositions in the sciences. In this sense language is the medium for knowledge, and all knowledge is linguistically mediated; language reflects the world or is in some relation of correspondence with the world, such that the utterances or propositions that we devise are allegedly tested for their truth-value against states of affair in the world.

It is this view of humanism as one of the underlying ideologies of modernity that postmodern philosophy contests; it contests both the underlying view of the humanist subject as rational and universal and also the view of science and society built upon it. In this book I begin to examine counseling theory in terms of this debate. Its implications are enormous, for if the notion of the humanist subject is in error or up for reevaluation, then so is counseling's humanist construction of both the "client" and the "counselor."

COUNSELING THE "SELF"

Notions of the self and identity have been important themes for counseling since its inception, although many counseling theorists and practitioners have not always been sensitive to the philosophical or historical treatments of the self or how they inform different counseling theories. The guidance counseling profession often combines various strands, such as psychological testing, biological developmentalism, and philosophical and practitioner orientations, some of which have gained particular prominence and favored status at different times. But central to all are notions of what human nature is and curiosity about how and why people do what they do. These are sometimes split between essentialist and nonessentialist notions about the existence of an inner essence, soul, or spirit of the human being.

When counseling was introduced into schools in the 1960s in Britain, the United States, Canada, and New Zealand, it was mostly known as "guidance counseling." Guidance counseling combines two different and somewhat competing notions about the self: on the one hand, notions centered on "guidance," and on the other, notions centered on "counseling." The differentiation between the two has become more marked over time, especially since the 1980s, with the increased professionalization of counseling. Counseling has tended to become separate from guidance.

Counseling is very much concerned with "knowing" the self, but it is not necessarily expressed in these terms. This "knowing" is not just for the client; it is very much part of the requirements expected of the counselor as well. For the client, "knowing" the self forms part of their therapeutic work in the counseling process as part of creating meaning in their lives. For the counselor, learning about the self is part of a personal and professional identity that is established in counselor education courses. It does not stop there; it is expected to continue with ongoing professional development with supervision, so that the counselor maintains a high degree of personal reflectivity. Furthermore, although it is often not spelled out and, in fact, seems to be almost studiously ignored in an attempt to be inclusive and nonjudgmental, counseling is inherently a moral activity, not in the narrow prescriptive sense of laying out rules of behavior, but in its broader understanding concerning the promulgation of human values. It is all of these facets that the counselor needs to reflect on as part of "knowing" the self.

"Guidance" tends to be more directive than counseling because information, especially about careers or courses, remains a key component, but it is also concerned about the self (Brown, 1999; see chapter 6). Guidance has often drawn upon a liberal–humanist educational philosophy that traditionally believes in the importance of and respect for the "individual personality" and the notion that individuals can do things to improve themselves by making rational choices to develop the self and, thereby, also increase their fulfillment in life. Guidance philosophy seemed to view itself as "holistic," focusing on the "whole" person—the child's intellect, emotions, physique, socialization, vocational choices, and aesthetic, moral, and spiritual values (Jones, 1977; McGowan and Schmidt, 1962). The guidance movement, certainly in its early phase, as schools grew bigger and more impersonal in the era of mass education and of large classes, could be considered an attempt to provide the "personal touch" by treating students as "individuals" rather than as a mass.

One can detect and deconstruct the "liberal" philosophical assumptions about the nature of the self that are reflected in McGowan and Schmidt's (1962) text of readings, which was widely used for guidance counselor education in the 1960s and 1970s. McGowan and Schmidt (1962) outline eleven principles of counseling, which were not only widely accepted by counselors in the 1960s but also explicitly or implicitly underlie most guidance and counseling texts and codes of ethics even today.

1. Recognition of the dignity and worth of the individual and his/her right to help in a time of need.
2. A client-centered approach is required, concerned with the optimum development of the whole person for individual and social ends.
3. It is a continuous, sequential and educative process and therefore an integral part of education, not just an adjunct.
4. Counsellors have a responsibility to society as well as to the individual.
5. One must respect a person's right to accept or reject any help offered.
6. Guidance is about co-operation, not coercion.
7. It implies giving assistance to persons in making wise choices, plans, interpretations and adjustments in critical situations of life.
8. It demands a comprehensive study of the individual in his cultural setting by the use of every scientific technique available.
9. It should be entrusted only to those who are naturally endowed for the task and have the necessary training and experience.
10. The focus should be on helping the individual to realise his best self rather than on solving isolated problems of the individual, school or institution.
11. It must be under constant scientific evaluation in terms of its effectiveness. (McGowan and Schmidt, 1962: 95–96)

While the intense focus on the individual has been challenged in the later twentieth century by systems-oriented counseling, such clear statements at what were the formative stages of counselor education still have relevance today and are discussed in the paragraphs that follow. While this list may appear to be only a brief synopsis, the rationale it provides is important for portraying how guidance counseling was philosophically positioned in the 1960s. Unless there is critique that results in new sets of principles, notions such as this are likely to persist. Hence in the next few paragraphs, I unpack the list to uncover some of its inherent assumptions.

This list of principles shows how counseling theory was conceived to rest fundamentally upon a notion of the "individual," which functions as a "primitive." A primitive is not a description of an individual, but a philosophical presupposition beyond which we cannot go or an element that functions as an unquestioned premise of the argument. McGowan and Schmidt (1962) outline how the "individual" is the prime concept for counseling, is endowed with "rights," and is perceived in humanistic terms to have "dignity" and "worth." These assumptions are, in part, a product of Judeo–Christian culture and the cultural development of humanism through the Renaissance, where the values of "dignity," "worth," and "respect" for human beings was elevated to a philosophy. This was subsequently synthesized to become the basis for the European culture of human rights after the Second World War. The notion of the right to help and the expectation that one will offer it in a life-threatening situation, if there is no substantial risk to one's own life, is derived from and extends ancient Jewish notions of *hayyav,* related to a personal duty to give assistance and portrayed in the parable of the good Samaritan.

What this brief analysis begins to reveal is the culture-boundedness and cultural specificity of this Western Euro-centered conception of the "individual" that has passed through various stages and reformulations.

Eugene Kamenka (1978) argues, for instance, that the notion of human rights and that of the "individual" on which it rests is a culturally specific product of Western civilization:

> The concept of human rights is a historical product which evolves in Europe, out of foundations in Christianity, Stoicism and Roman law with its *ius gentium*, but which gains force and direction only with the contractual and pluralist nature of European feudalism, church struggles, the rise of Protestantism and of cities. It sees society as an association of individuals, as founded—logically or historically—on a contract between them, and it elevates the individual human person and his freedom and happiness to be the goal and end of all human association. In the vast majority of human societies, in time and space, until very recently such a view of human society would have been hotly contested; indeed, most cultures and languages would not have had the words in which to express it plausibly. (Kamenka, 1978: 6)

It is difficult for many people to put in brackets or stand outside their cultural beliefs and to problematize notions that are part of them, of their very constitution and of their identity or the ways in which they have come to understand themselves. This is especially so for those who are closely entwined in the Western hegemony[2] Rose's (1989, 1998) argument shows how the dominance of psychological discourse in twentieth-century culture has informed notions of how we envisage and talk about the self and identity. Certainly, for counselors operating in multicultural and often postcolonial states (like the United States, Canada, Australia, New Zealand), this requirement for problematizing the prevalent Western hegemony of beliefs and cultural assumptions concerning the "individual" and his or her constitution and rights is now becoming more and more critical. The hegemonic position is something that various minority groups frequently challenge.

The notions of "client-centeredness" and the "whole person" mentioned in the above list are more recent formulations in counseling, springing from Rogerian analysis and the human potential movement that developed in the United States in the mid- to late twentieth century. These notions have been interpreted positively, on the one hand, as forms of personal liberation, and negatively on the other, by some as being inherently manipulative, shaping the individual to fit into the system rather than the reverse (see Items 2 and 7) (see, for example, Illich, 1977; Foucault, 1973, 1990; Rose, 1989, 1998).

Counseling itself is seen as "educative"—that is, as part and parcel of the process of the "individual" learning about themselves, their relationships, and their world; it is defined as a "continuous" and "sequential" process. Yet these very terms are left undefined and seem to reflect an implicit understanding that counseling echoes the process of individual development defined as "stages of growth" in influential psychological texts by scholars such as Piaget and Havighurst.[3] The assumption is that there is a normal cycle of development, which is invariant and is cross-culturally valid. Many theorists, including Walkerdine (1984, 1986), have seriously challenged this assumption. The idea of an educative element does, however, provide a clear theoretical justification for the place of guidance counseling within education, not just as some frill that could or should be located outside it.

There is some conceptual "slippage" in this list of principles. For instance, the notion of "individual" in Items 1 and 4 becomes "person" in Items 2 and 5, although it is clear that in philosophical terms these notions are not the same. "Person" is a more developed notion in the sense that it assumes the moral status of "personhood"—that is, an appropriate object of direct moral concern such as is involved in the ascription of rights. In his Essay *On Liberty*, John Stuart Mill's ([1854] 1961) view was that "personhood" and its associated freedoms were not available either to children or to madmen. No such considerations of rights apply to the notion of "individual." As another example, Item 5 describes the "individual" in terms of "person's rights"—in other words, modern rights discourse is appealed to, in order to define the person—a very contemporary notion, as can be seen from the comment by Kamenka above.

One might begin to trace the different strands that make up this composite list of principles as including Kantian talk of rights based upon ascriptions to "persons," along with more recent American counseling discourses. While "clients" are "persons" who are ascribed certain "rights," counselors are perceived as having certain "responsibilities"— a "responsibility to society as well as to the individual" (Item 4) though these "responsibilities" are left unspecified. Among the rights of a person/client is their right to "accept or reject help," as mentioned above, and an implicit acceptance of "respect" for the individual's autonomy and choice-making capacity. Counselors need therefore not only to be aware of the multiple layers of responsibility to the person and to society, they also need to be able to make ethically based decisions about which responsibility takes priority. This can pose ethical dilemmas that have no simple solutions but require considerable wisdom, experience, and often consultation with supervisors. After all, who decides the priority of responsibility, and on what basis?

Item 6 indicates the "guidance" side of the "guidance counselor" formulation: "Guidance is about co-operation, not coercion." Yet this simple statement, with which most of us would agree, tends to minimize the ethical difficulties that face both the "client" in a school that he or she compulsorily attends, and the counselor, who is employed by the State or the school board, and who, like all teachers, is considered to be in *loco parentis*.[4] This item implies that guidance counseling should be nondirective, but it does not spell this out. Under the term "guidance," subtle forms of coercion and manipulation are very difficult to discern. Perhaps it is with this in mind that today school guidance counseling has tended to move away from the directive aspects that comprise "guidance"— educational and vocational testing and advice—to focus more on the nondirective, personal counseling aspects that are part of the more generic profession of "counseling" (certainly in New Zealand).

Guidance counseling, in the conception outlined in the principles above, is conceived as "giving assistance to persons in making wise choices . . . in critical situations of life." This view certainly endorses a picture of the Kantian autonomous adult who is capable of self-directed activity and is able to exercise his or her choices responsibly, and of a child who might be developing such skills. The question of how a counselor might "give assistance," apart from suggesting possible options, is left unexamined, and it is up to the counselor to decide on the basis of their theoretical orientation and professional skill. Just how directive that assistance might be is not spelled out. What is meant by "wise" and wise for whom is similarly left unstated, open, and ambiguous and hence is open to interpretation.

There is a focus on contextualizing counseling and possibly a concession to the scientific outlook in Item 8, where the individual is to be "studied" in "his [sic] cultural setting" This reflects on how the professional identity of counseling is expected to involve client-centeredness, inclusiveness, empathy, and understanding of others. Without these, one could scarcely be considered to be "counseling." Item 9 refers to the necessary training and characteristics of counselors, in particular those who are "naturally endowed," and seems to imply some essentialist theory of the "counseling self" as distinct from other persons. To be suitable to be a counselor requires a combination of personal attitudes, enhanced by training. Personal attributes are not enough. This notion is still strongly endorsed by all the universities requiring certain personal attributes and aptitudes before one is selected for counseling courses.

The focus for counseling "should be on helping the individual to realize his [sic] best self rather than on solving isolated problems of the individual, school or institution" (Item 10). What "best self" means here can be both literal and metaphorical. It implies that each individual has either more than one self, or different sides to the one self, over which the individual—with some help—can choose. In other words, individuals have some agency in shaping their self or choosing which aspect or which self they wish to develop or display. Individuals may be thought of as having different sides to their self; people often express this metaphorically as "my good side" or "my dark side" in referring to and making judgments about their feelings and behavior. But if the individual literally has different selves, the implications are more serious, since this tends toward fragmentation of the self and mental illness associated with schizophrenia or multiple personality disorders. In this situation there is little element of choice about styling the self. The focus at this point in the early history of counseling was more on the individual than on the system in which the individual was located, which might be the group, the family, or the institution. In recent years, an overemphasis on individualizing notions has been seriously challenged with the development of contextualizing and systems theory as applied to counseling, particularly in dealing with family therapy and with people from ethnic minorities.

The final item reflects very current "scientific" understanding for the evaluation of the "success" of the process and its effectiveness, and it possibly also reflects the demand for professional and public accountability. While the type of "scientific" evaluation is not spelt out, counseling in its early days was closely linked with the positivistic type of evaluation involving pre- and posttesting that is common in psychology. The testing aspect has been somewhat discredited, especially in relation to intelligence testing, and has been largely dropped from the present-day counseling repertoire. Evaluation requires counselors to be reflective about their practice and about themselves in this process, hence it points to the need for supervision. It also implies remaining up-to-date with current research and methods through ongoing professional development. This is partly why the NZAC Code of Ethics has supervision and professional development requirements (see chapter 6 and <www.nzac.org.nz/>). One does not just learn to be a counselor in one training course, leaving it at that and thinking that one knows it all. After all, what is the point of "doing" counseling or using certain counseling methods if they do not work and make a positive difference in the lives of clients. This becomes part of the counselor's duty to their profession and to society, as in Item 4.

I have spent some time unpacking and analyzing these eleven principles to demonstrate the state of counseling theory in the formative stages of counselor education as the profession was established in the 1960s. Counseling largely expects its clients to become self-reflective and hence it is only reasonable for the profession itself to be similarly reflective of its self, of its philosophy and its history. This analysis therefore supports the notion that counseling theorists and practitioners must become more aware of the philosophical and historical elements that have helped to shape their profession and their discourse.

MICHEL FOUCAULT: CARE OF THE SELF

Technologies of Domination

The earlier sections of this chapter have delved into a consideration of various conceptualizations of the self and of identity in different discourses—philosophical, psychological, anthropological, and feminist. These have been undertaken as a means of understanding key issues that are, I would argue, largely missing in the counseling literature. Although ethics is dealt with in some detail in counseling discourse, it tends to be in a somewhat instrumental manner around applications of ethical codes and how counselors practice rather than examining philosophical underpinnings and issues of ethical self-constitution (as discussed in chapter 6). This next section, then, looks in particular detail at Foucault's notions of the self, which not only provide quite a shift from earlier discourses on the self but also bring in notions of disciplinarity, governmentality, freedom, and ethics to understandings of the self.

In Foucault's body of work there are considered to be differences or breaks between his earlier work and his middle and later period. Foucault's earlier notions of the self conceived of individuals as "docile bodies" in the grip of disciplinary powers and technologies of domination. Foucault introduces notions of corporeality, politics, and power and its historico-social context into understandings of the self. In his later work he extends and more fully explains the idea of agency through technologies of the self and ethical self-constitution that overcomes some of the problematic political implications in his earlier work. By then Foucault sees individuals "as self-determining agents capable of challenging and resisting the structures of domination in modern society" (McNay, 1992: 4). The earlier and middle Foucault is considered to include *Discipline and Punish* (1977) and *The History of Sexuality,* Vol. I (1980a). His later work includes *The Use of Pleasure: The History of Sexuality,* Vol. II (1985) and *The Care of the Self: The History of Sexuality,* Vol. III (1990). The notions of "technologies of the self" and "governmentality" appeared around 1978/79. In discussing his work late in his life, Foucault says:

> My objective for more than twenty-five years has been to sketch out a history of the different ways in our culture that humans develop knowledge about themselves: economics, biology, psychiatry. Medicine, and penology. The main point is not to accept this knowledge at face value but to analyze these so-called sciences as very specific "truth games" related to specific techniques that human beings use to understand themselves. (1988b: 17–18)

He sets out a typology of four interrelated "technologies," each "a matrix of practical reason" and each permeated by "a certain type of domination" and implying some form of "training and modification of individuals":

(1) technologies of production, which permit us to produce, transform or manipulate things; (2) technologies of sign systems, which permit us to use signs, meanings, symbols, or signification; (3) technologies of power, which determine the conduct of individuals and submit them to certain ends or domination, an objectivizing of the subject; (4) technologies of the self, which permit individuals to effect by their own means or with the help of others a certain number of operations on their own bodies and souls, thoughts, conduct, and way of being, so as to transform themselves in order to attain a certain state of happiness, purity, wisdom, perfection, or immortality. (Foucault, 1988b: 18)

It was the last two of these that Foucault analyzed. In "Truth, Power, Self: An Interview," Foucault (1988a) points out that having worked through the following three questions in "Technologies of the Self" (Foucault, 1988b), he has returned to the first of these:

(1) What are the relations we have to truth through scientific knowledge, to those "truth games" which are so important on civilization and in which we are both subject and object? (2) What are the relationships we have to others through those strange strategies and power relationships? And (3) what are the strategies and relationships between truth, power, and self? (Foucault, 1988a: 15)

Foucault's genealogical critique that questions the "subject" aims at revealing the contingent and historical conditions of existence. Foucault historicizes questions of ontology, substituting genealogical investigations of the subject for the philosophical attempt to define the essence of human nature. The first question is addressed in the second subsection of this chapter, "Technologies of the Self."

Part of the answer to the second question is found in *Discipline and Punish* (1977), where the focus is on technologies of domination and disciplinarity and the way the self is produced by processes of objectification, classification, and normalization in the human sciences. Here Foucault describes situations where discipline creates the self with a form of individuality that comprises four characteristics (see chapter 1). Foucault uses "calculable" almost interchangeably with "normalized" in referring to individuals, in a way that "should be understood in terms of governance or controlling the outcomes of behavior" (Marshall, 1997: 38). For Foucault, both "technologies of domination" and "technologies of the self" produce effects that constitute the self. They define the individual and control his or her conduct (Marshall, 1997). These technologies are harnessed "to make the individual a significant element for the state" through the exercise of a form of power, which Foucault defined as governmentality, in becoming useful, docile, practical citizens. As Foucault notes, "what I have analyzed was always related to political action" In this case it "is concerned with social principles and institutions" (Foucault, 1988a: 14). "Discipline increases the forces of the body (in economic terms of utility) and diminishes these same forces (in political terms of obedience). In short, it dissociates power from the body; on the one hand, it turns it into an aptitude, a capacity, which it seeks to increase; on the other hand, it reverses the course of energy, the power that might result from it, and turns it into a relation of strict subjection" (Foucault, 1977: 138).

The disciplinary rationality—the objectives, means, and effects—of the carceral system that Foucault analyzes used technologies of domination that established a new economy of power or a "political anatomy." "Docile bodies" were created through a complex set of relations between power, knowledge, and the body. In *Discipline and Punish*, Foucault (1977) describes and analyzes a political system with the king's body at its center. Foucault suggests that a new principle—the "body of society"—emerges in the nineteenth century. The social body is protected through a series of dividing practices involving the segregation of the sick, the quarantining of "degenerates," the schooling of boys and girls, and the exclusion of delinquents. From the eighteenth to the beginning of the twentieth century, the disciplinary regimes of schools, hospitals, barracks, and factories involved the "heavy, ponderous, meticulous and constant" investment of the body by power. By the 1960s industrial societies realized that they could exist with a much looser form of power over the body. Different societies need a different kind of body, and we should set aside the commonly held notion that power in our capitalist societies has denied the reality of the body in favor of the mind or consciousness. So, Foucault quite clearly conceives of an embodied self, person, or individual.

In his analysis of "disciplinary blocks," Foucault (1977) identifies and substitutes the word "disciplines" for what are normally termed "professions" and "professionals" (doctors, psychiatrists, psychoanalysts, teachers, warders, the military), thereby challenging the way they are usually perceived and unmasking them. Foucault plays with the duality in the notion of "discipline" as both a subject area and a method of social control as applied to education. In the "disciplines" there are three interconnected notions of power, which, Marshall (1997) suggests, cannot be dissociated: power relationships, as between partners who interact and modify each other's actions; the power to modify, use, consume, or destroy things; and symbolic power.

Foucault's notion of the way we become subjects—people with a particular view of ourselves—as being in the form of "disciplinary blocks," which not only develop power-knowledge but also exercise this "according to knowledge which has itself been the product of the exercise of power" has immense implications for education (Marshall, 1997: 36). Marshall (1997: 37) provides an example of the interconnectedness of all three in schools, where "the adjustment of people's abilities and resources, relationships of communication, and power relationships, form regulated systems." The conditions required for such power to be exercised involve space, time, and capacities—for example, in the disciplinary block of a school it requires rooms, a timetable, and learning activities. Normal patterns of expectation become established via techniques such as exams, observation, placement, streaming, and remedial work, so that the knowledge that is gained through the exercise of power produces "normalized individuals."

Foucault's Nietzschean approach suspends the standard liberal normative framework where notions of rights are grounded in the humanist conceptions of human nature. Power involves a plurality of incommensurable discursive regimes, each with its multiplicity of "micropractices," which ultimately directs us to study the "politics" or power relations of everyday life and the way power is inscribed upon the self and body. Nietzsche inspired Foucault to analyze the modes by which human beings become subjects without privileging either power (as in Marxism) or desire (as in Freud).

Technologies of the Self

Foucault (1988b: 19) considers that he may have concentrated "too much on the technology of domination and power." So, in his later works, he moves to technologies of the self: "the interaction between oneself and others and in the technologies of individual domination, the history of how an individual acts upon himself." Foucault's definition of technologies of the self has been provided in the previous section. In his work on sexuality Foucault does not present a sociological account of the history of morality, or sexual practices. Instead, he is concerned with problematizing how pleasure, desire, and sexuality, the regimes of power–knowledge–pleasure as components of the art of living or "an aesthetics of existence," have become discourses that shape our construction of ourselves through the revelation of "truth" of our sexuality and of ourselves (Foucault, 1985: 12).

Volume I of *The History of Sexuality* (1980a) presents a change from technologies of domination. A common assumption of Western culture, that the body and its desires—its sexuality—reveal the truth about the self, is explored in this book. From this assumption it is then proposed that if one tells the "truth" about one's sexuality, this deepest truth about the self will become apparent, and then one can live an authentic life that is in touch with one's true self. Foucault (1988b: 16–17) says: "the association of prohibition and strong incitations to speak is a constant feature of our culture." As a result his project became: "a history of the link between the obligation to tell the truth and the prohibitions against sexuality. I asked: How had the subject been compelled to decipher himself in regard to what was forbidden? It is a question of the relation between asceticism and truth" (Foucault, 1988b: 17).

The main technologies in *The History of Sexuality* (1980a) are the examination and the confessional or therapeutic situation, where the psyche or emotions are addressed when a priest or therapist exerts her or his expert knowledge to reinterpret and reconstruct what the client says. Various professionals in the psy-sciences or helping professions (e.g., priests, doctors, psychiatrists, psychologists, psychoanalysts, counselors, etc.) are sought in order to help one to access this inner self or inner truth. They do this by administering certain "technologies" for speaking, listening, recording, transcribing, and redistributing what is said, such as examining one's consciousness, the unconscious, and confessing one's innermost thoughts, feelings, attitudes, desires, and motives about one's self and one's relationships with others (see chapter 1 on confession). However, in gaining this form of self-knowledge, one also becomes known to others involved in the therapeutic process. This can, in turn, control the self.

Foucault (1980a) argues that power operates through the discursive production of sexuality. He challenges the repressive hypothesis and how power operates through this. The incitement to talk about sexuality is closely related to notions of liberation from repression (see chapter 7 for a discussion of repressive hypothesis and liberation). In his historical analysis Foucault points out that Christianity has emphasized the importance of confession and of verbalized sexual matters. In the eighteenth and nineteenth centuries sex became a matter of "policing"; regulating sex through public discourses led to an emphasis on heterosexual monogamy and a scrutiny of "unnatural" forms of sexual behavior (e.g., masturbation, homosexuality). Sexual conduct was revealed and incorporated into discourse, with sexual prohibitions existing side-by-side with the development of scientific discourses about sexuality. The Victorians of the nineteenth century did not refuse to recognize sex, but they put in place an entire machinery for producing true discourses concerning it that aimed at formulating a uniform truth of sex. Discourse on sex became incorporated into medicine, psychiatry, criminal justice, and a series of social controls that emerged at the end of the nineteenth century: "which screened the sexuality of couples, parents and children, dangerous and endangered adolescents—undertaking to protect, separate and forewarn, signaling perils everywhere, awakening people's attention, calling for diagnoses, piling up reports, organizing therapies" (Foucault, 1980a: 30–31). The effect was that people became intensely aware of sex as a constant danger, "and this in turn created a further incentive to talk about it" (Foucault, 1980a: 31).

Some clinical and psychiatric examinations required the person to speak while an expert in both observation and interpretation determined whether or not the truth, or an underlying truth of which the person was unaware, had been spoken. Foucault (1980a) points to a shift from the medical model of healing, where a patient "confesses" the problem and inadvertently reveals the "truth" as part of the diagnostic clinical examination, to a therapeutic model, where both the confession and the examination are deliberately used for uncovering the truth about one's sexuality and one's self. In the process the therapy can create a new kind of pleasure: pleasure in telling the truth of pleasure. But speaking the truth is not only descriptive. In confession one is expected to tell the truth about oneself—a basic assumption that most counselors continue to make about their clients. Because language has a performative function, speaking the truth about oneself also makes, constitutes, or constructs forms of one's self. By these discursive means and through these technologies a human being turns him or herself into a subject.

Historically there have been two great procedures for producing the truth of sex. Many societies have an *ars erotica* [erotic art], whereby truth is drawn from pleasure itself. Western society, however, has *scientia sexualis*, procedures for telling the truth of sex, which are geared to a form of knowledge-power found in confession. In confession, the agency of domination resides not in the person who speaks, but in the one who questions and listens. Sexual confession became constituted in scientific terms through "a clinical codification of the inducement to speak; the postulate of a general and diffuse causality; the principle of a latency intrinsic to sexuality; the method of interpretation; and the medicalization of the effects of confession" (see Foucault, 1980a: 59–70).

Foucault challenges the chronology of the techniques relating to sex in the fields of medicine, pedagogy, and demography and argues that they do not coincide with the hypothesis of a great repression of sexuality in the seventeenth century. Concerns about sexuality first occurred within the upper classes because of worries about their own class survival, which were expressed in terms of vigor, longevity, progeniture, and techniques for maximizing life through an affirmation of self. There was a steady growth of methods and procedures around sexuality that did not at first see the ruling classes limiting the pleasures of others, but successive shifts and transpositions extended sexuality from being just the concern of the bourgeoisie to involve other classes.

Over time, the mechanisms of power in relation to the body and the self have changed considerably in the West. The ancient right of the sovereign "to *take* life or *let* life was replaced by a power to *foster* life or *disallow* it to the point of death" (Foucault, 1980a: 138). From the seventeenth century onward, two poles emerged over which power over life became organized: an "anatomo-politics of the human body" as a machine operated on by the power of the disciplines and a "bio-politics of the population" of regulatory power that control the body of the species (Foucault, 1980a: 139). From the eighteenth century on, the politics of sex combined "disciplinary techniques with regulative methods" that revolved around the themes of the descent of the species and collective welfare (Foucault, 1980a: 146). Discipline focused on four issues: "the sexualization of children" where a campaign against precocious sexuality was concerned about health of society, the race, and the species; "the hysterisation of women" that thoroughly medicalized their bodies and sex in the name of responsibility to the family and to society; the institution of birth control and the "psychiatrisation of perversions" (Foucault, 1980a: 146–147). These four issues formed specific mechanisms of power-knowledge that centered on sex, which became the focus of the individual "body" and the aggregated "population" of a state. The mechanisms of power became organized around the management of the body, sex, and life rather than death at the hands of a sovereign power (see Foucault, 1980a: 136–147): "bio-power was without question an indispensable element in the development of capitalism; the latter would not have been possible without the controlled insertion of bodies into the machinery of production and the adjustment of the phenomena of population to economic processes" (Foucault, 1980a: 140–141).

In *The History of Sexuality: The Use of Pleasure,* Vol. II (1985), Foucault points out that his study shifts to the "arts of existence," which are those actions by which men not only set themselves rules of conduct, but also seek to transform themselves, to change themselves in their singular being, and to make their life into an *oeuvre* that carries certain aesthetic values and meets certain stylistic criteria. These "arts of existence," these "techniques of the self," no doubt lost some of their importance and autonomy when they were assimilated into the exercise of priestly power in early Christianity, and later, into educative, medical, and psychological types of practices. (Foucault, 1985: 11)

In "Technologies of the Self' (1988b), Foucault's emphasis shifts to "the hermeneutics of the self' in "(1) Greco-Roman philosophy in the first two centuries A.D. of the Roman Empire and (2) Christian spirituality and the monastic principles developed on the fourth and fifth centuries of the late Roman Empire" (Foucault, 1988b: 19). What Foucault argues is that the Delphic moral principle, "know yourself' [*gnothi sauton*], has become overemphasized and has now taken precedence over another ancient principle and set of practices that were "to take care of yourself," or "to be concerned with oneself' [*epimel√sthai sautou*] (Foucault, 1988b: 19). According to Foucault, care of the self formed one of the main rules for personal and social conduct and for the art of life in ancient Greek cities. The two principles were interconnected, and it was from this principle that the Delphic principle was brought into operation as a form of "technical advice, a rule to be observed for the consultation of the oracle" (Foucault, 1988b: 19). In modern-day Western culture the moral principles have been transformed, perhaps partly as a result of "Know thyself' being the principle that Plato privileged, which subsequently became hugely influential in philosophy. Foucault argues that "know yourself' is the fundamental austere principle nowadays, because we tend to view care of the self as immoral, as something narcissistic, selfish, and an escape from rules. Although there is no direct continuity from ancient to present times, Foucault's genealogy of sexuality does indicate some continuities and some of the Ancient Greek roots of our sexual ethics. First, Christianity adopted and modified themes from ancient philosophy and made renouncing the self the condition for salvation, but "to know oneself was paradoxically the way to self-renunciation" (Foucault, 1988b: 22). Second, our secular tradition "respects external law as the basis for morality," in contradiction to more internalized notion of morality associated with concern for the self. Echoing Nietzsche (in *Genealogy of Morals, 19*56), Foucault (1988b: 22) says: "Know thyself' has obscured "Take care of yourself' because our morality, a morality of asceticism, insists that the self is that which one can reject." Furthermore, theoretical philosophy since Descartes has positioned "knowledge of the self (the thinking subject) . . . as the first step in the theory of knowledge" (Foucault, 1988b: 22). Foucault argued for the return of the ancient maxim of "care of the self' because since the Enlightenment the Delphic maxim became overriding and inextricably linked with constituting subjects who are able to be governed.

Peters (2001b) discusses truth-games that Foucault elaborated in a series of six lectures given at Berkeley in 1983, entitled "Discourse and Truth: The Problematization of Parrhesia."[5] In the classical Greek, the use of *parrhesia* and its cognates exemplifies the changing practices of *truth-telling*. Foucault investigates the use of *parrhesia* in education to show that education was central to the "care of the self," public life, and the crisis of democratic institutions. He states that his intention was "not to deal with the problem of truth, but with the problem of truth-teller or truth-telling as an activity" (65/66). He claims that truth-telling as a speech activity emerged with Socrates as a distinct set of philosophical problems that revolved around four questions: "who is able to tell the truth, about what, with what consequences, and with what relation to power." Socrates pursued these in his confrontations with the Sophists in dialogues concerning politics, rhetoric, and ethics. These lectures reveal how Foucault thought that the "critical" tradition in Western that is "concerned with the importance of telling the truth, knowing who is able to tell the truth, knowing why we should tell the truth" begins precisely at the same time as an "analytics of truth" that characterizes contemporary analytic philosophy. Foucault says that he aligns himself with the former "critical" philosophical tradition rather than with the latter (65/66).

In this set of lectures Foucault utilizes Nietzschean genealogy to problematize the practices of *parrhesia* in classical Greek culture—a set of practices, culturally speaking, that are deep-seated for the West and take various forms. He demonstrates that these practices link truth-telling and education in ways that are still operative in shaping our contemporary subjectivities. They are therefore relevant in understanding the exercise of power and control in contemporary life.

A shift occurred in the classical Greek conception of *parrhesia* from a situation where someone demonstrated the courage to tell other people the truth to a different truth game, which focused on the self and the courage that people displayed in disclosing the truth about themselves. This new kind of truth game of the self requires "*ask√sis,*" which is a form of practical training or exercise directed at the art of living [*techne tou biou*]. The Greek practice of *ask√sis* differs significantly from the Christian counterpart of ascetic practices. In the Greek, the goal is establishing of a specific relationship to oneself—of self-possession, self-sovereignty, self-mastery. In the Christian, it is renunciation of the self. Thus Foucault continues the arguments he put up in "Technologies of the Self" (1988b) that Christian asceticism involves detachment from the world, whereas Greco-Roman moral practices are concerned with "endowing the individual with the preparation and the moral equipment that will permit him to fully confront the world in an ethical and rational manner" (55/66). The crucial difference in the ethical principle of self consists of ancient Greek *self-mastery* versus Christian *self-renunciation.*

Foucault had earlier elaborated on both the Greek (Platonic and Stoic) and Christian techniques. The Stoic techniques include, first, "letters to friends and disclosure of self," second, the "examination of self and conscience, including a review of what was to be done, of what should have been done and a comparison of the two," third, "*ask√sis*, not a disclosure of the secret self but a remembering," and, fourth, "the interpretation of dreams" (Foucault, 1988b: 34–38). He points out that this is "not renunciation but the progressive consideration of self, or mastery over oneself, obtained not through the renunciation of reality but through the acquisition and assimilation of truth . . . that is characterised by *paraskeuaz›* " [to get prepared] (Foucault, 1988b: 35).

In fact, it transforms truth into a principle of action or *ethos,* or ethics of subjectivity, that involves two sets of exercise—the *melet√* (or *epimel√sthai*) or meditation, and the *gymnasia* or training of oneself. The *melet√* was a philosophical meditation that trained one's *thoughts* about how one would respond to hypothetical situations. The *gymnasia* is a *physical* training experience that may involve physical privation, hardship, purification rituals, and sexual abstinence. Foucault (1988b) remarks that despite it being a popular practice, the Stoics where mostly critical and skeptical about the interpretation of dreams. It is interesting to note the reemergence of many of these practices of the self in the different psychotherapies the nineteenth and twentieth centuries, and Foucault does a real service in pointing us to the philosophical and historical roots of some of these.

In his exploration of the main techniques of the self in early Christianity—a salvation-confessional religion—Foucault determines both continuities and discontinuities. Christianity links the notion of illumination with truth and disclosure of the self:

> "an ensemble of truth obligations dealing with faith, books, dogma, and one dealing with truth, heart and soul. Access to truth cannot be conceived of without purity of soul. Purity of the soul is the consequence of self-knowledge and a condition of understanding the text; in Augustine: *Quis facit veritatem* to make truth in oneself, to get access to the light). (Foucault, 1988b: 40)

In early Christianity two main forms of disclosing self emerged: first, *exomolog√sis,* then *exagoreusis.* Despite being very different—the former a dramatic form, the latter a verbalized one—what they have in common is that disclosing the self involves renouncing one's self or will. Early on disclosure of self involved *exomolog√sis* or "recognition of fact," with public avowal of the truth of their faith as Christians and "a ritual of recognizing oneself as a sinner and penitent" (Foucault, 1988b: 41). Foucault, points out the paradox that "exposé is the heart of *exomolog√sis* . . . it rubs out the sin and yet reveals the sinner" (Foucault, 1988b: 42). Penance became elaborated around notions of torture, martyrdom, and death, of renouncing self, identity, and life in preferring to die rather than compromising or abandoning one's faith. Foucault points out that Christian penance involves the refusal or renunciation of self, so that "self-revelation is at the same time self-destruction" (Foucault, 1988b: 43). Whereas for the Stoics the "examination of self, judgement, and discipline" lead to "self-knowledge by superimposing truth about self through memory, that is, memorizing rules," for Christians, "the penitent superimposes truth about self by violent rupture and dissociation." Furthermore, "*exomolog√sis* is not verbal. It is symbolic, ritual and theatrical" (Foucault, 1988b: 43).

Foucault asserts that later, in the fourth century, a different set of technologies for disclosing the self—*exagoreusis*—emerged in the form of verbalizing exercises or prayers that involve taking account of one's daily actions in relation to rules (as in Senecan self-examination). With monastic life, different confessional practices developed, based on the principles of obedience and contemplation, and confession developed a hermeneutic role in examining the self in relation to one's hidden inner thoughts and purity. Foucault concludes by emphasizing that the verbalization techniques of confession have been important in the development of the human sciences. They have been transposed and inserted into this different context, "in order to use them without renunciation of the self but to constitute, positively, a new self. To use these techniques without renouncing oneself constitutes a decisive break" (Foucault, 1988b: 49).

An Ethics of Self-formation

In Foucault's later works the emphasis on the self shifts further, so that one no longer needs the expertise of the priest or therapist, one is able to do it for oneself, to ethically constitute the self (McNay, 1992).

"The Ethics of the Concern for Self as a Practice of Freedom" is an interview that was conducted with Foucault in 1984—the year of his death—by H. Becker, R. Fornet-Betancourt, and A. Gomez-Müller. Foucault is initially questioned concerning the change in his thinking about the relationship between subjectivity and truth. Foucault explains how in his earlier thinking he had conceived of the relationship between the subject and "games of truth" in terms of either coercion practices (psychiatry or prison) or theoretical-scientific discourses (the analysis of wealth, of language, of living beings, especially in *The Order of Things*). In his later writings he breaks with this relationship, to emphasize games of truth not as a coercive practice, but, rather, as *an ascetic practice of self-formation*—"ascetic" in this context meaning an "exercise of self upon the self by which one attempts to develop and transform oneself, and to attain a certain mode of being" (Foucault, 1997a: 282).

"Work" completed by the self upon itself is an *ascetic* practice that is to be understood not in terms of more traditional left-wing *models of liberation,* but rather as (Kantian) *practices of freedom.* This is an essential distinction for Foucault because the notion of liberation suggests that there is a hidden self or inner nature or essence that has been "concealed, alienated, or imprisoned in and by mechanisms of repression" (Foucault, 1997a: 282). The process of liberation, according to this model, liberates the "true" self from its bondage or repression. By contrast, Foucault historicizes questions of ontology: there are no essences, only "becomings"—only a phenomenology or hermeneutics of the self—the forging of an identity through processes of self-formation. To Foucault, liberation is not enough, and the practices of freedom do not preclude liberation, but they enable individuals and society to define "admissible and acceptable forms of existence or political society" (Foucault, 1997a: 283).

Foucault describes the notion of *governmentality* as "the relationship of the self to the self" covering "the whole range of practices that constitute, define, organize, and instrumentalize the strategies that individuals in their freedom can use in dealing with each other" (Foucault, 1997a: 300). In this lecture he rejects Sartre's idea that power is evil. He states instead: "Power is not evil. Power is games of strategy" (Foucault, 1997a: 298), and that the ways of avoiding the application of arbitrary, unnecessary, or abusive authority "must be framed in terms of rules of law, rational techniques of government and ethos, practices of the self and of freedom" (Foucault, 1997a: 299).

Foucault is drawing a contrast between two different models of self-interpretation: liberation and freedom. He suggests that the latter is broader than the former and historically necessary once a country or people have attained a degree of independence and set up political society. There may well be some translation difficulties between the French and English languages around notions of liberation and freedom. For example, a person in chains is not free, and although he or she may have some choices, these are severely limited by their lack of freedom. They have to be liberated or freed from their total domination in order to have the freedom to practice their own ethics. Freedom that equates with liberation is therefore a precondition of ethics, since ethics are the practices of the "free" person. In a particular example, Foucault uses questions of sexuality and suggests that the ethical problem of freedom in relation to sexuality is politically and philosophically more important than a simple insistence on liberating sexual desire. In other words, he wishes to understand freedom as the ontological condition for ethics, especially when freedom takes the form of a kind of informed reflection. This general understanding he begins to outline in terms of the ancient Greek imperative of "care for the self."

Foucault's discussion has strong and obvious relationships to counseling models, and it has clear applications to counseling in a school context. Here, the model of the self in relation to practices of freedom seems to promise a philosophical approach that offers counselors a model that is both historically accurate and ethically suitable to the way counselors have attempted to define their profession. Foucault's account also offers a Kantian-like basis for ethics based upon the way in which choices we make under certain conditions create who we become. He also offers a very useful theory of power. Yet at the same time Foucault is not immune to criticism, and counselors, if they are to make use of Foucault's work, must also be aware of his faults or limitations.

SOME CRITICISMS OF FOUCAULT

Three areas of criticism are dealt with in this section. First, I raise some of the feminist criticisms against Foucault's work. It is clear that he does not entertain the possibility that he might display a bias against women; for instance, Foucault (1997a) twice refers to the husband as governing his wife and children in terms of power relations. This indicates that he can be criticized, therefore, for his conservative, patriarchal position, which does not in any way consider feminist discourses already in existence (e.g., see McNay, 1992; Ramazanoglu, 1993).

Second, in his discussion of ancient Greek (Plato, Socrates, Xenophon) philosophical notions of "care of the self," Foucault (1997a) does not seem to discuss the idea that "care of the self" involves "care for others," or that "care for others" is an explicit ethic in itself. He states that "care for others" as an explicit notion in itself became an explicit ethic later on and should not be put before "care of the self" (see Foucault, 1984e, 1998b, 1997a). He accepts that the ancient Greek notion embodied in "care of the self" is an inclusive one that precludes the possibility of tyranny because a tyrant does not, by definition, take "care of the self," since he does not take care of others. Foucault seems to display a remarkable naïveté about the goodness of human beings in depicting how "care of the self" involves a considerable generosity of spirit and benevolent relations for a ruler of others, be they one's slave, wife, or children. Yet the argument that Foucault develops is so compressed that it needs some elaboration or teasing out to check out the major premises of what he does mean that is examined later in this section.

Third, there is a set of historical criticisms that revolves around Foucault's scholarship concerning his "readings" or interpretations of the ancient Greeks and, particularly, his emphasis on "care of the self." I deal with each of these criticisms or points in turn.

First, various feminist writers have emphasized that Foucault's work provides a critique of gendered power relations and a challenge to biological essentialist constructions of "women," "girls," and "femaleness." Yet, at the same time as offering a challenge to contemporary feminist theory, Foucault has also become the object of criticism (see, e.g., McNay, 1992; Ramazanoglu, 1993). Lois McNay (1992) argues that Foucault's early emphasis on the body and his later emphasis on the self has provided conceptual frameworks for understanding the gendered self. Foucault's analysis of power in relation to the body, McNay suggests, helps to explain women's oppression. She argues that Foucault's early work, with an emphasis on the body, tends to focus upon a docility and passiveness that robs the subject of any agency or autonomy. As such, this tends to be at odds with the aim of the feminist project of emancipatory politics, which is to recognize and rehabilitate the importance of women's experience. His later work, including *The History of Sexuality*, particularly Volumes II and III (*The Use of Pleasure* and *The Care of the Self*), McNay argues, overcomes these limitations of his early work, allowing for both self-determination or agency—or, more precisely, self-regulation or "ethical self-constitution"—and a notion of power that is not simply based upon repression, coercion, or domination. Foucault himself defended the "determinist" emphasis in *Discipline and Punish*, admitting that not enough was said about agency, so he redefined power to include agency (see Afterword in Rabinow, 1997). Foucault's understanding of what he calls "technologies of self" serves to balance his earlier emphasis of technologies of domination.

While some criticisms can be made of Foucault's early work from a feminist perspective, it is also clear that his notion of the "disciplinary society" has very strong implications for any critical understanding of school counseling, which in his terms, historically, might be considered a form of disciplinary apparatus of "schooling." The feminist appreciation of Foucault's later work tends to provide a gendered understanding of counseling and how important questions of female identity, subjectivity, and the institutional formation of the female subject have been (see Middleton, 1998).

On similar grounds to the feminist critique, concerns have been raised about Foucault's work and its capacity to address questions about the construction of "racial" or ethnic identity, or even the question of cultural difference per se. Certainly, some anthropologists have raised criticisms against Foucault for his Eurocentrism and his apparent lack of theoretical attention to the question of cultural imperialism. Yet it is the use of Foucault's work by the postcolonial theorists such as Edward Said (1978, 1993), Homi Bhabha (1990), and Gayatri Spivak (1999) that has enabled Foucauldian postcolonial accounts to be developed (see also Stoler, 1995).

The second area of criticism about "care of the self" can be better understood by elaborating the very compressed argument that forms Foucault's position. Rabinow (1997) provides a useful summary of the steps in Foucault's argument, and I present them here as a series of related premises in summary form:

Premise 1: "What is ethics, if not the practice of liberty, the considered practice of liberty (Foucault, 1997a). "Freedom is the ontological condition of ethics. But ethics is the considered form that freedom takes" (ibid.).

Premise 2: In the western tradition, "taking care of oneself requires knowing oneself." "To take care of the self is to equip oneself with these truths (p. 281); thus, as Rabinow (1997: xxv) points out quoting Foucault (1997a), "ethics is linked to the game of truth."

Premise 3: Ethics is a practice or style of life, and the problem for Foucault is to give "liberty the form of an ethos" (Foucault, 1997a).

Premise 4: The subject "is not a substance. It is a form, and this form is not primarily or always identical to itself" (Foucault, 1997a). As Rabinow (1997: xxvi) explains, "'self' is a reflexive pronoun, and has two meanings. *Auto* means 'the same,' but it also conveys the notion of identity. The latter meaning shifts the question from 'What is the self?' to 'What is the foundation on which I shall find my identity?'"

Premise 5: So the emphasis shifts to the historical constitution of these forms and their relation to "games of truth." "A game of truth is a set of procedures that lead to a certain result, which, on the basis of its principles and rules of procedures, may be considered valid or invalid." "Why truth? . . . And why must the care of the self occur only through the concern for truth? [This is] *the* question for the West. How did it come about that all of Western culture began to revolve around this obligation of truth . . . ?" (Foucault, 1997a). Rabinow (1997: xxvi) comments that given these premises, one must conclude equally that "one escaped from a domination of truth" only by playing the game differently.

Premise 6: "the relationship between philosophy and politics is permanent and fundamental" (Foucault, 1997a).

Premise 7: Rabinow (1997: xxvi) remarks, "Philosophy, understood as a practice and a problem, is a vocation. The manner in which liberty is taken up by the philosopher is distinctive, differing in intensity and zeal from other free citizens."

In Rabinow's formulation of Foucault's argument, it is clear that the overriding emphasis is on "care for the self," and there is no explicit discussion about "care for others" or the possibility of inferring the latter from the former (see Foucault, 1984e). Perhaps this emphasis on the centrality of truth in relation to the self is to be developed only through the notion of "others" as an audience—intimate or public—that allows for the politics of confession and (auto)biography.

With regard to the third point, Arnold Davidson (1997) makes it clear that Foucault, especially in his later work, *The Care of the Self* (1990), drew heavily on Pierre Hadot's[6] work on "spiritual exercises." Davidson suggests that Foucault owed Hadot an intellectual debt, especially with regard to what Foucault called "ethics" or the self's relationship to itself or what might be called "ethical self-constitution." He suggests that Foucault's four main aspects of the self's relationship to itself are an appropriation of Hadot's fourfold framework for interpreting ancient thought:

> the ethical substance, that part of oneself that is taken to be the relevant domain for ethical judgment; the mode of subjection, the way in which the individual established his relation to moral obligations and rules; the self-forming activity or ethical work that one performs on oneself in order to transform oneself into an ethical subject; and, finally, the telos, the mode of being at which one aims in behaving ethically. (Davidson, 1997: 200–201).

Hadot emphasized that in ancient schools of thought philosophy was considered to be a way of life, a quest for wisdom, a way of being, and, ultimately, a way of transforming the self. Spiritual exercises were pedagogy designed to teach its practitioners the philosophical life that had both a moral and an existential value. These exercises were aimed at nothing less than a transformation of one's world view and one's personality, involving all aspects of one's being, including intellect, imagination, sensibility, and will. Hadot claimed that in the figure of Socrates we find a set of dialogical spiritual exercises that epitomized the Socratic injunction, "Know thyself!" and provided a model for a relationship of the self to itself that constituted the basis of all spiritual exercise. In this model, Hadot draws our attention to the primacy of the process one adopts to a problem rather than the solution. Hadot's ([1987] 1995) major work, *Exercises spirituels et philosophie antique,* shows how this set of dialogical relations of the self (with itself) is at the very center of a total transformation of one's being (see Davidson, 1997). In a clear and important sense, Hadot's work provides school counseling with an ancient philosophical basis or model that is at once transformative, ethical, dialogic, and pedagogical. It is a model that could both complement and correct certain emphases in Foucault's later thinking about truth and subjectivity.

Hadot takes Foucault to task for the inaccuracies of his interpretation of Greco-Roman ethics as "an ethics of the pleasure one takes in oneself" (Hadot, [1987] 1995: 207). He criticizes Foucault for making too much of "pleasure" in relation to ancient Greek understanding of the self, truth, and subjectivity. We must ask: How far is Foucault's account historically astray? And to what extent do Foucault's possible historical errors of scholarship (according to Hadot) matter for the philosophical formulations and understandings based upon them? (This book does not seek to resolve these important questions.) Foucault's (1997b) essay, "Writing the Self," clearly draws on Hadot's groundbreaking work. This essay is part of what Foucault calls his studies of "arts of the self," which are designed to explore the "aesthetics of existence" and to inquire into the government of self and others that characterizes his later work. Foucault's essay analyzes a passage from Athanasius's *Vita Antoni*: "Here is one thing to observe to ensure that one does not sin. Let us each take note of and write down the actions and movements of our souls as though to make them mutually known to one another, and let us be sure that out of shame at being known, we will cease sinning and have nothing perverse in our hearts" (cited in Foucault, 1997b: 234).

Foucault notes that this "self-writing" . . . "offsets the dangers of solitude" and exposes our deeds to a possible gaze; at the same time the practice works on *thoughts* as well as actions, which brings it into line with the role of confession (in the early Christian literature). It permits, at the same time, a retrospective analysis of "the role of writing in the philosophical culture of the self just prior to Christianity: its close tie with apprenticeship; its applicability to movements of thought; its role as a test of truth" (1997b: 235).

One element that we might derive from Foucault and Hadot is the importance of "writing" and "reading" the self to counseling, alongside the more conventional conversational or dialogical forms that it takes. In other words, while acknowledging their current existence as counseling techniques, the emphasis in school counseling might be widened to reemphasize the forms of bibliotherapy, diaries, journal writing, personal narratives, autobiographies, biographies, together with the educative impulse of all forms of fiction, poetry, and drama or role play—both in film and television—that focus on the self.

This chapter began by providing some philosophical perspectives on the self and identity before turning to investigate these concepts in school counseling. It then examined new approaches to the concept of identity, exploring the ways in which structuralism and poststructuralism have rejected modernist notions of the essential or authentic self in favor of the notion of identities that are socially constructed, chosen, multiple, and fragmented. The chapter then went on to discuss the ways in which the notion of the humanist self has underwritten forms of counseling. Finally, the chapter introduced Michel Foucault's "care of the self," discussing in turn "technologies of domination," "technologies of the self," and "an ethics of self-formation," before raising some criticisms of Foucault. From a focus on philosophical understandings of the self and of identity, the book now moves to uncover how the terms "adolescence" and "youth" have been theorized in both psychological and sociological discourses in chapter 3 and chapter 4, respectively.

CHAPTER 3

PSYCHOLOGIZING ADOLESCENCE

INTRODUCTION: WHAT IS "ADOLESCENCE"?

After examining notions of the self and identity in some detail in chapter 1, this chapter poses the questions: "What is 'adolescence'?" "How has adolescence been constructed?" Allison James, Chris Jenks, and Alan Prout (1998) theorized childhood in a way that included adolescence. They contend that nowadays traditional understandings and certainty about children's social status are being undermined as a result of intense scrutiny, as childhood has become "popularized, politicized, scrutinized and analyzed in a series of interlocking spaces" (James, Jenks, and Prout, 1998: 3). Discourse on childhood no longer remains confined to parents, teachers, or developmental psychologists.

The chapter proceeds with an "archaeology" to uncover some of the ways in which Western societies have constructed the notions of adolescence/youth in the twentieth century. Since psychological discourse has had a major impact on both education and on counseling theory and therapies, three major areas of psychology—developmental, behaviorist, and humanist-existential psychology—are each assigned a section surveying a selection of key theorists. Psychologized discourses, especially developmental and humanist orientations, have profoundly influenced how we think of young people and have become the dominant discourse within the institution of the school, in pedagogy, and in counseling (Baker, 2001; Winslade and Monk, 1999; Wyn and White, 1997).

It seems that from some combination of these many different theoretical positions, and partly defined against philosophical notions of the "normal" adult self as a rational, responsible, autonomous being—a highly value-laden view of what adults are or should be—society constructs a meaning of "adolescence" or "youth." Chronological age is often used in describing adolescence, but it has limitations, mostly reflecting status, and somewhat arbitrary and convenient bureaucratic conventions. Biological definitions generally equate the start of adolescence with attaining sexual maturity. But gender differences are apparent, with menarche a clear-cut event for girls, whereas for boys there is no such observable event. Menarche tends to occur about two years earlier than any of the criteria—first ejaculation, development of pubic hair, growth spurt—used to describe puberty for boys. With a considerable chronological age variation for these events according to gender, ethnicity, and socioeconomic level, biological definitions are of limited value in discussing the notion of adolescence. This introduction therefore begins with a less contentious note: an etymological outline of the term adolescence and its related words, "teenager" and "youth."

Etymological derivations are particularly apposite, with "adolescence," "pubescence" and "puberty" all derived from Latin: *adolescere*, meaning "to grow into maturity," *pubescere*, meaning "to grow hairy," and *puberta*, meaning "the age of manhood." The *Shorter Oxford Dictionary* notes that "adolescence" comes from Middle English via French, dated at 1482 at its earliest, and means "growing from childhood to maturity." "Puberty" is the time when sexual maturity occurs; pubescence, often referred to as "early adolescence,"is the period approximately two years prior to puberty. "Teenagers" refers to the specific age group of 11–19 years; it was a term that came to prominence in the Second World War. "Youth" is a rather less precise and more flexible term. *The Shorter Oxford Dictionary* notes "youth" as coming from Old English, its earliest use (by Shakespeare) dated 1580; it means "being young (vigour or enthusiasm or inexperience or other characteristics of) period between childhood and adult age." It is sometimes used to include all those between childhood and adulthood but is often used to describe late adolescents and older teenagers. Nowadays, with the prolongation of adolescent dependency in the developed world, but probably for bureaucratic convenience, the World Health Organization has extended "youth" to include young adults up to 24 years of age (see Beautrais et al., 1998, for WHO statistics on youth suicide). This situation may well reflect the situation of "dependency" in the developed world, but it certainly does not reflect the reality of the developing world.

The word "adolescence" tends to be used more in the psychological literature, while "youth" has been the more favored in the sociological and postmodern literature. In this *categorical* approach, adolescents are commonly viewed as having essential characteristics based on age and the assumed link between physical growth and developmental tasks that they need to complete in order to achieve a stable personality and identity as mature adults (Wyn and White, 1997). Adolescence is seen as a time of preparation for a future "real" life as an adult. Categorical approaches are limited by being ahistorical and static, with insufficient attention paid to difference, processes, and change. They tend not to see that the norms established are often those of white, middle-class males. Continuities and discontinuities over time are ignored. They do not acknowledge that growing up involves relationships between young people and between young people and adults and is a process that young people both negotiate and have imposed on them (Wyn and White, 1997).

"Youth" is more favored in the sociological and postmodern literature, where it is conceptualized as *relational*—as "social processes whereby age is socially constructed, institutionalized and controlled in historically and culturally specific ways" (Wyn and White, 1997: 11). Youth is idealized and institutionalized as a deficit state of "becoming" that exists and has meaning in relation to the "adult" it will "arrive" to be. Power relations become clearer in taking this viewpoint.

The next section examines how notions of adolescence have changed over time and the influence of several key theorists in the twentieth century. The impact of the work of theorists from different fields of psychology—in particular that of Stanley Hall and Arnold Gesell—and of psychoanalysts Sigmund Freud and his daughter, Anna Freud, has been significant. Biological, psychiatric, and psychoanalytic notions of adolescence form a medical model of adolescence, which, while drawing from psychology, strongly emphasizes the biological aspects and time-specific notions of maturation. It sets up standardization and normalization notions and then critiques young people against these. Gesell and Ames (1956) was influential in establishing norms, and in doing so he considered that the discovery of the self was the central task of adolescence. Donald Winnicott (1971) tended to view adolescence itself as an affliction that the adolescent grows out of as maturity occurs. Seeing adolescence itself as an afflicted life stage reflected in part Hall's (1905) ideas of emotional storm and stress, and in part Freudian concepts. But medical-model views tend to portray adolescence as a disorder with a particular symptomatology, as indicated by the increased number of definitions and disorders related to adolescence in the *Diagnostic and Statistical Manual IV* (*DSM IV*).[1] This tends to pathologize adolescence to a large extent rather than accepting and understanding that many of the perceived difficulties of the young person might be part of "normal" growing up. Such definitions emerge from highly value-laden, hence strongly contestable, adult viewpoints. In defining adolescence as something largely outside adult society's norms and values, it is positioned almost as something "abnormal," which in turn points to the need for, and ways of, controlling adolescents. What is "normal" adolescence and what is not are also brought into question.

The impact on the notion of adolescence of developmental psychologists Jean Piaget, Erik Erikson, and Robert Havighurst has been enormous. Their theories, along with the work of Vygotsky and Bronfenbrenner, are discussed in a later section. The field of developmental psychology established notions of distinct stages and developmental tasks that form part of many psychological definitions of childhood and adolescence in terms of behavioral, cognitive, and developmental changes that occur at each life stage. Criticism of such definitions centers on the vagueness of the tasks and the age at which they are considered to start and end, on the cultural and ethnic biases inherent in such normalization, and on the oppressiveness of these (Morss, 1991; Walkerdine, 1987). An overview of such critique is presented in this section.

Behaviorist psychologists base much of their work on Skinner's and form a very distinct branch of psychology, which emphasizes the influence of the environment on an individual's behavior. This is examined in the fourth section. The work of cognitive behavioral therapists Albert Ellis and William Glasser is also considered. Both these latter theorists have developed therapies that have been widely applied as interventions in dealing with adolescent problems, especially by educational psychologists.

The fifth section surveys the way humanist-existential theorists emphasize growth, the need for positive regard, empathy, and genuineness to achieve this, and the importance of an individual's perceptions as the foundation of their sense of reality. The key theorist in this area has undoubtedly been Carl Rogers, whose humanist-existential emphasis and person-centered therapy was the predominant mode of counseling when school guidance counseling began in the 1960s in places like the United States, the United Kingdom, Australia, and New Zealand.

This chapter concludes by examining the strongly Foucauldian perspectives of Nikolas Rose's arguments that show the profound impact of the "psy" sciences, which became key ways of understanding the self, childhood, and adolescence as families came under increased regulation during the twentieth century, especially after the Second World War. Rose did not pretend to provide a full or definitive consideration of psychological discourse, but he did provide some interesting and valuable insights into its influence. He contended that the soul of the young citizen has become the *object* of government—the government of the self and the government of the state—through professional and, particularly, through psychological expertise. He argues that psychology discourses, especially after the Second World War, have provided the language to describe, diagnose, and categorize childhood subjectivity and parenting and its problems. These have established the difference between the normal and the pathological. Psychology, in turn, has invented technologies and developed professional expertise for the intervention, cure, and normalization that regulates childhood (Rose, 1989).

The use of the term "adolescence" and the definition thereof has been much debated. It has been considered a way of describing the particular characteristics of individuals in the transitional period between childhood and adulthood, when one can no longer be considered either a child or an adult, having, rather, an interim status, which sometimes results in adults holding parochial attitudes toward adolescents and in the marginalization of adolescents in social policy making. In this sense it can have negative definitional aspects, being neither one thing nor another and defined against notions of the "normal" adult self. But since there seem to be a set of characteristics in common for those grouped under the label "adolescent," there has now emerged a set of positive identifications and definitions involving biological, cognitive, emotional, social, moral and vocational criteria. By the 1990s there was very much seen to be a separate adolescent or youth culture, the emergence of which as a postwar phenomena, constructed in sociological and post-modern discourse, is discussed in chapter 4. However, the impact of the psychologically oriented discourses has been profound on how we have come to understand and to deal with childhood and adolescence, in education and in counseling. Hence this chapter provides a broadly sweeping overview of how the work of many theorists has "psychologized" adolescence.

NOTIONS OF ADOLESCENCE THROUGHOUT HISTORY

Some of the different notions that this section explores are: the evil vs. the innocent child, the relatively recent emergence of a distinctive category of "adolescence" in Western societies, a biological focus on adolescence (Stanley Hall), an interest in the *psyche* that accompanied Freudian explorations, the "scientization" and establishment of norms as exemplified in Gesell's work, and psychiatric notions of pathology, as classified by the *DSM* categories.

Conceptions and notions of adolescence and its problems existed in different societies in the past. In the eighth century BC, the Ancient Greek poet Hesiod worried about the future if society depended "on the frivolous youth of today, for certainly all youth are reckless beyond words" (Côté and Allahar, 1994: xi). George Bernard Shaw's famous complaint that youth is wasted on the young further highlights some of the tensions between young and old. Adults frequently complain about the irresponsibility and immaturity of youth and respond to such complaints with increased surveillance and regulation of them. In his study, *Centuries of Childhood*, Philippe Ariès (1962) asserted that childhood, as we know it, has not always had the same meaning. He suggested that it was in the mid-eighteenth century that adults began to think of children as different from themselves, with the result that an "age-based hierarchy and eventual dichotomy was becoming institutionalized in the relationship between adults and children and the defining characteristics of these differences were, by and large, oppositional" (James, Jenks, and Prout, 1998: 4). Ariès contended that because children were not given any special status in mediaeval times, being viewed as miniature adults, they were often treated in what we would consider harsh and inhumane ways. He noted that although the first written mention of adolescence was in a thirteenth-century translation of ancient Byzantine writings, the roots of the notion of adolescence were in the sixteenth-century youth academy schools in France.

James and colleagues (1998) pointed out the origins of two competing discourses, which continue to this day, in terms of "the evil child" and "the innocent child." The former began with Christian notions of Adam's "original sin," which saw the child enter the world as unintentionally willful, potentially harboring dark (and even demonic) forces that might be unleashed if adults, through either dereliction or inattention, allowed children to veer away from the "straight and narrow" path. James and colleagues (1998) considered that as part of the Puritan tradition, Thomas Hobbes's *Leviathan* (written in 1651) formed the philosophical antecedent of the "evil child" by advocating that to maintain good conduct and social order, the monarch has absolute power over the people, as parents, in turn, have over their children. For without such power over them, children, who have neither power nor rights, would become unruly, wild, and anarchic. Children were compared to wild animals and similarly in need of taming and domestication. Hence the rationale was set for maintaining oppressive, antidemocratic states[2] and harsh, punitive, and even violent practices by parents and institutions, aimed at controlling and restraining children for what was believed to be their own good, according to the prevailing morality (see Marshall and Marshall, 1997). In this manner, the Christian injunction to "spare the rod and spoil the child" was played out.

The discourse of the "innocent child" arose out of philosophies of individual liberty. Robertson—in de Mause's (1974) edited collection, *The History of Childhood*—credited Jean-Jacques Rousseau, the Enlightenment philosopher, with bringing the needs of children to the attention of adults. Rousseau opposed notions of "original sin," arguing that children have natural goodness, innocence, and wisdom that should be treasured. In Rousseau's *Émile*, "the child was promoted to the status of person, a specific class of being with needs and desires and even rights" (James et al., 1998: 13). This set the seeds for concern about children as individuals, as not just on the part of their family, but also on the part of society as an investment in its economic and social regulation. The child's growing up and education was part of the issue of progress that so concerned the age, and clearly adults came to be seen to have responsibilities for this. The child's innocence needed to be preserved. The child should not be mistreated, nor left to its own devices—hence the notion of child-centeredness. Competing discourses about the nature of the child continue to this day, as displayed in comments about the "breakdown of the family," the "loss of family values," and in how some peers and neglectful adults are seen to seduce or corrupt innocent young people who are considered "at risk." In response, various measures and programs are often proposed to maintain innocence—especially sexual innocence—right through adolescence.

The nineteenth century changed the way children were thought of; during this time "public bodies began to think of children as children, with special needs because of their helplessness and vulnerability, rather than as small adults with the right to hire themselves out for sixteen hours a day, or as chattels of their parents" (Robertson, 1974: 428). However, de Mause (1974) presented a highly questionable account of a particularly depressing, psychogenetic picture of childhood, noting abuse of children by their parents and caregivers from ancient times until today. Such abuses included infanticide, neglect, abandonment, swaddling, deliberate starvation, beatings, solitary confinement, sexual abuse, and overwork. In his historical but very one-sided gaze, de Mause unconsciously supported progressivist notions, since he implied that generally today's parenting is far better, but he can be criticized for providing little evidence for this. His ideas highlight the danger of imposing twentieth-century values and concepts of childhood and adolescence on earlier times.

Children became objects of philosophical interest in the eighteenth and nineteenth centuries, when it was thought that they might reveal the presence or absence of innate ideas and qualities, or show the effect of sensations on the development of human attributes. But in the late nineteenth and early twentieth centuries a new scientific gaze focused upon the young child from the perspective of evolution. The development of a particular interest in and concept of childhood enabled the notion of adolescence to evolve.

In Western societies before the twentieth century, young people were thought of differently than they are today, with no sharp distinction between the status of adolescence and adulthood. Adolescents could and did assume adult roles in what today we would consider were the teenage years: depending on gender and age, they could work, marry, have children, and enter military service. They did not, however, reach adulthood until the age of 21—the "coming of age" when they were considered to have reached their legal "majority." Before the era of universal suffrage, if they were male and landowners, they also gained voting rights.

Many researchers would contend that while some reference is made to adolescence earlier, it is first mentionned in the late nineteenth century but is more a phenomenon of the twentieth century. By 1900, with more than a third of the population of the United States living in cities, concern was being expressed about the low level of morality in such places:

> Drinking, sexual immorality, vagrancy, and crime were not only intrinsically threatening to orderliness but were also particularly distressing influences on the young. . . . As a result of these conditions, three major movements developed, all of which conspired to make a social fact out of adolescence: compulsory (and characteristically public) education, child labor legislation, and special legal procedures for "juvenile." By the specific citation of a precise chronological age, the legislation associated with these three areas essentially eliminated the vagueness of all previous ideas of the time at which adolescence terminates. Thus adolescence became a period between pubescence, a concrete biological occurrence, and the age specified by law for compulsory education, employment and criminal procedure. (Bakan, 1971: 12)

Compulsory education enforced the separation of adolescents from other parts of society and from employment. Along with other specifically targeted legislation, this indicated adolescents as a special case, somewhat problematic and in need of education, guidance, protection, and family and community support. At the turn of the twentieth century, largely influenced by Stanley Hall's ideas (as discussed later), young people were seen as not fully developed socially, psychologically, emotionally, or morally, prone to weaknesses and moral perversions, and hence in need of the control and guidance of parents and other adults. Thus, industrialization and legislation created and defined the notion of adolescence in a manner that, some writers would contend, limits their power and assigns them minority status.

While the impact of the industrial age increasingly led to both dependency and to relative leisure for adolescents early in this century, in recent decades this has been considerably increased. In the post–Second-World-War period, not only were women initially sent back into the home when men returned to peacetime jobs, but with increased mechanization on farms and greater urbanization, the labor of adolescents was no longer needed. As the school, leaving age rose and the importance of a tertiary education burgeoned in the late 1960s, adolescents became dependent on their parents for much longer. Nowadays, however, in many Western countries those adolescents who opt for a tertiary education in the hope of attaining high-paying professional careers are frequently being saddled with large student loans. In the sense of "dependence," in the late 1980s and 1990s adolescence could be seen as being extended beyond the teenage years, into the early twenties: "The delay is characterized by economic and social marginality; sequestration into age-segregated groups, and extended financial and emotional dependence on parents. The young are also subject to manipulation and control by a variety of groups formed by adults who are out to protect their own interests" (Côté and Allahar, 1994: xv).

Early theorists on adolescence were strongly influenced by Darwinian ideas and the role of instincts, and so they emphasized the biological aspects of adolescence. According to Rose (1989), Darwin, Sully, Stanley Hall, Claparède, and Baldwin all observed infants, describing and documenting changes in their emotions, words, and movements over time. The aim of this type of study was to shed light on the nature of human evolution, establish characteristics that distinguish man from animals, discover the extent to which human emotions and expressions are innate or learned, and possibly support doctrines of recapitulation.

In the late 1800s, young people came under the gaze of the emerging social sciences of psychology, anthropology, and pedagogy as objects of study. G. Stanley Hall is acknowledged as the "father of adolescence" following his scientific study in his two-volume work, *Adolescence: Its Psychology and Its Relations to Physiology, Anthropology, Sociology, Sex, Crime, Religion, and Education* (Hall, 1905). It is interesting to note the inclusion in the title of sex, crime, and religion, none of which are social science disciplines but are, instead, concerned with legal and moral issues and so tended to problematize and define the notion of adolescence in relation to such issues. It was the perceived problem of the deviance of young people in the industrial age that saw social scientists viewing adolescence as a distinct stage in the life cycle, an inevitable part of growing up, when adolescents are controlled by their biological impulses, resulting in emotional turmoil, storm, and stress. Since this was seen as an inevitable stage, difficulties and moodiness were to be expected and accepted.

Hall proposed a theory of recapitulation, strongly influenced by Darwinian evolutionary ideas of biologically innate stages, whereby all people symbolically trace a progressive cycle of humanity that is summarized as follows:

- *Infancy* (0–4 years): the child develops sensorimotor skills, repeating the stage of human evolutionary development from being on all fours to standing upright;
- *Childhood* (4–8 years): playing with toys, hide-and-seek, building forts, playing cowboys and Indians, and enjoying outdoor activities like camping symbolizes the hunter–gatherer stage of human evolution;
- *Youth* (8–12 years): the ability to cooperate with others and to respond to discipline, routines, and training drills develops akin to the semibarbaric stage of about a thousand years ago;
- *Adolescence* (12–25 years): a time of storm and stress, with emotional upheaval, suffering, passion, and rebellion against adult authority symbolizing modern civilization's rapid change and great advances.

If these stages are "natural" and biologically determined and if the environment itself has little influence, it is argued that there is no point in trying to change their onset or completion. Because each of Hall's stages offered unique opportunities and challenges for the individual, this resulted in suggestions for some profoundly different ways of dealing with children and adolescents. These new ways were more lenient and permissive than the current practices of child rearing and were designed so that the child would fully experience each natural stage. Infants should be able to roam freely, touching, tasting, and smelling things at will. Youth should be taught and trained extensively so that cooperation with others developed and behavioral routines were established. Adolescents should be given time and space to deal with their moods, and their challenges to adult authority should be accepted as normal. Hall believed that the appropriate educational experiences should be available during adolescence if society was to advance. The influence of these ideas no doubt partly contributed to the establishment of compulsory secondary education in Western societies.

Scientifically oriented approaches to conceptualizing childhood and adolescence evolved out of Darwinian notions of natural selection. The emphasis was particularly on the biological, as ways were sought to understand evolution. Not only did Hall's theory of the psychology of adolescence have biological underpinnings along with the notion of stages of development, so did Sigmund Freud's, Anna Freud's, and Arnold Gesell's work, although Freud would by no means be considered "scientific" as such (for Wittgenstein's arguments see Cioffi, 1973; Fromm, 1982; and Peters and Marshall, 1999).

There was an enormous explosion of interest in the mind, in the *psyche* and how it worked, in the late nineteenth and in the twentieth centuries, much of which was influenced by the pioneering work of Sigmund Freud. This, in turn, has clearly influenced how we think not only of ourselves, but also of childhood and of adolescence. Sigmund Freud's work was instrumental in providing a new set of notions, terminologies, and techniques for describing and understanding the self. Freud (1953) systematically developed ideas to understand the mind, the unconscious, behavior, and personality and how these develop. It is from his work and from the body of research building upon this that notions of stages of human personality development were formulated and from which both psychoanalytic and psychodynamic counseling approaches subsequently developed.

If Hall was considered the "father" of "adolescence," Freud was considered the "father" of psychoanalysis and psychotherapy. In recognizing the power of the past, the hidden, and the unconscious to shape the present, psychodynamic counseling approaches have their foundations in Freud's work. Subsequently, neo-Freudian theorists—Carl Jung, Alfred Adler, Erik Erikson, Erich Fromm, Karen Horney, Harry Stack Sullivan, and Jacques Lacan—adapted and modified Freud's ideas. Psychodynamic counseling approaches are not the same as Freudian psychoanalysis and are many and varied, developing out of the work of theorists such as Eric Berne (transactional analysis), Fritz Perls (Gestalt), Melanie Klein (object relations theory), and others (Ivey, Ivey, and Simek-Downing, 1987).

Freud (1953) provided a developmental theory that suggested that the personality was made up of three elements: the id, the ego, and the superego, which constantly deal with two conflicting impulses or "drives" within the individual—a life instinct (sex) and a death instinct (aggression). While the id involves biological urges or the "pleasure" principle seeking immediate and constant gratification of the drives, the ego and the superego involve societal and environmental constraints. These restraints become internalized in adolescence, and inner conflict continues. The ego is the "reality" principle that seeks to control the id, to preserve the self, and to find socially appropriate ways of expressing the impulses and tensions of the two drives. The superego is the "conscience," a product of parental influences and societal values relating to the judgment of good and evil, seeking only socially acceptable behavior. Conflict between the id and the superego results in both neurotic and moral anxiety, which create painful tension that results in overly using defense mechanisms if the anxiety is not dealt with realistically. The three elements act differently, and individuals develop defense mechanisms (repression, suppression, projection, reaction-formation, sublimation, regression, rationalization) to hide the internal conflict between them from the self and others. These defenses are important for understanding adolescent behavior because they are particularly pronounced then. Freud theorized five stages of personality development— the oral, anal, phallic, latency and genital stages—three of which occur in childhood and two in late childhood and adolescence, respectively. At each stage libidinal energy is focused on erogenous zones that characterize the stage, with trauma at any stage due to overindulgence or deprivation resulting in fixation and unresolved conflicts centered on this stage (Ivey et al., 1987).

Freud's work effectively broke new ground and set the scene in general for many later researchers. What his model established was that childhood was the source of aberrant—abnormal, deviant, delinquent, and criminal—adult behavior. As a result, the parent–child relationship came to be seen as vitally important in itself and also for adult self-exploration and in how one constitutes the self. Freud "positions the child as no more than a state of unfinished business or becoming" that is "dispossessed of intentionality and agency. Instead, these are absorbed into a vocabulary of drives and instincts, with sexuality becoming the major dimension in the development of self and amnesia emerging, ironically, as the key to successful socialization" (James et al., 1998: 21).

The work of Freud's daughter, Anna Freud (1946), extended his theories, applying them specifically to adolescence and emphasizing how the dramatic increase in sexual or libidinal energy from biological maturation at this time focuses on genital feelings, sexual objects, and sexual goals. She suggested that this could lead to extreme hedonism or to two defense mechanisms—asceticism and intellectuality. "Asceticism" is a mistrust of personal instincts and a refusal to engage in any sort of pleasurable activity. "Intellectuality" is a preoccupation with abstract ideas about friendship, love, and marriage and often involves creative expressions of these in art, writing, and poetry. Implications for parents and other relevant adults are that they should help adolescents to cope with their sexual maturity and with their ineffective defense mechanisms by accepting their feelings and fears and by channeling their libidinal energy into socially acceptable outlets.

In the early part of the twentieth century the clinic and the nursery school played a vital role in studies in child and adolescent development. They enabled large numbers of children of different ages to be observed by skilled psychological experts under controlled, experimental, almost laboratory conditions. Thus they allowed simultaneously for standardization and for normalization. Arnold Gesell's work at the Yale Psycho-Clinic, which opened in 1911 for the assessment and treatment of children having problems at school, "left traces of the child—graphs, records, measurements, photos, inscriptions that together with those of many other children that have been accumulated, combined, correlated, graded and consolidated into the object of developmental psychology" (Rose, 1989:144).

From his observations of large numbers of children, Gesell developed a normative theory of behaviors that are typical of children at particular ages. His ideas centered on the primacy of the biological regulating mechanism of "maturation," which he considered determined both the order and the appearance of behaviors, rather than "acculturation" or the effect of the environment. Gesell and Ames in their work, *Youth: the Years from 10–16* (1956), provide descriptions of normative behavior for each of these years in terms of emotions, activities, interests, attitudes, ethics, relationships, self, school. For Gesell, the discovery of the self is the central task of adolescence, and from his observations he challenged Hall's notion that adolescence necessarily involves a stage of storm and stress. Gesell contended that if children were not hindered, they would develop "normally," parents should provide them with relevant experiences for each level of development of the self, and this normal, natural course should not be altered. The development of the self is described in age-based statements, such as:

- *Twelve* is in better balance; accepts others; sees both them and himself more objectively; but unevenly fluctuates from childish to more mature attitudes.
- *Thirteen* withdraws and inwardizes in order to focus more deeply upon his own thoughts, moods, and images in a manner reminiscent of Seven.
- *Fourteen*, more outgoing, and seeks to find himself by comparing himself to others, by matching and by imitation; he is less inwardly centered.
- *Fifteen* withdraws not physically but mentally to meditate, and to explore his own nature in relationship to ideas, ideals, and the opinions of others.
- *Sixteen* is more at ease and circulates more freely among age-mates and adults; seems more independent and self reliant (Gesell and Ames, 1956: 356).

Many researchers find it difficult to accept such precise, age-specific norms because they are not necessarily consistent with Gesell's own normative descriptions for each age group.

Although psychiatric notions of adolescence share much with psychology, they follow a more biological and scientifically oriented model that combines what might appear to be two separate and distinct discourses in what constitutes a medical model of adolescence. Donald Winnicott was particularly influential in advancing the psychiatric/biological model and seemed to be highly influenced by Gesell with respect to time-specific notions of maturation:

> There exists one real cure for adolescence, and only one, and this cannot be of interest to the boy or girl who is in the throes. The cure for adolescence belongs to the passage of time and to the gradual maturation process; these together do in the end result in the emergence of the adult person. This process cannot be hurried or slowed up, though indeed it can be broken into and destroyed, or it can wither up from within, in psychiatric illness. (Winnicott, 1971: 40–41)

Côté and Allahar (1994) concluded from an examination of empirical literature that biological assumptions linking hormonal affect with adolescent turmoil and delinquency—elaborated in Hall's notions of "storm and stress"—were very small at best and were not statistically shown to be more important than social variables. Biological approaches linking puberty with adolescence did not account for the increasingly early onset of hormonal changes that occur in early teenage years, and even in the preteen years for many girls. This left many years after puberty when young people were incorrectly perceived to be at the mercy of their hormones. Stereotypical views about adolescents behaving immaturely due to their biological immaturity and hormonal influxes all too easily resulted in the assumption that they are unable to act maturely, and therefore they need to be strongly controlled. Intensive control, especially as set by many schools, denies adolescents the experiences required to gain maturity and responsibility—something of a circular argument and self-fulfilling prophecy.

Côté and Allahar (1994) suggested that psychiatry tended to view adolescence itself as afflicted, as a disorder with a particular symptomatology and diagnoses, as evidenced by the separate section now devoted to disorders in adolescence in the latest version of the *Diagnostic and Statistical Manual IV (DSM IV*—APA, 1994). The first edition of what became the *DSM* was devised by William C. Menninger during the Second World War and was used by all branches of the U.S. military to screen and eliminate those who were mentally unfit for combat. Despite the *DSM IV* pointing out that the definition of mental disorder[3] "implies a distinction between 'mental' disorders and 'physical' disorders that is a reductionistic anachronism of the mind/body dualism" (APA, 1994: xxi), they proceed with their definition and classification scheme. Numbered codes are provided for medical record-keeping with the stated purpose of providing "clear descriptions of diagnostic categories in order to enable clinicians and investigators to diagnose, communicate about, study and treat people with various mental disorders" (APA, 1994: xxvii). In subsequent editions of the *DSM*, catagorization was extended from defining 60 disorders in 1952 to 230 in 1980; the latest, the 1994 *DSM IV*, has headings for 56 types of mental disorder, each including several different categories. It is widely accepted as an authoritative document by the medical, psychiatric, and psychotherapeutic establishment but is also highly contentious (Caplan, 1995; Rose, 1989, 1998; Szasz, 1973). Psychiatrists, clinical psychologists, psychotherapists, and social workers use DSM categorization to diagnose who will be hospitalized, who will get insurance cover (in the United States), who is judged competent or abnormal. Paula Caplan (1995) has criticized not only the dangers of labeling, but that a small number of people from the most powerful mental health association in the world (1,000 contributors to *DSM IV* from the American Psychiatric Association) define what is abnormal. She maintained that the diagnoses masquerade as scientific and as "truth" when they are in fact riddled with personal, cultural, gender, and political bias. She contended that this reflected an ongoing tendency for the public to accept as "truth" the opinions of high-status medical scientists and practitioners.

The separate section for mental disorders occurring in early childhood and adolescence sets out eight disorders, each including some four further types. These are: mental retardation, reading, mathematics, learning, written expression, motor skills, communication-expressive, autistic, childhood disintegrative, Asperger's syndrome, Tourette's syndrome, AD/HD, conduct, oppositional-defiant, disruptive behavior, and encopresis disorders, numbered and described on pages 13–24. They do not include other disorders such as those of drug and alcohol use and abuse, eating disorders, or schizophrenia, which are also described in the *DSM IV* (APA, 1994). Questions need to be asked: Is the definition of disorders now more precise and is it time, as some mental health psychiatrists have suggested, that 20% of adolescents really have a mental illness? (McGeorge, 1995). This raises the criticism of psychiatry and clinical psychology being self-serving for defining adolescence as a largely pathological state. Furthermore, the *DSM IV* classification of disorders is criticized for having such broad categories that "virtually all aspects of adolescent behavior that deviate in any way from the normative can be labeled as mental disease" (Sprinthall and Collins, 1984: 386). The effect of medical labeling that the *DSM* series enables and encourages can be devastatingly detrimental, particularly for adolescents, and especially if professionals see adolescence as "afflicted" and as a problem. If one's view of the world is dominated by the construct of "mental illness," then it is almost inevitable that one will construct the world in terms of mental problems and disorders.

Many of Hall's and Freud's assumptions, as described earlier, still inform psychological, psychiatric, and counseling theorizing about adolescents, despite numerous subsequent studies that show that adolescent turmoil is not universal to all cultures or to all adolescents and therefore cannot be an inevitable part of human development.

Such ideas were challenged and rejected by subsequent theorists. John B. Watson's behaviorist theories de-emphasized developmental notions, instinctual forces, and the role of biology in favor of the role of the environment. They formed the basis of the "nature" side of what became the extensive nature–nurture debate that occupied a huge amount of the time and energy of social scientists in the twentiethcentury. The work of the anthropologists Margaret Mead and Ruth

Benedict, as well as that of subsequent sociologists and of feminists, provided a critique and rejection of the "nature" side of the debate and informed the "nurture" or environment aspects.

Sociologists and anthropologists tended to theorize a "nurture" viewpoint whereby adolescence and its problems where considered to be the products of cultural and environmental contexts. This was initially promoted by Margaret Mead's controversial *Coming of Age in Samoa: A Psychological Study of Primitive Youth for Western Civilization* (1928). This study was controversial not only for the challenge to the biological determinists, but also because of the relatively recent challenge to her findings by Derek Freeman. Freeman (1983) provided evidence that Mead was not told the truth by those whom she interviewed when she was conducting her research and challenged her portrayal of sexual freedoms for adolescents. What Mead's work did suggest, though, was that a relatively smooth transition to adulthood can occur when adults provide a structure of consistent beliefs and clear roles for adulthood, so that the sorts of problems and rebellion that Hall and others have described are less likely to arise. This concept was also emphasized by Ruth Benedict's (1938, 1950) theory that the development process should be gradual from infancy to adulthood or the individual's growth will be distorted through the trauma of abrupt changes or "discontinuity," causing maladjustment in adolescence. She believed that parents and educators should provide "continuity," thereby preventing stress for adolescents by helping them to change slowly, safely, and securely with respect to sex, responsibility, and independence.

As this section has demonstrated, different concepts of "adolescence" have emerged over time. "Adolescence" is primarily a phenomenon of Western societies that has arisen in the context of urbanization and industrialization rather than in traditional feudal or tribal societies. Understandings about adolescence and theories about who they are, what constitutes them, and why they do what they do have burgeoned in the twentieth century, when one of the key ways of looking at people— children, adolescents, and adults—has involved psychological and related notions. These discourses form part of Nikolas Rose's theory of the "psy" sciences and have been adapted and used by various theorists forming what have become known as psychoanalytic and psychodynamic theories of human behavior. All of these notions have had profound impact on a variety of ways in which through "psychologizing" we have come to understand the self, adolescence, youth, and counseling.

DEVELOPMENTAL PSYCHOLOGY THEORIES

A considerable amount of psychological theorizing has centered on developmental theories that are described in terms of stages and tasks of emotional, cognitive, behavioral, and moral development from childhood through to adulthood. First, this section examines the work of three major figures—Jean Piaget, Erik Erikson, and Robert Havighurst— whose work in stage theories of development have had a profound influence on how we think of and describe childhood and adolescence. It then takes a brief overview of the theories of Vygotsky and Bronfenbrenner, who understood development in terms of an ecological, constructivist, systems approach.

Rose (1989) provided an explanation of how, after the First World War, concepts of childhood and adolescence became dominated by the establishment of norms. It was against these norms that young people were measured in order to ascertain whether they were advanced, average, or retarded in their growth and development. Rose highlights the very power of these notions to appear benign when in fact they are not: "But pretty soon psychometrics was joined by other normalized and normalizing visions of childhood that appears softer and more benign but which have become, by this very token, more pervasive. The most powerful of these was the notion of development" (Rose, 1989: 141).

Developmental psychology is based on the assumptions, first, that the child is a "natural" rather than a "social" being, and, second, that being "natural" leads the child inevitably through a process of maturation (James et al., 1998).

Jean Piaget (1952, 1954), writing between the 1920s and 1970s, has been probably the most influential developmental psychologist in the twentieth century (Morss, 1991):

> His work on genetic epistemology extended biology, quite successfully, into the vocabulary of the taken-for-granted and produced the most absolute, of materially reductive, image of childhood that we are likely to encounter. Ironically perhaps, he sets out from an idealism more deeply founded than Rousseau's but one tempered by a voracious empiricism. Piaget seeks to reconcile reason with fact. (James et al., 1998: 17)

Piaget propounded a stage theory of mental or cognitive and moral development that had huge impact on both psychology and education, especially from the 1960s onwards—once the influence of behaviorism in psychology had begun to wane in the 1950s (Morss, 1991). His theory of cognitive development considered that the basic mental structure was the result of the interaction between the individual and the outside world and comprised four stages of sequential learning processes of increasingly abstract complexity, following a predetermined timetable: The stages were fixed; through them children adapted to the surrounding world, achieving this first through action and then through cognitive processes. Each stage prepared the child for the next one, which would be better than the previous one. Piaget considered that although the environment could influence the acquisition of thought processes, it was the natural, biological development of maturation that most strongly influenced mental development; therefore it was inadvisable to attempt to accelerate a child's thinking processes.

86 Counseling Youth

0–1½ years		sensorimotor perception, recognition, coordination
1½–6 years	preoperational	preconceptual intuitive thinking, symbolic play
6–11 years	concrete operations	elementary logical thought
11–15 years	formal operations	propositional, hypothetical, deductive, inductive, reflective thinking

Piaget's work on moral development is somewhat similar, again being a stage developmental approach. It viewed moral growth as resulting from the interaction between the innate mental structure and the environment, with all individuals proceeding through a series of distinct stages in the same order, differing only in how soon and how far they developed morally. Piaget described two hierarchical levels of morality for children. First, "moral realism" leads to compliance with rules that are considered sacred and unalterable and are either totally right or totally wrong, depending on the consequences of physical punishment. Second, "autonomous reality" sees rules being viewed in terms of respect for others rather than in obedience to authority. The transformation from the former level of functioning to the latter depended on both cognitive or intellectual development and on the experiences of social interaction, through which a child examined its own perspectives in comparison with the expectations of others. Piaget's two stages were extended and amplified by Lawrence Kohlberg (1970, 1977) into a theory of six stages of moral development.

Rom Harré (1983) criticized both Piaget's and Kohlberg's theories of moral development by using playground evidence to argue that almost all of Kohlberg's stages could be found in children of five or six years of age, if the situation presented was suitable for them to consider. Harré suggested that rather than stages, there were various "strategies" or ways of interacting with other people. Harré's work concurred with that of Paul Light (Light and Simmons, 1983), who had examined children's drawings and concluded that "children are not working their way through a fixed sequence of mental states, finally reaching the state we call adult thinking" (Morss, 1991: 20).

A considerable body of research and critique has centered on the application of Piaget's theories and their implications for education and for parenting. His theories are relevant if it is assumed that the purpose of education is to assist a child to reach higher levels of intellectual functioning. They have influenced both how and when the curriculum is presented. They emphasized the need for interactive, experiential, and problem-solving methods in the learning process rather than just rote-style learning, and they de-emphasized IQ tests in favor of analyzing the ability to think. In effect, they have reinforced age-level classes. While Piaget's work on logical thinking during adolescence (alongside that of John

Dewey) brought about extensive changes in the teaching of science and mathematics (e.g., the introduction of "scientific method"), arguably his greatest impact was in developing the notion of "concrete operations."

John Morss (1991) provided a comprehensive account of criticisms of Piaget, and although the majority of these criticisms center on young children rather than on adolescents, the challenge to Piagetian thought is strenuous enough to affect Piaget's work on adolescence. Despite his long, productive career, "the claims which Piaget made have been proven to be misleading, simplistic, and in some cases simply wrong" (Morss, 1991: 10). Morss argued that Piaget's whole theory was based on two assumptions: "that problem-solving and intellectual activity are the most important aspects of human experience and that there is a gradual development in the mental structures that underlie this activity." In effect, "cognitive development" is a concept that Piaget invented (Morss, 1991).

There are several points of criticism. First, despite emphasizing the importance of experience in learning and developing, Piaget does not allow for the different experiences that people have in becoming adult— the actual diversity of culture, class, ethnicity, gender. Second, his concept of adulthood seems to mean the person "thinks like a Western scientist: setting up experiments, manipulating variables, and deducing general laws of nature" (Morss, 1991: 9)—a reflection of just who Piaget himself was. Again, diversity was not acknowledged. Third, children were believed to have a limited learning potential, depending on their level of development—that is, according to Piaget, cognitive development. Learning was considered to be subservient to development, development (as in "readiness") being required before learning could occur. Piaget's notion of development was a universal one, regardless of cultural or historical contexts, endorsing the Enlightenment project of the progression of mankind.

Morss argued that Piaget was wrong in his assertion that young children were incapable of "operational thinking," that they "are self-centered in their thinking; they can only think of one thing at a time; they cannot understand abstract concepts; they cannot understand or apply the simplest forms of logic" (Morss, 1991: 12). Piaget was saying that children could not think in an abstract way because they had limited language, and although they might appear competent in their everyday activities, in fact they were not. The implication of this endorsed parochial attitudes toward not just children, but anyone with limited cognitive abilities. Regardless of age, if one lacked intellectual competence, someone needed to act on their behalf until they achieved competency. Morss pointed out that several publications showed that "the supposed limitations of the young child could be at least partly attributed to the way the tests were presented" (Morss, 1991: 14): First, if crucial changes in presentation were made, young children were capable of passing Piaget's "conservation" test in its transformation of materials (Donaldson, 1978; Hughes, 1986). This test involved the researcher spreading out one of two rows of counters and asking the child whether the number of counters in the two rows was the same. Second, redesigning the "transitivity" task to reduce the amount of information enabled young children to perform logical tasks in developing inferences about measurement (Bryant, 1974). In the "transitivity" task, Piaget argued that preoperational children were unable to work out that if stick A was longer than stick B, and if B was longer than C, then A had to be longer than C. Piaget held that if the young child could not understand both the conservation of number and transitivity tasks, little mathematics could be learned before age 7 (Morss, 1991). Donaldson pointed out that despite Piaget's work seeming to be different and better than IQ tests, "the tests were in fact very similar, in that they both ignore the social context and the human understanding which is so crucial to any interaction between people" (Morss, 1991: 17).

Universalized stage theories of child and adolescent development, such as those of Piaget, Erikson, and Havighurst, were a potent force and possibly a dangerous one, too, in affecting how the adolescent was theorized for quite some time:

> Piaget's genetic epistemology has, through its measuring, grading, ranking and assessing of children, instilled a deep-seated positivism and rigid empiricism into our contemporary understandings of the child. Under the hegemony of developmental stage monitoring it is not just iniquitous comparison with their peers which children suffer through testing and league tables, but also a constant evaluation against a "gold standard" of the normal child. For those who fail to meet the standard, whether in educational, bodily development or welfare, the repercussions and sanctions are strong. (James et al., 1998: 19)

Valerie Walkerdine (1988) has pointed out that in the 1970s psychology involved a reevaluation of Piaget and the place of context. Several theorists—especially Walkerdine and Carol Gilligan (Brown and Gilligan, 1992; Gilligan, 1982; Taylor, Gilligan, and Sullivan, 1995)—have placed feminist discourse into the arena and pursued postmodern approaches to psychology. The critique by Morss and others suggested that Piaget's central notions were incorrect, and so his work "seems to belong to the history of psychology and not to its present or future" (Morss, 1991: 26). Since the late 1970s, attempts to address criticisms about the social and universalizing aspects have seen a contextualized approach, based on the work of Jerome Bruner (1986), Lev Vygotsky (Morss, 1996), and Urie Bronfenbrenner (1979, 1986) becoming favored. The emphasis on the social has major implications for how adolescents are understood as social beings who operate both individually and in groups, interdependently with others, and for the role that education has to play in their development. But the social context is still seen as adaptive and so still appeals either implicitly or explicitly to functionalist biology (Morss, 1996).

The second major figure in developmental psychology to be discussed also had a major impact on counseling—Erik Erikson. Erikson became one of the first psychoanalysts to practice as a child analyst in Boston. At the White House Conference on Children in 1950, his theoretical framework was accepted in total and became a national charter of child and adolescent development in the United States (Kroger, 1996). While he had a psychoanalytic background, Erikson criticized traditional psychoanalytic methods for not adequately dealing with identity, because "it has not developed terms to conceptualize the environment" (Erikson, 1968: 24). Erikson's work focused on notions of identity, and as part of his theories he developed a set of psychosocial stages.

By extending and reformulating Freud's five stages, Erikson (1963) developed his theory of eight psychosocial stages, each comprising developmental tasks that the individual must achieve at a critically specific time in becoming a healthy normal personality. The first four stages occur before adolescence and largely correspond to Freud's first four stages. Erikson considerably expanded Freud's "genital" stage that began in adolescence, to extend it into phases of adulthood. The key stage at adolescence centers on the self and issues of identity. Erikson's eight stages set up binary oppositions as follows:

infancy	sense of trust versus mistrust;
1–3 years	sense of autonomy versus shame or doubt;
3–5½ years	sense of initiation versus guilt;
5½–12 years	sense of industry versus inferiority;
adolescence	sense of identity versus role confusion;
early adulthood	sense of intimacy versus isolation;
middle adulthood	sense of generativity versus stagnation;
later adulthood	sense of ego integrity versus despair.

Erikson considered that in Western society, where there is no definite initiation of adolescents into adulthood, a "psychological moratorium" or sanctioned delay of adulthood is provided. This allows adolescents to work through issues of identity by trying out different styles of dress, philosophies, ideas, groups, religions, and relationships before committing themselves to a specific identity. It often involves conflict as adolescents attempt to meet societal expectations about appropriate adult behavior. Erikson's notion of identity involved "biological endowment, personal organization of experience, and cultural milieu all conspire to give meaning, form and continuity to one's unique existence," that was "rooted both within the individual as well as the communal culture" (Kroger, 1996: 16). In the Eriksonian view identity locates within the individual a sense of sameness and continuity that is partly conscious and partly unconscious. It is the past that forms the base for the future, so that the "process of identity formation depends on the interplay of what young persons have come to mean to themselves and what they now appear to mean to those who have become significant to them" (Erikson, 1977: 106). In other words, for Erikson, identity evolves from earlier stages of development, becomes a particular issue in adolescence, and continues to be reshaped throughout life. Several terms are used in the discourse around identity: *self*—the part of the person that one is aware of; *self-concept*—opinions and beliefs about the self; *self-esteem*—emotional evaluation about the self; *self-image*—a temporary self-concept. Various factors, such as social class, family and interpersonal relationships, body image, successes and failures, and peer acceptance influence each of these terms, and so these aspects of the self can vary from one situation to another and from one year to the next. In the Eriksonian view, during adolescence, significant adults can help by providing guidance and support, by giving adolescents the freedom to experience and experiment with different roles, and by listening to their concerns, hopes, aspirations, and opinions. Erikson noted that different cultures assist their young people through this stage in different ways, but he emphasized the importance nevertheless of providing such guidance.

According to Kroger (1996), while criticism of Erikson's theories came especially from empiricist researchers concerned about the imprecise, unclear way he explained identity, it was this very imprecision and breadth of his formulation of identity that has made his ideas acceptable and amenable to research by many social scientists. It is argued that Erikson's work displays cultural bias and is not applicable to children from extended families (Bettelheim, 1969). But it is his sexist views about women that are most strongly criticized (Caplan, 1979; Gilligan, 1982), especially his view that "anatomy is destiny and initially determines the style of engagement with the social milieu; reflecting sexual morphology, boys emphasize play, while girls focus on the inner space in their more peaceful, passive activities" (Kroger, 1996: 32). James Marcia (1966, 1980, 1993, 1994) has extensively researched Erikson's theories of identity in adolescence, proposing that four different personality types provide different identity resolutions, depending on the individual's attitude to crisis and to social roles. Despite the limitations highlighted in these critiques, Erikson's work, and that of subsequent researchers such as Marcia, still has much to offer to counseling and in understanding youth and their identity/identities as individuals and as members of various groups, cultures, and subcultures (see chapter 4).

There has been considerable time, effort, and research undertaken into issues of identity by many psychologists, since it is seen so widely to be central to the world of the adolescent and to problems with which the adolescent may have to deal with. Powerful emotions associated with sex, love, and romance pose problems and from part of the identity issues that adolescents face and have to deal with for the first time in their lives. Identity is not only an issue in psychology; it also seems to be central to the development of a youth culture in the latter half of the twentieth century, as James Coleman's (1961) work, which is discussed in chapter 4, suggests. The influence of the mass media on adolescents and on their formation of identity, their values, and their behavior is significant in both positive and negative ways, according to a growing body of psychological research.

The American psychologist David Ausubel (1954) supported universal notions of development in adolescence, but he did acknowledge environmental factors. He suggested that adolescence was a separate developmental period, not because of the span of years, but because of distinctive changes in the biosocial status and "a certain homogeneity of developmental content." This referred to the assumption of adult biosocial sex roles and an extensive personality reorganization that involved developing behaviors that were considered culturally appropriate for mature adults.

Therefore adolescence involved marked changes in learning, in social and economic roles and responsibilities, in changing attitudes, aspirations, behaviors, and relationships toward the self and others. These he conceptualized as *adjustment* difficulties that must be overcome before adult status can be attained. It was very much around notions of adjustment that the early models of school guidance counseling were centered.

Robert Havighurst (1972) theorized eight developmental tasks that form part of many psychological theories suggesting that adolescents needed to acquire the following skills, knowledge, functions, and attitudes:

1. accepting one's physique and using the body effectively;
2. achieving new and more mature relationships with peers of both sexes;
3. achieving a masculine or feminine sex role;
4. achieving emotional independence from parents and other adults;
5. preparing for an economic career;
6. preparing for marriage and family life;
7. designing and achieving socially responsible behavior;
8. acquiring a set of values and an ethical system as a guide to behavior, and developing an ideology.

Completion of such tasks was sequential and progressive, depending on individual effort and motivation, maturity, and societal expectation. Some that have a biological component were time-specific. Havighurst suggested that if they were not completed at the optimum age, the maladjustment from this would cause increased anxiety, social disapproval, and an inability to handle other tasks, such that they may not be able to be completed later. Unlike some other psychological theories, Havighurst did acknowledge the importance of culture and of ascertaining which specific tasks it required for adolescents, so that problematic areas were identified and dealt with to help them to adjust and cope. Criticism of Havighurst's work centered on the vagueness of the tasks, and when they were considered to start and to end.

Using the work of two Russian theorists—Lev Vygotsky (1962, 1978) and Urie Bronfenbrenner (1979, 1986)—Bruce McMillan (1991) puts notions of development into an ecological perspective, a position that seems to be quite favored as part of constructionist forms of psychology at the present time.

Vygotsky, born in 1896, the same year as Piaget, was writing in the Soviet Union in the 1920s, but his work has only recently been translated into English (McMillan, 1991). Vygotsky recognized the importance of language as a tool that both shaped and reflected culture and so could be used as a means of achieving goals. For him, development and learning needed to be matched to a certain extent, because, he believed, in a rather general sense children function according to the norms of development, in a form of "proximal development" that is not simply determined by age (Vygotsky, 1978: 86). For Vygotsky, development was not about biology but depended on the environment, where there was an overall pattern of continual progress, with rapid movements forward and even regression at times, especially in response to crisis. This is because the learning situation is a social one.

Bronfenbrenner (1979, 1986) emphasized the structural systems in which an individual operates and the subjective meaning that they make of their experiences as being important in their development. In his view, development is: "The process through which the growing person acquires more extended differentiated, and valid conception of the ecological environment, and becomes motivated and able to engage in activities that reveal the properties of, sustain, or restructure that environment at levels of similar or greater complexity in form or content" (Bronfenbrenner, 1979: 27).

Bronfenbrenner outlined a framework of four levels: microsystem, mesosystem, exosystem, and macrosystem. First, family, school, sports, church, or cultural groups provide the *microsystem* framework in which relationships, roles, and activities are experienced. He emphasized that the most significant learning occurs in "primary dyads"—that is, in relationships between two people who are emotionally significant to each other. Second, *mesosystems* are the indirect links or sets of connections that are formed by messages and information being transmitted between different settings, which in effect mediate between different systems. Examples of influences that are external to the primary dyad could be the way the sudden unemployment of a caregiver or the suicide of a friend of a parent might impact on a child or adolescent. The *exosystem* is the third level and involves systems that are external or not directly related to the primary dyad. Such things need to be two steps away from the dyad and would depend on "what the family or individuals within it perceive to be the links between socially acceptable practices, and their particular behaviors, as well as between the latter and actual changes in children" (McMillan, 1991: 35). The *macrosystem* involves systems that are beyond the control of families or their direct involvement and concern the overall system of sociocultural values, beliefs, and assumptions about the world and how it is and should be. McMillan (1991) pointed out that this systems theorizing focused on how individuals construct meaning, based on their perceptions of the systems with which they relate. Such systems might be the school-leaving age, attitudes to women, or sexuality.

Universalizing stage theories of child and adolescent development, such as those of Piaget and Erikson, were a potent and possibly a dangerous force in how the adolescent was theorized in individual, positivist, naturalist, and functionalist terms. The adolescent was seen as an individual trying on various personae in the search for an identity or true self that would become established for life. Linear sets of stages of development toward becoming a fully autonomous, independent individual do not fit women's experiences of growing up because women tend to seek connectedness or interdependence rather than independence in relationships (Gilligan, 1982; Johnson, 1993). Moreover, developmental models do not deal with "the construction of gendered identities in which power relations are central" (Wyn and White, 1997: 61), nor do they deal with ethnicity. The critique of universalizing aspects of stage theories of development has seen them largely rejected in favor of a contextualized approach. Development is now understood to be not just physical maturation, nor simply the achievement of individual goals, but, in the view of Vygotsky and Bronfenbrenner, to be "a process by which all members of a society are able to function satisfyingly and effectively together" (McMillan, 1991: 44). Clearly, then, Vygotsky's and Bronfenbrenner's emphasis on the social has major implications for how adolescents are understood as social beings who operate both individually and in groups, interdependently with others, and how counseling has a place to play in their development. While Eriksonian ideas have generally become part of psychodynamic counseling therapies, Vygotsky's and Bronfenbrenner's work has had particularly important implications for modalities of counseling that emphasize context and a systems approach—especially family counseling, but also constructionist therapies.

BEHAVIORIST AND COGNITIVE–BEHAVIORAL PSYCHOLOGY THEORIES

Behaviorist psychology is rooted in notions of modernity, progress, a devaluation of the past, and a belief in the scientific pragmatism that endorses the objectivity of science and its ability to solve human problems. It developed in the United States and is often seen as particularly "American," being "scientific, forward moving, optimistic and concerned with 'what works'" (Ivey et al., 1987: 223).

Behaviorists believe that explaining human behavior by searching for and dealing with underlying inner causes, as the psychoanalytic, cognitive, and medical model theories have done, neither increases our understanding of adolescence nor provides solutions. Behaviorism is antithetical to psychoanalytic and psychodynamic understandings about the self. Behavior is believed to be caused by external events in a person's environment. It is learned from past experiences with current experiences either weakening or strengthening the behaviors:

> Psychology as the behaviorist views it is a purely objective branch of natural science. Its theoretical goal is the prediction and control of behavior. Introspection forms no essential part of its methods, nor is the scientific value of its data dependent on the readiness with which they lend themselves to interpretations in terms of consciousness. The behaviorist, in his efforts to get a unitary scheme of animal response, recognizes no dividing line between man and brute. (Watson, 1913: 158)

Behavior problems can be changed through behavior modification techniques based on B. F. Skinner's (1953, 1961) theories of operant conditioning that describe the relationship between behavior and environmental events. This involves the following four types of contingent behavior: positive reinforcement (rewards), negative reinforcement (removal of an unpleasant consequence), punishment (imposing a penalty), and extinction (ignoring certain behaviors to weaken or remove them). Behavior can be shaped by immediately reinforcing small changes in behavior that match the overall goal. "Token" economies, using "points" (stars or tokens) as "rewards" for behavior that is acceptable to those in authority are used to achieve this. While this can be benign, it is certainly open to abuse by those who are concerned more with the administration of power and control than with therapy (Foucault, 1977; Rose, 1989). In abusive instances basic requirements (such as food or blankets) may be used as rewards rather than, as would seem reasonable, some luxury (phone calls or TV time). Behavioral modification techniques are often applied to adolescents and others who are in structured institutional settings—schools, residential centers, prisons, drug rehabilitation clinics, and mental institutions. They are also used in individualized adolescent treatment programs—with varying success, because adolescents often view those administering such programs with considerable mistrust.

In applying behavioral notions, behavioral counseling uses applied behavioral analysis that, first, establishes a relationship between counselor and client; second, defines the problem by operationalizing behavior—working out what the client does or how they behave; third, conducts a functional analysis—antecedents, behavior, consequences (ABC); four, establishes behavioral change or socially important goals for the client (Ivey et al., 1987). Assertiveness training, relaxation techniques, systematic desensitization, and relapse prevention are examples of behavioral counseling and therapy.

Variations of the strict behaviorist theories are cognitive-behavioral theories. Well-known cognitive-behavioral therapists include Albert Bandura, Aaron Beck, Albert Ellis, William Glasser, George Kelly, John Krumboltz, and Donald Meichenbaum (see Ivey et al., 1987 and others). This section looks briefly at the work of Kelly, Bandura, Ellis, and Glasser, who have developed their ideas into distinctive forms of therapy. They provide a more humanistic approach than do strict behaviorist notions and aim to integrate thought, action, and decision making. Cognitive-behavioral theories are described as "a beginning attempt to integrate the three major philosophical traditions of idealism, realism, and existentialism" (Ivey et al., 1987: 304). The emphasis is on responsibility and the choices made by individuals by encouraging them to examine and to change faulty belief systems as they are assisted in examining internalized identification and patterns of behavior.

The idea that individuals act upon how they perceive and then "construct" the world, acting in a way as scientists by constantly testing hypotheses to sort out the confusions of the world, led to George Kelly's (1955) pioneering "personal construct theory." For him, because each client was unique and strongly influenced by their culture and environment in how they conceptualized the world, it became imperative that counselors checked out the client's constructs before anything else— Kelly's *law of parsimony*. Therefore he presented a systematic way of diagnosing and assessing a client's language and behavior before working out any long-term treatment plan (see Kelly, 1955: 777–779).

Albert Bandura (1977, 1986, 1997) developed a more humanistic approach to behaviorist therapy through shared decision making between the counselor and the client, promulgating the notion of "self-efficacy." He stressed that the best growth occurs when individuals feel they are in control of their own destiny.

Albert Ellis (1971) developed rational emotive therapy (RET), which is generally considered to be a psycho-educational therapy. It focuses more on an individual's thoughts than on their feelings, maintaining that their irrational thinking patterns have made people victims of their thoughts. The "A–B–C" theory of personality is Elis's contribution to understanding the self in general and does not separate out adolescents from adults. A is the objective facts/event/ behavior that an individual encounters; B is the individual's beliefs about A; and C is the emotional consequence or how the individual feels about A. It is not so much the event that is troublesome; rather, it is how one experiences and thinks about it that is the problem. Ellis's theory has a connection to other theories that focus on how an individual creates meaning or interprets the world and in how they come to understand and create the self. In practical terms, how a counselor would use this theory would involve a confrontation of incongruities displayed by the client,, directives, interpretations, advice, and opinion, while downplaying listening skills of attending to and reflecting feelings. While RET has been favored somewhat in educational psychology circles, many school counselors are likely to feel some unease about the form of listening skills, the directiveness, and the conflict with notions of client autonomy that they are likely to consider important, whether dealing with teenagers or with adults. For adolescents who constantly have authority figures blaming them and/or directing, an RET-oriented counselor may well be just another in a line of authorities who tell them what to do and what and how to think, so that an appropriate level of trust may be precluded.

Since choice is not necessarily incompatible with strict behavioral notions, the work of William Glasser (1965, 1984), in what was initially called "reality therapy" and is now known as "control" or "choice theory," has evolved from and generally superseded the narrower behaviorist methods. It is also in line with some current directions in developmental psychology. Glasser's ideas, similarly to those of Ellis, have taken on considerable importance in schools that use variations of "assertive discipline" and in educational psychology, especially for dealing with behavioral problems and delinquency in adolescents, such as Resource Teachers: Learning and Behavior (RTLBs) in New Zealand. Glasser (1965) theorized that individuals who get into trouble "deny the reality of the world around them. . . . Therapy will be successful when they are able to give up denying the world and recognize that reality not only exists, but that they must fulfill their needs within its framework" (Glasser, 1965: 6). In practice, reality/control/choice therapy is confrontational and uses role play, goal setting, and teaching techniques. While it emphasizes that clients take responsibility for or "own" their actions, it pays scant attention to the unconscious, to transference, or to alienation of the "inner self." That the therapist is the one in a position of power and control may be overly emphasized in a school setting and may result in this form of counseling being counterproductive, somewhat similarly to the reservations described above in relation to RET. In comparing Ellis and Glasser, Ivey and colleagues sum up the former approach as "be rational and think about things logically," the latter as "take responsibility and control of your life and face the consequences of your actions" (Ivey et al., 1987: 324).

Behavioral and cognitive-behavioral technologies form a paradigm that developed not in relation to mental illness, but in dealing with the behavior of maladaptive aspects of personality. Psychological techniques related to specific goals can be applied to such problem-centered maladjustments as alcoholism, kleptomania, anorexia, bulimia, anxiety, obsession, phobia, stopping smoking, sex therapy, assertion training, and cognitive restructuring of values. These theories and the associated therapies are particularly, but not solely, applied to work with adolescents. The twin assumptions that the problem is within the person who has an incorrect perception of the reality of their environment and that the therapist, as an expert, has the correct perception of reality leaves these techniques open to criticism.

HUMANIST-EXISTENTIAL PSYCHOLOGY THEORIES

Abraham Maslow (1968), Carl Rogers (1961, 1969), Fritz Perls, and Viktor Frankl are known as humanist-existential or phenomenological theorists. Ivey and colleagues (1987) point to a continuum of humanist-existential therapists with Rogers and his nondirective, person-centered therapy at one end, the directive, "be-here-now" immediacy of Perls's gestalt therapy on the other, and Frankl's logotherapy emphasizing the search for the meaning of life somewhere in the middle. Their theories and therapies display different ways of reading the world, people, and the self, but they have evolved from two philosophies—humanism and existentialism[4]—that were discussed in some detail in chapter 2. A brief summary of these philosophies and what they imply about the self, the conceptualization of adolescence, and the implications for counseling and therapy is provided by Ivey and colleagues:

> Existentialism is concerned with the human *existence* and the infinite possibilities of life . . . founded on the belief that each person sees the world uniquely and constructs her or his own reality through transactions with the world. We can know our selves only through our relationship with others. There is general agreement that existentialism is the study of humankind's *being-in-the-world.* Thus existentialism is centrally concerned with examining the meaning of life and our place in the world . . . [asking] "What does that mean?" "Why did that happen?" "What really *is*?"
>
> One existential position sees difficulties and problems in life's many possibilities. The existential-humanist sees beauty, opportunities, and alternatives. The question of meaning is in the eye of the beholder. A humanistic choice is one which is positive and directed toward a possible

> future. Humanism is a philosophy that dignifies and conceptualizes people as making their own choices and decisions. (Ivey, Ivey, and Simek-Downing, 1987: 269)

The summary that Ivey and colleagues (1987) provide needs to be acknowledged as being for and by counselors, not what would be considered adequate for philosophers of education. The existential concept of "being-in-the-world," with individuals acting on it while it acts on them, leads on to other concepts: *alienation* as a result of separation from others and the world; *existential anxiety*, which may result from alienation or from not making decisions or choices; *existential commitment* when choices are made and action is taken. These are underpinned by *intentionality*, the notion in counseling that "sees choice as opportunity rather than problematic . . . that people can be forward moving and act on their world, yet must remain keenly aware that the world acts on them as well" (Ivey et al., p. 270). Ivey and colleagues (1987) argue that *intentionality* provides a bridge to humanism, a philosophy that values and dignifies humankind, as exemplified in the theories of Carl Rogers and Martin Buber.

Humanist-existential theorists contend that humans have a growth force that motivates and guides them to reach their full potential of mental health and desirable social behaviors or "self-actualization," the apex of Maslow's hierarchy of needs. The conditions enabling this growth to occur are described, particularly by Rogers, as involving positive regard, empathy, and congruence or genuineness. Humanist-existential theorists assume that perception is the basis of reality and behavior and that therefore, because of her or his unique perceptions, everyone has a different reality. While differences in perception result in individual behavior, there are broad similarities and common elements in human perceptual behavior. Some degree of pain, hurt, and struggle is inevitable in life, but if we can free ourselves from the negativity of bitterness, anger, hurt, and fear, we can find the strength to cope with disappointment and adversity and move on to higher levels of growth and personal fulfillment.

Abraham Maslow's (1968) hierarchy of needs suggested that growth involves movement toward fulfilling one's potential by at least partially satisfying these at lower levels before highe-level needs can be fulfilled. His five levels start with the physiological, safety and security, belongingness and love, self-esteem, and, finally, self-actualizing needs. Ivey and colleagues suggest that May, Binswanger, and Boss, who brought existential philosophies to the United States and to psychology and counseling in the 1950s and 1960s, were particularly influential figures. But after the Second World War the giant figure who provided a radical departure from the then current notions of psychoanalysis, developmental psychology, and psychodynamic and behaviorist counseling was Carl Rogers, who established humanist-existential theories. The influence of both Rogers and Maslow has been profound. Rogers was instrumental as part of the revolution in thought in the 1960s, in promoting empowerment for people, including adolescents, with his client-centered counseling approach.

Carl Rogers (1961, 1969) believed that what is good for an individual is good for society, and so he supported concepts of freedom. He assumed that if people were allowed the freedom to express their natural potential, they would live reasonably ordered, constructive lives without needing to be controlled by institutions and other social control mechanisms. He considered the self to be the most important aspect of psychological growth, and he contended that a healthy, positive self-concept grows from the unconditional "positive regard" or feedback from significant others (parents, friends, teachers, spouses). If significant others respect their thoughts and behaviors, even when they are disagreeable or differ from their own, children and adolescents learn to value and trust themselves, developing strong self-concepts than can readily grasp and embrace new experiences. They rapidly become fully functioning people. Those who don't experience warmth, genuineness, and understanding and who are rejected or are denied accurate, realistic information about themselves develop a negative self-concept. They can become defensive, with little hope, trust, and optimism, unable to reach out and positively grasp new experiences. They can become psychologically crippled, maladjusted, neurotic, and even psychopathic, using their energies to defend their fragile self from further damage and hurt.

Implications for adolescence from this theoretical approach emphasize freedom and growth in an ideal environment of positiveness, trust, acceptance, unconditional love, and minimal conflict and negative feelings. Growth in adolescence was seen as developing the maturity to not require external controls and threats to control behavior, but to respond to internalized control through developing self-discipline. Taken to extremes, it can result in a highly permissive environment with inadequate limits or boundaries and with behavior being controlled only by "natural" consequences rather than by rewards and punishments.

Psychological concepts, as outlined, have for the most part strongly emphasized an individual approach, paying attention to internal changes within the adolescent rather than examining the influence of the external on emotional and cognitive development. In ignoring the cultural and societal aspects that led to the emergence of adolescence, society, and psychology in particular, end up blaming the victim—that is, the adolescent. This is not to say that to a certain extent adolescents are not responsible for their actions and the choices they make. While it is important to look at the individual, it is also important to look at the structures within which they are situated when dealing with their problems. Psychologically oriented practices mostly deal individually with adolescents who have major problems, to help them to work through and understand the inner processes that affect their behavior. Individual approaches do little to change the societal issues that often have contributed to the problem—for instance, poverty, unemployment, and racism. What individual approaches can do is help adolescents to develop coping skills to deal with these circumstances. There is no professional requirement or suggestion that psychologists should lobby politically on such structural issues of social justice. If they do so, it is entirely their own individual choice. Psychological perspectives provide useful viewpoints for counseling, but what counselors engaged in dealing with adolescents need to take into account is the critique of psychological discourse as they continually update, refine, and integrate relevant notions into their practice.

THE BURGEONING OF THE "PSY" SCIENCES IN THE TWENTIETH CENTURY

Nikolas Rose, inspired by Foucauldian thought, used critical history in his works *Governing the Soul: The Shaping of the Private Self* (1989) and *Inventing Our Selves* (1998) to examine the relationship between society, the "psy" sciences, and the self. In the sense in which Rose uses "psychology," he does not mean "a body of abstracted theories and explanations, but an 'intellectual technology,' a way of making visible and intelligible certain features of persons, their conducts, and their relations with one another" (Rose, 1998: 10–11). Intellectual technologies involve governing a domain and developing theories within that domain through an intellectual mastery over a sector of reality, identifying its characteristics, processes, and features in ways that are "notable, speakable, writeable," and explainable (Rose, 1998). Modern democracies use economic, medical, legal, sociological, and psychological knowledge or intellectual technologies that are "assemblages of ways of seeing and diagnosing, techniques of calculation, and judgement" (Rose, 1998: 120). Rose sees psychology in a general sense as an activity that combines academic and practical "expertise," involving "a corps of trained and credentialed persons claiming special competence in the administration of persons and interpersonal relations, and a body of techniques and procedures claiming to make possible the rational and human management of human resources in industry, the military, and social life more generally" (Rose, 1998: 11).

Such a definition would clearly apply to school counseling, for it requires selected personnel with tertiary training in counseling theory, skills, and practice to deal with personal and interpersonal issues that, intentionally or otherwise, aim to have an enabling effect on the institution of the school and its students' lives. It encourages students to take care for themselves and to care for others, and it enables them to be managed by and within the institution they are part of as long as they are willing to visit the counselor. Counseling has clear links with the discipline of psychology, and in Rose's conception, it would certainly be considered one of the "psy" sciences. Although it is not psychology per se, it largely grew out of psychology and continues to use many psychological theories in its primary emphasis on emotional and psychological well-being.

During the twentieth century in the liberal democracies of the West, especially in the United States, Europe, and Australasia, "psychology, and all related "psy" knowledges, have played a significant role in the reorganization of the practices and techniques that have linked authority to subjectivity" (Rose, 1998: 18–19)—that is, to govern, in the broad Foucauldian sense, requires "knowledge" about what is possible, legitimate and effective (see Introduction for Foucault's term "governmentality"). It requires a range of knowledge or intellectual technologies, so that decision makers can know, calculate, and justify their choices in relation to "the facts." Rose (1989, 1998) maintained that psychological language and theories have provided not just a "science of behavior," but the central intellectual technologies in how we have come to relate to ourselves and think about ourselves, our social lives, and our interactions, as well as practical ways of transforming these.

The inscription[5] devices that psychology developed enabled both individuals and social life to become calculable. The war years were important to these developments, because they produced "a new set of social psychologies, psychotherapies and psychiatries that sought to document, interpret, and utilize these social relations in different ways" (Rose, 1989: x). The First World War stimulated the development and deployment of intelligence tests as the military sought to select appropriate personnel. The subsequent development of psychological tests combined individual attributes that were collated and compared to form norms that could then be calculated, evaluated, and judged, and that, in effect, "rendered visible the invisible qualities of the human soul, distilling the multifarious attributes of the person into a single figure" (Rose, 1989: 121). Testing became a vital mechanism where the "efficiency of an organization comes to be seen as dependent upon a rational utilization of the human factor" (Rose, 1989: 121). It also became an integral part of school guidance counseling when it was set up in New Zealand schools. Social psychological devices such as attitude scales, morale surveys, sociometric diagrams, and graphical representations of field theory inscribed social life in ways in which it could become calculable and, in turn, manageable. Both testing and social psychology have been used by education to stream students according to their abilities and by vocational guidance to allocate persons with certain traits to particular jobs.

Rose (1998) points to a number of references to democracy in social psychology texts (see Allport, 1954; Lewin, Lippitt, andWhite, 1939) to argue that the link between social psychology and democracy in the 1930s, 1940s, and 1950s was much more than rhetoric. He contends that social psychology involved a project to encourage and promote democracy in order to prevent the multiple horrors of fascism, genocide, and loss that had occurred during the Second World War. Such a link partly accounts for the development of social guidance for adolescents and the use of mental hygiene films (as discussed in chapter 4). Saving youth from itself and the negative aspects of the times was seen as a way of preventing a slide into fascism or dictatorship and as a foil to communism. Guidance counseling was positioned as providing one such mechanism to save youth from itself and, in turn, save society—a huge and largely unrealistic task.

Psychological expertise was considered vital for maximizing human resources in various institutions in the war years—a time of crisis when states demanded more accurate techniques for military recruitment and promotion and more efficient policy decision making. During the First World War intelligence tests had been developed and used. Rose (1989) argued that psychology's practical involvement and research activities during the Second World War were crucially important in how "the postwar technologies of subjectivity" were shaped (Rose, 1989: x). What emerged was the concept of the "group" as a fundamental field of analysis, therapy, and regulation that enabled people to be understood in terms of specific processes and could describe their relationships (Rose, 1998). New notions of subjectivity, especially "attitudes" and "personality," enabled individual value-related social actions (e.g., political preferences, racial prejudices, religious orientations, moral beliefs) to be ordered and measured by psychology (Rose, 1998: 120). Psychological language and norms were rapidly disseminated through the education of social workers, health workers, and teachers, and they became established in popular literature, the mass media, and advertising. This led to a proliferation of "psy" therapies such as psychoanalysis, clinical psychology, social work, psychotherapy, and counseling, and it developed what Rose contends is "the therapeutic culture of the self" (Rose, 1989: xii). Such new psychological "languages" and techniques enabled psychological expertise to claim a key role in any practice of the management of individuals in institutional life, be that prison, workplace, armed forces, factory, hospital, or school (Rose, 1989, 1998).

Since the mid-nineteenth century, the sphere of family and the objectives of government have gradually become more closely linked. The rearing and well-being of children has become of interest to governments concerned with the economic and social welfare of society at large. Incorrect or ignorant practices of child care within the family have at different times been blamed for all manner of social ills: vagrancy, addictions, vice, crime, delinquency, military defeat, and industrial decline. Solutions to these have involved a wide range of programs linking health, education, and welfare, as evidenced in movements such as eugenics, mental hygiene (as discussed in chapter 4), and public health programs. Around the welfare of the child and adolescent, the minute details of conjugal, domestic, and parental family practices have become available for scrutiny (Donzelot, 1980; Rose, 1989).

Since the Second World War, psychological discourse played a key role by increasingly providing the language for dealing with concerns about child-rearing, and for identifying problems, and it provided the types of expertise to solve them. In establishing norms of desirable childhood and adolescent development and behavior, psychology devised new means of describing and understanding the nature of childhood, thereby differentiating between normality and pathology. If a child does not attain these norms, parents or educators may become anxious and seek professional guidance to manage this perceived discrepancy. The tendency is to suggest that young people or their parents are deficient in some way, with all the attendant issues of blame. But at the end of the twentieth century such "truths" have become quite strongly contested (Rose, 1989). Furthermore, Rose suggests that there has been a shift from concern about "correct" child rearing practices, aimed at preventing psychological maladjustments, to an emphasis on the "proper" management of early relations with parents and the environment, so that both the emotional adjustment and the cognitive efficiency of the child are maximized. In the process, "Our selves are defined and constructed and governed in psychological terms, constantly subject to psychologically inspired techniques of self-inspection and self-examination. And the problems of defining and living a good life have been transposed from an ethical to a psychological register" (Rose, 1989: xiii).

This move has been reflected in a much tighter surveillance and regulation of family life and in a greater emphasis on education. It is not so much middle-class families that have come under scrutiny—rather, the regulation of families has tended to concentrate on social work interventions for poor, nonnuclear, solo-parent, and ethnic minority families. Governments rationalize their action in such forms of regulation, surveillance, and governmentality by aiming to keep costs to a minimum while maximizing the human resources they have power over (Donzelot, 1980; Lasch, 1979, 1984; Rose, 1989).

"Adolescence" is a notion that describes the growth to adult maturity and is largely age-defined, depicting a life-cycle stage that is part of modern Western culture rather than a universal and crossculturally valid concept. The arrival of puberty in Western society is usually considered the start of adolescence. The Western notion of "adolescence" is not applicable to traditional societies, where children are inducted into adult society once they reach a certain age, usually associated with the physiological indicators of the arrival of puberty. In traditional societies, there are frequently elaborate rituals as rites of passage and a new set of rules, expectations, and behaviors for these new adults, who are then required to contribute to the economic life of their community, to accept adult responsibilities, and to be married.

Psychologists suggest that adolescence itself is a developmental stage, and some scholars argue that it is not a single one but, rather, divisible into stages of early, middle, and late adolescence that are not entirely age-specific. Such stages are allegedly characterized by particular interests. Those in the early stage are considered to be as different from those in the later stage as an adult is considered different from a child. In many countries differences within adolescence are reinforced structurally by schooling patterns: intermediate schools, high schools, junior and senior high schools. Early adolescence is often focused on dealing with pubertal changes, a rapidly changing body, the impact of sexual drives, and therefore a changing self-image. Middle adolescence is often a time of experimentation with different values, sex, drugs, and challenges to authority. Late adolescence focuses more on the future, on career choices, relationships, and the meaning of life. But all are involved in issues around the self and around identity, in a more intensly conscious manner than in childhood. Some educators and counselors argue that extreme permissiveness from adults who set no limits for adolescents does a disservice to young people in search of their identity. It is suggested that a lack of boundaries and excessive freedom can cause insecurity and can almost "paralyze" that adolescents' growth as they search for someone significant to them, to show that they care enough to set limits and to set an adult identity against which adolescents can assert themselves.

This chapter has discussed notions of adolescence throughout history, focusing upon ways the discourses of the human sciences have conceptualized and constructed understandings about young people. It follows the Foucauldian Nikolas

Rose in describing the genealogy and burgeoning of the "psy" sciences in the twentieth century and how "psychological theories have played a key role in the birth of this new concept of the self and psychological techniques through which modern selves are constructed, sustained and remodelled" (Rose, 1989: xii). It has presented not only an overview of developmental, behaviorist, cognitive-behavioral, and humanist-existential psychology to argue that the discourse of adolescence has been profoundly "psychologized" in the twentieth century, but also some of the critiques of this discourse. In the light of anthropological and sociological critique that has clearly indicated that different cultures and different times have specified human capacities in different ways, it is argued that notions of the self are not universal. Although the universalist aspects of much of psychological discourse have now been revised to include the influence of culture on behaviors, many people involved in the "psy" sciences still consider adolescence a stage when cognitive and emotional development takes place amid emotional storm and stress (Baker, 2001; Hall, 1905). As a result, a focus on problems where young people do not reach expected norms has led to remedial/adjustment models to become dominant in dealing with adolescents in psychological practice and in schools. But these inadvertently blame the victim instead of suggesting how society should adjust to better accommodate the adolescent.

It was the remedial-adjustive notion that was prevalent when counseling was introduced into schools in Britain, the United States, and New Zealand and, not surprisingly, strongly influenced the identity of counseling, because training was initially provided by psychologists in university education departments. Schools as sites where young people negotiate class, gender, ethnicity, and other relationships need to become aware that the practices they adopt are derived from the hidden, unquestioned assumptions of development theories, where "the discourse of youth development actually provides a legitimation for denying young people rights which are provided for adults. By individualizing and essentializing young people, a highly judgmental approach can be justified, which ultimately marginalizes those who are the least powerful in our society" (Wyn and White, 1997: 71).

Psychological theorizing of adolescence has clearly had enormous impact on how we view young people and construct notions of adolescence, but it has been strongly challenged by the discourses that have emerged in the later part of the twentieth century and by sociology. Sociological understandings about adolescence/youth are examined in chapter 4.

CHAPTER 4

SOCIOLOGIZING YOUTH

INTRODUCTION: SOCIOLOGICAL PERSPECTIVES

An understanding of both sociological and psychological approaches to adolescence/youth and the assumptions of both discourses are important for enabling educators and school counselors to gain a better understanding of the issues of identity for their youthful clients. This chapter discusses some sociological notions of youth that emphasize the group and its identity by drawing on sociological theory and ethnography. These theories differ from psychological approaches that tend to focus largely on the individual, except for recent social, discursive, and constructionist psychological approaches. As noted in the previous chapter, psychologically oriented discourses tend to use the term "adolescence," while sociological ones tend to favor "youth." Both are used interchangeably in this book, but this chapter, in focusing on the sociological, mostly uses "youth."

Sociological approaches can be classified into: functionalist studies, political economy, and cultural/subcultural studies. This chapter begins with an overview of functionalist and political economy sociological perspectives about youth. The second section focuses on what Gordon Tait (2000) argues is the dominant paradigm of cultural/subcultural studies of youth conducted in the 1970s in Britain at the Birmingham Center for Contemporary Cultural Studies (CCCS). These studies are central to this section because youth only emerged as a specific category for ethnographic study in the 1970s. The CCCS studies displayed a radical shift from the sociology on the 1950s that focused on integration, coherence, difference, and discontinuity between dominant and subordinate value systems, as indicated by a shift from functionalist to Marxist language. Subcultural theory evolved out of a combination of functionalist anomie and deviancy sociological theories and urban ethnography in a political context of disillusionment with the welfare state (Cohen, 1980). These studies utilized ethnographic methods and Marxist analysis to describe the contours of youth culture and subcultures in the postwar period—a time when youth came to be seen as a social problem that reflected considerable social change in lifestyle and values. Subcultural studies focused on the interplay of ideology, socioeconomic status, and culture, positioning working-class male youth as resisting the dominant, hegemonic adult middle-class culture (Cohen, 1972; Hall and Jefferson, 1976; Willis, 1977, 1978). They have subsequently been criticized from feminist and other perspectives (Cohen, 1980; McRobbie, 1991; Tait, 2000) for romanticizing youth and for universalizing from studies that focused only on working-class males, using notions of "counterhegemonic struggle, generational consciousness, and style as discourse" (Tait, 2000: 54).

Once there was a full-bodied theoretical concept of youth culture, it became possible to write critical histories of its emergence by projecting the notion backward to excavate the layers of the past in terms of genealogies of values represented in "moral panics." The section concludes by suggesting that a distinct youth culture, with its own subcultures, has developed. Alongside, there is now a deeper theoretical sense and an appreciation that youth are largely perceived with more tolerance than they were in the 1950s and 1960s.

Postmodern approaches to youth and the influence of Foucauldian critique are briefly discussed in the last section by using several exemplars. These include notions of a globalized youth culture (Giroux, 1990; Luke, 2000), feminist viewpoints (Lesko, 1996; Nava, 1991), and youth movements (Kahane, 1997).

Sociology emphasizes that all beings are *social* and, therefore, need to be examined within their social contexts. Much of the focus in classical sociology is on the transitional period between the dependency of childhood and the independence and autonomy of adulthood, together with an examination of the tensions inherent in such a phase. Sociological perspectives include divergent viewpoints but tend to support the underlying assumption that adolescence is a cultural construct based on the social expectations of that particular culture that are beyond the control of the adolescent. These perspectives tend to take the side of "nurture" in the nature–nurture debate about adolescence.

Sociologists examine how the primary relationships with family, peers, and school help to form a core identity that develops in adolescence and underlies social activities as an autonomous self in adulthood. However, the notion of a free, rational, conscious, choosing, autonomous self (as discussed in chapter 2) is not universal. It is a creation originally of Ancient Greek society and more recently of Western capitalist democracies—that is, a product of a particular culture. Furthermore, what is meant by "dependence" and "independence" is contestable, changing in different societies and at different times.

The functionalist sociological approach centers on the impact of social changes due to industrialization and urbanization, which have significantly changed the period between childhood and adulthood in Western societies. The following two effects have extended adolescence at both ends in ways that did not happen before industrialization. First, the secular trend, considered to be the result of improvements in public sanitation, in nutritional quantity and quality, and in health care and medicine, describes the increased lowering of the average age for the onset of puberty. This is now about four years earlier than it was in 1850, being at approximately age 12 for females and 14 for males, compared with 16 and 18, respectively, in 1850 (Côté and Allahar, 1994). Second, young people's labor is less required in industrialized societies, so rather than being considered economic assets, as they were in agricultural societies, children and adolescents are often seen as economic liabilities in urbanized, industrialized societies. One consequence has been a dramatic fall in birth rates in such societies. With fewer children in a family now, there is, arguably, a more intense emotional attachment between parents and offspring. Ariès (1962) argues that intense attachments did not arise in earlier centuries because so many children died young and hence were not worth the emotional investment. Offsetting the notion of economic liability, the young have been positioned differently in terms of ideology and institutions: "These ideologies include the importance of protecting the young from the evils and hardships of the adult world; the institutions include the education system and various government agencies entrusted with enforcing this separation from the adult world" (Côté and Allahar, 1994: 17).

The impact of change from an early industrial society that focused on manufacturing to a service-based economy of postindustrial society today has further prolonged adolescence at the adult end. Tertiary education, while not a guarantee of employment in the current era of credential inflation, has nevertheless become the required standard to enable youth to enter well-paid service-related and professional careers and to not remain unemployed, underemployed, or in low-paying jobs. Côté and Allahar (1994) contend that while this functionalist view is convincing and useful, it is too descriptive and fatalistic in accepting the inevitability of social order and social change and in assuming "a natural evolution of society" (Côté and Allahar, 1994: 20).

Critical political economy perspectives center on the notion that adolescents are a disenfranchised class, without economic, political, or social power. This is what causes them to react either to form their own subculture or to be conditioned into false consciousness, supporting structures that work against their own interests and lead to alienation rather than to creative individualism and self-determination. The emphasis here is on the causes rather than a description of the reaction of adolescents. Côté and Allahar (1994) suggest that to mask this disenfranchisement and to ensure that young people do not mobilize as a reaction against their exploitation, it has been necessary for the state to impose a long period of indoctrination into acquiescence and acceptance of existing power structures as normal, natural, good, and benign. The state does this in capitalist societies because it directly serves the interests of capital and those who control it. This indoctrination is accomplished mainly through the educational system, but other institutions such as the media also enter into complicity with it. (Côté and Allahar, 1994: 25)

"Indoctrination" of this sort (see chapter 4 for further discussion) occurs when society emphasizes neoliberal notions of choice and self-responsibility. It unwittingly leads adolescents to believe that their sense of alienation is normal. Because they are responsible for choices they have made, they end up blaming themselves or their peers rather than examining the system to see whether something is wrong. From a functionalist perspective, those that are acquiescent and unquestioning of existing power structures would be considered to be well socialized. Adolescents who resist such control and manipulation are often subjected to interventions by various state-funded social agencies (teachers, deans, psychologists, counselors, social workers, courts) to encourage compliance and acceptance, without the agents noting or assigning any blame to the system. These people (including school counselors) can unwittingly and unthinkingly become agents for social control, supporting dominant economic interests against the very group that they are meant to be helping. According to Snook (1972), it may not be defined as "indoctrination" if intent is not involved. Regardless, though, of how one defines it, the effect on youth can be very negative.

From the political economy sociological perspective, the capitalist system that aims to maximize profits regardless of social costs is particularly controlling of adolescents who have been marginalized from adult society and sequestered into age groups at school, and who are searching for an identity. They are subject to exploitative, menial jobs with low-paying youth pay rates. They are targets of massive marketing campaigns aimed to play on their emotional insecurities, cynically endorsing the notion of "youth culture" by encouraging them to buy fashion, music, art, sport, and consumer goods that confer identity, only to have these goods or styles made deliberately obsolete the following year. The market (and their peers) may require them to buy the latest to be "in" or to be acceptable to their group, but it is the company that benefits financially.

The sociological viewpoint that sees adjusting adolescents to fit their environment, as many psychological and socialization developmental theories imply, ignores the possibility of adjusting the environment to fit some or all of the people. This perspective requires changes in how adolescents are perceived, so programs and institutions are developed to fit their needs, including recognizing their level of development, maturity, and autonomy and that some of the problems that youth present may not result from individual inadequacy, but from problems in the wider structures of society. Such problems may involve challenges to societal values and a move to a more humanistic society.

Sociological interest in the topics of childhood and adolescence, considered in their own right rather than as part of studies of the family or of deviance, has led to the emergence of distinctive discourses since the 1970s (James, Jenks, and Prout, 1998). Allison James, Chris Jenks, and Alan Prout (1998) assert that until recently the notion of "socialization" had been unchallenged in its dominance of sociological understandings about social development in a way that had close parallels to psychological notions of cognitive maturation and development. Socialization is a process through which individuals—especially children and adolescents—learn what social norms are and how to conform to them. Allison Davis's (1944) theory describes the socialization process whereby adolescents are motivated by anxiety about punishments, threats, and the withdrawal of love and affection, to become what their culture expected of them in terms of ideas, beliefs, values, and norms. In this way the social order and the transmission of culture ("acculturation") from the older to the younger generation was allegedly established and maintained. For sociologists holding this viewpoint, society is a complex phenomenon that shapes the individual. Children and young people are seen as not fully formed, but as having the potential to become fully functioning adults once they have been taught how; hence the institutions of family, church, and school are believed to be of prime importance.

Talcott Parsons (1951), in his classic work, *The Social System,* defines socialization as "the process of child development," which supports the idea that "the stablest and most enduring [aspects of the learned personality] are the major value-orientation patterns" (Parsons, 1951: 101). There is much evidence that these are "laid down" in childhood and are generally not subject to drastic alteration during adulthood (Parsons, 1951). His notion is a universalizing one that assumes an exact fit or congruence between the individual and a society, with the individual being determined by the structure of society and not by their personal agency. Many studies in "structural sociology" are formed on this premise. According to this view, because the child or adolescent was not fully formed, was incomplete or incompetent, the notion of applying remedial action or interventions came to prominence, as was the case with much of psychology and of school guidance counseling in the 1960s and 1970s (Hermansson, 1990; Wadsworth, 1970; Winterbourn, 1974).

Parson's theory of socialization, though path-breaking, is only one example. G. H. Mead developed his theories of socialization as "symbolic interactionism" that involved social psychology and group dynamics and has resulted in many ethnographies of small groups and communities. Socialization was considered an element of interaction or transactional negotiation in terms of the language and skills that were acquired as individuals negotiated their way into groups they joined. It was contended that "the basic theory of the acquisition of language and interactional skills is based very much on an unexplicated behaviorism, and in the final resolution of the matured relationship between the individual and the collective other (that is the "self" and "other") is a thinly disguised reworking of Freud's triumph of the super-ego over the id" (James et al., 1998: 25).

James and her colleagues (1998) suggest that socialization theories account for the way neither childhood nor adolescence were positioned as topics of study in their own right. Adolescence was not considered a suitable topic of study unless it was part of the investigation of *deviance*. Until the 1970s, adolescence/youth had been positioned in the sociological literature as an object of study in terms of criminology, delinquency,[1] and deviance, and this says a great deal about how adults perceived them and were, to a certain extent, fearful of them. Historically, in much of the psychological literature, youth were studied in terms of clinical problems and stage theories, with initial research tending to have a pathological bias, focusing on the "problem" population—the "clinical." The research findings were then generalized to the major or "normal" population (Rose, 1989, 1998). While some elements of this persist, sociological research tended to broaden in the 1970s to become culturally based.

SUBCULTURAL THEORIES OF YOUTH, 1960s–1990s

This section surveys notions of "youth culture" and subculture because they are instrumental in shaping the identity of youth. It is essential to have some understanding of youth, subcultures, their context, and their forms if one deals predominantly with youth, as secondary schools and school counselors do.

Cultural and subcultural theories developed out of the nurture aspect of the nature–nurture debate that has been briefly referred to in chapter 3. James S. Coleman, writing in the 1960s, developed a "youth culture theory" that identified the significance of a youth culture that had evolved in our society by the 1960s and 1970s. He suggests that pop music was partly responsible for this, in uniting youth and giving them a form of expression that was different from that of the adult generation. Some of the characteristics he identifies are the need for love, security, and acceptance that results in intense, close personal relationships, a push for autonomy and a consequent support for those who challenge adult cultures, concern for change, stemming from the perception of being outside adult cultures, and idealistic hopes of creating a better world in future. Youth culture strongly influences adolescents in their choices of political affiliations, lifestyles, clothing, music, heroes, and role models through focusing in on itself, giving youth a reference point, guidance, approval, and acceptance—or the reverse of these. Coleman's work points out that membership in a youth culture influences how adolescents relate to adult society, identifies the importance of peers for adolescents, establishes their dominant values at this point in time, and ascertains that social class and family background influences achievement in school. His research in ten high schools in the 1960s in the Midwestern United States found that popularity and acceptance by peers were prime motivational forces, with athletic ability and good looks being more important than academic achievement. He summarizes what adolescents said it took to get into the leading crowd in these schools:

> it takes a lot of things; academic success is not one of them. It takes athletic prowess, knowing how to dance, owning a car, having a good reputation, or liking to have fun. It takes being a good date, liking parties, and often not being a prude (for girls) or a sissy (for boys). Good grades and intelligence are mentioned, but not very often, and not as often as the other items. (Coleman, 1965: 19)

Coleman posits a structuralist argument contending that high schools themselves were partly responsible for this heightened peer culture, because youth are together in age groups for so many hours a day that the peer group becomes central to many activities and provides social reinforcement:

> Youth are segregated from adults by the economic and educational institutions created by adults. They are deprived of psychic support from persons of other ages, a psychic support that once came [to them as children] from the family. They are subordinate and powerless in relation to adults, and "outsiders" [in relation to] dominant social institutions. Yet they have money, they have access

> to a wide range of communications media, and control of some, and they are relatively large in number. (Coleman et al., 1974: 125)

Although Coleman is identifying youth as a distinct group from others, his ideas also seem to have resonance in the light of the April 1999 multiple killings at Columbine High School, Denver, U.S.A., which resulted from many forces operating, including gun culture and favorable attitudes to violence. Social ostracism and exclusion led to the formation of separate and very different peer subgroups with ideas and values not only in opposition to the popular group, but also with murderous intent and actions toward those very peers, focusing the attack on athletes and blacks and popular students.

Rather than being passive, the adolescents in Coleman's study were very active in defining their social milieu in schools through developing their own newspapers, clubs, and organizations. Therefore, Coleman suggests, schools and the community have an important part to play in harnessing the positive aspects of youth peer culture to motivate youth to behave in positive and constructive ways that benefit society.

A further development of this viewpoint is the subcultural or peer group view of adolescence, derived from symbolic interactionism theory, which contends that interaction is based on our ability to share meanings through both verbal and nonverbal communication. It examines how adolescents develop meaningful identity through developing their own subcultures in response to marginalization, incompleteness, and meaninglessness in the roles that adult society grants them. The effects of race and social-class background can increase this marginalization. The more mainstream adult culture ignores youth subcultures, the more these will use symbols such as language, clothing, music, jewelry, and behavior to reject and negate conventional adulthood. The problem is that the more involved with and the more radical the subculture, the less able is the adolescent to enter mainstream society, and consequently social dislocation becomes entrenched. This subcultural viewpoint, while highlighting the problems of adolescent marginalization and adjustment, in effect only deals with a minority of adolescents.

According to Stuart Hall and Tony Jefferson in the seminal text, *Resistance through Rituals* (1976), although youth had been highly visible for some time, it was in postwar Britain that this group emerged as a specific category for study, as a social problem something ought to be done about, and as what the authors considered was "one of the most striking and visible manifestations of social change" (Hall and Jefferson, 1976: 9). This social change is pictured in terms of basic lifestyle and values "premised on the view that what happened to 'youth' in this period is radically and qualitatively different from anything that happened before" (p. 15).

The Second World War and the years following it mark a period of massive change in the Western world. All manner of traditional values were challenged: families and attitudes to marriage, sex, and divorce changed; the influence of the church and organized religion declined enormously; there were huge advances in mass technologies, mass media, and mass tourism; the world of work and leisure altered; gender, race, and class issues changed consciousness, social relationships, and expectations; and there was a considerable increase in disposable income available for youth—more so for boys than for girls in the 1950s. In addressing the effect on youth culture of such enormous changes, Hall and Jefferson (1976) examine social action and reaction by focusing on "the idea of style as a coded response to changes affecting the entire community" (p. 80). They use Gramsci's concept of "hegemony" to interpret "the succession of youth cultural styles as symbolic forms of resistance; as spectacular symptoms of a wider and more generally submerged dissent which characterized the whole post-war period" (Hebdige, 1979: 80).

The social change that Hall and Jefferson discuss reflects the idea that a youth culture that was distinct from adult culture had developed and within this youth culture, there were subsets of subcultures that focused around particular activities. But there were also suggestions that youth were in fact a subculture rather than a culture (Hall and Jefferson, 1976). Subcultural theories of youth reflected Marxist notions of class struggle, focusing on how a hegemonic, dominant adult culture impacted on working-class youth (Cohen, 1972; Hall and Jefferson, 1976; P. Willis, 1977, 1978). This located youth in structural terms—in a society with features that were beyond individual control: "History and political economy became open rather than hidden; the 'problem' of the working class adolescent was seen not in terms of adjustment, or providing more opportunities to buy a larger share of the cake, but of bitter conflict, resistance, and strife. The delinquent changed from 'frustrated social climber' to cultural innovator and critic" (Cohen, 1980: iv).

Dick Hebdige, in *Subculture: The Meaning of Style* (1979), criticizes many writers of the time for overemphasizing the intergenerational opposition in the relationship between young and old and omitting "any idea of historical specificity, and explanation of why these particular forms should occur at this particular time" (Hebdige, 1979: 73). He suggests that many subcultural groups arose as a series of mediated responses by white working-class youth to the emergence of a sizable black community in Britain following extensive postcolonial immigration in the period from the 1950s to the 1970s. However, this would only account for white youth and for male subjects, who were the ones almost exclusively studied in much of the sociological research into youth culture of the 1970s. The lack of attention to girls partaking in youth subcultures unthinkingly supports the patriarchal hegemony, as Angela McRobbie critically points out in two essays (McRobbie, 1980; McRobbie and Garber, 1976). It would not account for the emergence of distinctive groups that emerged within the black community around reggae, soul, and Rastafarianism, or for the participation of girls and the development of "girl-power" in the 1990s. The study of youth groups has focused on particularly localized phenomena and has attempted to draw broader universalized conclusions from these, for which they are criticized and largely found wanting. In social science research there are often particular difficulties: value judgments and hidden moral agendas are often implied, but not acknowledged; some researchers romanticize the delinquent adolescent and others unashamedly use their case for political ends:

> The subculture is observed and decoded, its creativity celebrated and its political limitations acknowledged—and then the critique of the social order constructed. But while this critique stems from a moral absolutism, the subculture itself is treated in the language of cultural relativism. Those same values of racism, sexism, chauvinism, compulsive masculinity and anti-intellectualism, the slightest traces of which are condemned in bourgeois culture, are treated with a deferential care, an exaggerated contextualization, when they appear in the subculture. (Cohen, 1980: xxvii)

The proposition that in the West in the late twentieth century youth culture is a subculture is open to challenge, for it would appear that not simply one but, rather, a number of distinct subcultures have emerged, flourished, and disappeared in different places over time. Youth subcultures in the postwar period have included: teddy boys, bodgies, widgies, mods, rockers, punks, skinheads, Rastafarians, hipsters, beatniks, hippies, hip hoppers, rappers, surfies, homies, metallers, and more. Such names are notable since they seem to focus on the particular style of dress, mannerisms, and type of music that provide some of the cohesiveness for the named groups and invoke images of particular types of behavior, which is usually perceived by adults as rebellious, negative, and even violent. The focus on style and life-style in the construction of youth subcultural identity is the focus of Hebdige's work.

Hebdige (1979) draws widely from the work of sociologists, anthropologists, epistemologists, and semiologists (such as Stuart Hall, Phil Cohen, Stan Cohen, Paul Willis, Louis Althusser, Roland Barthès, Claude Lévi-Strauss, Umberto Eco, Julia Kristeva) to explore the notion of youth subculture by examining several case studies of "spectacular" youth subcultures from the 1950s to the late 1970s. What distinguishes "spectacular" subcultures from surrounding subcultures is their visibility, their being "*obviously* fabricated" in ways that "display their own codes (e.g., the punk's ripped T-shirt) or at least demonstrate that codes are there to be used and abused (e.g., that they have been thought about rather than thrown together)" (p. 101). From case studies (including punk, Rastafarians, mods, rockers, teds, glam rockers) Hebdige extends the notion of youth culture as one of "style" that, in responding to the conjuncture of specific historical conditions, involved a series of transformations of an initial set of items (clothes, dance, music, argot) unfolding through an internal set of polarities (mod v rocker, skinhead v greaser, skinhead v hippie, punk v hippie, ted v punk, skinhead v punk) and defined against a parallel series of "straight" transformations ("high"/mainstream fashion). Each subculture moves through a cycle of resistance and defusion and we have seen how this cycle is situated within the larger cultural and commercial matrices. Subcultural deviance is simultaneously rendered "explicable" and meaningless in the classrooms, courts and media at the same time as the "secret" objects of subcultural style are put on display in every high street record shop and chain-store boutique. Stripped of its unwholesome connotations, the style becomes fit for public consumption. (Hebdige, 1979: 130)

In being expressive social forms, subcultures to a certain extent play out the tensions between those in positions of power and authority in society and those who are not, who are subordinate, oppressed, and repressed by the hegemony of the ruling ideology. Hebdige (1979) interprets subculture as "a form of resistance in which experienced contradictions and objections to this ruling ideology are obliquely represented in style" (p. 133). Youth subcultures tend, then, to be positioned as responses that involve a refusal of the hegemony, a move away from the consensus—a notion held dear in Western democracies—and which become unwelcome challenges to society since they highlight difference. As a result, society tends to react to the subculture initially with hostility, rage, fury, and rejection, often invoking frenzied moral panics (as in the Mazengarb Report, as detailed in chapter 5). Subsequently the panic or opposition subsides, and the subculture becomes defused of its challenge, accepted, incorporated into the mainstream, and dismissed as a phase young people are going through, part of growing up, a distraction from the serious or "real" issues that young people will eventually have to deal with as fully fledged adults. In this way there is a continual process of recuperation that repairs and restores the fractured social order.

Hebdige (1979) points out that the incorporation of youth subcultures occurs in two ways—through "commodity forms" and through "ideological forms." The "commodity form" involves consumption and the conversion of subcultural signs, such as dress and music, from private, small-scale creation into mass-produced objects in the fashion market. In turn, the new commodities become "frozen," then "passé," and this leads to the subculture's subsequent demise, since it is no longer new and challenging. The cultural and commercial aspects are closely interwoven. After their initial shock and challenge, youth subcultural styles become "codified, made comprehensible, rendered at once public property and profitable merchandise" and "end up establishing new sets of conventions; by creating new commodities or rejuvenating old ones" (p. 96). The "ideological form" involves various labeling and redefinition by dominant groups such as the media, police, teachers, clerics, politicians, and academics. The ways that youth are represented by the media become central because the media not only records youth subcultural resistance and places youth "within the dominant framework of meanings" (p. 94), but also returns youth to their "place" in relation to family, work, and society—that is, to a place where they are largely accepted. In this way, the impact of the media on identity cannot be underestimated, and the media could be considered to have steadily colonized both cultural and ideological realms of society since they are responsible: "a) for providing the basis on which groups and classes construct an image of their lives, meanings, practices and values of *other* groups and classes; b) for providing the images, representations and ideas around which the social totality composed of all these separate and fragmented pieces can be coherently grasped" (Hall, cited in Hebdige, 1979: 85).

Stanley Cohen's (1980) *Folk Devils and Moral Panics*, originally written in 1972 and based on a transactional model of deviant behavior, shows how the media handled the conflict between "mods" and the "rockers" (this is elaborated further in chapter 5). While the notion of "folk devil" highlighted societal fears of the "Other" as threatening one's existence and the tabloid sensationalism involved, it also pointed to the way youth subcultures can very readily be "demonized" and seen as "evil." In the mass media, a considerable proportion of "news" readily pays attention to negative behavior and violence and to "deviance" in sensational terms of strange happenings, bizarre behavior, scandals, and exceptional crimes. Whenever youth fall into any of these categories, they usually become newsworthy objects, and so a negative portrayal reinforces existing perceptions and prejudices, and a resultant adult public outcry often ensues. The current catch phrase, "youth at risk" sums this up. Youth are yet again positioned as "problems," as per the clichés, "mad, bad and dangerous to know" and being only interested in "sex, drugs and rock and roll." Through emphasizing deviance in general, the media not only provide information and possibly vicarious pleasure, but also display society's moral norms and expectations of right and wrong and what falls outside the bounds of acceptability. In this way the media define and shape society and social problems. While well aware that sensational events "sell" and so not above exaggerating these, the media may well act out of and express moral indignation and outrage. In turn, the media are used by moral crusaders to get their concerns and messages across and to gain public support for their cause. As a result, youth culture could perhaps be considered to be, to some extent, morally constituted by the media.

Hebdige suggests that, paradoxically, the media represent subcultures as being "both more and less exotic than they actually are" (Hebdige, 1979: 97), in a way that parallels Barthès's notions of the "Other" being, on the one hand, "trivialized, naturalized, domesticated" (p. 97) and, on the other hand, being transformed into exotica, animals, spectacles, or clowns. McRobbie (1991) points out that despite the way Hebdige uses the Barthèsian notion to highlight inadequacies in the moral panic argument of how the media portray youth, this remains a gendered account with: "the shock of subcultures being partially defused because they can be seen as, among other things, boys having fun" (McRobbie, 1991: 27). In positing the reaction if the *Sex Pistols* had been an all-female band, spitting, swearing, vomiting, taking drugs, McRobbie (1991) said, "the response would have been more heated, the condemnation less tempered by indulgence. Such an event would have been greeted in the popular press as evidence of a major moral breakdown and not just a fairly common, if shocking occurrence" (pp. 28–29). Then—as is probably still largely the case—it was far more acceptable to society for boys to act in outrageous ways than it was for girls. Clearly, this says a great deal about the moral constitution of youth identity in terms of gender relations and sexuality.

Much of youth subculture seems to be about constructing an alternative identity, about negotiating an alternative space between the culture of parents and the dominant hegemony and about communicating this difference or "Otherness" to the world. In this respect there is an element of seeking autonomy, of breaking away, of creating a space and a place, and of developing and/or having one's own power/knowledge that largely excludes the adult world. Spectacular youth subcultures use style to communicate both their differences from the Other and their similarity as part of their group identity.

"Style," as understood by Hebdige, is a signifying practice that youth subcultures construct through a form of *bricolage* and *homology*. Bricolage is a concept developed by Claude Lévi-Strauss in his anthropological work, *The Savage Mind* (1966), to show how "primitive" cultures used magical modes (superstition, sorcery, myth) to make their own sense and meaning of the minutiae of the physical world in ways that are different and confusing to the Western world. The concept was extended to the way youth appropriate objects from the everyday world, radically adapting and subverting them to new and different usage that makes sense to them and not necessarily to outsiders. Hebdige used two of Umberto Eco's statements to describe how this applies to the spectacle of clothing style, "I speak through my clothes" (p. 100) and "semiotic guerrilla warfare" (p. 105), with examples being the punk use of the union jack as clothing, and the safety pin as jewelry and to hold deliberately torn clothing together. Thus bricolage could be considered a means of creating the visible difference from other groups in society, but the coherence of internal values within the group can be seen as a form of *homology*. Homology is another of Lévi-Strauss's concepts and was applied by Paul Willis in his 1978 study of hippies and bikies, *Profane Culture*. Homology can be understood as "the symbolic fit between the values and life-styles of a group, its subjective experience and the musical forms it uses to express or reinforce its focal concerns" (p. 113). For example, hippie culture focused around alternative, back-to-nature, free love, communal, antiwar values, drug use, especially marijuana and LSD, colorful, flowing clothes and hair, and rock music.

While the hippie subculture may have appealed more to middle-class youth, the focus of the most sociological studies of the 1970s (including that of Willis, Hebdige, Hall), largely from a neo-Marxist viewpoint, examined ways the researchers considered working-class males resisted and displayed their opposition to dominant values and institutions. Feminists contend that since universalizing notions are frequently developed from studies of particular groups, the voices of males as authors, as subjects, and as male structures are traditionally heard at the expense—intentional or otherwise—of female voices and perspectives (see McRobbie, 1991; Moi, 1986; Rowbotham, 1973). Females are thereby ignored, silenced, and rendered invisible. McRobbie (1991) was particularly concerned that neiher Willis nor Hebdige was aware of the inherent sexism in his studies, neither included the personal authorial aspects, as in the feminist notion, "the personal is political," and neither acknowledged the politics of selection. Their studies paid homage to masculinity and emphasized disrespectful male discourses toward females, as exemplified in the unambiguously degrading language toward women and sex and the aggressive attitudes of young men as they kicked against the oppressive structures they inhabited—home, school, work:

> Questions around sexism and working-class youth and around sexual violence make it possible to see how class and patriarchal relations work together, sometimes with an astonishing brutality and at other times in the "teeth-gritting harmony" of romance, love and marriage. One of Willis's "lads" says of his girlfriend, "she loves doing fucking housework. Trousers I brought up yesterday, I took 'em up last night and she turned 'em up for me. She's as good as gold and I wanna get married as soon as I can." (McRobbie, 1991: 18)

According to McRobbie (1991), the very notion of subculture had become so masculine that it excluded women, especially when the media tended to focus on and sensationalize the more extreme forms, particularly violence of and by males. "The objective and popular image of a subculture is likely to be one which emphasizes male membership, male focal concerns and masculine values" (McRobbie, 1991: 5), despite it being clear that girls did take part in youth subcultures. They certainly listened to the music, went to concerts and dances, formed fan clubs, and adopted dress styles of the group to which they belonged. But although present, McRobbie (1991) suggests that women retained their cultural subordination as being marginal to not only the male subcultures but also to work, because where women were central and pivotal was in the subordinate realm of the home and family. Whereas the teddy-boy culture used the street and café as an escape from the strictures of home and work, 1950s sexual double standards tended to see these locales as largely unacceptable for girls. If they did frequent such places, girls were perceived as "easy," promiscuous, and ultimately not desirable marriage material. Males could "sow their wild oats," but females had to not "get into trouble," since despite many "shotgun marriages," the consequences for the different genders were often vastly different. Being an "unmarried mother" and bearing an illegitimate child in the 1950s was considered shameful: "The difficulty in obtaining effective contraception, the few opportunities to spend unsupervised time with the opposite sex, the financial dependency of the working-class woman on her husband, meant that a good reputation mattered above everything else" (McRobbie, 1991: 5).

Furthermore, McRobbie underlined that although things have now changed, "before the emergence of the women's movement in the early 1970s, the notions of escaping from the family, the bourgeois commitments of children and the whole sphere of family consumption formed a distinct strand in left politics" (1991: 19). While males could escape into a subculture, this was much more difficult for girls, and, in any case, the male escape was often from girls, women, and family, to a peer group "whose consciousness and pleasure frequently seem to hinge on a collective disregard for women and the sexual exploitation of girls" (p. 20). Furthermore, because the focus was on the public sphere and on leisure-time activities, the 1970s studies of subcultures ignored the private sphere of relationships with family, peers, and girlfriends.

Girl subcultures, although style-oriented, tended to focus more on hair, make-up, clothes, fashion, music, getting a boyfriend, and marriage in ways that saw them organize their social activities from the safety of their bedrooms at home, avoiding the high-risk aspects of the dominant male subculture. It also saw them form extremely close-knit friendship groups, where they would discuss and share goods and ideas related to the latest style in fashion and music and, of course, talk about boys. While the 1960s saw mod culture evolve into the "swinging sixties" with "liberated dolly-birds," some increased independence, and the advent of the contraceptive pill, girls still saw work as an interim before their real careers of marriage and children began (McRobbie, 1991). McRobbie suggests that the 1970s "teeny-bopper" culture idolizing young male pop stars such as David Cassidy and Donny Osmond was a way of girls forming their own distinctive subculture. McRobbie concludes: "Female participation in youth cultures can best be understood by moving away from the 'classic' subcultural terrain marked out as oppositional and creative by numerous sociologists. Girls negotiate a different leisure space and different personal spaces from those inhabited by boys. These in turn offer them different possibilities for 'resistance,' if indeed that is the right word to use" (McRobbie, 1991: 14).

The CCCS form of subcultural analysis of youth tends to essentialize their cultural formation, at times romanticizing and other times overemphasizing differences and dichotomies of domination/subordination, expression/repression or regulation and normal/delinquent in its focus on styles. Furthermore, it ignores female perspectives, commonalities, continuities and personal agency, and the active choices that young people make (Cohen, 1980; Wyn and White, 1997). Personal agency is circumscribed by the diversity of structures, institutions, values, family, and peers with whom one interacts. At the same time as there are universalizing generalizations that suggest a distinct, separate, homogeneous "youth culture" that has developed since the Second World War, there are studies that are focus on the particular differences of subcultures often resulting in problematizing youth. Youth and their subcultures themselves do not remain static. They often shift from one subculture to another, so that by the time young people reach their twenties, they may have defined themselves and belonged to a number of different subcultural groups. Yet adults could certainly also be categorized in such a manner. Furthermore, some of the wider socioeconomic and cultural forces and processes, such as sexism and racism, are shared regardless of age. Like notions of youth, notions of cultures and subcultures are complex and contestable.

POSTMODERN APPROACHES TO THE STUDY OF YOUTH

There have been different issues and problems generated for and by young people in Western societies that have led to the development of various helping professions and their associated technologies, with "each asserting its virtuosity in respect of the self, in classifying and measuring the psyche, in predicting its vicissitudes, in diagnosing the cause of its troubles and in prescribing remedies" (Rose, 1989: 2–3).

School counseling is but one of these. In counseling theory and practice, I have suggested, it is necessary to supplement psychological accounts of growth and development of adolescence with sociological and ethnographic accounts focusing upon subcultural analysis. This is particularly important, I would argue, when analyzing youth in "the postmodern condition," because more and more we can see the influence of globalized cultural and subcultural styles of life impacting upon youth, particularly since mass consumer culture has strengthened and developed after the Second World War.

Young people in modern Western societies have limited legal rights, and limited economic resources, and they are (except for particular criminal actions after a certain age) not considered to be fully responsible for their actions and treated as incomplete, not yet full-formed people. Côté and Allahar (1994) argue that in the postmodern world youth face the problem of how to formulate a viable and stable identity in a world that is uncertain and even hostile, where circumstances limit their access to resources that enable the ego or self to grow and remain strong.

Postmodern approaches do not reflect any single viewpoint; they tend to reject objectivist accounts of adolescence as a universal life-stage. Postmodern approaches emphasize the subjective, or how things are *experienced,* rather than "objective reality," because objective reality is rejected as unknowable or inaccessible to the human mind, especially when considering social reality. While Foucault was at pains to describe himself as not a "postmodernist,"[2] many of the postmodern approaches to youth have developed out of sociological discourse and are particularly influenced by his work. Postmodern approaches tend to hold that the self is fundamentally social, and therefore they problematize the category "adolescence" as a reflection of a Western humanist psychology that largely ignores its own power/knowledge (Foucault, 1977, 1980a, 1997a). Postmodern approaches are likely to see adolescence less as a universal category of growing-up than as an aspect of the culture of advanced consumerism. The phenomenon of the categorization of "youth," particularly in relation to the market—be it the young cosmetics and beauty market, the youth fashion market, or the latest music fad—is highlighted as a sociocultural construction based on the concept of style and life-style. This emphasis on "style," "life-style," and what Foucault called the "aesthetics of existence" typifies both the influences of Heidegger and Nietzsche, who are often considered the forefathers of postmodernism. Foucault, echoing Heidegger, talked of making one's life a work of art (Foucault, 1990). A Nietzschean–Heideggerian–Foucauldian approach to questions of style of youth would seem to provide promising theoretical leads to those ethnographers who wish to explore a line different from traditional Marxist-inspired sociology. Postmodern approaches tend to emphasize the dual cultural processes of constructing youth identity, through the market and through the agency of youth themselves. This final section, then, discusses some aspects of post-modern approaches to youth through three major exemplars.

The first exemplars form what we might call studies of the globalization of youth culture, arguing that postmodern youth cultures are emerging due to the impact of globalization, the mass media, and information technology, rather than simply as a result of the processes of marginalization or alienation. For example, Henry Giroux (1990) argues that the new information and communication technologies, through emphasizing individualism, create both a sense of alienation and of boredom with school, which can no longer compete with such exciting technology. Yet through the globalizing effects of postmodern marketing, consumerism, and mass media, adolescent perceptions, expectations, and experiences in many countries are linked and sometimes become homogenized. Giroux (1990) argues that a postmodern youth culture is emerging due to the impact of globalization, the media. and information technology. Similarly, Allan Luke (2000) describes the emergence of "world kids" as new kinds of youth for whom growing up is "about navigating through a sea of texts" . . . "becoming your own hybrid, blending and shaping and putting together something that's a range of cultures" (Luke, 2000: 24). Giroux's and Luke's viewpoints stand in opposition to traditional sociological studies that tend to emphasize the marginalization and alienation of adolescents.

A second set of postmodern exemplars builds on the work of Michel Foucault (1988a) and the need to examine regimes of truth about social practices. As discussed in previous sections, Foucault characterizes social control in contemporary society as having shifted from repressive practices to practices of normalization where populations and problems were identified, defined, measured, and compared, and where scientifically based norms were established. Alongside a focus on the abnormal, deviant, clinical, and pathological, a construction of unproblematic, "normal" childhood and adolescence emerged. Foucault (1980a) argues that through various institutional programs, the state regulates adolescents and how they should spend their time. Such programs classify adolescents as normal, abnormal, successful, and so on according to a matrix of norms. This viewpoint is based to a certain extent on psychological notions of identity, that an individual must construct an adult self, and that it is a task of adolescence to work on the self to become self-governing.

Postmodern feminist perspectives strongly challenge the existing "truths" and theoretical constructs as being primarily patriarchal and universalist assumptions that ignore the particular experiences of females and that position adolescents as a single group whereby the female is subsumed under what have been mostly male norms (Lesko, 1996; Nava, 1991). Mica Nava (1991) examines the regulation of adolescents and gender differences. She argues that because adolescent females are more regulated and controlled, especially in their sexuality, than young males, they occupy public spheres to a lesser extent. In the home, which is considered the main source of control, females are more regulated than males. Schools and the peer group reinforce regulation and control. Young males within the peer group participate in regulating the females because they hold notions of femininity that include particular modes of sexual behavior, deference, and compliance. Nava (1991) considers that gender is as significant as social class in structuring how adolescent males and females experience youth and the process of entering adulthood.

Nancy Lesko (1996), following a Foucauldian viewpoint, questions "how scientific knowledge about adolescent nature, located primarily in the field of psychology, participates in constructing and maintaining boundaries for what may count as normal and deviant teenagers" (p. 142). She examines the sociohistorical context to challenge the accepted discourse about the nature of adolescence and naturalizing assumptions in three common characterizations: "coming of age," being hormonally driven, and being peer-oriented. Lesko deconstructs the predominant recurring notion of adolescence as a "natural," universal, ahistorical stage with immutable characteristics, arguing that the prevailing discourse ignores the social processes and constructs that created the notion of adolescence and that can and do change over time. If these aspects are ignored, adolescence becomes defined as problematic, out of control, and needing to be constrained by adults who assign blame. This is an easier solution than examining and changing the social and organizational practices that contribute both to the problems that arise for adolescents and to the way they are defined (Lesko, 1996). The postmodern emphasis is very much on the construction and mutability of what has mostly been assumed to be "natural." Theories of "adolescence" can be considered as the effects of certain sets of social practices of power/ knowledge that occur across numerous contemporary social domains— the family, school, law, medicine (Walkerdine, 1986, 1987). Lesko (1996) points out that how educators think of adolescents, of their nature and needs, leads to new and different policies and practices in education— constructing systems such as homerooms, mentoring, role models, peer leadership programs, age-based and gender-based classes, guidance, and counseling. For example, schools situate children and adolescents in age-based classes and seem largely to accept the notion that adolescents are hormonally driven individuals who are at the mercy of peer pressure in ways that are often negative in how they envision the self (selfesteem, self-concept, self-image, and their attitudes, etc.) and in how they behave (drugs, sex, gangs, impulsivity, immediate gratification, changeability, etc.). In response to such a sense of what adolescents are like, schools institute different disciplinary and surveillance structures and regimes.

A third exemplar examines postmodern youth in terms of "movements." For example, Reuven Kahane, in *The Origins of Postmodern Youth* (1997), points out that although youth have usually been studied within developmental-psychological, transitional, and subcultural paradigms, these are no longer adequate as ways of explaining youth behavior and their perceptions of the world in the late twentieth century. According to Kahane:

> In striving to construct an authentic, meaningful model of life in a rapidly changing, complex world, the behaviour of "postmodern youth" centers around

> symbols of freedom, spontaneity, adventurism and eclecticism. This pattern has gradually emerged since the rise of the youth movements . . . at the beginning of the century, and later underwent changes with the emergence of the pop youth subculture, the student movements of the 1960s, and the recent rock-disco cultures. These expressions of youthfulness constitute a new code of informality, a fluid type of order that is a response to the chaotic nature of the postmodern world. Yet despite the awareness of this shift toward informality, the essence of this trend has not been fully grasped or explained. (Kahane, 1997: 1–2)

Kahane suggests that there have been three stages in the concept of youth in the twentieth century: "from an immature, hot-blooded, heavily controlled group, to an autonomous entity, to an informal authentic culture" (p. 3). He maps changes in the relation between youth and society, arguing that youth movements in the early part of the twentieth century were adaptations that attempted to create a new social reality out of chaotic elements and rapid social changes. Subsequent to this type of adaptation to and maintenance of the social order, youth turned to protest and rebellion in the 1960s, to behavior that was often misunderstood by adults and was reflected in the then current notion of a "generation gap," and to "moral panics" (Cohen, 1980). Youth were described as alienated, uncommitted, undisciplined, unwilling and unable to distinguish between work and play, "as reflected in their dress, beatnik lifestyle, and 'meaningless' travels" (Kahane, 1997: 2). They were described by the adult culture in terms of its own codes of values and understandings of the world, rather than in terms of a code of youth themselves.

Kahane argues that the postmodern world is chaotic, pluralistic, and existentially disordered, and it is unlike the traditional sociological one that Parsons (1951) considered. The world in which postmodern youth have grown up, entails a technologically sophisticated, urbanized industrial society where notions of welfare, democracy, and rapid social change have become institutionalized and the norm. Postmodern youth behavior is based on a new code of "informality" that is "a symbolic and behavioral construct with which individuals or groups strive to maximize what they perceive as their genuine self-expression" (p. 3). Kahane proposes the following model of an informal postmodern youth code of behavior with "components that operate in tandem to create an open framework" (p. 30), stressing the values of autonomy, freedom, and spontaneity:

> The ideal-type informal order (or organization) has eight basic structural components: voluntarism (constraint-free choice); multiplexity (wide range of activities equivalent in social value); symmetry (exchange based on equal distribution of power and therefore on mutually accommodated expectations); dualism (coexistence of contrasting orientations); moratorium (provision of opportunities for experimentation or trial and error with a variety of rules and roles); modularity (interchangeable clusters of activities); expressive-

> instrumentalism (coexistence of immediate and delayed rewards); and pragmatic symbolism (conversion of symbols into deeds and vice versa). (Kahane, 1997: 3)

According to Kahane, such an informal code institutionalizes liminality[3] and reduces marginality, promotes identity diffusion, enabling individuals to express and cope with confusion and doubts about the self, encourages corporate role development, fosters the development of value commitments and a sense of justice and trust, and enables freedom, spontaneity, and authenticity to emerge and become routine. The five conditions that seem to give rise to the emergence of informality are: "(1) when basic cultural paradigms undergo rapid change; (2) when structural complexity increased; (3) when pluralism emerges out of a lack of clear criterion of evaluation; (4) the more open the political system; and (5) the greater the material affluence" (Kahane, 1997: 34).

Through informal codes of behavior, youth construct their own fluid reality that makes sense and meaning of their experiences of the world and in turn enables them to develop their own sets of values. But if such informal frameworks are strong, they tend "to resist both external pressures for order and internal processes of 'oligarchization' and bureaucratization" (p. 35), whereas if they are weak, informality can be undermined (Kahane, 1997).

More could be said about each of these exemplars, yet I have said enough to indicate their respective theoretical emphases and research directions. I would argue for the importance of all four approaches to counseling theory and practice. The globalization of youth culture, the Foucauldian examination of the regimes of truth about social practices, feminist accounts, and youth considered as social movements all contribute valuable understandings to counselor education.

Considerable ambivalence and negativity toward youth resulted in serious concern and much publicity around the notion of a "generation gap" in the 1960s and 1970s, but such expression seems to have waned now at the turn of the century (Goldson, 1978; Lavelle, 1990; Molloy, 1993). It may well be that the parents of teenagers today, who were mostly teenagers in the late 1960s, 1970s, and 1980s, having themselves been objects of such negativity, are keen to avoid this with their own children and so have a different parenting style from that of their parents. They may also see that they and their peers negotiated to a greater or lesser extent successfully their teenage years, various subcultures, protests, rebellions, and sexuality issues, contrary to how adults saw them at the time. It may well be that fear of moral chaos, of rebellion by the youthful generation, has been considerably defused in the current era. Apart from concerns around particularly serious problems, such as abuse, drugs, and suicidality, it seems that youth are now perceived much more favorably in general. Though it is by no means seen as nothing to get too worried about, it is considered more as something to work through. The majority of youth seem to pass through these years not without problems, but emerge largely unscathed, so that being an adolescent is generally seen as putting on a new and different style—a stage that kids go through, which adults hope and pray they will manage successfully.

Ethnographies of youth culture can provide important qualitative data on processes of identity formation and contemporary trends in style that affect young people. Group attitudes to the presentation of self, to sexuality, to drug-taking, and to many other contemporary youth issues can be usefully elucidated by ethnography. Counselors need to avail themselves of these insights and insider-views both in their professional training and in their ongoing professional development as school counselors. Ethnographies can also provide methodological insights. Most counselor education involves the presentation of case studies that parallels the use of an ethnographic type of methodology. Both counseling and ethnography are concerned with the problem of understanding and communicating with the "other" in empathic terms in order for clients to make changes for the better in their lives. However, both ethnographies and case studies involve the researcher in observation, whether or not as a participant. As several theorists argue (Quine, 1963; Sellars, 1963), the observation of events is never innocent, and events never speak for themselves. On this point, Peter McLaren writes:

> Every description is ideologically loaded, codified, and intertextually related to larger interpretive contexts. Nothing that can be observed or named is ideologically neutral or innocent. No thoughts, ideas, or theories are transparent, autonomous, or free floating; to say that they are, is a middle-class mystification that seeks to disguise the social interests being served. Ideas are always and necessarily tied to particular interests and enciphered in particular relations of power, and tied to particular power/knowledge configurations. Absolutely nothing is of unmediated availability to human consciousness. To "know" anything is always an effect of power/knowledge relationships. The crucial question is: Who has the power to make some forms of knowledge more legitimate than others? (McLaren, 1989: ix)

Therefore, it behooves school counselors to consider seriously the caution implied here: to be critically self-reflective in considering "knowing" in their methodological use of case studies in their training and subsequently in their practice. They need to be aware of how their own power–knowledge operates in relationships, and of the role of their own ideology when they conduct case studies, observe their clients, and interpret what they say and how they say it. They need to ensure that they do not inadvertently silence the voice of their clients. As much as is humanly possible, counselors need to become very aware and "knowing" of their own "self" and the self that the "other" (the client) is presenting as well as the social context for both. For school counselors, this means coming to "know" the culture and subcultures of the adolescents with whom they are dealing, "knowing" the school culture, and "knowing" the social culture. This is not a knowing that is simply factual and instrumental or interpreted only through the counselor's cultural lens; it is a knowing that casts a self-reflective, critical eye on all of those components. Through such a knowing counseling can empathize, affirm, understand, and perhaps help clients to analyze their experiences and voice in their creation of meaning in their lives and in their formation of identity and sense of self. School counselors need to understand the cultural and social forms through which their adolescent clients learn to define themselves, how the social world is experienced, mediated, and produced by adolescents, and how attitudes and behavior result from the multiple discourses and subjectivities that students experience. However, this is not about always unqualifiedly endorsing or legitimating all experience—after all, abuse, violence, racism, and sexism for example, are not things counselors are likely to endorse uncritically. When they do find these displayed by their clients, they need to have ways of constructively challenging them. In this way counseling can move further toward fulfilling its aims in terms of being an ethical profession involved in empowerment and social justice.

Postmodern views are helpful when analyzing youth in advanced industrial societies, where increasingly we can see the influence of mass consumer culture and globalized cultural life-styles. But postmodern perspectives are sometimes criticized as restating previous sociological concepts (e.g., global village, consumerism, alienation, and fragmentation of self, gender roles) in a new terminology. Sociological notions of youth differ from most psychological approaches that—with the exception of recent social, discursive, and constructionist psychological approaches—mostly focus on the individual. But sociological perspectives are criticized for reducing all behavior to social structural causes. There needs to be an acknowledgment that we are all humans, and we have a biological basis, which differs for males and for females. In response, societies have often structured gender roles differently at different times, according to sets of culturally accepted beliefs. While structures will have a role in the governance of society in general and for youth in particular, we need to acknowledge the impact of agency, the capacity for acting intentionally in our modern world. Understandings about youth are meaningful only in relation to the politico–socioeconomic contexts in which they exist (Wyn and White, 1997). I have suggested that an understanding of *both* sociological and psychological approaches to adolescence/youth and the assumptions of both discourses are important for enabling educators to gain a better understanding of their youthful clients. But more than understanding, we also need to question and critique accepted "truths" and dominant discourses. "The challenge in rethinking youth, is to maintain a balance between recognising the importance of physical and psychological changes that occur in young people's lives and recognising the extent to which these are constructed by social institutions and negotiated by individuals" (Wyn and White, 1997: 12).

This chapter has described how sociology has preferred the term "youth" over that of "adolescence" and has focused more on group identities than individual notions of self or identity to conceptualize youth in their social context. A major contribution to our understandings of youth identities has been provided by the theories of the 1960s to 1990s, which portrayed youth largely in terms of distinct cultures and subcultures. Youth subcultures do not remain static, nor do adolescents, who often change allegiances as they grow up, shifting from one subculture to another. Indeed, one of the salient characteristics of youth culture in general is that by the time young people reach their twenties, they may have defined themselves having belonged to a number of different subcultural groups. Subsequent to subcultural theorizing, particularly in the 1990s, postmodern notions of youth have emerged that emphasize the subjective and that challenge and reject universalist assumptions. Exemplars from a selection of postmodern theorists were used to elucidate these recent approaches that emphasize how young people define and construct their identities. Counselors need not only to understand individual issues of identity in relation to the self, as discussed in chapter 2, but also to have an understanding of the processes and formations of group identities—the individual's relation to others, to class, gender, sexuality, family, culture, subculture, peer group, and so on. Chapter 5 delves into the sociohistorical contexts that led up to and existed when the idea of school counseling came to be seen as a way of managing and helping adolescents in many schools in the Western world.

CHAPTER 5

THE MORAL CONSTITUTION OF YOUTH

INTRODUCTION

This chapter presents a picture of how young people and their moral state has been viewed since the Second World War. It outlines how and by whom their moral behavior has been regulated—in other words, it analyzes some of the disciplinary technologies and the understandings that have been invoked in the moral constitution of youth. It takes a largely sociological approach but adds a Foucauldian slant by firstly examining Foucault's comments on morality.

In contemplating the moral constitution of youth, I find myself wondering about why our society seems so concerned about this and in providing guidance for them. Foucault provides something of an answer in his discussion of the link between political rationality and the emergence of the social sciences, but also in his work on morality. The chapter explores the link between pedagogy and morality in the use of disciplinary technologies to shape and constitute and control the morality of youth.

It is not surprising that at times society expresses profound fears about the moral constitution of youth, some of which became constructed as "moral panics" by sociologists in the 1970s. Yet there is nothing new about episodes of threat, crisis, fear, panic, and the varied responses to these in society. One could draw up a considerable list: for example, the plague in the Middle Ages, venereal diseases in Victorian times, the nuclear threat in the cold-war era, and, more recently, Aids, BSE (Bovine Spongiform Encephalopathy), and CJD (Creutzfeld-Jakob Disease). Often the physical and the moral become intertwined in fears about social disorder; in the 1970s they became constructed as moral panics. Society frequently focuses on the actions of certain segments, most notably youths, as immoral and threatening to the accepted cultural norms and practices. Foucault provides the example of a moral panic that resulted in the social control of sexuality:

> The restrictions on masturbation hardly start in Europe until the eighteenth century. Suddenly, a panic-theme appears: an appalling sickness develops in the Western world. Children masturbate. Via the medium of families, though not at their initiative, a system of control of sexuality, an objectification of sexuality allied to corporal persecution, is established over the bodies of children. But sexuality, through thus becoming an object of analysis and concern, surveillance and control, engenders at the same time an intensification of each individual's desire, for, in, and over his body. (Foucault, 1980a: 56)

Much later, during the 1950s and 1960s, there was widespread concern over the influence of rock'n'roll music with fears that it led to promiscuity and antisocial behavior. The drug culture of the 1960s led to far-reaching anxiety, and it was widely believed that an entire generation would become "crazed" addicts.

Prior to this time, especially from the late nineteenth century to the middle of the twentieth century, concerns about managing the health and well-being of the population was constructed in terms of "mental hygiene," a term that had connotations of mental cleanliness and was eventually replaced by the term "mental health." Mental hygiene provided the antecedents and setting for the development of social guidance. Mental hygiene films were one of the teaching resources endorsed by progressive educational methods used in school guidance. Both of these provided part of the impetus for the guidance aspect of school guidance counseling. By the end of the twentieth century, social guidance in New Zealand became formalized into a compulsory strand of the national curriculum as the *Health and Physical Education in the New Zealand Curriculum* (Ministry of Education, 1999b). So pedagogy and the policing of morality have become formally encapsulated in the discipline or subject matter of health education—a form of disciplinary technology with, of course, benign intent. Nevertheless, social guidance programs, in dealing with morality, leave themselves open to the possibility of indoctrination. Since guidance counselors are frequently involved in social education programs, especially in teaching the sexuality component, they need to be vigilant about whether guidance programs are about education or about indoctrination—notions that are examined in the second section. Mental hygiene is also covered in this section.

The third section refers mostly to the social situation in the United States and to the use of mental hygiene films, some of which were also used in New Zealand schools. The technology of film was new and "progressive" at the time and is—in the form of video—still extensively used in health, social education, and guidance programs. There are still "hidden agendas" in some curren-day health videos—for example, some that encourage sexual abstinence may promote religious agendas, others that may promote "safe sex," or yet others that may be produced by manufacturers of feminine hygiene products (e.g., Johnson and Johnson). It is argued that today the early form of social guidance as a form of social engineering would be considered quite contrary to the *intent* of school counseling and counseling in general. Early social guidance films used psychologically manipulative techniques adapted to education by film producers who, as experts in advertising and magazine publishing, were adept at using marketing and sales techniques. Such attempts at controlling the social condition and the moral constitution of youth by what is now largely considered to be indoctrination are polar opposites to counseling's ethical position, which emphasizes autonomy, choice, honesty, and truth.

Moral panics about youth form the last section of this chapter because it has been from moral panics, concerns, and research about youth, their morals, and their problems that various "technologies" have been developed and been applied. For

Foucault, "technology" is the actual practice of power that involves "the government of individuals, the government of the souls, the government of the self by the self, the government of families, the government of children, and so on" (1984b: 256). School counseling is one of these technologies. Others include guidance and social education or life-skills programs and mental hygiene films.

Society often perceives the moral constitution of youth quite negatively in ways that can be considered a moral panic. The seminal sociological work on moral panics, that of Stanley Cohen (1972, 1980), examines the case of Mods and Rockers in England in 1964. In 1954, in postwar New Zealand, deep and widespread concern for the moral well-being of youth and for the future of society arose in response to sex scandals in what is now considered to have been a "moral panic." Parliament set up an inquiry, which resulted in the Report of the Special Committee on Moral Delinquency in Children and Adolescents, known as the Mazengarb Report (1954). This report presents an official viewpoint of the sociohistorical context within New Zealand and the setting for the introduction of the pilot guidance counselor scheme five years later, in 1959. It provides a snapshot of the way youth were constituted as moral beings in the mid-1950s, and it is presented as a case study in the fourth section. As a case study, New Zealand represents a small, highly literate country that has often been seen as something of a social experiment in the Western world. It was the first country to enfranchise women (1893); it was also the birthplace of the welfare state in 1935, under the first Labour government, and of the reversal of this after 1984, under the fourth Labour government, when radical neoliberal economic theories were applied. Neoliberalism and its impact on the professionalization and the ethical constitution of school counseling are explored in chapter 6.

The case study reflects the importance the public placed on the moral integrity of youth and provides a picture of what the society of the time thought of itself and what held it together. It shows how some of the official adult voices reacted to the perceived negative factors and aspects in the emergent youth culture. The way in which society wished to constitute youth was displayed in the way they tried to regulate them— in terms of self, external controls, and institutional controls. What was not recognized but can be seen with the benefit of hindsight is that the in 1950s New Zealand was party to some major social changes that included urbanization in general, with Maori shifting to the cities amid the rapid development of new, poorly resourced suburbs, a postwar "baby boom", the shift from British to American cultural influences that had begun when American GIs had been stationed in New Zealand during the war, increased consumerism, including labor-saving devices and mass entertainment systems in the form of film, radio, pulp fiction, and comics; and the emergence of a new, distinct, U.S.-influenced youth culture that was at odds with what many of the older generation considered to be acceptable and proper. In this way it uncovers a point of view against which late-twentieth-century attitudes to youth that have been informed by sociological, feminist, and postmodern notions can be positioned.

CHAPTER 5

FOUCAULT—POLITICAL RATIONALITY AND MORALITY

Foucault outlines and discusses two aspects of morality: ethical self-constitution, which operates at an individual level, and the political technology of individuals, which operates at a societal level (Foucault, 1988c, 1997a). The former emerges at the intersection of questions of truth, power, and subjectivity, the latter is a form of political rationality (governmentality) that emerges with the development of liberalism and is directed through the notion of policing and administration at the governance of individuals. Administrative practices in the early manuals and encyclopedias of policing practices focused on morals, health, public safety, factories, and the regulation of the poor (Foucault, 1988c). The governance of youth as an aspect of the political technology of individuals is aimed at questions of pedagogy and the policing of their morality. In his studies of madness, psychiatry, crime, and punishment, Foucault has shown how we have indirectly constituted ourselves through the exclusion of others— criminals, mad people, and delinquents. In his later work he goes on to show how we directly constitute our identity through ethical techniques of the self, some of which have their origins in antiquity. Thus, he provides three lines of inquiry through, first, "dividing practices" (i.e., the indirect constitution of our selves through the exclusion of others), second, ethical self-constitution, which preserves a notion of agency, and, third, the development of a political rationality of governance. This governance focuses on the question of the integration of individuals in a community and the relationship between processes of individualization on the one hand and those of totalization (i.e., group constitution) on the other. In relation to the third line of inquiry, Foucault links the emergence of social science with the rise of this new political rationality of governance (Foucault, 1988c). In what follows it is clear that all three lines of inquiry are involved when we come to talk about the moral constitution of youth through the emergence of mental hygiene, social guidance, and what has been called "moral panics."

Foucault conceptualizes the modern political rationality or "reason of state" that developed in the transition from precapitalist to capitalist society in the seventeenth and eighteenth centuries as involving new forms of social control and techniques of government. In modern capitalist societies, there developed a new political technology of individuals that enabled us "to recognize ourselves as a society, as part of a nation or of a state" (Foucault, 1988c: 146). Government "entails more than just implementing general principles of reason, wisdom, and prudence"—it also needs "concrete, precise, and measured knowledge as to the state's strength" through statistics or "the knowledge of the state, the knowledge of different states' respective forces" (Foucault, 1988c: 151). It became important for states like France and Germany to find new ways of integrating the individual as useful to the state. "Police" (a term that in France and Germany at this time had a different meaning from the English sense of police) referred to "the specific techniques by which a government in the framework of the state was able to govern people as individuals significantly useful for the world" (Foucault, 1988c: 154). That is, police became a new administrative technology of government that was involved in "taking care of individuals living in society" with the aim of "permanently increasing production of something new, which is supposed to foster the citizen's life and the state's strength" (Foucault, 1988c: 158–159):

> the true object of the police becomes, at the end of the eighteenth century, the population; or in other words, the state has essentially to take care of men as a population. It wields its power over living beings, and its politics therefore has to be a biopolitics. Since the population is nothing more than what the state takes care of for its own sake, of course, the state is entitled to slaughter it, if necessary. So the reverse of biopolitics is thanatopolitics. (Foucault, 1988c: 160)

As a result of the focus on the population, new "policing" strategies developed, involving, first, general surveillance, such as gathering statistics, producing social surveys, collecting public records and other means of storing information, and developing laws and regulations that affect and shape the spaces in which life can be conducted. In this manner, Foucault argues, the state has provided a rationale for increasingly intervening in the lives of its citizens. Furthermore, he states, "the emergence of social science cannot, as you see, be isolated from the rise of this new political rationality and from this new political technology" (Foucault, 1988c: 162).

Policing the population also involves forms of disciplinary technologies, such as the range of programs in nineteenth-century institutional life that provided training to produce "the obedient subject, the individual subjected to habits, rules, orders; an authority that is exercised continually around him and upon him and which he must allow to function automatically in him" (Foucault, 1977: 227). Power is used to manage the population, to render them "docile, productive and useful for the state's preservation, expansion and felicity" (Foucault, 1988c: 148). Taking life or destroying bodies is wasteful. Power would be used to ensure not only that bodies would be made useful, but also that there would be no wastage, with no one being allowed to stand outside society as outcasts, rebels, outlaws, and so on. Sexuality and the influence of eugenics in the development of sexual discourses from the early years of the nineteenth century became important as a means of regulating the conduct of individual bodies and of ensuring the health and efficiency of the population as a whole (Foucault, 1980a). Power needed to be exercised to reconstitute those who departed from "the norm" as "docile bodies," so they would be able to conform and contribute to the patterns of production of capitalist society. Foucault (1988c) points out that alongside wars of mass slaughter like the Second World War, there emerged great welfare, public health, and medical assistance programs (e.g., the Beveridge program in United Kingdom). Hence, although the welfare state may have been wound back somewhat by current neo-liberal policies, there remains a continued and profound interest in the morality of youth, in forging them into "docile bodies" and useful citizens by ensuring that they are included in society and are not "at risk" of their lives being "wasted" in the perils of sex and drugs.

In his analysis of sexuality, Foucault points out that morality has by no means been universal, nor has it been applied to all people, and that although "From a strict philosophical point of view, the morality of Greek antiquity and contemporary morality have nothing in common. On the other hand, if you take them for what they prescribe, intimate and advise, they are extraordinarily close" (Foucault, 1989d: 323).

At first ancient morality concerned only the very small minority of "free" people; by Marcus Aurelius's time it had spread to be a matter of choice for people but was not obligatory, so that "we are thus very far from the moral conformities schematized by the sociologists and historians who study an assumed average population" (Foucault, 1989d: 320). While writing Volume 1 of the *History of Sexuality*, Foucault wondered: "why have we made of sexuality a moral experience?" Before producing the later volumes he again looked to "what happened in Antiquity in order to see how sexuality has been manipulated, lived, and modified by a certain number of participants" (Foucault, 1989d: 328–329). He points out that he has tried to "uncover how what we call Christian morality was embedded in European morality, and not since the beginnings of the Christian world, but since the morality of Antiquity" (Foucault, 1989d: 330–331). He argues that in antiquity the form of morality was "essentially a search for a personal ethics," but with Christianity morality became obedience to a code or a system of rules (Foucault, 1989c: 311). He points out that in thinking about antiquity, he tried to think this morality in the same form in which its contemporaries had reflected upon it, to wit, in the form of an *art of existence* or rather let's say a *technique of life*. It was a matter of knowing how to govern one's own life on order to give it the most beautiful form possible (in the eyes of others, of oneself, and of the future generations for whom one could serve as an example). That's what I tried to reconstitute: the formation and development of a practice of self whose objective was to constitute oneself as the worker of the beauty of one's own life. (Foucault, 1989c: 298)

Foucault acknowledges that in his last two books, *The Use of Pleasure* (1985) and *The Concern for the Self* (1990), the "truth" takes a very different form from that of his earlier works. Problematization as a set of discursive or nondiscursive practices on "an object for thought" remains a common theme (see chapter 1). The last two books are about "how one 'governs' oneself . . . to show how the government of self is integrated with the government of others" by exploring the history of thought (Foucault, 1989b: 296):

> The history of thought—that means not simply a history of ideas or of representations, but also the attempt to respond to this question: How is it that thought, insofar as it has a relationship with the truth, can also have a history?

> . . I try to respond to a specific problem: the birth of a morality, of a morality that is a reflection on sexuality, desire, pleasure.
>
> . . . I am not making a history of mores, of behaviour, a social history of sexual practice, but a history of the manner in which pleasure, desires and sexual behaviours have been problematized, reflected upon and thought about in Antiquity in relation to a certain art of living. (Foucault, 1989b: 294)

Making this study, Foucault's genealogy uncovers the way in antiquity notions of sexuality have been "transposed, metamorphosed and profoundly modified in Christianity" (Foucault, 1989b: 294). According to Foucault, "sexual activity is perceived and represented as a violence and thus problematized from the point of view of the difficulty in controlling it" (Foucault, 1989b: 300). Self-mastery as a style of morality becomes a fundamental ethical form of behavior that in antiquity involved "three distinct principles: (1) the relationship to the body and the problem of health; (2) the relationship to women, or rather to the woman who as wife to her husband is part of the same household; (3) the relationship to particular individuals who are adolescents and who one day may become free citizens" (Foucault, 1989b: 301).

One of the great changes was from the positioning of self-mastery in antiquity as "a problem only for the individual who must be the master of himself and master of others and not for those who must obey others" to an "ethics of the flesh that will hold in the same manner for both men and women" in Christianity (Foucault, 1989b: 301). But a general concern for self-mastery and the responsibility that adults have in this has to a large extent remained today. As a result, and because we tend to see youth as our hope for the future, society has continued to be concerned with the moral constitution of youth, and with governing their moral behavior by devising and harnessing technologies that teach, encourage, control, and enable youth to have mastery or governance of self.

INCULCATING MORAL VALUES IN YOUTH: SOCIAL EDUCATION AND MENTAL HYGIENE— EDUCATION OR INDOCTRINATION?

All education is indoctrination. The real question is whether indoctrination shall be confined merely to the mores and taboos of the past, or whether it shall be directed toward solving the problems of the future. In time, parents will recognize that the hope of a better world lies in such a new curriculum (H. M. Barr, Director of Research, Portland, Oregon, Public Schools, 1947, cited in Smith, 1999: 25).

The conception of education as a form of indoctrination of societal values amid hopes for a better world in the aftermath of the Second World War largely paralleled the notion of mental hygiene and its role in preventive medicine and social control. It portrayed how some adults and some educators viewed their place as controlling the world of child and adolescent behavior and how the choices and power were within the realm of adulthood, not in that of the adolescent. This section provides an overview of ways in which moral values considered important by society have been inculcated in youth in the fields of education and mental hygiene. It traces how social guidance is considered an important part of both fields. These display how youth and their moral state have been viewed, and how and by whom their moral behavior has been regulated. The section outlines how child guidance clinics provide one way of dealing with child mental health and how the collaborative model that was a key to the operation of such clinics has continued in different formulations to this day. Although the terminology may have changed, it was under the rubric of mental hygiene that social guidance programs began in U.S. schools in the postwar period, prior to the advent of school guidance counseling. Despite being endorsed by progressive education, the mental hygiene films that are discussed in the next section were more a form of "indoctrination" than "education."

The concept of education as indoctrination has been roundly criticized on the grounds that there are important conceptual differences between the terms "education" and "indoctrination" (Siegel, 1991; Snook, 1972; Spiecker, 1991). To indoctrinate is to imbue one, via teaching, with a doctrine or set of beliefs that involves intentionality on the part of the teacher. It is inherently ideological and suggests "that someone is taking advantage of a privileged role to influence those under his charge in a manner which is likely to distort their ability to assess the evidence on its own merit" (Snook, 1972: 66). On the other hand, education, at least the liberal theory of education promoted by philosophers such as John Dewey and R. S. Peters, is concerned with broadening the mind and developing rationality and a critical world view, which is epitomized in terms of problem solving, decision making, or scientific method (Peters, 1967). Snook (1972) concludes (in the gendered language of the day) that part of the difficult job of an educator, be they parent or teacher, is to balance the conceptual issues between indoctrination and education: "He must initiate immature minds into a cultural heritage, and train unformed consciences to know and love what is good. At the same time he is bound to respect the rationality, potential or actual, which these young people embody" (Snook, 1972: 110).

The tensions in these competing streams of educational thought have also been played out in how youth, school guidance, and counseling have been conceptualized in different institutions and at different points in time. Some school educators have seen and will continue to see guidance and counseling as a form of social engineering toward conformity in showing, telling, modeling, or persuading young people toward a "right" way of behaving amid informing them of the consequences of "bad" behavior or unwise choices. Others will view it in more humanistic terms as a form of nurturing personal development, encouraging growth, and tapping potential and difference, so the individual has the freedom to become his or her "true" self (which are themselves open to criticism, as chapter 7 discusses).

NZAC[1] provides a contemporary viewpoint about guidance and counseling in schools:

> "Guidance" refers to the growth, development and learning of the whole person—cognitive, emotional, social, spiritual and physical. It works to develop self-knowledge as a pre-requisite to social adjustment. It encourages empowerment, rather than offering direction or advice, creating opportunities for the development of life-long decision-making skills. Good individual guidance occurs in settings where guidance values permeate the organizational climate and where guidance principles are used in the development of structures, systems and policies. These principles should be evident in relations between staff, as well as in the services and programmes for students. Guidance provisions assist in the ordinary learning and development of all in a school environment, as well as paying special attention to those with particular needs. "Counselling" is a specialised activity, offered within the guidance networks of most secondary schools and available to the whole school community. The role requires additional training. The secondary school guidance counsellor provides counselling for all those who wish it and acts as a focus point and facilitator for the overall guidance network. (NZAC, 1997: 25)

Although this NZAC viewpoint is not necessarily one that all school counselors would subscribe to, especially in its use of notions of "adjustment," what it makes clear is that indoctrination is not what guidance or counseling are about in New Zealand secondary schools today.

Snook (1972) suggests that although "there are few conceptual limits to the subject matter that can be indoctrinated" (p. 68) it is in the realm of morals, religion, and politics that indoctrination is most likely to occur because, "informed people" differ in how they perceive these and how and what they believe young people should be taught. At one extreme, some would argue that all moral and social training should be avoided until the child has developed sufficient rationality to assess, evaluate, and form reasonable conclusions about various moral ideas. Such a position seems permissive but does not necessarily equate with freedom in that it may ensure a negative freedom—that is, a freedom from some custom—but it does not ensure a positive freedom, a freedom to do something. It makes the erroneous assumption that rationality is something that a child acquires at a certain age, denying that rationality is the result of the child experiencing and working through their reactions to a range of social and moral situations and dilemmas. Denying a child such experiences is, as Snook (1972) suggests, "to stunt his rationality" (p. 70); it is therefore also likely to stunt his or her moral development.

Snook comments on the great dilemma of education as how to transmit cultural values and traditions in which rationality is defined without indoctrination and without stunting the rationality of the child in the process. The question then becomes one of the *form* the education should take once the child is considered educable, and what form it should take prior to this. Snook endorses the work of John Wilson,[2] who argued that children should be taught to be rational about morals because "there is a style of moral argument just as there is a style of mathematical argument" (p. 71). Although procedural rules require further work,

Wilson argues that a program of moral education could not "be called indoctrination since its whole purpose is to encourage children to weigh the evidence, consider the consequences, and so on, all of which is the very antithesis of indoctrination as we have defined it" (p. 72). Snook considers that Kohlberg's (1970) work, in extending Piagetian thinking and involving philosophical thought on the nature of morality, may also provide a way through the dilemma. He notes, without discussing, Kohl-berg's assertion that his theory of stages of moral thinking that children pass through is "culture-neutral and quite independent of the particular content of the morality in question" (p. 72). This, in fact, highlights one of the key criticisms of Kohlberg's theory (as discussed in chapter 3).

Social guidance is a form of moral and social education. In the immediate postwar period, film was a very modern, future-oriented technology, which became linked to liberal notions of education, preventive notions of mental hygiene, and a sense of moral duty on the part of educators, politicians, and parents to save America's youth. Western nations were traumatized by war and fearful of communist takeovers and the possibility of nuclear annihilation, and they were facing youthful rebellion. Young people were largely seen as bad-mannered, disrespectful, impolite, and, at worst, as delinquent. Hence, the scene was set for the development of systems of guidance and counseling in schools as the means to sort out these "difficult" young people. To what extent this sorting out was about moral development and to what extent it was about social control and the assertion of the power of adult authority is somewhat blurred and contradictory and in the early postwar years reflected notions of mental hygiene.

The term "mental hygiene" was first used in the United States in the mid-nineteenth century, amid concerns about the effects of unsanitary conditions after the Civil War (Mandell, http://mh.jhsph.edu/) and came to prominence during the Second World War. In 1893 Isaac Ray, a founder of the American Psychiatric Association, defined mental hygiene as the art of preserving the mind against all incidents and influences calculated to deteriorate its qualities, impair its energies or derange its movements. The management of the bodily powers in regard to exercise, rest, food, clothing and climate, the laws of breeding, the government of the passions, the sympathy with current emotions and opinions, the discipline of the intellect—all these come within the province of mental hygiene. (cited in Mandell, http:// mh.jhsph.edu/)

Mental hygiene was related to the now discredited eugenics movement, and as a result, this connection is now largely downplayed.[3] The link with eugenics was fairly clear as in the above clause on "laws of breeding." Eugenics[4] is currently [2000] described as the study of methods to improve inherited human characteristics. It is directed chiefly at discouraging reproduction among those considered unfit (or those carrying genetic diseases) and encouraging it in the fit, although there are many difficulties in defining which traits are most desirable. The first half of the 20th century saw extreme coercive applications of such principles by governments ranging from miscegenation laws and enforced sterilization of the insane in the U.S. and other nations to the holocaust of Nazi Germany. In recent years, interest in eugenics has largely focused on genetic screening, although China enacted restrictions on marriages involving persons with certain disabilities and diseases in 1994. (http://www.encyclopedia.com/ printable/04265.html)

With the eugenic element now deleted, mental hygiene is defined as: "the science of maintaining mental health and preventing the development of psychosis, neurosis or other mental disorders" (*Encyclopaedia Britannica)* and "the science of promoting mental health and preventing mental illness through the application of psychiatry and psychology" (*The Columbia Encyclopedia*, 5th edition). In the twentieth century in the United States various individuals and groups (e.g., Clifford Beers, Adolf Meyer, Paul Lemkau, William White, Bronson Crothers, Connecticut Society for Mental Hygiene, National Committee for Mental Hygiene) promoted the notion of mental hygiene as a means of improving the quality of care for the mentally ill, preventing mental illness where possible, and ensuring that accurate information regarding mental health is widely available. This resulted in public education programs about mental hygiene, reforms in institutional care, and the establishment of child guidance clinics that apply a combination of psychiatry, psychology, and social work. Mental hygiene is partly about preventive medicine, public health, social engineering, and social control. Although "mental hygiene" is not used widely today, having been superseded by the term "mental health," it still appears in the names of a few U.S. organizations.[5]

Child guidance clinics became established partly because child mental health concerns were either overlooked by psychiatrists who mostly spent their time with severely ill adults, or were deflected because of time constraints in busy medical practices. These clinics were separated from medical practices but used a clinical medical model that stressed a collaborative interdisciplinary approach that continues today. Practitioners are likely to include mental hygienists, pediatricians, psychologists, psychiatric social workers, and psychoanalysts. The focus is on the "whole child"—on positively influencing its emotional development and on helping with parenting skills. A recent initiative in child and youth health and well-being in New Zealand is the Strengthening Families program of interagency cooperation that began in 1998.[6] Another example, but located in the medical arena, is the Community Child Adolescent and Family Service (CCAFS) that is part of Auckland Health-care (Hospital). It includes several teams: a youth early intervention service that diagnoses mental health disorders, a community team that deals with issues such as phobias and eating disorders, a child and adolescent liaison service that operates between the hospital, child, and family unit and school to reintegrate young people back into school if they have been ill and out of school for some time, a school–CCAFFS liaison team that operates a consultancy service, and special-purpose groups, such as stress management. Guidance counselors are the personnel with whom such teams primarily liaise at secondary schools. The link that counselors have with mental health services, as well as their knowledge, understanding, and expertise about mental health issues, therefore forms a vital component of their work. Very often it is the school counselor who becomes aware of symptoms that indicate possible mental illness in young people. School counselors require knowledge in how to deal with this, and in where to refer those clients withwhom they are unable to deal .

PROGRESSIVE EDUCATION AND MENTAL HYGIENE FILMS: DISCIPLINARY TECHNOLOGIES OF THE YOUTHFUL SELF

The youth culture that began to appear in the United States in the 1940s and 1950s revolved mostly around the high school—around music, clothes, dating, cars, and particular verbal codes, such as "cool, hep, hip, fab, gear." Frank Sinatra and other crooners were the focus in the 1940s, skiffle groups and then Elvis Presley and rock and roll in the 1950s. Many popular musicians received considerable criticism from adults who were appalled at their appearance and overt sexuality. Elvis's famous hip swivel and pelvic thrusts were particularly shocking to adults, especially because it made the girls scream in delight and lets boys to imitate him. Pop music certainly had an impact on New Zealand youth as well as on their overseas counterparts (see Yska, 1993).

The development of mental hygiene films coincided with the birth of a distinctive youth culture in the years following the Second World War. In the United States and in Britain, with fathers away at war and mothers out working on the war effort, teenagers had more freedom and less supervision and restraint than had earlier generations. After the war, such freedom was rapidly curtailed, as mothers returned into the home and fathers into jobs vacated by women. New Zealand youth probably had less freedom in the war years than did their British and American counterparts, because although many men were away, married women with children tended not to work outside the home, and there simply were not the large-scale industrial factories harnessed to the war effort as there were elsewhere. New Zealand's war contribution was geared to its pastoral economy rather than to manufacturing industries and associated factories. New Zealand society was not yet as highly urbanized as were those of Britain and the United States, but that would change rapidly during the postwar years. Nevertheless, there was considerable concern about a rise in juvenile delinquency associated with the war and youth freedoms (see Yska, 1993).

In his book, *Mental Hygiene: Classroom Films 1945–1970*, Ken Smith (1999) researched the genre and the social setting in the United States that gave rise to mental hygiene films. Thousands of mental hygiene educational films were produced, especially in the American Midwest, over a 25-year period between 1945 and 1970, for use in teaching guidance in various curriculum areas, such as health and safety, sociology, psychology, civics, and home economics. While many mental hygiene films have been all but forgotten or were lost or destroyed, Smith (1999) spent considerable time researching the topic, and he provided synopses of 250 of them in his book. He considered mental hygiene films to be "a uniquely American experiment in social engineering, the marriage of a philosophy—progressive education—and a technology—the instructional film" (Smith, 1999: 19). In a pledge to American educators in 1946, a mental hygiene filmmaker said that he considered it an "honored privilege" and even a "sacred trust" to produce films that would produce "finer men and women" and would, in turn, lead to better worldwide understanding. He pledged that these films would motivate students to think constructively while using realism rather than artifice to maximize their interest (Smith, 1999).

That the American Midwest was the location for film production was partly because wealthy entrepreneurs looking for new ventures, such as David Smart (Coronet) and William Benton (Encyclopaedia Britannica Films), two of the biggest producers of educational films, were from Chicago. The University of Chicago was a major center for progressive education, which advocated using visual resources. Popular accounts suggest that Smart, a keen amateur filmmaker, who was rich from magazine publishing (*Apparel Arts, GQ, Esquire*) either saw during a trip to the Munich Olympics (1936) or read about how the Nazis used the powerful force of films in their classrooms to shape youth behavior, and subsequently he set up a studio over two acres in Glenview, Illinois. Benton, the wealthy founder of an advertising agency, became vice president of the University of Chicago, and he was clearly linked with progressive educators. He provided finance for the university to buy Encyclopaedia Britannica, then purchased a catalogue of 500 classroom films from two other companies to form Encyclopaedia Britannica Films, which, in turn, made sufficient money to finance a film studio (Smith, 1999).

Progressive educationalists, well aware of the success of film as a teaching tool during the Second World War, were anxious to see a change in pedagogy from the existing systems using repetition, textbooks, and lectures toward more Dewey-influenced, child-centered, active learning methods that developed critical methods of thought. Broadly speaking, the aims of progressive education were for all boys and girls to be inculcated with ideals and attitudes that would enable them to meet the complexities of modern life and to take their place as effective members of a modern democratic society. Progressive education became prevalent in the United States until 1959, when Deweyan ideas were severely criticized and unfairly scapegoated by President Eisenhower, Vice Admiral Rickover, and others for causing the "sputnik crisis" (Hook, 1968). Progressive, child-centered education came to prominence in New Zealand after 1935 under the influence of Clarence Beeby (director general of education), and despite criticism it has remained the predominant style of pedagogy in New Zealand. The use of film as a modern technology fitted, therefore, the progressive education project, with Smith quoting Ivah Green, supervisor of rural education, Iowa Department of Public Instruction: "It's a perfectly delightful way to learn. The motion picture . . . [is] literally knocking at school doors, ready and eager to make learning more rapid, more meaningful, more lasting, and—dare we mention it?—more fun!" (Smith, 1999: 22).

Mental hygiene films, however, became a pervasive form of cultural indoctrination until the late 1960s, when the growing sophistication of a generation of television-watching adolescents saw them become outdated and outmoded.

These films, which could be considered forms of social engineering, preventive medicine, and cultural indoctrination all rolled into one, were aimed at shaping the behavior of adolescents to conform to the adult-directed norms of the time by extolling proper behavior. Their vast range included such topics as proper dating procedures, proper personal style and presentation, the consequences of drug use, of early marriage, of premarital sex (pregnancy and VD), and the effects of dangerous driving, juvenile delinquency, and the atom bomb. They were seen by millions of American schoolchildren, and some were bought by the National Film Library and used as part of New Zealand guidance programs. The list of 20 films provided for the first national course for guidance counselors in 1964 includes three that Smith (1999) describes in his book: *The Other Fellow's Feelings* (1957, Centron, 8 min.); *The Procrastinator* (1952, Centron, 12 min.); *Emotional Health* (1947, McGraw-Hill, 20 min.). The rest may have been "mental hygiene films," but they were not on Smith's list (Besley, 2000).

Smith (1999) identifies eight genres: "fitting in; cautionary tales; dating; girls only; drugs; sex education; bloody highways; sneaky sponsors" (p. 9). The rationale for such a division is not discussed, but it is largely based on the descriptive content. The "girls only" category includes films on menstruation and on home economics, which were considered the domain of females at the time. But there was a certain amount of overlap with "sneaky sponsors," who encouraged young people to use their products, be they feminine sanitary products or cuts of meat. Certain types of films had particular prominence at different times over this period, depending on the influence of educational theorists and public demand.

Smith suggests that films about dating and manners were predominant for fifteen years, from 1945 to 1960. Survival films—those concerned with the effects of atomic war—peaked in 1951, and films on juvenile delinquency in 1955. Antidrug films featured both in the early 1950s and from 1965 to 1970. Road safety films featured continuously and do so to the present day.

Four of the film producers and production companies (Coronet, Encyclopaedia Britannica Films, Sid Davis, and Centron) are discussed by Smith; all of them were private providers—"a peculiarly American, profit-making approach to social engineering" (p. 14)—and only some of whome used educational consultants. Sid Davis, who made over 150 films, receives particular mention for his excesses, exaggerations, and distortions, which went unchallenged because, unlike other filmmakers, he did not have a committee of educational advisors or a peer group overseeing his work. Davis's films focused on misery (child molestation in *The Dangerous Stranger*, 1950); injuries (impaled on scissors in *Live and Learn*, 1951), and often ended in violent death, simply because a boy had driven too fast (*The Bottle and the Throttle*, 1968) or hitched a ride with a homosexual (*Boys Beware,* 1961).

Smith's final section provides comments and brief synopses of about 250 films. He indicates how the social and moral fabric of teenagers was shaped. Teenagers viewing these films were taught the negative consequences of being delinquent, selfish, arrogant, and undemocratic. For example, *Last Date* and *Keep off the Grass* used scare tactics to discourage self-destructive, rebellious behavior, while encouraging conformity. Conversely, being popular, having fun, and surviving into their twenties were the positive consequences for teenagers who followed the accepted societal rules, as in *Dinner Party* and *The Prom: It's a Pleasure!* Other films, such as *Are You Popular?* and *A Date with Your Family*, showed teenagers as clean-cut, obedient team players, suggesting that by imitating such behavior, they, too, would be happy. There were also "discussion" films that focused on social problems. Some of these were intended to provoke class discussion and so ended with a difficult, unresolved situation.

Films such as *Act Your Age* (1949), *Control Your Emotions* (1950), and *Other Fellow's Feelings* (1957) provided tips on emotional development. Some of the road safety films went to extremes, showing not only actual dead bodies, but also scenes of people dying in road crashes. *Mechanized Death* (1961) opens with an audio of a dying woman coughing up blood as she is pried from her wrecked car and continues with "just grainy handheld footage of accident scenes and incessant, droning, judgmental narration" (Smith, 1999:182). The placement and blame for the problems addressed in these films was always the teenagers' fault, never that of society and its rules. Many films were highly exaggerated or even blatantly untrue, especially those about drugs. For example, in *Narcotics: Pit of Despair* (1967) a boy joins a hip crowd by going to a pot party and becoming "psychologically dependent" after one puff; he quickly starts mainlining heroin, ending up screaming in agony with withdrawal symptoms on a dirty mattress. He takes full responsibility for his actions in wanting to "fit in," realizing too late that "by joining to belong, he's now more alone than ever" (p. 188). No comment or blame is assigned to his parents, who were seldom at home and left him unsupervised and feeling lonely (Smith, 1999).

Smith (1999) comments that in tone, these films might teach with a smile, a scowl, or a sneer, and although some had progressive messages promoting family planning or opposing prejudice, many were preachy, dogmatic, and often alarmist, coming as they did from an era that held rigid beliefs about right and wrong and about how adults thought young people should behave. The filming techniques involved presenting a strategically scripted scenario of a perfect world that isolated the targeted issue from everyday life. While they copied Hollywood stagecraft in order to appear realistic, they deliberately used unrecognizable local personnel[7] rather than Hollywood actors. A few actors from these films subsequently went on to Hollywood.[8]

The effectiveness of this huge body of educational technology is questionable. With most mental hygiene films being just over 10 minutes long and certainly no longer than 25 minutes, they were often not used quite as intended. They were meant to be accompanied by classroom discussion and exercises in self-examination to shape and inculcate the "right" attitudes, but it seems that they were often used to break classroom boredom. " Without postscreening reinforcement, the messages delivered by these films often failed to sink in" (Smith, 1999: 31).

Smith suggested that in the 1950s, when teenagers were mostly compliant about conforming, the films were effective, but by the late 1960s, with a generation accustomed to television and the most rebellious teenage group ever, they were no longer effective. In the late 1960s and early 1970s teenagers became very involved in protesting about positive moral causes such as the Vietnam War, women's liberation, civil rights, and environmental conservation issues. Teenagers then were dressing more sloppily, taking more drugs, having sex, and protesting about values largely held by the older generation, and one wonders whether in the end the mental hygiene films might have resulted in reverse social engineering. Not only might they have shown teenagers how to do "bad" things, but teenagers might also have thought that kids doing "bad" things looked cool, while those doing the "right " thing looked nerdy or square, according to the norms of the current youth culture.

This section has shown some ways used by those concerned about the behavior of youth to attempt to control and channel them into developing socially acceptable values and ways of behaving. Although Smith's work discusses the situation in the postwar United States up until the 1960s, there were parallels in other Western countries. Both New Zealand and Britain worried about what was happening in the United States. In the 1950s in New Zealand, how youth were perceived became critical for the subsequent setting up of guidance counseling services. To a certain extent, New Zealand adopted imported fears and concerns about the "youth problem" and delinquency amid a reaction to postwar incursions of American pop culture in a society that still largely privileged Britain as "home" and consequently British culture as superior to American culture. There was a popular perception that New Zealand was following a path similar to that of the United States and Britain and that what happened there would eventually arrive in New Zealand (see Yska, 1993). The genre of mental hygiene films, their tone and content illustrate how society at the time perceived what adolescents were and what they should be, in terms of their moral constitution. Despite a change from the notion of mental hygiene, the medium of film and now video is still a popular means of presenting social guidance and health programs. Acknowledging that film is a powerful medium and that it can and has been used for indoctrination purposes is something of which educators and school counselors need to be aware. The next section looks at societal reaction and fears about what was considered to be unacceptable youth behavior and how this has been theorized as at times being "moral panic."

"MORAL PANICS" AND THE "MAZENGARB REPORT"— A CASE STUDY OF THE MORAL CONSTITUTION OF YOUTH IN THE MID-1950S IN NEW ZEALAND

Mental hygiene films were one way in which education responded to adult concerns about the youth of the times, their morality, their behavior, and the dangers they faced. But this was not the only sort of response to youth. Another response is embodied in that of a "moral panic." The notion of "moral panic" is a sociological one, developed in a 1972 book, *Folk Devils and Moral Panics: The Creation of the Mods and Rockers,* by Stanley Cohen ([1972] 1980), that built on ideas from American sociological theories of deviance, labeling, and interactionism. In the United States, the notion became focused more on episodes of collective behavior that involved some perception of threat but turned out to be not particularly damaging when actually measured by concrete indicators (Goode and Ben-Yehuda, 1994).

But the very words used—both "moral" and "panic"—are problematic. "Panic" has negative connotations of irrationality, overemotionality, fear, manipulation, stampede, people are reacting to insufficient information or being manipulated by selected information. Once something comes to be labeled a panic and so as irrational, the very situation or behavior that has been highlighted can easily be dismissed. The notion of "moral" is derived from the philosophical study of morality and from notions of "goodness" and "right action." But it is commonly positioned around conservative, religious (Christian) values that relate to the regulation of conduct, to ideas of right and wrong, but especially to sexual behavior, violence, and honesty. Moral panics usually center around uncontrollability, especially with regard to children and youth, in terms of sexuality and crime, a lack of morals, of discipline, and of respect for authority, concerns about "soft" punishment, and suggestions that "unteachable" young people result in high truancy rates and suspension from school. Cohen provided a comprehensive definition:

> A condition, episode, person or group of persons emerges to become defined as a threat to societal values and interests; its nature is presented in a stylised and stereotypical fashion by the mass media; the moral barricades are manned by editors, bishops, politicians and other right-thinking people; socially accredited experts pronounce their diagnoses and solutions; ways of coping are evolved or (more often) resorted to; the condition then disappears, submerges or deteriorates and becomes more visible. Sometimes the object of the panic is quite novel and at other times it is something which has been in existence long enough, but suddenly appears in the limelight. Sometimes the panic passes over and is forgotten, except in folklore and collective memory; at other times it has more serious and long-lasting repercussions and might produce such changes as those in legal and social policy or even in the way the society conceives of itself. (Cohen, 1980: 9)

"Moral panic" contextualizes the situation where the media, as the self-appointed champion of public morality, tend to focus on the perceived misbehavior and criminality—in this case, of young people. In such a situation, the media become not just the reporters, but also the major instigators of public panic as a result of the way that they obtain some information and describe, sensationalize, exaggerate, inflame, and generalize from this point. In the process, this media usually call on the police, judiciary, politicians, educational and welfare authorities, and concerned citizens to voice their concern. Seldom is the subject of the panic—that is, youth—consulted and if they are, their voice tends to be selectively aimed at backing up the media story. The description that the media provide of the behavior tends to produce the behavior itself in that it virtually tells young people of a way to behave, albeit a way that is unacceptable to authorities. Hence the media tend to perpetuate or enable the behavior to happen, in turn enlarging the panic even further. According to Cohen (1980), moral panics tend to highlight what can become "folk devils"—that is, individuals or groups fulfilling roles and occupying positions that society considers should be avoided.

Moral panics tend to occur in times of profound social change and may be used by those in power to divert public attention away from policy and funding inadequacies. Moral panics are sustained campaigns that are lead by politicians, lobbyists, and the media wanting official— usually government—action to suppress threats to social order and especially to the family, which is often positioned as the cornerstone of society. They "appeal to people who are alarmed by an apparent fragmentation or breakdown of the social order, which leaves them at risk in some way" (Thompson, 1998: 3). The ideal is often portrayed as some past, halcyon time of moral certainty, so there is often an appeal to a simplistic "back to basics" and even to fundamentalism. But in the post-modern condition, morality is no longer a singular set rules prescribed by the Church and set out in laws—it is largely challenged and negotiable. Since the late twentieth century, while still keeping some control, the state has tended to remove itself from the private morals of the individual and the family, especially on issues such as abortion, homosexuality, and attempted suicide. The discourses of popular culture, politics, and professional groups often become intertwined in the creation of moral panics. Popular culture in terms of television programs, soaps, magazines, tabloid press, pubs, the workplace, as well as politics in terms of neoconservative values, privileges the nuclear family of husband wife and children and professional groups claiming more resources. Thompson argues that "the 'at-risk' character of modern society is magnified and takes the form of moral panics in Britain due to the undermining of the authority of traditional elites and the loss of deference on the part of the lower classes, allied to the centralized and 'incestuous' character of the mass media" (Thompson, 1998: 7).

Moral panics often result in hastily pulled-together conferences, special committees, and legislation seeking "solutions" to the "problem" as a means to control the "youth problem" and reaffirming society's consensus of morality. The following case study portrays what is now seen as a moral panic in the 1950s in New Zealand. On 23 July 1954, the government appointed a Special Committee[9] on Moral Delinquency in Children and Adolescents, chaired by Dr. Oswald Mazengarb Q.C. (NZ Parliamentary Debates, July 1954). The committee produced a 70-page document, the "Mazengarb Report," gleaned from public submissions, available literature, and research. It provided a statement about the moral constitution of youth in the 1950s—of what was acceptable and unacceptable sexual behavior for them and of how adults in authority should manage or control. particularly, female sexuality.

Concerns about the morals of young people came to the fore in New Zealand in

1954, when newspapers reported a sex scandal involving a large group of adolescents in the Hutt Valley, a new suburb. Newspapers reported that 57 young people (41 boys, 16 girls, some aged 13–15 years) were arrested for sexual misconduct in the form of carnal knowledge and indecent assault, which had apparently occurred in private homes and movie theaters. This was revealed following an admission to the police by a 15-year-old girl that to be popular she had repeatedly had sex with members of a "milk bar gang" (see Mazengarb Report, 1954: 11–12). The public became increasingly concerned about what seemed to be a new breed of "teenagers," "milkbar cowboys," "bodgies," and "widgies," who increasingly displayed the influence of American popular culture on what was then a predominantly British-focused New Zealand (Yska, 1993). There was also concern about how this seemed to be happening in a newly established predominantly-working class state housing area.

But the 1954 context for the moral panic built on more than one incident. There was already a history of some earlier adolescent sexual misbehavior in 1952. On top of this there were sensational murders by teenagers: the Parker-Hulme bashing in Christchurch by supposedly lesbian teenage girls in 1954 and the "Jukebox" shooting in Auckland in 1955 (see Yska, 1993). Parallel with the emergence of rock 'n' roll was a teenage or youth culture that challenged adult expectations (Molloy, 1993; Shuker, 1987; Shuker, Openshaw, and Soler, 1990; Soler, 1988, 1989; Yska, 1993). Yska (1993: 82) points out that the report "allowed the Government and other traditional bodies to dismiss the new postwar social values (coming mostly from the United States) as being of little importance and just a passing influence" and instead to set out the conventional moral values that New Zealand seemed to be abandoning. However, this is only part of the story, and what the report reveals is how adolescents were conceptualized and identified in the 1950s.

An analysis shows that in addition to two committee members having clear religious affiliations, a preponderance of witnesses were from the religious sector, indicating the enormous influence of religion on morals in the mid-1950s. Yska (1993: 70) criticized the Committee for comprising only "Anglo-Saxon, middle-class professionals" with "strong moral and religious codes" and for excluding "social workers, educationalists, or those with 'hands on' experience of 'problem' adolescents." The voice of youth was categorically omitted, perpetuating a form of institutionalized silence—perhaps none too surprisingly, in an age of paternalistic attitudes to young people, as exemplified by the cliché, "children should be seen and not heard." No young people and certainly not those who were involved in the scandals were interviewed, because "it was thought undesirable" (Mazengarb Report, 1954: 11). Much of the report's evidence was from adults who were considered "reliable" but who provided second-hand evidence. The youth involved had already been judged as being "delinquent" and, by definition, bad, criminal, and unreliable compared with the morally upright, professional adults. This report was about the externalized moral regulation of youth by others — that is, adults —

rather than an internalized self-discipline in the form of an ethical self-constitution (see Foucault, 1997a).

While it acknowledged the limitations of secondary and hearsay evidence and of statistics, the report still presented its evidence as strongly accurate and factual, with only some qualification at times. It scarcely acknowledged that the sensationalist newspaper reports were about a tiny fraction of the youth population (see also Yska, 1993) or that despite an increase in juvenile delinquency rates during the war, these had returned to the lower prewar rate.[10] But it seems that if such things were happening to a few, they might be only the tip of the iceberg.

A list compiled from the table of contents and the first three pages of the report, displays the negative attitudes toward the sexual behavior of adolescents in the terms and phrases used to connote and describe the central category of *moral delinquency* in adolescents: juvenile immorality, sexual misbehavior, indecent assault, carnal knowledge, immoral conduct, sexual crime, abnormally homosexual behavior, sexual orgies, juvenile delinquency, sexual delinquency, lowered moral standards, sex cult, lewd rituals, grossly obscene acts, gross act of indecency, indecent exposure, sexual assault, sexual indulgence, and illicit sexual practices. From this list and from the central category of *moral delinquency*, it becomes apparent that this term is a conflation of three discourses—the discourse of *morality* from Christian religion, the discourse of *delinquency* from psychology and sociology, and the discourse of *offending/crime* from law. It is the running together of the religious morality and psychology with the notion of deviating from the norm in ways that may or may not involve criminal offences, depending on how the law is defined (for it differed in its application for male and female), that provides a very conservative, biased, judgmental, punitive, stigmatizing, and controlling view of the behavior of adolescents and their parents.

The second part of the report formed the major part and focused on searching for the cause of the decline in moral standards. It comprised 10 sections that were particularly wide-ranging and included some visual and auditory influences, the school, community influences, the home environment, information on sex matters, the influence of religion on morality, the family, religion, and morality, changing times and concepts, the law and morality, and child welfare in New Zealand. The blame for the decline in moral standards resided with the child, with bad parenting, and with bad publishers and their pulp material. In a way that echoed the indoctrination and social control aspect of the mental hygiene films, film censorship was endorsed. Radio was criticized for its crime serials and suggestive love songs, for which adolescents craved the sheet music as a means of obtaining the words. But that was only part of the problem. Once it was switched on, the radio stayed on, so that children not only lost sleep but also heard programs not intended for them. Parents were blamed for being too lax and "should select their children's programs and see that their listening hours are reasonably restricted" (p. 26). Interestingly, in the 1950s both the problem and the solution of youth access to the media was described in ways that are almost identical to public concerns about television and Internet viewing today—in both instances it is a case of control and exercise of that control by parents as part of their parental responsibilities.

Some causes emanating from school involved the relationship between teacher and child. Increased urbanization was blamed for having largely put paid to teachers living within the same community as their students and so to a knowledge and understanding of local conditions and tensions that a child might face. Now that knowledge had to be acquired from within the school and "is of great importance in diagnosing maladjustment that might lead to delinquency" (p. 27). Surprisingly for such a conservative document, coeducational schools were not blamed for immorality, even though witnesses had asserted that they provided the opportunity. The evidence presented indicated that the students on whom the report centered, were "already concerned in immoral acts outside the school or that they had home circumstances conducive to delinquency" (p. 29). Progressive education, with its "play way" and "free expression" and concentration "on the development of the personality of the child—a development which could lead to licence" (p. 31), supplanted "traditional external discipline" but was not conclusively a cause of immorality.

"Defects" in the community undid good teaching and satisfactory "home training" and were factors promoting juvenile delinquency, whereas "the more normal and well balanced a community is, the greater are the child's chances of developing a well-balanced personality" (p. 31). Due to full employment and a growing economy, in the 1950s New Zealand society was becoming a consumerist one. A stable, peaceful family life, owning your own home in the suburbs or at least having a state house, were a reality for many. It was the rapidly created urban communities, which were "just an aggregation of houses" (p. 34) with a high proportion of children and youth reflecting an "abnormal distribution of population" (p. 32), that were "defective." New areas featured an "absence of community spirit" because "churches, schools, halls, and monuments are entirely non-existent or very new" (p. 33). There were "streets of overcrowded homes unsuitable for family life," so young people tended to "seek their pleasures away from their home and district" (p. 33) and to form local groups or gangs where the "influence for good of the better among them is often outweighed by the misbehaviour and dangerous propensities of others" (p. 34). The dearth of organized recreation, sport, clubs, and entertainment was perceived as a particular problem. Such a litany provides clear evidence of a middle-class cultural bias and a victim-blaming mentality of the committee and its witnesses against young, poorer communities.

The importance of the family was stressed, but its problems were highlighted as being insecurity, absent mothers and fathers, high wages, inadequate parenting. Being unloved, unwanted, or less cared for than other family members was criticized for promoting feelings of insecurity that "renders the child more susceptible to influences leading to delinquency" (p. 37). "The mother's attitude to the child is of prime importance" (p. 37), as is the parents' love, which should be "affection combined with wisdom" in a family where "all the members—father, mother and children—are in a proper relationship, the one to the other"

(p. 37). Divorce, separation, and remarriage leading to emotional disturbances, poor discipline, lack of parental training, and lack of responsibility by parents were all believed to contribute to delinquency. Mothers who were frequently absent from home were condemned as thoughtless, be they working, socializing, or playing sport. Mothers who worked but economically did not have to were particularly singled out for opprobrium. Since nearly a third of the delinquents presented had working mothers, this was held up as a clear indicator of potential delinquency. Fathers did not escape criticism if they showed no interest in their children once they returned home after being at work all day. Clearly the start of a consumer society was starting to hit and this was frowned upon for its effect not only on wives, but also on adolescents. The high wages paid to adolescents who did not save but spent their money on luxuries was also condemned, so "a compulsory savings scheme should be instituted to guard young people from the evils of misspent leisure and to develop in them that sense of reliability which is so often lacking" (p. 40). This subsequently resulted in the Post Office Savings Bank operating in schools. In fact, family and parenting were considered fundamental, since the committee noted that the delinquency cases presented involved either a lack of parental responsibility or an inability to guide and control their children: "a remedy must be found before this decline [in morality] leads to the decay of the family itself as the center and core of our national life and culture" (p. 45).

Sexual activity was definitely not counterbalanced for young people, even if they were over the age of consent (then, as now, 16 for girls, but not specified for boys), but when, how, and by whom sex education was to be taught was considered very important. For adolescents contraception and instruction about using contraceptives remained taboo and in the sphere of medical practitioners until the passing of the Contraception, Sterilisation and Abortion Act in 1977. Adolescents may be sexually mature and capable of reproduction, but socially they are considered as children, emotionally immature and without sufficient financial means to be parents, so they are not "permitted" to be sexually active. Until the 1970s, sex was expected to remain only within marriage—otherwise one was considered to be "fallen," "promiscuous," or "living in sin." During adolescence, the individual is expected on the one hand to increase her or his level of responsibility but is seldom actually given much real responsibility, legally, economically, or socially.

The report displays a real lack of transparency about itself in considering what a moral code is and how it is formed. It explains this as meaning that while the law is not about a coercion to follow a certain moral code of conduct, it is concerned with the effects of sin and immorality on others, so it seeks to restrain people from offending "those who do observe the principles of religion or of morality" (p. 50). But in such restraint, clear messages about a moral code are present, even if in the form of what not to do. Some things—sex, smoking, drinking, and gambling—are acceptable for adults, but not for children. Offenses against religion include blasphemy and disturbing public worship; offenses against morality include indecent exposure, publications, prostitution, carnal knowledge, rape, and abortion.

Suicide being "a result of sin and a breach of morality" (p. 51), suicide attempts were punishable with up to 2 years' imprisonment under the Crimes Act, 1908. Attempted suicide ceased to be an offense with the passing of the Crimes Act, 1961, but aiding and abetting suicide was and still is an offense. There was not only a "limit on the right of the individual to do what he likes with his own person," but, in an astoundingly mercenary statement, suicide was also an expenditure issue because "the State spends so much money on the education and health of the people" (p. 50)—that is, suicide is a waste of such resources. The lack of understanding of human suffering and mental illness that might be involved for someone who attempts suicide is amazing. One can only wonder what the committee might make of New Zealand's current infamous youth suicide statistics.

When it came to the law on indecency, carnal knowledge, and indecent assault, the committee wanted to see it operate fairly for both genders, because at this time girls could not be charged with such offenses. The issue of consent in sex cases was such that there was no defense of consent allowable if girls were under the age of 12; in the case of girls in the 12–16 age group, if a girl was the same age as or older than the accused, or if the jury thought a girl appeared to be 16, this could be a defense. A girl might appear to be over the age of consent if "the nature of her clothing, red on her lips, the fact that she is said to smoke and drink, and evidence on other similar matters, enable a verdict of acquittal to be given" (p. 52). The committee did not contest this attitude to appearance, but they also noted concern about the "failure of the law to make it an offence for a sophisticated girl to entice a male into carnal knowledge of her" (p. 52). Girls were clearly perceived as being capable of being seducers and sexually active in ways that were totally unacceptable. The attitude was that if they looked sexy, they probably were sexually active. According to Molloy (1993), Mazengarb's pattern of questioning witnesses followed the notion that the girls were the aggressors, leading the boys astray.

There was no discussion in the report about sexual abuse or incest and its effects, despite the repeated use of four terms or euphemisms that indicated this: "initiate, seduce, corrupt, interfere" (Molloy, 1993: 9). Molloy (1993) noted that despite evidence from social workers that many girls were initiated into sex by older boys and men in what would now clearly be considered to be sexual abuse, this was ignored by the committee. The underlying position was that female sexuality was "illicit, incipient and dangerous to the girl herself and to society. Even in the case of sexual abuse of young girls by older men the act was described in terms which suggest that harm is done by unleashing female sexuality prematurely rather than in direct harm to the person of the girl" (Molloy, 1993: 9).

Psychologists attested to the dangers of female sexuality and the difference between male and female sexuality, where sexual urges and activity, including masturbation, were described as "normal" for adolescent males but not for adolescent girls, in whom it was believed to result from insecurity. In other words, in girls it was a sign that they had psychological problems. The idea that female sexuality, "awakened" through sexual abuse, might involve "violence, transgression of the girl's autonomy or abrogation of a trusting relationship" (Molloy, 1993: 10) was beyond the conceptualization of the times. Despite evidence to the committee, this was ignored, and the discourse of sexual abuse remained part of the silent underbelly of society until the rise of feminism some twenty years later.

The Mazengarb Report posed the moral constitution of adolescence as requiring new laws, new regulations, and stricter administration of these to allay the existing moral panic. This meant no sex, not too much leisure, and certainly no unstructured activities, a life well regulated by adult authorities in school, home, or welfare, not too much money, and regular savings if they did earn money, censored media, and new offenses for adolescents. What was not recognized but can be seen with the benefit of hindsight was that the 1950s were a time of major social changes—urbanization in general, with Maori shifting to the cities amid the rapid development of new, poorly resourced suburbs, a postwar "baby boom", and the emergence of a new and distinct youth culture that was at odds with what many of the older generation considered to be acceptable and proper interests and behavior.

In subsequent reflection and research, the Mazengarb Report has been criticized for being an overgeneralized, overly moralistic document, reflecting Victorian moral values and an exaggeratedly negative view of the youth of the time (Glazebrook, 1978; Molloy, 1993). Glazebrook (1978) questions the public's ability, let alone right, to legislate on morality where youth are rejecting the moral standards of their parents' generation. The excessive media attention given to moral delinquency on the part of a handful of adolescents reinforced the level of mistrust and negativity of adults toward adolescents and adolescence that largely remains today (Lavelle, 1990). Although Goldson (1978) largely endorses the opinion that the Mazengarb Report reflects moral panic, her focus is that the problem for youth in Western societies is one of identity because of the lack of clarity about what constitutes the transition from childhood to adult status. She argues that unlike other societies, in Western society there are no clear, public rites of passage—no puberty rites. no initiation rites, and some very clear contradictions, especially in terms of sexuality. Molloy (1993) argues that societal attitudes in 1954 put an extreme emphasis on domesticity as a counter to the upheavals of war, idealizing the role of the mother as nurturing national prosperity through being the prime influence and nurturer of children—the future of the country. These notions were particularly influenced by Bowlby's work on attachment and loss, which, in turn, focused on maternal deprivation as a source of juvenile delinquency (see Bowlby[11], 1947, 1953, 1969, 1979). Not only did such a notion support the existing patriarchy and women's place as being in the home, it also reflected a fear of female sexuality and the belief that once awakened, it was a powerful and potentially destructive force that needed to be controlled within the confines of marriage. The sexually active adolescent girl was perceived very negatively as being outside family control and authority and hence a threat to public order and decency (Molloy, 1993).

In the 1950s, the commitment to Victorian values meant that adults applied their authority from home, church, and school with a firm and often physically punishing discipline (Ausubel, 1960; Marshall and Marshall, 1997; Ritchie and Ritchie, 1970, 1981, 1990). Ausubel (1960) criticized the way schools in New Zealand controlled and disciplined adolescents by using corporal punishment, the prefect system, school uniforms, and the segregation of the sexes. Along with the exaggerated deference that teachers expected, the disciplinary regimes of the time contributed to the rise of resentful, antiadult, antisocial behavior in youth. He asserted that instead of corporal punishment, in a democratic society the major emphasis in disciplining adolescents should be on self-control, on developing concepts of equity and reciprocal obligation, and on the use of sanctions from democratically elected peers rather than imposed by the hierarchy (Ausubel, 1960). It was a change in focus that saw these very notions becoming adopted with the increased use of social guidance programs and the advent and wider use of school counseling as legislation in the mid-1970s forced New Zealand schools to abandon corporal punishment.

While the 1950s may have witnessed a moral panic regarding the behavior of youth, the late 1960s and 1970s saw many youth in outright rebellion. This era—the "pill" era, the hippie era, the counterculture, and so on—provided a considerable break with the morality of the past. Alongside concerns about a generation gap, the concept of a distinct youth culture and subcultures came to prominence and was studied and theorized as such by sociologists (chapter 4). In the 1990s a succession of moral panics brought it to prominence again after it had largely slipped from sociological interest in the 1980s as the impact of neoliberalism came to the fore. Moral panics have become characteristic of our post-modern society, when major changes create anxiety and the sense of being "at risk" includes economic restructuring, deregulation, immigration, feminism, multiculturalism, new technologies, and new ways of thinking about ourselves. Moral panics are often symptomatic of "tensions and struggles over changes in cultural and moral regulation (Thompson, 1998: 142). Uncovering who produces and disseminates discourses has become important because knowledge is no longer seen as value-neutral or separate from power. Foucault (1980a) points out that the regulation of sexual practices has moved progressively from Victorian repression not to one of deregulation and permissiveness, but to new forms of regulation—of governmentality—managing the conduct of conduct and new technologies of the self. "Moral panics about sexuality, and other issues, represent power struggles over moral regulation" in our contemporary society, where there are multiple and competing "discourses about sexuality and the regulation of bodies, each with different moral implications" (Thompson, 1998: 26). The mass media reflect and amplify these conflicts, which often spiral into a "moral panic," especially when "several examples of deviant behavior can be linked to some general risk from moral degeneracy, such as a threat to children from child abusers, pornography, video nasties, homosexuality, violence on television etc." (Thompson, 1998: 26). However, Cohen has cautioned that new, unnamed moral panics and folk devils will be created, "not because of some inexorable inner logic but because our society as present structured will continue to present problems for some of its members—like working-class adolescents—and then condemn whatever solution these groups find" (Cohen, 1980: 204).

The Mazengarb Report was so concerned about controlling the behavior of youth and their parents, so specific about legislative changes and censorship of popular culture, and so scathing about new social and psychological ideas, yet surprisingly it did not make recommendations for dealing with problem pupils in secondary schools. It left this for the Department of Education to decide, which it did five years later, when it introduced a school guidance counseling pilot scheme. The focus of the next chapter moves to school counseling—one of the prime sites for counseling youth.

CHAPTER 6

SCHOOL COUNSELING: THE ETHICS OF PROFESSIONAL SELF-REGULATION

INTRODUCTION: ETHICS, CODES AND COUNSELING

The chapter shifts the focus of previous chapters from looking at the client of school counseling—youth—to examining the school counseling profession itself. The chapter concerns being and becoming "professional." It focuses on the development of a professional identity through a code of ethics, which we might call, after Foucault, a form of professional ethical self-constitution. In the third section, the chapter examines the double-edged sword of professionalization—that is, the issue of professional autonomy versus the pressures of surveillance and of compliance to the requirements of external agencies in the name of accountability. It focuses on the development of "technologies" and a form of "governmentality" that regulates the "conduct of conduct," thus exercising a form of power/knowledge that helped to shape and direct the activities of counselors (Foucault, 1979b, 1982). Just as Foucault uses the terms "government" and "discipline" in different senses (see Introduction), he uses "conduct" in the sense of both "being led" or "being conducted" and as "behavior" or "conduct." While the chapter briefly discusses aspects of "professionalism" and the process of "professionalization," its main focus centers on describing ethical self-regulation as a major feature of the professionalization of counseling in general and school counseling in particular.

This chapter makes use of Foucauldian terminology and insights to raise the question of ethics in relation to questions of professional self-regulation in school counseling. Foucault provides a clear model for tracing the genealogy of values (and ethics) within the "caring" professions, or the "psy" sciences. Foucault provides us with some substantial clues about the relationship between the sociological fact of codes of ethical practice in general and ethical theory—clues that come to us from the connections he draws among the notions of "truth," "subjectivity," "power," "governmentality," and the development of the disciplines or professions that are discussed in section two.

Because school counselors tend to form a specialty of a larger, umbrella professional association, their professional and ethical standards are generally subsumed under a generic professional code of ethics (e.g., ASCA as part of ACA, NZAC, BACP, CAC[1]). In this chapter, then, unless specifically pointed out, "counseling" and "school counseling" are used interchangeably. As in the previous chapter and for the reasons already outlined, the New Zealand situation and NZAC is frequently used as an exemplar and case study. School counseling in New

Zealand has at times been strongly influenced by counseling and guidance ideas from both the United Kingdom and the United States. British influences, especially that of Cyril Burt and the National Institute of Industrial Psychology, and American vocational guidance emphases were all influential in how guidance evolved in New Zealand schools (Winterbourn, 1974). While there was no formal advice or consultation, their writings and ideas greatly influence counseling in New Zealand, which in time developed its own distinctive systems. There are some clear parallels that counselors from other countries will be able to ascertain.

In addition to New Zealand, the chapter also uses some aspects of the American professional organizations—ACA and its school counselor division, ASCA—as exemplars. This is not to provide a detailed comparative study, but to highlight particular points of similarity and difference and how different times and different social contexts give rise to different forms of codes of ethics and to how counselors are constituted in terms of these ethics (Mabe and Rollin, 1986). In other words, counseling codes of ethics are not universal, nor value-neutral—they can and do change over time and are context-sensitive. The American Counseling Association (ACA) was established in 1952, and the American School Counselor Association (ASCA) was chartered in 1953, the first of what are now 17 specialty divisions of ACA. ASCA currently has a membership of over 12,000. ASCA requires its members to belong to ACA, but although ACA members can join one or more specialties, they are no longer required to do so. Compared with their counterparts in New Zealand, school counselors in the United States are subject to much more formal state control in their professional practices, being regulated by state and federal laws, by case law, and by certification and school-board rules. By 1999, 45 states[2] and the District of Columbia had counselor licensure or certification, providing increased protection for the public and increased professionalism for counselors (<www.counseling. org> 2001).

The notion of ethics is not a twentieth-century construction, although its expression in a *code* of ethics by a profession may well be. Ethics has its antecedents in ancient philosophical traditions that involve the belief systems of individuals and society. As a branch of philosophy, the word "ethics" is often used interchangeably with "morality." Ethics can have a wide meaning, referring to the overall subject matter of this field, or it can have a narrower meaning to refer to the moral principles of a particular individual, group, or tradition. The field is often divided into meta-ethics, applied ethics, and the metaphysics of moral responsibility—the general study of "goodness" and of "right action." It is within the field of ethics that questions are posed about what ends human beings ought to choose to pursue the good life and what moral principles ought to govern these choices.

A traditional account of ethics that makes assumptions about human nature and assumes that we naturally seek the good life has led to the development of a theory of human well being. Accordingly, questions posed about the components of the good life are fundamentally questions about what ends we ought to pursue. In contrast, the other major approach makes no assumption about human nature; it proceeds by arguing that whatever is good in itself is worth pursuing. On the basis of this argument the theory of intrinsic value has developed. The philosophical traditions of hedonism, as espoused by Epicurus and J. S. Mill, and of moral perfectionism, as espoused by Plato, Aristotle, the Stoics, and Nietzsche, form different branches of a theory of well being that first originated in ancient Greek ethics and was known as *eudaimonia*, translated as "happiness" and "flourishing." Both theories are important to counseling, and their adoption leads to quite different conceptions of practice.

Codes of ethics attempt to ensure that behavior accords with societal and organizational belief systems. Yet ethics is both more than and different from simply codes or rules of behavior. In the traditional Western milieu:

> Ethics was good character and what that entailed—good judgment, sensitivity, openness, reflectiveness, a secure and correct sense of who one was and how one stood in relation to other people and the surrounding world. Ethical theory was the study of the best way to *be*, rather than any principles for what to do in particular circumstances or in relation to recurring temptations, or the correct philosophical basis for deriving or validating any such rules. (Cooper, 1999: x)

This statement reflects what is expected of a counselor in terms of personal development, world view and ethical behavior. According to this definition of ethics or morality, counseling is a profession that is permeated with ethical issues and characterized by ethical practices. Perhaps more than any other profession, counseling is constituted in terms of ethical principles, at least ostensibly, for it is conceived as helping or enabling their clients to make choices—often moral choices— for themselves. Hence, counseling at its ethical heart involves implicit claims about the ethics of freedom construed as autonomy for the client—a liberal-humanist orientation. Also, it is clear that as one of the "caring professions, counseling embraces the ethical principle of "care"—of promoting the "interests" of the client above those of anyone else. Certainly, these two principles can be seen to involve the metaphysics of moral responsibility—the counselor has moral responsibilities to the client, which are set in action once a professional counseling relationship is formally established—and a conception of applied ethics, embodying ethical practice. It is in the latter sense that many professional "caring" organizations have begun systematically to formulate codes of practice and of ethics as described for counseling in New Zealand and the United States in the last section.

The current NZAC Code of Ethics is very much in line with this ancient tradition as outlined above. It combines both philosophical and practical components that center on what Kitchener (1984) describes as the five fundamental ethical principles of counseling. After outlining these, it becomes somewhat more practical in detailing fifteen situations in relation to client rights in counseling that spell out more clearly what to do—or, in fact, what not to do—in the counseling relationship. In contrast, the ACA Code of Ethics does not provide any list of ethical principles but, rather, eight sections that provide practical detail (as discussed later).

Ethics can involve ethical appraisal of policy, teaching ethical values as a part of moral education, and professional ethics (Strike and Ternasky, 1993). Professional ethics are distinguishable from, but connected to the other categories. Yet professional ethics has figured very little in the educational literature or counselor training programs until relatively recently. The recent upsurge of interest in professional ethics is related to a range of factors, including public scandals concerning the inappropriate behavior of some counselors, the assumption that increased professionalization would make counseling more effective, and the link with neoliberalism and managerialist notions of accountability as they were developed in the United States, the United Kingdom, and New Zealand since the 1980s (the Reagan–Bush–Thatcher years).

An explanation of some terms is appropriate when discussing ethics and professional standards because some are used almost interchangeably. Corey, Corey, and Callinan (1993) point out that while "values" refer to what is good and desirable, "ethics" involves what is right and correct, particularly in terms of the behavior and conduct of individuals and groups, especially professional organizations. Values may not necessarily always be ethical, but ethics always involves values. Professional standards may or may not involve ethical behavior. For example, it would be unprofessional to use alcohol while at work, but it is not necessarily unethical behavior. Ethical codes usually involve practical components in the form of "mandatory ethics" or behavior that must be complied with to ensure safe practice and to avoid censure. They sometimes involve philosophical or "aspirational ethics" of ideal standards that reflect on the intentionality of the intervention for clients, as in the five principles of the NZAC Code.

Codes of ethics are often pragmatic guides to action that help to regulate the profession by providing guidelines and standards of practice to follow. These codes enable clients to identify malpractice and conflicts of interest and to seek redress through a complaints or disciplinary procedure. While not often discussed in critical terms in the literature, it is the case that codes of ethical practice constitute important sociological criteria for the professionalization of a discipline or activity. A later section looks at this aspect as it examines codes of ethics as a form of self-regulation. In other words, the development of a code of ethical practice forms a framework that allows the profession to reflect upon its own practices, to gain status, power, and credibility in the public realm, and to regulate itself. Ethical codes tend to reflect and embody current societal normative orientations, and they function to institutionalize the profession, often creating a bureaucracy that concerns itself solely with management, organization, and disciplinary functions. In this sense, codes, being pragmatic, tend to be less interested in the relationship between codes of ethical practice, on the one hand, and ethical theory, on the other. Yet it is precisely this relationship that requires close examination if one is to understand larger issues concerning the "governmental," political, or "disciplinary" role that the profession might play within the wider society. To do this, codes of ethics can be "unpacked" in terms of Foucauldian notions, so the next sections outline those very notions and explore them further.

FOUCAULT: A POSTSTRUCTURALIST APPROACH TO SUBJECTIVITY, POWER, AND ETHICS

In this discussion and analysis, a Foucauldian "analytics" of power and his notions of ethical self-constitution and self-regulation are used to inform the discussion of professional autonomy. From a Foucauldian viewpoint, the hallmarks of a profession are ethical self-constitution and ethical self-regulation. These twin concepts refer to the traditional Kantian notion of autonomy, especially in relation to professional practice and accountability. Ethical self-regulation is reflected in codes of professional conduct or codes of ethics by most professions. In addition, it is now customary that the profession institutes a complaints procedure, where charges of professional misconduct or negligence can be heard and dealt with according to established procedures. If the real political task facing our society is to criticize the working of institutions, especially those institutions that appear to be both neutral and independent, as Foucault (1984a) suggests, then counseling, its professional practices, and its codes of ethics are certainly open to scrutiny.

The effect of traditional philosophical questions, such as "What is the world? What is man? What is knowledge? How can we know something?"(Foucault, 1988c, p. 145), has been a focus on knowing and speaking the "truth" of what we are, of our essence or human nature. Foucault derives these notions, the "will to truth," from Nietzsche's *The Genealogy of Morals* (Nietzsche, [1887] 1956). Nietzsche has been influential in contemporary thought in providing a critique of traditional Christian morality, especially of those forms that derived their justification for absolute or eternal values directly from God, as a transcendental guarantee outside the system of values, so to speak. Nietzsche's "method" of genealogy provides a model of historical critique and evaluation of morals that Foucault adopts in *Discipline and Punish* (1977) and in other works. Nietzsche's history of the question of European nihilism provides the theoretical background for the reappraisal of humanism, in both its Christian and its atheistic forms (where man has replaced God) for Heidegger and Foucault.

Poststructuralism, as outlined in chapter 2, challenges the traditional philosophical questions of liberal humanism and structuralism. Foucault links the will to truth "with the success of the professional disciplines in the production of the great meta-narratives of human nature and human development" (White, 1997: 222). Foucault suggests that rather than traditional philosophical questions, as above, there is a change to focus on "the historical reflection on ourselves," and he asks "What are we today?" (Foucault, 1988c: 145). Foucault's ruminations open up interesting possibilities for exploring how our lives—both professional and personal—are produced through cultural knowledges and practices. Traditionally, counseling, at least in its humanist modes, has anchored itself in grand narratives of human nature and development. These grand theories have in large part constituted the body of knowledge and expertise as the basis of professional knowledge and practice. When, along with Foucault, we question theories of human nature, we are, ipso facto, also questioning a body of professional knowledge and a set of professional practices based upon these theories.

The questions "What is man?" and "What is knowledge?" go to the heart of counseling as a profession. Both questions answered in traditional humanist terms give answers that fix both human nature and our understanding of it, essentializing and universalizing "man," "knowledge of human nature and development," and therapeutic or professional practices derived from these theories. Indeed, theories of human nature also form and dictate to us the ethical framework for practice, because ethical protocols are derived or inferred from theories of human nature—that is, theories of morality are often predicated or based upon or assume a theory of human nature. Rather than predicate professional counseling practices and bodies of knowledge upon a theory of human nature (that is, what it is to be human), a Foucauldian approach substitutes a critical reflection on who we are today, replacing questions of ontology with genealogical narratives concerning the social and historical construction of subjectivities—in the plural. Thus, a Foucauldian approach to professionalism and professionalization in counseling is two-edged. Not only does it question "what is man?" and "what is knowledge" in relation to counseling theory and practice, but it also turns the historical gaze back on counseling as a professional, suggesting that all that can be expected is a series of genealogical narratives about the growth of counseling as a profession.

Foucault's earlier work, with its archaeological orientation, fails adequately to explain "agency"—that is, the ability of a person to act and to transform the world. His earlier analysis of power is developed more fully later on with a return to the Kantian subject and to notions of human freedom, of agency, and of the ways in which we ethically constitute or regulate ourselves (Foucault, 1985, 1990, 1997a). The later Foucault does not abolish the self, but he questions the essentialism and humanism underlying the Cartesian-Kantian subject. He returns to the historical production and reproduction of subjectivity as an object of discourse actively constituted at the intersections of truth and power (Foucault, 1988a,b). The notion of the self as the center of narrative gravity stresses the discursive production and reproduction of the self while at the same time preserving a notion of narrative agency, which embodies some aspects of traditional humanism.

The Foucauldian notion of power as formulated in his later work is not a repressive one, as power is usually conceptualized in traditional liberal sociology and in Marxist political thought. For Foucault, it is the "juridico-discursive" conception that is repressive (Foucault, 1980a: 82). Foucault's understanding is that power is not only repressive or negative, but also "positive," not in the sense of being good or benign or something to aspire to, but in the sense of being constitutive in the shaping of people's lives and ideas. Foucault addresses issues of repression and emancipation in his analysis of power relations and its parallel in forms of resistance, in how power operates in a capillary fashion, not simply as a binary opposition between rulers and the ruled (Foucault, 1980a,b, 1984f).

Foucault (1980a) raises *three* distinct doubts concerning the Freudian "repressive hypothesis":

> First doubt: Is sexual repression truly an established historical fact? . . . Second doubt: Do the workings of power, and in particular those mechanisms that are brought into play in societies such as ours, really belong primarily to the category of repression? . . . Third and final doubt: Did the critical discourse that addresses itself to repression come to act as a roadblock to a power mechanism that had operated unchallenged up to that point, or is it not in fact part of the same historical network as the thing it denounces (and doubtless misrepresents) by calling it repression (Foucault, 1980a: 10)?

Foucault (1997a) also warns that the notion of liberation needs to be scrutinized and treated cautiously, otherwise one runs the risk of falling back on the idea that there exists a human nature or base that, as a consequence of certain historical, economic and social processes, has been concealed, alienated, or imprisoned in and by mechanisms of repression. According to this hypothesis, all that is required is to break these repressive deadlocks and man will be reconciled with himself, rediscover his nature or regain contact with his origin, and re-establish a full and positive relationship with himself. I think this idea should not be accepted without scrutiny. (Foucault, 1997a, p. 282)

Foucault tends "to move less toward a "theory" of power than toward an "analytics" of power: that is, toward a definition of the specific domain formed by relations of power, and toward a determination of the instruments that will make possible this analysis" (Foucault, 1980a: 82).

Foucault is primarily interested in *how* power is exercised—in "actions upon actions," which constitute power relations (Foucault, 1982: 220)—and how it involves creative aspects in terms of relationships, discourses, and consciousness (see Introduction). Thus, a Foucauldian interpretation provides a way of understanding the actions of professional counseling associations like ACA and NZAC, as "actions upon the actions" on the part of counselors and school counselors.

The project of ethics that informed Foucault's later work was the liberation of human beings from constraints masked as unsurpassable *a priori* limits and the contemplation of possible alternative forms of existence: "I believe that the concept of governmentality makes it possible to bring out the freedom of the subject and its relationship with others which constitutes the very stuff [*matière*] of ethics" (Foucault, 1991: 102). He analyzes ethics in terms of the free relationship to the self [*rapport à soi*], emphasizing the historical and conceptual relations between truth, freedom, and subjectivity. As Rabinow (1997: xxvii) explains, Foucault examines such a relationship through four basic categories that are to be found in any historical configuration: ethical substance, mode of "subjectivation," ethical work, and *telos*.

Ethical substance is understood in terms of "the will to truth" and refers to "the way that the individual has to constitute this or that part of himself as the prime material of his moral conduct" (cited in Rabinow, 1997: xxix). Mode of subjectivation is understood as "self-stylization or form-giving" and refers to "the way in which the individual establishes his relation to the rule and recognizes himself as obligated to put it into practice" (p. xxx). Critical work constitutes "critical activity" or "thought experience"—that is, "The work one performs to attempt to transform oneself into the ethical subject of one's behaviour" (p. xxxiii). Finally, *telos* stands for "disassembling the self"—as Foucault writes: "The place an action occupies in a pattern of conduct. It commits an individual . . . to a certain mode of being, a mode of being characteristic of the ethical subject" (cited in Rabinow, 1997: xxxviii).

Subjectivation, in particular, has application in understanding not only the processes by which clients "become" subjects, but also how counselors become professionals. Both are concerned with subject making—the making of an autonomous subject, on the one hand, and a professional subject, on the other. It also concerns how individual counselors establish a relation to a rule, practice, or ethical protocol set by the professional organization that obligates them and acts as a template for practice. Thus the crucial element of this cycle of reflection is as a form of *professional self-knowledge* that not only helps to set the parameters within which the counselor engages with the client, but also sets in process the learning processes by which the counselor, in helping others, constitutes him- or herself as a professional.

GOVERNMENTALITY, NEOLIBERALISM, AND THE PROFESSIONALIZATION OF SCHOOL COUNSELING

Governmentality and Neoliberalism

Foucault (1977) suggests that the operation of institutions such as prisons, factories, and schools can be understood in terms of techniques of power that are a form of "power/knowledge" that observes, monitors, shapes, and controls the behavior of people within these institutions. Disciplinary mechanisms, such as "hierarchical observation, normalizing judgement and the examination," develop within disciplinary institutions and enable disciplinary power to be achieved by both training and coercing individual and collective bodies (Smart, 1985: 85).
This enables an understanding of how school counseling, as a profession, involves a form of disciplinary power with its own form of power/ knowledge—a set of practices and techniques operating within schools that assists students to "take care of the self" at best, but imposes a form of domination at worst.

On top of this earlier formulation, Foucault's later analysis of power as a form of ethical self-constitution and governmentality allows us to understand counseling's recent developments under neoliberalism with its demands for accountability and professionalization. Foucault's notion of governmentality, its link with the sociohistorical context and with one instrument of the disciplinary technology of power—the "examination"—that enabled psy sciences like counseling to emerge, was described in the Introduction to this book. The notion of governmentality in this section serves to analyze the professionalization of school counseling.

In Foucault's view, "governmentality" means the complex of calculations, programs, policies, strategies, reflections, and tactics that shape the conduct of individuals, "the conduct of conduct" for acting upon the actions of others in order to achieve certain ends. Governmentality is not simply about control in its negative sense (such as controlling, subduing, disciplining, normalizing, or reforming people) but also in its positive, constitutive sense, in its contribution to the security, health, wealth, and well-being of society.

The formal governance of school counselors is conducted by various authorities, such as professional associations to which the counselor may belong, legislation, and employing authorities. The general purpose of formal governance is to avoid negative effects on clients. Informal forms of governance involve feedback from clients, their relatives, peers, friends, and others who associate with them and who judge the counselor as third parties. Foucault's questions about "how to govern oneself, how to be governed, how to govern others, by whom the people will accept being governed, how to become the best possible governor" have implications for the governance of professionals such as school counselors (Foucault, 1991: 87).

What constitutes a profession has by no means remained static over time or place. Occupations considered to be professional vary from one country to another. Some countries apply the term more broadly than do others. The expansion of the number of occupations assigned the status of "profession" over time largely reflects the concerns of the relevant age. Some professions have maintained a place (medicine, law, architecture), while others (e.g., dentists, veterinarians, accountants) have been added, and still others (e.g., railroad surgeons, psychological mediums, gynecological neurology) have become deprofessionalized and even disappeared (Abbott, 1988). In the eighteenth century the few professions at the time, such as medicine, law, and the clergy, held jurisdiction over health, justice, and the soul, respectively. The industrial age added accountants, bankers, and engineers to the list of professions. The late nineteenth and the twentieth centuries, under the influence of the "welfare state," added teachers, academics, scientists, psychiatrists, psychologists, psychotherapists, counselors, and social workers. The "market" economies of the late twentieth century have seen the rise of enterprise, marketing, and financial professionals, and all those associated with information technology.

Although there is no complete consensus in defining the attributes of a "profession," certain characteristics are common to most professions and distinguish them from other occupations (Abbott, 1988; Caplow, 1966; Etzioni, 1969; Vollmer and Mills, 1966). In contemporary Western society, professionalism requires, first, an appropriate formal tertiary level of education as a minimum standard for entry. This is often in the form of a general undergraduate degree, which is followed by specific professional training, usually at postgraduate level. A major distinguishing characteristic of a profession is the combination of theory and practice—the attempted integration of "academic" and "professional" education into a coherent program for the profession. Second, in some instances entry to a profession is restricted by government regulation and/or by a professional organization. Third, professionalism demands the development of an esoteric body of knowledge, theory, and skills over which professionals have a monopoly. A monopoly in this instance does not imply that there are not overlaps nor instances of shared skills and knowledge and expertise, but that there are some aspects that are separate and distinctive in how these are applied or operate for a particular profession. Fourth, there is autonomy and self-regulation regarding the terms and conditions of practice that may or may not be modified by state or legal regulations. Fifth, a professional organization or association develops with a form of collegial authority that devises and upholds a code of ethics and a complaints procedure that are in many ways specific to that profession. In this respect it can act to discipline members who breach the required codes of ethics and of practice. Sixth, a profession upholds a commitment to a service ideal. An underlying theme is that the relationship between the professional and the client is based on trust, a sense of moral responsibility, and the ideal of serving the interests of the professional community and society as a whole rather than the self-interests of the individual. Seventh, a particular orientation to the profession's clients, which often occurs within the framework of a collegial organization or association, prohibits competition within and withstands challenges to it from outside the profession, all the while aiming to protect both clients and members. All of these features emphasize the special nature of professional power/knowledge and indicate how the professions can act as disciplinary bodies. In this respect they use dividing practices to exclude those who do not meet their criteria for being considered "professional" and disciplinary practices to control those who are considered to be professional. Apart from legislation, the other main means of disciplining professionals is through the rules and activities of governance of professional organizations and associations.

Counseling and, by extension, school counseling in the United States, Britain, and New Zealand largely fit the characteristics of a profession. In New Zealand counseling had achieved three of the four steps listed by Caplow (1966): first, forming a professional association; second, changing the association's name to differentiate it from lower-status occupations; third, promulgating a code of ethics (Miller, 1994). Caplow's fourth step, political lobbying for legislation involving accreditation and credentialing to protect the association, began with NZAC's ratification in 1991 of a process of accreditation of members but has not as yet (2002), despite discussion about registration, been taken further. With the extensive revamp of the membership process from 1997 onwards, and with outside agencies (e.g., the Accident Compensation Commission [ACC], which funds counseling for sexual abuse survivors) recognizing the professional status of NZAC members, the need for accreditation became subsumed under the new membership procedures, which themselves constitute a form of accreditation.

Government regulation and legislation are frequently formulated to ensure that the practitioners of certain professions are both suitably qualified and competent, because their field involves specialized personal services dealing with public health, safety, and well-being. The state often defines and legislates training and registration procedures and awards professional privileges that limit who can legitimately call themselves the relevant professional name (e.g., doctor, lawyer, psychologist, nurse, real estate agent, motor vehicle salesperson). It is noteworthy that neither teachers nor counselors are included in this category.

The ACA provides a lay person's guide to "professional counseling" to distinguish its members from other people who use the term "counseling" that was approved by the ACA Governing Council, October 1999:

> Professional counseling is the application of mental heath, psychological or human development principles, through cognitive, affective, behavioral or systemic interventions, strategies that address wellness, personal growth, or career development, as well as pathology.
>
> Professional counselors undergo extensive education and training which includes at least a master's degree and field training with a solid foundation in human growth and development, career and lifestyle development, social and cultural foundations, group work, practice and internships. Licensure is required in 44 states and the District of Columbia. Professional counselors serve at all levels of schools and universities, in hospitals, mental health agencies, rehabilitation facilities, business and industry, correctional institutions, religious organizations, community centers and private practice. (<www.schoolcounseling.org> 2001).

In the United States counselors are subject to far more government regulation than are those elsewhere. As the official ACA website indicates, most U.S. states have credentialing laws, but licensure does not have a common meaning. Although state regulatory boards mostly use the term "Licensed Professional Counselor," the title of the law does not make it clear what is being regulated. In some states licensure only regulates the use of titles of who may call themselves "professional counselor," in others counselors are certified and the practice of counseling is also regulated (<http://www.counseling.org/resources/licensure_legislation.htm> 2001). For clarification, the ACA provides the following definitions:

> *Certification:* Webster's Dictionary meaning to "vouch for the truth of." Certification is often referred to as a "title control" process because it gives standardized recognition of competence by a professional group or governmental unit but does not grant authority to the holder to practice a

profession. Certification can be awarded to individuals who have met certain minimum qualifications specified by voluntary associations, agencies, or government bodies such legislatures and departments of education. While the concept of certification is fairly simple, the realities of professional certification are more complex. Depending on the type of organization that grants the certificate, the process of certifying professionals can be statutory or nonstatutory. Examples of nonlegislative certification agencies include state departments of education (granted to school counselors and teachers) and independent professional organizations (granted to individuals such as professional counselors, physicians, and social workers). Regardless of the process involved, certification in this study refers to the process whereby professionals are granted the use of a title by verifying that they meet certain qualifications. It does not involve the authorization to practice a profession nor does it regulate the profession.

Licensure: Licensure, unlike certification, is always a legislatively established process of credentialing. Typically, licensure grants a practitioner the legal right to practice through law, while restricting this right to only those persons who hold a license. It is important to note that state laws vary. In some states, state legislated certification may protect both the title and practice of a profession. These states require licensure to render counseling services to the public and the laws are typically referred to as "practice acts or laws." Similarly, some states grant licenses that act more like certification laws by protecting only the title granted to practitioners but not regulating the practice of the profession. These laws are usually referred to as "title acts or laws."

National Board Certification: refers to a certificate granted by nonlegislative, professional organizations and is not tied to any one jurisdiction. There are currently two such national boards that certify professional counselors. These are the National Board for Certified Counselors (NBCC) and the Commission on Rehabilitation Counselor Certification (CRCC). (<http://www.counseling.org/resources/licensure_legislation.htm> 2001)

The ACA further points out the dangers of a situation where the buyer must beware if there is no state certification of counseling. Because people are usually vulnerable when they seek counseling, they should be protected: an untrained, unqualified person counselor might cause greater trauma that is "difficult to reverse" (<http://www.counseling. org/resources/licensure_legislation.htm> 2001). Yet, certification sets minimal standards of effectiveness. Once one has passed examinations in the requisite knowledge and is granted the appropriate certification to practice, all that can be implied is that the person has attained the minimum criteria for entry to the profession. It may well be that they have superior skills and abilities, but this cannot be determined through certification. It then is left to an employer or a client to ascertain more about the person's abilities. Employers do this by observation and through referees' reports, while clients are usually left with only the option of word-of-mouth from other clients or the recommendation of another professional—for example, a referral from a general practitioner to a specialist. Proponents of certification often suggest or assume that the knowledge acquired for achieving certification equates with adequate performance, when this can clearly be demonstrated to be incorrect. Therefore, any effective certification model must include performance standards in its criteria. Just how this is to be done is open to question, since measurement itself poses problems. Knowledge components can usually be assessed via some sort of test, whereas performance components require on-the-job observations. In applying for certification, trainees should be allowed more than one chance to reach this. Counseling trainees need to ascertain their own readiness in applying for certification by checking against the required criteria and by consulting with their trainers (for debates on certification, see Everts, 1987; Hoyt, 1991; Manthei, 1989). Certification involves a considerable extension of the surveillance of counselors and of the policing function of professional associations.

Since 1998, NZAC has been exploring the possibility of reassessing members annually to provide a practicing certificate as a means of maintaining professional standards. However, the association is primarily run by volunteers and only two paid employees, and such a move would involve considerable extra costs in terms of administration and, in turn, an increase in the cost of membership subscription. In the light of the huge amount of work involved with the new membership criteria and the requirement for a supervisor's report for renewal of membership, not to mention some objections from members, NZAC has dropped this proposal (see NZAC, 1998). In lieu of the lack of state regulation of counseling in New Zealand, NZAC has developed a comprehensive set of procedures to ensure the professional accountability and ethical practice and behavior of its members, which is extremely important, given the private nature of the relationship between the counselor and the client. Despite the private nature of counseling, its efficacy is often judged publicly by others, based on what the client may have reported to others and/or how the client is subsequently seen to behave. In this way the counseling activity may be judged publicly by parents, family, caregivers, the client's friends, teachers, deans, principals, school boards, outside agencies, NZAC. Yet this may be quite unfair on the counselor who is hardly able to contest this because of confidentiality requirements.

In New Zealand, while anyone can call himself or herself a "counselor," only counselors who are NZAC members can identify themselves by using the initials MNZAC after their name. In New Zealand, to date, political moves to legislate to either protect the name, "counselor" or to require credentialing have not been a focus for either the government or NZAC. As relative "parvenus," counselors in New Zealand have no legally constituted registration requirements (with the exception of school counselors, who are required to be registered as "specialist teachers"), nor protection of the name of their profession. In 2001, the center-left coalition government is proposing a Health Professional Competency Assurance Bill (HPCA) that will apply to counselors working in the medical and health milieu. At the same time, social workers are seeking registration through legislation; therefore notions of certification and registration are again being debated by NZAC. This is quite a change from the neoliberal political context that prevailed until 2000 and when NZAC had previously debated certification.

During the 1980s, neoliberalism was adopted by many Western governments (e.g., the United States, Britain, and New Zealand—the Reagan/Bush/Thatcher years) to legitimate the attack on the bureaucratic welfare state. Neoliberalism promotes an agenda that is characterized by competition, privatization, and the reform of public institutions using managerialist ideologies that emphasize the four "D's"—decentralization, devolution, deregulation, and delegation—and codifying policy and accountability. Neoliberal ideas have been largely shaped by the political and economic theories of Friedrich von Hayek (1944) and some prominent economists who subsequently established the "Chicago School"[3] (Friedman, 1962). With it, the main strands of American neoliberalism—public choice theory (Buchanan and Tullock, 1962), and human capital theory (Becker, 1964)—were established. Hayek (1944) focuses on the problems of the planned socialist economy where the absence of a pricing system prevents producers from knowing the true production costs and other possibilities and warns of the political dangers of socialism and totalitarianism. After the Second World War, Hayek was concerned that welfare-oriented governments fettered the free market, consumed wealth, and infringed the rights of individuals. Hayek's theories emphasize methodological individualism, the doctrine of spontaneous order, and the notion of *homo economicus* [economic man], based on assumptions of individuality, rationality, and self-interest. Neoliberalism involves an economic rationalization or liberalization that abolishes subsidies and tariffs, floats the exchange rate, frees up of foreign investment controls, and restructures the public sector through corporatization and privatization. It often leads to "downsizing," "contracting out," and a concerted attack on the unions, replacing wage bargaining with individual and collective employment contracts, site contracts, and performance targets. Perhaps most importantly for education, neoliberalism involves the dismantling the welfare state through commercialization, contracting-out services, targeted services, and the promotion of notions of self-responsibility. Under the political doctrine of neoliberalism there is nothing distinctive or special about education or health— rather, they are services, products, commodities to be treated like any other, to be traded in the marketplace (Peters, 1999, 2001a).

The neoliberal commitment to the free market involves, first, the claim that efficiency of the market is a superior allocative mechanism for the distribution of scarce public resources and, second, that the market is a morally superior form of political economy. Yet, although neoliberal policies are identified with a fiscal austerity program that is designed to shrink the public sector, the negative effect in many countries (e.g., New Zealand, the United States, Britain) has been one of increasing the gap between rich and poor and the growth of poverty—hardly what could be argued as "morally superior" results (Boston and Dalziel, 1992). The political philosophy of neoliberalism involves a competitive, possessive form of individualism that is often construed in terms of "consumer sovereignty" and emphasizes freedom over equality and individual freedoms over community freedoms (Peters and Marshall, 1996). The notion of freedom is often individualistic, with negative implications in terms of "freedom from" rather than "freedom to"—especially freedom from state interference. This implies an acceptance of inequalities that are generated by the market. Clearly, such notions have implications for education and for school counseling in terms of counseling as a profession and in terms of the world with which the counselor's clients have to deal.

The extent of state regulation reflects, first a concern that unless the activities of a selected group of occupations is controlled, the public is likely to be at risk of unacceptable practices, and, second, the way society sees the role of the state. A leftist welfare state is often seen as one that strongly values state regulation and control, whereas a neoliberal state is positioned as being more concerned with limiting the power of interest groups and professions through deregulation and decentralized control. Neoliberal governments have promoted competition through the reform and removal of restrictive practices in business and in trade unions, but, largely because of the power and strength of many professional associations, they have had little success in dealing with restrictive professional practices. In a neoliberal environment it is unlikely that lobbying on the part of a professional association for government regulation would be accepted; instead, it would probably be dismissed as representing "self-interest" and "provider-capture." The emphasis on deregulation and competition means that neoliberal governments are unlikely to legislate for registration of counseling unless there is considerable clamor and lobbying from many public bodies (possibly a "moral panic") and probably evidence of highly contentious, unethical, unprofessional practice by people calling themselves "counselors," whether or not they are professional association members.

External, government regulation has traditionally granted many professions a high degree of autonomy and the privilege of self-regulation. Professional self-regulation usually requires members of a profession to join a professional association and abide by a set of professional standards of competence and a code of ethics to ensure the protection of the public. Professional groups that are subject to government regulation have generally achieved high levels of very secure remuneration through being able to control both the supply of its professionals and competition between them (e.g., doctors, lawyers, dentists, accountants). The intent to protect the public inadvertently results in enabling and endorsing professional self-interest and at times results in conflict between these two impulses (for example, criticisms of medical councils and bar associations). Simply being a "professional" has traditionally implied a high level of trust, but in the present era, with a far better educated public, traditional structures, regulations, and privilege are being challenged. Restraints on competition are believed to lead to a lack of innovation, insufficient information for clients, and excessive costs for services, all amidst accusations of professionals promoting their own interests ahead of the public good. Nowadays clients are often less willing to defer without questioning the professional and are far more prepared to complain or even seek legal redress when errors are made. As a result, professional indemnity insurance has become a necessity for both professionals and their employers, and many professional associations have developed more stringent professionalization and accountability procedures. From a neoliberal, managerialist perspective, on the one hand, it could be argued that more stringent professionalization and accountability procedures, such as the monitoring of membership and supervision that has emerged for NZAC members, are about accountability. Yet, on the other hand, from a Foucauldian perspective, they would be considered an example of policing or turning the gaze back on its own profession. If one assumes that counselors are generally on the political left, as some writers do, it may seem somewhat incongruous that they would embrace the sort of training and membership criteria of that characterize right-wing, neoliberal values and economics (Sweet, 1997).

Professional Counseling Associations

How a type of work becomes established as a "profession" with a professional identity is often referred to in the literature as "professionalization." This usually involves the foundation of a professional organization that provides a combination of support, advocacy, and disciplinary measures for its members. The organization sometimes controls entry to the profession. In some instances, membership implies a form of recognition or informal registration that means that only those who belong can lay claim to specific words, such as "professional counselor." It usually develops stringent professional membership criteria, formulates a code of ethics and/or a code of professional practice, has input into the training of prospective members, outlines a set of minimum professional standards for members, promotes itself by distinguishing itself from other related professions, and often produces a professional journal that promotes academic exchange and recent research on theory and practice and/or a newsletter to act as a forum for information, viewpoints, and discussion about professional issues.

A professional organization often deals with demarcation issues. Counseling has attempted to establish itself as a profession in its own right, distinct from psychologists, social workers, and others in the helping area, despite not having a monopoly over the body of knowledge, theory, and skills involved—unlike, for example, law, medicine, or architecture. This body of professional knowledge is used to a greater or lesser extent by psychotherapists, psychologists, social workers, and others in the human services areas, many of whom consider that they "counsel" clients. A professional association has a part to play in encouraging appropriate working conditions for counselors, but not in a uniontype sense, with negotiation and bargaining. Its role is more in terms of lobbying relevant government departments and ministries (e.g., health education, welfare), unions, and other agencies on behalf of counselors to ensure that they work under conditions that are as conducive as possible to act ethically, safely, and professionally. When an association has a large number of its members obtaining a proportion of their counseling income from third-party funders such as insurance companies and HMO's, it may be pushed into focusing on client safety through a discourse of increased professionalization, competence, credibility, accountability, and quality control issues through credentialing and stringent membership criteria (Manthei, 1997a; Miller, 1996). Although not driven by the needs of salaried school counselors, such concerns about issues of professionalism and accountability have an impact on school counseling and on how codes of ethics and professional standards apply to them.

School counseling has changed as a result of many factors, including changes within the counseling profession with the way professional counseling associations have increasingly emphasized professionalization, the introduction of new modalities like narrative therapy, and changes in how youth are perceived, especially in their rights to autonomy and confidentiality. These changes and developments are best described and analyzed in the form of actual cases, so the remainder of this section focuses on some of the changes in two professional associations—ACA/ASCA and NZAC.

School counseling was mostly known as "guidance counseling" when it was introduced into schools in the 1960s in Britain, the United States, Canada, and New Zealand. As counseling changed and developed into a generic profession, guidance counseling became a specialty within this field. For example, in 1990 in New Zealand, the professional counseling association was renamed the New Zealand Association of Counsellors[4] (NZAC), and its focus extended to encompass counseling beyond the educational setting. It had previously been an organization set up by and for mostly school guidance counselors, the New Zealand Counselling and Guidance Association (NZCGA), and the change saw references to "guidance" being dropped (Besley, 2000; Hermansson, 1999). Even in naming the earlier association, the main emphasis was on the term "counseling" rather than on the specific educational connotations of "guidance," hence the order of names, with "counseling" preceding "guidance"; as a result counseling was emphasized in the context of guidance rather than the reverse, which is the more traditional order (Hermansson, 1999). In New Zealand, prior to the advent of school guidance counseling, "guidance" comprised extramural specialist support services for school students, centered on health, welfare, employment, and special education (e.g., school medical officers, district nurses, school dental nurses, visiting teachers, welfare officers, social workers, vocational guidance counselors, educational psychologists). Within schools, "guidance" embraced notions of pastoral care, with teachers getting to know students as individuals and being aware of the educational, social, and personal difficulties they may be having (Small, 1981; Winterbourn, 1974). The job title of "guidance counselor" is an indication of the fairly directive nature of the job in the early years. In line with current NZAC nomenclature, some schools now have replaced it with the title "school counselor," especially where other personnel have taken on the guidance aspects and career advice in large urban schools.

The de-emphasis on guidance did not only occur in New Zealand. The forerunner to ACA, the American College Personnel Association, as the American Personnel and Guidance Association (APGA) was formed in 1952 at a convention of four independent associations: The National Vocational Guidance Association (NVGA), the National Association of Guidance and Counselor Trainers (NAGCT), the Student Personnel Association for Teacher Education (SPATE). The aim was to provide "a larger professional voice." In 1983 "guidance" was dropped as APGA changed its name to the American Association of Counseling and Development. The association was further renamed, in 1992, the American Counseling Association (ACA) "to reflect the common bond among association members and to reinforce their unity of purpose" (<www.counseling.org/join_aca/history.htm> 2001). ASCA is one of ACA's 17 divisions and 56 branches.

> The American School Counselor Association is the national organization representing the school counseling profession. ASCA focuses on providing professional development, enhancing school counseling programs and researching effective school counseling practices. With ONE VISION ONE VOICE, ASCA emphasizes its commitment to all school counselors and all students.
>
> ASCA believes in one vision and one voice and works to ensure it meets the needs of all professional school counselors, regardless of setting, experience level or needs.
>
> With a membership of more than 12,000 school counseling professionals, ASCA focuses on providing professional development, enhancing school counseling programs and researching effective school counseling practices.
>
> ASCA's mission is to represent professional school counselors and to promote professionalism and ethical practices. (<www.schoolcounseling.org> 2001)

While the first professional counseling organization in New Zealand, NZCGA, was set up in 1974, largely as a support group for guidance counselors, its transformation into NZAC in 1990, despite maintaining supportive aspects, arguably involves the administration, policing, and surveillance of members to some extent (Manthei, 1997a,b; Winslade, 1997). It is argued that this role constitutes a form of governmentality at a specific institutional site of power. It is not mandatory for either a counselor or a school counselor in New Zealand to belong to a professional counseling organization like NZAC, but the same membership criteria, and ethical and professional standards apply to all members. Most New Zealand school counselors are not only professionally qualified and registered teachers, but are also professional counselors, and therefore they have at least one and frequently two sets of professional standards to uphold: those of the government and those of NZAC, if they are members. It has been largely taken for granted that guidance counselors are "professional" because until 1996 they had to be teachers of some years standing prior to becoming counselors. As teachers, these counselors were already considered to be "professional" (Besley, 2000). New Zealand school counselors are relatively autonomous and self-regulate the terms and conditions under which they practice within the bounds of their code of ethics and the requirements their work-place.

NZAC does not control entry to the counseling profession as a whole. What it does control is the formulation of the criteria for membership to its own organization, which become a key component in the formation of professional identity and professional practice. But by setting these standards and in turn becoming recognized as *the* organization for counseling in New Zealand, to a certain extent it does exert informal control over the profession. Even the Ministry of Education (1997, 1999a,c) upholds NZAC's professional standards and supervision reports as exemplars for school counselor performance management systems. This is in no small measure the result of the association lobbying government agencies following the removal of their protected status in 1996, when, without any critique or consultation of guidance counseling apart from a report on career guidance (Ministry of Education, 1995), in 1996, all of the previous staffing formula was removed. As part of its deregulation agenda, the neoliberal government of the time repositioned school counselors to be simply part of a global staffing formula, rather than recognizing, as now is the case, that school counselors are "specialist teachers" (Besley, 2000). NZAC has attempted to create an organization whose members operate ethically and professionally, where membership indicates to clients and the public appropriate standards of probity and accountability. This gives NZAC and its members professional credibility against those who call themselves counselors but are not members of any professional organization.

NZAC's concern for professional standards and accountability for all counselors has resulted in the development a wide range of systems and policies. The first is a code of ethics; if the code of ethics is breached, it may result in the member being subject to a complaints procedure that is monitored by an ethics committee and may result in the member being disciplined. A code of supervision must be upheld as part of ethical practice because supervision forms the prime means of facilitating and monitoring ethical counseling practice. Full-time counselors must have regular, fortnightly supervision. Strict membership criteria, administered by a membership committee, have been applied since 1997, and only members can use the initials MNZAC. Apart from special circumstances, members must be trained in theory, skills, and practice at tertiary-level courses that have been approved by the training approval group. Criteria for recognizing supervisors have been developed. Although they have been recently dropped, because they were superseded by the revised membership criteria, accreditation criteria had been formulated for members who displayed advanced counseling skills. For continued membership, existing members are required to accompany their annual subscription with a annual supervisor's report, outlining the fulfillment of ethical requirements about amount and type of supervision and professional development undertaken. As a self-regulatory measure for retaining membership, it clearly relies not just on the integrity of the counselor, but also on that of the supervisor, thus setting up a system of checks and balances. NZAC has formulated a policy on the role of school counselors in relation to the Ministry of Education's national education and administration goals and guidelines. It sends an appointments kit to schools advertising for new school counselors that includes a sample job description, person specification, and training and supervision requirements (Besley, 2000).

Moves for changes in professional standards and in association membership criteria are more often than not reactionary rather than proactive measures. Associations act in response to perceived threats from sources such as inadequate training programs, territorial issues where competing professions challenge the existing standards of counseling practice as a means of justifying excluding counselors from the milieu, concern about the practice of some counselors, clients' complaints about poor or unethical service from association members, defending counseling practice against powerful critics, and in response to government requirements. Associations often decide to take action to circumvent any criticisms that have become too damaging for the association and the profession.

As the organization's membership grew extremely rapidly in the late 1990s, NZAC members became increasingly concerned about client safety, accountability, the quality and effectiveness of counseling, and the quality of the vastly increased number of counseling training providers. The impetus was not simply due to notions of "progress" or "improvement" in counseling, but in response to the requirements of neoliberal managerialist ideology in the name of accountability in an increasingly lower trust environment that seeks to minimize risk in all sorts of ways. The sociopolitical context of the 1970s and until the mid1980s was very different. It was a welfare state that only began to be rolled back or contracted after 1984, when neoliberal managerialist ideology was applied in what became known as the "New Zealand experiment" (Boston, 1995; Kelsey, 1993, 1995). Limitations were noted in the existing process for approving and retaining membership, supervision of members was not rigorous enough, the complaints procedure needed tightening up and the code of ethics was in need of review in order to clarify ethical standards for NZAC membership in the increasingly deregulated and competitive neoliberal environment. Considering that counseling occurs in a private setting where a relationship with the client is central to the work undertaken, "counselling can only ever be safe in the hands of a self-regulating autonomous professional" Webb (1998: 13). NZAC developed a series of professionalization and accountability measures in the late 1990s. These measures involved establishing new subcommittees that devised and implemented new policy and criteria, including tightening the criteria for both new and ongoing membership, setting criteria for "recognized supervisors", upgrading the complaints procedures, and establishing criteria for approving training courses.

One of the key changes for NZAC has been in the criteria for both new and ongoing membership. The former were huge, the latter more in terms of evidence than of changed substance. In the 1970s and 1980s, membership criteria for NZCGA and the early NZAC were vastly different from the detailed criteria that have been required since 1997. The membership criteria for NZCGA were:

a. persons who are, to the satisfaction of the National Executive Committee, engaged for 12 hours or more per week in the area of counselling and/or guidance in an educational institution or related service;
b. persons who are engaged in or who have satisfactorily completed a course of full-time professional training in the area of counselling and guidance;
c. persons who are invited to become members by resolution of the National Executive Committee (NZCGA Constitution, 1977, cited in Hermansson, 1999: 34–35).

In the NZCGA era, the only formal counseling training was at postgraduate level and only for trained teachers appointed as guidance counselors or vocational guidance counselors. Once the association became the NZAC, with membership open and available to counselors from other than the education sector, university training was no longer a given. Counselors who were in private practice or in agencies other than education may or may not have received training from various sources and have built up a high level of skills over many years in practice. So, after 1997, the new NZAC membership criteria are as follows:

NZAC Membership Criteria, 1999
Member: The following shall be eligible for membership

1. *Through approved training.* A person who:
has completed a cohesive and comprehensive counselling training through a course approved by the Association, and has a record of bi-cultural learning and/or experience, including marae experience, has sensitivity to treaty of Waitangi issues, and can demonstrate an understanding of Tikanga Maori, and has completed a self-awareness and personal growth component including counsellor as client and group therapeutic process, and has completed face to face practice as a counsellor (400 hours), and has submitted a recent satisfactory report from a supervisor acceptable to NZAC who has been the candidate's supervisor for at least 6 months, and has had their suitability for membership confirmed in an interview by a panel of Members on behalf of the Membership committee.
Notes: An approved training programme is of a minimum one-year full time equivalence and integrates relevant cultural and social awareness and sensitivity; theoretical knowledge; skills training; personal awareness; professional practice; and practice supervision components. Of the 400 hrs of counselling practice, a minimum of 100 hours is to be completed and supervised during training and a minimum of 200 hours post-training. The post-training face-to-face counselling is to have been supervised for at least 20 (1 hour) sessions with a supervisor acceptable to NZAC.

2. *Through particular circumstances.* A person who:
   is granted membership based on the person's particular circumstances and presents with the qualities, knowledge, skills and experience of a candidate who qualifies under (1) and has a record of bi-cultural learning and/or experience, including marae experience, has sensitivity to treaty of Waitangi issues, and can demonstrate an understanding of Tikanga Maori, and has completed a self-awareness and personal growth component including counsellor as a client and group therapeutic process, and has a record of satisfactory face to face practice as a counsellor (400 hours), and has submitted a recent satisfactory report from a supervisor acceptable to NZAC who has been the candidate's supervisor for at least 6 months has had their suitability for membership confirmed in an interview by a panel of Members on behalf of the Membership committee.
   Notes: This option is a vehicle for recognising personal development, learning and experience from a variety of sources, including extensive supervised counselling practice, which the candidate has been able to integrate to form their own professional foundation for counselling work. The onus is on the candidate to demonstrate that they have acquired in other ways, the awareness, theoretical knowledge skills and experience normally found in an approved training programme, achieved appropriate levels of competency and integrated different sources of learning. Detailed information and evidence must be provided.

3. *Through special invitation.* A person who is invited to become a member by resolution of the National Executive. (see Hermansson, 1999: 156–157)
   Part of the changed criteria involved an interview for the membership candidate at the final stage, at the discretion of the membership committee. Another change allowed members to take temporary leave from active membership of NZAC; this was needed in an environment that saw supervisors' reports being a requirement to accompany subscriptions to maintain ongoing membership (Besley, 2000).
   A set standards and competency levels has been developed for "recognized supervisors," but as yet not all counselors who provide supervision are expected to be "recognized." An NZAC Recognized Supervisor must be an NZAC member for at least two years have been trained in supervision, and be very experienced in counseling supervision and being able to demonstrate their skills to the accreditation committee (NZAC, 2000).

Another set of measures established an ethics committee and developed a much more rigorous complaints procedure "to protect, not only the interests of the Association, but also the rights of individual members including those against whom complaints have been made" (NZAC, 1992: 6). The only sanction provided prior to this was termination of membership if the member was found guilty of bringing the association into disrepute (Crocket, 1992). The NZAC ethics committee has a threefold role: to "process complaints brought against members of the Association; to advise the National Executive on ethical issues and to stimulate discussion and thinking about high standards of ethical care among members of the Association" (Winslade, 1998: 32). To date there has been no research published that details the number of complaints, what sector they are against (e.g., private practice, agency or school counselors, new or established counselors), or which parts of the code are the focus of complaints. This would provide useful information in updating the code and the complaints procedure. It would also provide an indication to members and other interested parties of the level of professional self-regulation and of accountability that is provided by membership of NZAC. Despite the lack of formal research, until 1999 complaints to the Ethics Committee[5] have been inadvertent actions whereby the counselor was caught up in either their own personal situation or agenda or in a community situation, especially in a small town. Good-quality supervision might have prevented these problems, so this was often the recommendation of the ethics committee in cases that did not go to formal complaints hearings.

That most complaints have been against counselors in private practice and only one or two against school counselors should not be surprising. The counselor in private practice is often working alone, without the support of an agency or institution to ensure accountability and supervision. Furthermore, clients of agency and school counselors are likely to complain first to the institutional authorities who would be expected to resolve things satisfactorily, before or even instead of complaints being taken to NZAC. School pupils and their parents are probably less likely to know about the code of ethics and the existence of a complaints procedure than are adults in other counseling situations. After all, unlike the health sector, where posters outlining client rights adorn walls, schools seldom, if ever, do this. Schools have tended to be quite self-protective and to keep things in-house, but this may change in the current era that highlights client rights in many public sectors.

Is setting professional standards a form of surveillance or a policing of members? In answer to this, serious questions are posed about the role of a professional association, its aims, philosophy, beliefs, form, and structure, and whom it represents. Is it practical, let alone desirable, for a professional association to police individual members' behavior and professional practices? (for a discussion of this in NZAC, see Manthei, 1997a,b; Sweet, 1997; Winslade, 1997). An association's decisions are often made at annual general meetings (AGMs), where the actual numbers voting reflect an extremely low proportion of the membership— something that, despite being an avowedly democratic process, could be argued to be undemocratic. Yet most associations send out remits to members prior to their meetings, allowing for proxy votes to be submitted. Furthermore, any changes that are total anathema to the membership can be overturned at subsequent AGMs. Some associations now attempt to address this by instituting postal voting. Such are the issues of democracy at work in the governance of professional organizations. Like many organizations, as NZAC becomes larger and more professionalized, it risks becoming more bureaucratic, with some members perceiving a distance between themselves and those holding power as office-holders of the association. Criticism of the changes is oriented and informed by Foucauldian notions. What is not spelled out in these criticisms is just how powerful NZAC has become, and how this is bound up with a form of governmentality that uses its power-knowledge in a system of surveillance of members.

CODES OF ETHICS AS PROFESSIONAL SELF-REGULATION OF SCHOOL COUNSELING: ACA AND NZAC

Counseling codes of ethics serve several purposes: to provide a set of standards to guide the counselor's professional practice by clarifying the counselor's responsibilities to clients and to society as a whole, to state how clients rights are protected, and to guide a counselor's behavior through a process of ethical decision making. Several other purposes, though seldom stated explicitly, are to establish an association's professional identity, to differentiate itself to a certain extent from other professions, to improve its professional status in the workplace, and to establish a form of accountability and acceptable professional standards of service delivery with implications for legal liability, especially in malpractice and negligence cases Wilcoxon, 1987). Yet the ACA is explicit about how its code will be used "as the basis for processing ethical complaints initiated against members of the association" (ACA Code of Ethics, 2001).

A code of ethics, while it may differentiate one profession from another, also has a role to play in bringing a profession into line with the standards of related professions. There is always a danger of a code being a set of motions that one simply goes through to fulfill the criteria of being a professional. But the hope of many professions is for it to be more of a "living" document, more of a way of life, so there is a high degree of congruity between members' professional ethical practice and their behavior and "responsibleness" in their personal life, beyond their professional life. This is very much an expected characteristic of a counselor.

It is sometimes suggested that the development of codes of ethics and education in professional ethics are signs of a profession's "coming of age" or maturity. The counseling profession in New Zealand (NZCGA) has had a code of ethics since 1976—not necessarily a point in time when counseling would be considered "mature" (Abbott, 1988; Hummel, Tal-butt, and Alexander, 1985). Hummel and colleagues (1985) point out that for counseling, maturity is not just about professional maturity; it also requires personal maturity, because of the interpersonal nature of the counseling relationship. Adopting a developmental stage model is not particularly useful, because considering that as such codes change over time, so an association's maturity also changes, and that is debatable.

To illustrate how codes of ethics change over time and in different contexts, the 1976 NZCGA code provides an example. Bob Manthei, an American, formulated the NZCGA Code of Ethics in 1976, basing it somewhat on the codes of similar associations (the American Psychological Association and the American

Counseling Association).[6] It remained in place for the next fifteen years. A review of this code and the establishment of more clearly defined complaints procedures have occurred since NZCGA became NZAC in 1990. The NZAC code is again under review, so that after widespread membership consultations, a new code was adopted in June 2002 (NZAC, 2001). In New Zealand it was because of the special nature of the job that school guidance counseling developed and pushed for its counselors to adhere to a code of ethics long before the managerialist ethos of the neoliberal environment of the mid-1980s encouraged the development of this in education and in other areas.

Although many codes of ethics seem to be written with autonomous adults in mind, the NZCGA code was written primarily for school guidance counselors, yet it did not provide specific guidelines or recipes for the behavior of guidance counselors. The NZCGA code consisted of six principles relating to autonomy, confidentiality, beneficence, fidelity, and professional development—some, but not all, of the principles that became part of NZAC's 1991 code and its amendments. The NZCGA code reflected the fact that NZCGA was primarily an association for counselors in educational institutions—mostly guidance counselors dealing with adolescents in secondary schools, who would not have been considered to have rights of confidentiality at this time. Furthermore, it had a very different, looser definition of confidentiality than the current NZAC code, and it did not provide sufficient protection for clients. It did not deal with nonmaleficence, social justice, or supervision, nor did it state that sexual intimacy between counselor and client was unethical. It implied a high level of sharing of information within the school and to parents, which would have been acceptable at the time because the guidance orientation was directive, compared with today's attitude which emphasizes autonomy. This code refers particularly to relationships with employers and professional colleagues and is not particularly specific in describing the relationship with clients. It emphasizes the role of counselor as change agent in their institutions. The counseling relationship and client rights were expanded considerably in the code that was subsequently revised.

The usefulness of codes highlights a major tension over philosophical and practical elements and has an impact on how the identity of a profession is formulated. Should the code have a philosophical orientation with an expression of broad principles and guidelines that may be open to various subjective interpretations and misinterpretations? Or should it be essentially a practical code, dealing precisely with situations with which professionals frequently have to deal? The answer does not need to be an either/or but tends to be—and perhaps needs to be— context-sensitive. Codes can encompass both, as has the NZAC code for counselors in contrast to the earlier NZCGA code and the ACA code.

The ACA Code of Ethics (1995) is extensive and seems to attempt to cover almost every eventuality in a country where all forms of counseling exist in a highly litigious milieu; it also has a related set of standards of practice. On top of these, ASCA provides a set of 32 position papers on issues such as child abuse/neglect prevention, confidentiality, critical incident response, discipline, and group counseling to clarify how its members are expected to deal with children and young people (<www.schoolcounseling.org> 2001).

The CAC Code of Ethics (1999) contains six fundamental ethical principles: respect for the dignity of persons, not willfully harming others, integrity in relationships, responsible caring, responsibility to society, and respect for self-determination (<www.ccacc.ca/coe.htm> 2001). This is followed by a set of six steps that should be considered in ethical decision making. The NZAC Code of Ethics (1995) covers five fundamental principles of counseling—autonomy, doing no harm (nonmaleficence), beneficence, justice, and fidelity—and fifteen situational principles regarding the counseling relationship and client rights that are provided in full on the website (<www.nzac.org.nz>). The five fundamental principles are:

NZAC Code of Ethics, 1995
The Five Principles

1 *The principle of autonomy:* Counsellors shall respect the dignity and worth of every individual, the integrity of families/whanau and the diversity of cultures. This implies respect for people's right to make decisions that affect their own lives, to choose whether or not to consent to anything that is done to them or on their behalf and to maintain their own privacy. Exceptions to the principle of autonomy occur when there is clear danger to the client, counsellor or public at large and when the individual's competence to make a decision is clearly limited.

2 *The principle of not doing harm:* Counsellors shall avoid any diagnostic labels, counselling methods, use of assessment data or other practices which are likely to cause harm their clients.

3 *The principle of beneficence:* Counselling is a helping profession which expects counsellors to act in ways that promote the welfare and positive growth of their clients. In situations where there is the possibility of both harm and benefit the responsibility is on counsellors to ensure that their own actions are chosen with a view to bringing about the greatest balance of good.

4 *The principle of justice:* Counsellors shall be committed to the fair andequitable distribution of counselling services to all individuals and social groups. Counsellors shall also promote social justice through advocacy and empowerment.

4. *The principle of fidelity:* Counsellors shall be honest and trustworthy in all their professional relationships. (NZAC, 1995: 21–22)

The principle of autonomy involves notions of clients' rights to choice and taking responsibility for their actions, so long as they and others are not endangered. This implies rights of privacy, informed consent, and confidentiality. Nonmaleficence derives from medicine and obliges counselors to provide services that not only do no harm but have positive outcomes for clients. Beneficence is critical to counseling because of the flow-on effect: since clients benefit, society permits the profession to operate because counseling is perceived to be good for humanity. As a corollary, incompetent, dishonest counselors undermine the profession by bringing it into disrepute if the public lose faith in counseling. The notion of justice centers on the assumption of equity, with all people deserving equal access to services, but it is consistent with acknowledging diversity. Fidelity involves faithfulness, keeping contracts, loyalty, and honesty. Without these, others' rights cannot be respected.

The code expands these five principles to cover the counseling relationship and client rights in fifteen situations: access, consent, confidentiality, discrimination, impartiality, group counseling, abuse of power, sexual harassment, fees, referral, termination, competence and professional development, responsibility to the wider community, responsibility to colleagues and the profession, and relationship with employing institutions. These situations all have important implications for the manner in which school counselors perform their work, and they are therefore components to be considered in terms of their relationship with adolescents, their professional identity, and their accountability.

Since many of the ethical dilemmas that counselors will face are likely to be unique, ethical principles should address broad issues and not be legalistic, because dealing with every possible circumstance that may arise is an impossibility. Counselors needed to develop their own moral conscience or sense of "responsibleness" that extends beyond the notion of "responsibility," which denotes an obligation to an external standard or authority—that is, a code of ethics or a set of professional standards. If it is not codified, can counselors then act freely and unethically?—not if they follow broad ethical principles and use a sense of "responsibleness" (Bond, 1992, 1993; Tennyson and Strom, 1986).

Yet it is in an environment that is fraught with legalistic challenges and what has become almost a tradition of seeking to assign blame and suing for vast amounts of money as compensation or damages that the ACA have formulated their code of ethics. This code is extensive and makes an attempt to cover all sorts of eventualities—perhaps not surprisingly, considering not only the context in the United States, but also that ACA represents some 60,000 members form seventeen different divisions of counseling specialty (e.g., Association of Adult Development & Aging [AADA]; Association of Counselor Education a & Supervision [ACES]; American Mental Health Counselors Association [AMHCA]; National Career Development Association [NCDA]). The ACA Code of Ethics comprises eight sections: "the counseling relationship; confidentiality; professional responsibility; relationships with other professionals; evaluation, assessment, and interpretation; teaching, training, and supervision; research and publication; and resolving ethical issues." (ACA Code of Ethics, 2001). Each section has several subclauses. ACA members must adhere to both the code of ethics and the interlinked standards of practice which provide minimal behavioral statements of each section of the code. The code of ethics provides "further interpretation and amplification of the applicable Standard of Practice" (ACA Code of Ethics, 2001).

What is of particular interest for school counseling is how these codes position children and young people. Although all sections of the ACA code apply to children and youth, only one makes specific reference to them:

B.3. Minor or Incompetent Clients.When counseling clients who are minors or individuals who are unable to give voluntary, informed consent, parents or guardians may be included in the counseling process as appropriate. Counselors act in the best interests of clients and take measures to safeguard confidentiality.
(See A.3.c.)

In the United States, "minor" has varying definitions under different legislation, but it mostly refers to persons under the age of 18. In the Children's Defense Act of 1999 (H.R.2036) a "minor" is defined as any person under the age of 17 years, and in the Parents' Empowerment Act (HR 5045) a minor is under the age of 18. In the Child Custody Protection Act (H. R. 1218) "the term 'minor' means an individual who is not older than the maximum age requiring parental notification or consent, or proceedings in a State court, under the law requiring parental involvement in a minor's abortion decision" (<http://thomas.loc.gov/> 2001). ASCA's 32 position papers provide much more amplification of dealing with issues related to counseling children and youth. The ethical challenges that arise usually involve consent, confidentiality, and ability and competence, parent/caregiver rights, and child rights. The notion of informed consent depends on what and how information is presented and anticipates a rational approach to relatively unknown outcomes or risks. In the light of this, when and whether children become sufficiently "understanding" to be able to give their consent freely and autonomously and have sufficient ability to make a wise choice in their own interests invokes notions of "competence," which often rest on developmental presumptions about how decisions are made and on responsibilities that are attributed to the individual. Because of their age, immaturity, and presumptions about their intellectual and moral reasoning, children and youth are often perceived as incompetent or of diminished responsibility. But chronological age and competence are by no means the same thing, and assumptions about limited reasoning and maturity are open to debate. Article 12 of the UN Convention on the Rights of the Child links a consideration of children's views and feelings in procedures affecting them to a combination of their age and their competence. The ACA Codes of Ethics highlighted in this chapter attempt to address competence rather than age in dealing with young people.

How do counselors learn about ethical codes and behavior? One could assume that this comprises a paper or part of a paper in counselor education courses. Yet, interestingly, such courses seem to have only relatively recent emerged, especially since the neoliberal politico-economic environments of many Western countries in the mid-1980s emphasized accountability for professionals and challenged and de-emphasized existing notions of trust of professionals.

The idea that ethical conduct can be developed via professional ethics courses is open to critique. While intended for people to behave better in their professional life, many professional ethics courses ignore the importance of character, which is "usually formed over many years and is at least as much a matter of habituation and training as it is of cognition and reflection" (Strike and Ternasky, 1993: 5). Courses that only signal what is unacceptable behavior without encouraging a genuine commitment to reasonable moral standards and those that do not examine the institutional structures, "their prevailing ethos, and the pursuant socialization that initiation into the profession provides" are inadequate (Strike and Ternasky, 1993: 6). This is because a professional ethics course may not necessarily counter a morally unhealthy ethos and may, in fact, be a substitute for critique and reform. It must therefore be with such reservations and concerns in mind that appropriate and effective professional ethics courses are structured.

The importance of ongoing professional development is clearly recognized by NZAC and is enshrined the code of ethics, although the hours and acceptable types of ongoing professional development are not spelled out. Professional development is important because the useful life span of the knowledge components of formal vocational training is considered to be about five years. As knowledge shifts, expands, deepens, and broadens and as counseling theories change, with some gaining or losing favor, counselors need to keep abreast of these and may need to develop new skills. They need a systematic maintenance, improvement, and broadening of knowledge, skills, and personal qualities that are not just a blanket openness to the new, but are also a critical evaluation of these and of earlier theories. Experience, too, is important, because it enables a counselor to recognize what knowledge and skills are important to develop and retain and how to use both existing and new knowledge more effectively. Therefore the notion of lifelong education and training becomes an essential part of counselor professional and ethical behavior.

While NZAC had a code of ethics right from its inception, it was only later that it developed a code of supervision. An ethical requirement listed under "competence and professional development" requires members to uphold the code of supervision and to have regular supervision. This code sets out standards for supervisors to meet so that counselors seeking supervision are informed and protected about what to expect in the relationship. The "Preamble to the code of supervision" sets out the intent and the need for supervision:

> The NZAC Code for Supervision is intended to promote the professional development of counsellors in order to best meet the needs of clients. It is therefore intended to be consistent with the Code of Ethics and Objects of the NZAC. In keeping with this, it is based on an absolute commitment to respecting the dignity and worth of each person, in particular of our clients, our colleagues, and ourselves. The NZAC Code of Ethics states that all Members and aspiring members of the association must have regular supervision with professionally competent supervisors. The need for supervision does not decline with experience or training, although the type of supervision may change. (NZAC, 2000: 27)

The code of supervision comprises six sections: the nature of supervision, responsibility in supervision, competence in supervision, management of supervision, and confidentiality in supervision. A full-time counsellor is required to have fortnightly supervision. For part-time counselors (less than 10 client contact hours per week), supervision is prorated. But regardless of the amount of time spent counseling, a counsellor is still expected to have supervision at least monthly. The supervisor is expected to belong either to NZAC or to another similar professional body with a code of ethics and to be familiar with counseling.

Counseling supervision is aimed at ensuring safety for clients by ensuring that the counselor is competent and behaves ethically. The supervisor provides support in a collaborative environment for the counselor and is able to be apprised of counseling issues, skills, and problems that the counselor may present through case studies, verbatims, or audio or video tapes. These are critiqued with the counselor, who is enabled to consider alternative or better practices, to examine any difficulties, transference, and parallel processes that may be involved. To protect the privileged nature of the counseling relationship, the code of supervision requires that supervisors maintain confidentiality. One surprising exception is:"Where it is clearly stated otherwise in a supervision contract" (NZAC, 2000: 29). Why this clause should exist is open to both criticism and question. Other exceptions are when there is serious concern about the client's welfare and the counselor is unable or unwilling to deal with this, and when disciplinary action is being pursued against the counselor.

The NZAC Code of Supervision is almost as long as the code of ethics and is quite detailed, being both descriptive and prescriptive about what, who, and how supervision is to be conducted and by whom. It provides more detail of the "what" and "how" of supervision than the code of ethics does about counseling, probably because the concept of supervision was not enshrined in the NZCGA Code of Ethics until the revamp of NZAC's code in 1991. It probably reflects something of what those who formulated believed was required for informing counselors about supervision. One of the proposed changes in the current review is that the code of supervision be abbreviated and incorporated into the code of ethics.

Supervision can become a disciplinary practice particularly if the supervisor is expected to provide an evaluation report to employing organizations or third-party funders—(such as ACC, schools)—as a means of appraisal and accountability. A perhaps less feasible but more appropriate check of accountability would be to ask clients about the quality of the counseling they receive. If power is assigned to supervisors to act in an overseeing, evaluative, hierarchical, judgmental manner, then there is a danger that counselors will stop disclosing their vulnerabilities and difficulties and will no longer seek help. To maintain the impression of competence, they will, instead, present only their best work in supervision. Instead of ensuring client safety, supervision would become primarily a disciplinary relationship. For supervision to remain a supportive, open, trusting, nonevaluative relationship, counselors need to separate out clinical supervision from line management supervision within their employing agencies.

But in professional associations, if the evaluative gaze tends to focus more on individuals than on training programs, it can create anxiety that undermines the professional confidence of members and can, in turn, inadvertently lower professional standards instead of raising them. Rather than an association's role being one of policing, members should be made aware of required ethical and professional standards and should be expected, as part of what constitutes being "professional," to take responsibility for their own ethically competent practice.

Policing members involves a burgeoning cost financially. There is no easy, effective, or affordable way of policing or ensuring that a professional association's annual check on every member can ensure that each is practicing according to some mythical standard of safety. In the process of policing its members, an association can become increasingly controlling and exclusionary, not only about who qualifies for membership but also about how members practice counseling, through more stringent and restrictive requirements for training, membership, and supervision. In Foucauldian terms, these practices could be seen as "dividing practices."

While a complaints procedure exists to deal with serious ethical issues of client safety, where should the responsibility lie in ensuring that association members meet the requirements of the codes of ethics? Should the onus be on members, their supervisors, or the association? Despite changes to the code of ethics, questions remain about the actual quality and standard of professional counseling that is achieved.

Foucault (1988a, 1997a) noted that in our modern world, when ethics are referred to, it is usually in the sense of sets of rules or codes that govern the conduct of conduct, rather than in terms of personal ethics. The professional disciplines take up the notion of institutional rather than personal ethics in an effort to ensure safe professional conduct. For counseling, ethics are couched in terms of client safety, the avoidance of harm or exploitation, and harnessing top-down forms of accountability that hierarchies or management might require as part of their performance management systems. Many counselors whose income is derived from third-party funders are forced to belong to a professional organization that has ethical codes, professional standards, and complaints procedures in place. But top-down accountability may not prevent and may, in fact, mask the very exploitation it is intended to counter. Taken-for-granted assumptions could be challenged by harnessing a principle of transparency that is "based on a commitment to the ongoing deconstruction of our own actions . . . ways of being in this work [therapy] . . . ways of thinking about life . . . that requires us to situate our opinions, motives, and actions in contexts of our ethnicity, class, gender, race, sexual preference, purposes, commitments, and so on" (White, 1997: 150). In this way we can "identify and challenge the practices and structures of domination of our culture" and develop an alternative, bottom-up form of accountability in the form of partnership and collaboration with people or groups that is constitutive of our lives and "brings many possibilities for us to become other who we are" (White, 1997: 150).

Although codes of ethics tend to be reactive rather than proactive, the way they change over time makes it clear that they are not set in concrete and that professional counseling organizations are, and need to be, self-reflective so that their codes are reviewed from time to time. There is often tension and confusion about what constitutes a code of ethics and a code of practice. It is within the latter that ethical dilemmas and guidelines for ethical decision making can be elaborated in exploring issues of right and wrong, of morality, and of what constitutes "a good life." Ensuring ethical, culturally sensitive practice requires more than just a knowledge of a code of ethics It does, at least, provide a starting point, but a code is not a substitute for active, reflective professional and personal ethical decision making.

CHAPTER 7

FOUCAULT, NARRATIVE THERAPY AND SCHOOL COUNSELING

> It may be that one of the defining characteristics of European approaches to the development of narrative-informed counselling and psychotherapy is that being philosophically grounded represents an alternative to the pragmatic, empiricist, instrumental therapies and health-care systems that have come to dominate the global psychotherapy scene in recent years. (McLeod, 2000a: 333)

INTRODUCTION

In this chapter I explore the impact of the work of Michel Foucault on "narrative therapy" as initially developed by Michael White (Adelaide, Australia) and David Epston (Auckland, New Zealand) in *Literate Means to Therapeutic Ends* and *Narrative Means to Therapeutic Ends* (White and Epston, 1989, 1990).[1] Their work shows that European strands of narrative-informed therapy are by no means alone in being informed by philosophy. Furthermore, narrative therapy is part of a broader movement within philosophy, the humanities and the social sciences—the linguistic turn (Rorty, 1967)—which promised agreement among philosophers by shifting discussion to the metalevel to study the language of representation rather than the referents or objects themselves. The change to "narrative," while part of the wider linguistic turn, can also be seen as a response to the formalism and scientific pretensions of structuralism by poststructuralist thinkers (Onega and Landa, 1996). Poststructuralism's affinities and divergences with structuralism were outlined in the previous chapter. The second section of this chapter outlines the notion of "narratology"—the science of narrative.

What is significant is that this new form of counseling emerged from the study of the work of a group of social science theorists with post-modern and poststructuralist orientations, rather than from traditional therapy sources in the psychological oriented discourses. The third section of this chapter highlights several poststructuralist theorists and earlier Foucauldian themes that influenced White and Epston's pioneering formulation of narrative therapy. The importance of language and meaning to counseling, as exemplified by structuralist and poststructuralist modes of thought, is profound and had been largely unexplored by counselors until narrative therapy emerged. On this account, it is held that language not only affects how we frame our notions of the self and identity, but also how counselors deal with people and their sense of meaning of the in which world they live.

Narrative therapy takes up the Foucauldian critique of the assumed neutrality of education and school counseling—institutions that often seem unaware of their power-knowledge relationships (see Marshall, 1996). As McLeod (2000a) indicates in the opening quotation, narrative therapy challenges humanism and the dominant discourses in the "psy" sciences, such as psychology, psychotherapy, and counseling, by examining questions of self, cultural contexts, power, and the way power relations help to shape, legitimize, and constitute personal narratives (McLeod, 2000a; Rose, 1989, 1998). Narrative therapy's challenge to psychological discourse and humanist counseling becomes the focus of the fourth section.

Since the late 1980s, various strands of narrative-informed therapy have developed in Australia, New Zealand, the United States, and Europe, along with a burgeoning literature (see for example, Freedman and Combs, 1996; McLeod, 1997; Monk et al., 1997; Parry and Doan, 1994; Payne, 2000; Smith and Nylund, 1997; Speedy, 2000; White and Epston, 1989, 1990; Winslade and Monk, 1999). The earlier theories of White and Epston have been developed further by many other writers and practitioners, so once the opening sections of the chapter have dealt with philosophical grounding and influences on the emergence of narrative therapy, the fifth section of this chapter provides a brief overview of the general set of notions and terminology that are used in particular ways in the practice of narrative therapy.

Although it was initially developed for family therapy, the promise held by narrative therapy of providing a way of addressing power and ethical issues through harnessing the metaphor of narrative saw it being taught in the counselor education program at Waikato University, New Zealand, and applied in some New Zealand secondary schools in the 1990s. Almost all New Zealand secondary schools, state and private, have at least one school counselor who deals with students' personal issues. They or other staff may deal with vocational and educational guidance. In the school setting, narrative therapy not only presents a new form of counseling, but also provides an indicator to a different way of dealing with students in the classroom. It can be enabling, empowering, and educative in the way it models how to deal with power-sharing in relationships and so can positively influence the whole climate of a school. The chapter concludes by outlining how narrative therapy can and in fact has been applied in schools.

NARRATOLOGY

The "turn" to narrative is briefly discussed here along with the concept of narrative itself. The development of narrative therapy did not occur in isolation. Interest in "narrative" was something that already existed. For example, Freud contributed indirectly to the analysis of narrative in the way he conceived "the whole process of the development of the self, as well as the process of psychoanalytic therapy as narratively structured" (Onega and Landa, 1996: 34). Furthermore, by encouraging his clients to tell their stories freely, Freud could even be considered to be the first "narrative" therapist, despite his attempts at interpretation of an "underlying foundational theory of truth" (Parry and Doan, 1994: 8). The modernist quest for self was typified by Freud's idea that by looking deeply enough into the self, and by probing the unconscious, people would find what they were looking for and be liberated.

Narratology, as the science of narrative, really has its roots in the Russian formalists (for example, Propp, 1968; Shklovsky, 1991), who were reacting against impressionist and historicist approaches to literature. The formalists, rethinking Aristotelian concepts, developed new approaches to narrative, borrowing from the structuralist linguistics of Jakobson and Saussure (Onega and Landa, 1996). Poststructuralist accounts of narrative can be seen as a reaction against the formalist development of a general *science* of narrative, one that preserves the structuralist decentering of the subject but at the same time reintroduces the historical and dynamic back into analysis.
According to Onega and Landa (1996), contemporary narratology can be divided into a number of theses, each dealing with a different subject matter:

- *Authorship*: for example, who is the author and what is the author function?
- *Enunciation*: for example, what are the different levels of enunciation or voice in the text or story?
- *Action* or *fibula*: for example, how can we classify events and actions?
- *Story* and *narration*: for example, how should we analyze time, structure, plot, point of view and presentation?
- *Reception*: how should we understand communicative speech acts and the reader's or viewer's creative responses to a text or story?
- *Self-referentiality* and *intertextuality*: for example, how should we analyze reflexive story-telling or metafiction (that is, fiction which experiments with its own way of making meaning)?

In relation to school counseling, narratology involves questions of applied narratology that attempt to formulate more precisely the relations between narrative, society, history, and ideology, and to theorize the relationship between narrative on the one hand and social structures, institutions, and cultural phenomena in general. Such approaches cannot therefore escape questions of power and the way power relations help to shape, legitimize, and constitute personal narratives. This is why Foucault's work has proved so fertile and attractive to scholars and practitioners working in the "psy" sciences or related fields, in their attempts to develop a counseling therapy that is relevant in the post-modern era—an era that challenges notions of "expert" knowledges, accepted notions of truth, and the tyranny of metanarratives of dominant discourses.

Yet Foucault himself was at pains to avoid being described as a "postmodernist," as he was at pains to avoid the limitations of binary dichotomies, such as modern versus postmodern, telling an interviewer that "he was unclear what the word 'modern' (let alone 'postmodern') means" (Gordon, 1991: xxxv; Foucault, 1984b, 1989a). Foucault referred to architecture, where postmodernism found one of its earliest forms of expression, when he described his opposition to the sort of sentimentality that romanticized and venerated a supposedly better past in the name of an antimodern form of postmodernism. He objected to the general, simplistic way in which events in the immediate past were seen "as the primary enemy, as if this were always the principal form of oppression from which one has to liberate oneself" (Foucault, 1989a: 268). He is suspicious of "anything that claims to be a return" (Foucault, 1989a: 269) since this is illogical, and although his historical analysis enables people to "criticize the present," he objects to "a historicism that calls on the past to resolve questions of the present" (Foucault, 1989a: 268).

White and Epston's use of Foucault's neo-Nietzschean notions and of narrative that is part of postmodern discourses in many fields is seen as a significant contribution to the world of therapy. But Parry and Doan (1994:19) argue that "White's use of narrative does not make use of the unique implications of work with families, particularly for the postmodern dimensions of the story." They seem to be referring to Foucault's earlier work when suggesting that instead of using the "ideologically informed pessimism of Foucault and Derrida," it would be more appropriate to use "those who, like therapists, live their professional lives in the domain of stories" (Parry and Doan, 1994: 19). Two of the post-modern writers referred to are Thomas Pynchon and William Gibson. Parry and Doan suggest that White and Epston in fact work within the discipline of *hermeneutics* or interpretations in what could be called "clinical hermeneutics" (Parry and Doan, 1994: 22), agreeing with Fredric Jameson (1981: 13) that narrative is "the central function or instance of the human mind." They argue that narrative provides a sort of "master code by which a person interprets her/his life in order to give it meaning. But since a person's life connects with the lives of so many others, her/his stories are, more precisely, the code according to which the person deciphers the meaning of life as text" (Parry and Doan, 1994: 24).

Hermeneutics (from Hermes, messenger of the gods) is the name for a general theory of interpretation. It has its origins in forms of scriptural interpretation and later became a method characteristic of the human sciences [*Geisteswissenschaften*] that required reference to human intention in order to interpret human action. With Heidegger's ([1927] 1993) *Being and Time*, hermeneutics became the preferred term—in the place of phenomenology—for analyzing temporality as the essence of Being. Finally, with Gadamer (Heidegger's student), hermeneutics became elevated to a philosophy itself. Clinical hermeneutics is a "depth psychology" that allegedly reveals the self by examining, in a principled and systematic way, how people construct or fail to construct meaningful lives.

The turn to narrative is often associated with the movement of postmodernism, particularly since Lyotard (1984) used the phrase "suspicion toward metanarratives" as a way of describing the postmodern ethos or attitude. What he meant by this was a suspicion or skepticism concerning the "big narratives" that the state or other ideological agencies, like the Church or party, used to promulgate its own ideological ends. He asserts that these metanarratives—such as the Christian "story" of martyred souls or salvation of the few, or the tale of capitalist technoscience of unlimited technological progress, the generation of wealth, and its "trickled-down" distribution, or the liberal story of enlightenment through knowledge, or the Marxist metanarrative of history as the emancipation of the working class—are no longer credible. They have lost their unifying political effects and their ideological justification. In contrast, Lyotard maintains that the "*petite recits*"—the little narratives or individual life histories—are quintessential of the postmodern condition (Lyotard, 1984). He is supporting the micronarrative of the individual, the family, and the cultural group as being more significant today, both politically and existentially, than the metanarrative, which has exhausted its resources. Thus, each of us lives our life at the intersection of many different language games, and we construct our lives accordingly.

Lyotard's turn to narrative to characterize "the postmodern condition" is representative, more generally, of a view that underlies the development of social sciences and cultural studies in the latter half of the twentieth century. We can describe this view in terms of the twin methodological imperatives: the linguistic turn, including the significance of representation and the "social construction of reality," on the one hand, and, the attempt to overcome the dualisms, the search for certainty and essences, and the subjectivism that is the legacy of the Cartesian thought, on the other.

The term "social construction" was used in the late 1960s by the sociologists Berger and Luckmann in *The Social Construction of Reality* (1966), which utilized the methods of phenomenology to describe the social world. The term was soon also used by social psychologists in the 1970s to describe how the acquisition of language was a *cultural* process. Some of this work appealed to the Russian theorist Vygotsky to criticize the biological determinism of Piaget. Bruner (1990), for instance, used the functionalist, adaptive, survival aspects of Vygotsky's work (Morss, 1996), and the social psychologist, Harré (1983, 1986), following G. H. Mead and Wittgenstein, criticized the biological determinism of Piagetian stages theories of development. These theorists, in contrast, offer a sociocultural model of cognitive development, often drawing on discursive and sometimes narratives and conversational modes directly.

Similar views—also utilizing Wittgenstein, among other theorists— were advanced by Shotter (1993) and by Gergen (1991, 1995), both of whom were instrumental in linking social constructionist psychology with the postmodern turn. Yet the "postmodernism" of Shotter and Gergen, while critical of the *universalist* explanations of modernist (discursive) psychology, tended to embrace a form of (liberal) humanism, emphasizing a form of individualism and the faculty of choice. The poststructuralist orientation of the critical psychologists, utilizing the work of Michel Foucault in particular (e.g., Walkerdine, 1984), criticized the alleged humanism, individualism, and liberalism underlying social constructionism (see

Morss, 1996).

Some scholars have claimed that narrative is a universal cultural practice or "metacode" for making sense of the world (White, 1987). Others suggest that children have an innate, predisposed capacity for grasping the structures of the language they grow up within and readily use narrative as a means of organizing their thoughts and experiences.

Bruner (1990: 138), for instance, argues that there is a universal predisposition to think in narrative terms and to produce stories with a coherent sequence of events—indeed, a "push to narrate" that "promote negotiation and avoid confrontational disruption and strife" (Bruner, 1990: 67). He argues, for example, that children are "predisposed naturally and by circumstances . . . with models and procedural tool kits for perfecting those [narrative] skills," and he maintains that "without those skills we could never endure the conflicts and contradictions that social life generates. We would become unfit for the life of culture" (Bruner, 1990: 97). Such a highly idealistic suggestion as to the function of narrative assigns it a high moral value and a role in the smooth and peaceful functioning of society. Bruner elevates his cognitive studies into evolutionary and universal tendencies that are theoretically alleged to be inherent in the notion of narrative itself. In other word, narrative becomes the central instance of the functioning of the human mind, and narrative competence becomes the major goal of individual growth. Thus, narrative is essentialized and also given a central value for individual growth and the development of a civilized society.

In its early formulation, narrative therapy tapped very much into Bruner's ideas and needs to be aware of this sort of criticism that it may itself face, especially at the hands of practitioners who unquestioningly adopt it without critically examining its philosophical foundations and assumptions. Yet, on the other hand, narrative or "storying" does seem to be universal, although it takes many different cultural forms. In particular, story-telling forms what seems to be an essential way of communicating informally and formally about themselves and their culture in societies that do/did not use written forms of language (e.g., Aboriginal song lines and dream-time; Maori *korero, whakatauki, whakapapa*[2]). In the West, the ancient craft of story-telling or "storying" has not disappeared, though it may not be tied to its older formulaic structures and purposes or be governed to the same extent by rules of hierarchy of who speaks and when. If anything, the narrative form has proliferated and diversified. Narrative has developed its many different forms in so-called "literate cultures" (the forms of the novel, biography, autobiography, confession, etc.), and different media forms have developed the scripted narrative in film, television, and video as new communication technologies have emerged. In personal life we all seem to have our own self-stories that we tell ourselves and sometimes to others. We tell "stories" that are true and factual as we see them and others that are not—that may consist of lies, fantasies, fables, allegories, yarns, jokes, and so on. As we age and experience so many different things, it seems, we often construct multiple, complex stories but are unable to remember every single one fully: some are forgotten and become dull or distorted; others remain sparklingly clear and vivid. Narrative therapy often uses the metaphor of a map that we present or show as we tell our stories, autobiographies, personal accounts, or self-narratives about our lives.

POSTSTRUCTURALIST AND FOUCAULDIAN THEMES IN NARRATIVE THERAPY

This section examines the philosophical foundations of White and Epston's form of narrative therapy as pioneered in the late 1980s and subsequently developed by them and other writers in the 1990s. White and Epston point out that while the "text analogy provides a frame for consideration of the broader sociopolitical context of person's lives and relationships," it is Foucault's analysis of power-knowledge that provides some details of the sociopolitical context (White and Epston, 1990: 27). The resonance of the broad sense of the political in "some of Foucault's thought on power and knowledge" (White and Epston, 1990: 1) was discussed in the Introduction and in the first chapter of their books. They point to the way that Foucault's ideas provided a way out of what had become an impasse over the debate about power in family therapy.

Apart from Foucault, the major influences in narrative therapy include the family therapist David Epston, the anthropologist Gregory Bateson, the ethnographer Edward Bruner, the psychologist Jerome Bruner, the philosopher Jacques Derrida, the social constructionist Kenneth Gergen, the anthropologist Clifford Geertz, the sociologist Erving Goffman, and the anthropologist Barbara Myerhoff (Payne, 2000; White, 1989, 1997; Winslade and Monk, 1999). By 1997, White firmly rejects the structuralist notions of permanent deep structures such as human nature and the unconscious that have universal application amidst surface or superficial cultural differences (Payne, 2000). White (1997) suggests that metaphors for the experience of "surface and depth" might be replaced by Gilbert Ryle's concepts of "thin and thick" or "thin and rich" that are discussed by Geertz (1983). Moreover, by 1997, White states that "the tradition, thought and practice that has informed its [narrative therapy's] development—that is, the tradition of poststructuralist thought" (White, 1997: 217). The dominant poststructuralist thinkers who have influenced narrative therapy have been Michel Foucault and, to a lesser extent, Jacques Derrida. In evolving from a synthesis of these diverse influences, narrative therapy can be considered to be a postmodern, poststructuralist form of therapy positioned within the social constructionist[3] domain of social psychology (Gergen, 1995, 2001; Harré, 1986; Monk and Drewery, 1994; Payne, 2000; White, 1995, 1997). The following paragraphs briefly review some of the diverse influences on narrative therapy before addressing Foucault's influence.

Michael White and David Epston explore "meaningful" forms of therapy, arguing that problems are produced or manufactured in social, cultural, and political contexts that serve as the basis for life stories that people construct and tell about themselves (Epston, 1989; White, 1989, 1991, 1992, 1995, 1997, 2000; White and Epston, 1989, 1990). White and Epston assume that people generally seek therapy for their problems: "when the narratives in which they are 'storying' their experience, and/ or in which they are having their experience 'storied' by others, do not sufficiently represent their lived experience, and that, in these circumstances, there will be significant aspects of their lived experience that contradict these dominant narratives" (White and Epston, 1990: 14–15).

From this assumption, and because of concern about how people inadvertently contribute to their problems by the way they construct specific meaning of their experiences, White and Epston explore the way alternative stories open up new possibilities for clients. In doing so, the notion of "meaning" is important, and it is argued that the meaning that people attribute to events determines their behavior (White and Epston, 1989, 1990). Meaning is produced through language and its context, and the way that language is used to convey thoughts, emotions, and histories. It is not made for us. Meaning is produced by context rather than being something given that is then applied in a context. The way that narrative therapy explores meaning and finds alternative stories that can open up new possibilities for clients positions it within the constructionist psychology domain, in opposition to many systems and biologically based psychological theories that assume that some underlying structure or dysfunction determines behavior (see the table of analogies, White and Epston, 1990: 6). But by taking on Foucauldian thought, critique, and concepts that deal with the political, narrative therapy addresses some of the criticisms about humanism and liberalism in Shotter and Gergen's forms of social constructionism (see Morss, 1996).

The broad concept of language underlying narrative therapy is indebted to Ludwig Wittgenstein. For Wittgenstein (*Philosophical Investigations,* 1953), meaning is not just *found* in the world; people make and give meaning to what they encounter. For him, language is part of a culture; it is based on public criteria or rules (agreements in practice), and these rules cannot be learned explicitly, as they are the products of deep cultural agreement that forms the background against which sentences make sense. In other words, we become socialized into a language and a cultural system, and we cannot assign just any meaning to language as we see fit, as a radical constructionist viewpoint might argue.

The notion of objective reality and the interpretation of events is important for narrative therapy. David Epston's application of "the story analogy in novel ways to a wide range of presenting problems" (White and Epston, 1990: xv–xvi) was combined with White's interest in text analogy, with which he was familiar from the work in "interpretive method" of the anthropologist Gregory Bateson (1972, 1980). It is not psychoanalytic interpretation, but is about objective reality which argues that "since we cannot know objective reality all knowing requires an act of interpretation," that is determined by how things fit "into the known pattern of events" (White and Epston, 1990: 2)—that is, the interpretation of events depends on the context in which they are received. But furthermore, events that cannot be located in a context would not be selected and so would not exist or be noted for us as facts. To highlight how the temporal dimension was generally missing from therapy, White and Epston cite Bateson's notion that "human sense organs can receive *only* news of difference, and the differences must be coded into events in *time* (i.e., into *changes*) in order to be perceptible" [bold in original] (Bateson, 1980: 79, cited in White and Epston, 1990: 2). In this way, Bateson argues, we can work out that things are different or change by noting "news of difference" over time. White and Epston argue that because stories are relatively indeterminant and are constitutive in shaping people's lives and relationships, they are open to interpretation and multiple meanings. There is room for ambiguity and a range of diverse perspectives (Bruner, 1986). Narrative therapy uses this form of interpretation to help clients to see both dominant and alternative stories that in turn help to "reauthor" their stories and to clarify what choices they may have and wish to make (Winslade and Monk, 1999).

In narrative therapy the understanding of text analogy is based on a combination of ideas, including Gergen and Gergen's (1984) notions about "storying" or "self-narrative" and Bruner's (1986a,b) idea that the interpretation of current events is as much future-shaped in terms of endings as it is past-determined in having a beginning. The text analogy not only "enables a consideration of the broader sociopolitical context of persons whose lives are situated in many texts, it also enables us to include a consideration of *power* in its operation and effects on lives and relationships" (White and Epston, 1990: 18).

Despite the similarities between text analogy, maps, and narrative, narrative has an advantage by having a temporal dimension: "narrative emphasizes order and sequence, in a formal sense, and is more appropriate for the study of change, the life cycle, or any developmental process. Story as a model has a remarkable dual aspect—it is both linear and instantaneous" (Bruner, 1986a: 153, cited in White and Epston, 1990: 3).

Furthermore, narrative is selective and can never encompass all of one's lived experiences, so there are some isolated experiences that are always omitted. This is because we may not understand what we are experiencing, or because the experiences are not able to be told or "storied," or because we lack the vocabulary or performative and narrative resources. White and Epston (1990) argue that through "storying" their experiences, people make meaning of them and of their lives, so stories are constitutive in shaping people's lives and relationships and are open to interpretation and multiple meanings. Since they relate to all texts that are themselves relatively indeterminant, there is room for ambiguity and a range of diverse perspectives (Bruner, 1986)—that is, they are open to interpretation and multiple meanings: "The text analogy is distinct from those analogies that would propose an underlying structure or pathology in families and persons that is constitutive or shaping of their lives and relationships" (White and Epston, 1990: 12). Text analogy suggests, first, that people's lives are situated in and within texts and, second, that with each telling of their story, "through its performance, is a new telling that encapsulates, and expands upon, the previous telling" (White and Epston, 1990: 13).

Jacques Derrida's (1982) notion of "deconstruction" is used to externalize the dominant "problem-saturated" descriptions or stories of a person's life, to listen for spaces, gaps, hidden meanings, or conflicting stories. For narrative therapy, deconstruction involves the application of social constructionist ideas that enable us to become more aware of the different ways of life and thought that shape our existence. Our self-narratives, our dominant cultural knowledges about self and relationships, and our discursive cultural practices become known through "procedures that subvert taken-for-granted realities and practices; those so-called 'truths' that are split off from the conditions and context of their production, those disembodied ways of speaking that hide their bases and prejudices, and those familiar practices of self and relationship that are subjugating of person's lives" (White, 1995: 122).

By externalizing the dominant "problem-saturated" descriptions or stories of a person's life, the influence that problems have in their lives can be explored and mapped. Separating the problem-saturated descriptions from the habitual reading of the dominant story enables people to identify what Goffman (1961) called "unique outcomes"—as adopted by White and Epston (1989, 1990). Unique outcomes are people's experience that falls outside the dominant stories about their lives and relationships. Through using carefully framed questions about how the problem has been affecting their lives and relationships, people can see dominant and alternative stories and can clarify what choices they may have and wish to make. People are invited to ascribe meaning to the unique outcomes and actively to "reauthor" their stories. They "experience a sense of personal agency" and "a capacity to intervene in their own lives and relationships" to construct alternatives that reauthor, reconstruct, or renarrativize their lives (White and Epston, 1990: 16). People "experience a sense of personal agency" and "a capacity to intervene in their own lives and relationships" to construct alternatives that reauthor, reconstruct, or renarrativize their lives (White and Epston, 1990: 16). Personal agency and the survival of alternative stories is enhanced by "inviting persons to be an audience to their own performance of these alternative stories" (simultaneously acting as performer and audience). This might involve using "therapeutic documents" and enlisting feedback from how an "external" audience has experienced the new performance and stories of identity (see Payne 2000; White and Epston, 1990; White, 2000). The context of reflexivity that this process engenders enables people to discover and engage new choices in their lives (White and Epston, 1989, 1990).

So just how Foucauldian is narrative therapy? White and Epston (1989, 1990) make it clear that narrative therapy is considerably informed by Foucauldian notions. They argue that notions of power have been "much overlooked in the therapy literature generally, and in the benign view that we frequently take of our own practices" (White and Epston, 1990: 18). Analyses of power in therapy literature, "have traditionally represented it in individual terms, such as a biological phenomenon that affects the individual psyche or as individual pathology that is the inevitable outcome of early traumatic personal experiences, or in Marxist terms as a class phenomenon" (White and Epston, 1990: 18–19). It was feminist discourse that alerted many therapists to issues of abuse, exploitation, and oppression in a gender-specific and repressive analysis of power. But therapy has not considered the more general problematics of power—both its repressive and constitutive aspects and the operation of power-knowledge (Foucault, 1980a,b).

In establishing narrative therapy, White and Epston's (1990) text used texts from what McNay (1992) would describe as Foucault's middle years that focus on notions of genealogy: *Madness and Civilization* (1965), *The Birth of the Clinic* (1973), *Discipline and Punish* (1977), *The History of Sexuality* (1980a), *Power/Knowledge: Selected Interviews and Other Writings* (1980d), "The Subject and Power" (1982), "Space, Knowledge and Power" (1984b), and "Nietzsche, Genealogy, History" (1984c). Insofar as this early version of narrative therapy was developed prior to the publication of Foucault's later works, White and Epston (1990) were at this stage, not able to explore fully Foucault's later theories of power-knowledge and ethical self constitution (Foucault, 1997). But in subsequent writings, White has pursued Foucault's work more closely and sought to integrate it into narrative therapy (see White, 1995, 1997, 2000).

Foucault's earlier archaeological orientation fails to explain "agency" adequately, and his earlier analysis of power was developed more fully later on with a return to the Kantian subject and to notions of human freedom and the ways in which we ethically constitute or regulate ourselves (Foucault, 1985, 1990, 1997a). The 1990 formulation of narrative therapy outlines Foucault's understanding that power is not only repressive or negative, but also "positive," not in the sense of being good or benign or something to aspire to, but in the sense of being constitutive in the shaping of people's lives and ideas:

> According to Foucault, a primary effect of this power through "truth" and "truth" through power is the specification of a form of individuality that is, in turn, a "vehicle" of power. Rather than proposing that this form of power represses, Foucault argues that it subjugates. It forges persons as "docile bodies" and conscripts them into activities that support the proliferation of "global" and "unitary" knowledges and, as well, the techniques of power. (White and Epston, 1990: 20)

White and Epston (1989, 1990) point out that for Foucault "truth" did not mean objective or intrinsic facts about the nature of people; rather it meant that in constructing ideas that are ascribed the status of "truths," they become "normalizing" in the way they shape and constitute people's lives. They discuss Foucault's notions of the inseparability of *power-knowledge* and how the "truths" of traditional notions of knowledge position one form of knowledge in ascendancy over another. They also explore his notions about techniques that recruit the individual into actively participating in their own subjugation as "docile bodies" and how we live in a society where evaluative and normalizing judgments form an omnipresent, objectifying "gaze" that is the primary mechanism of social control, rather than the judicial forms and torture of the past (see Foucault, 1977).

In doing so, they focus on four features: orientation in therapy, separating from the unitary knowledges, challenging the techniques of power, and resurrecting the subjugated knowledges. "Orientation in therapy," means an orientation that challenges the "scientism" of the human sciences and how therapeutic practices have often been situated within these. They suggest that if we accept that power and knowledge are inseparable . . . and if we accept we are simultaneously undergoing the effects of power and exercising power over others, then we will be unable to take a benign view of own practices. Nor will we be able to simply assume that our practices are primarily determined by our motives, or that we can avoid all participation in the field of power/knowledge through an examination of such personal motives. (White and Epston, 1990: 29)

Therefore, therapists "are inevitably engaged in a political activity," in the sense that they must continually challenge the "techniques that subjugate persons to a dominant ideology" (White and Epston, 1990: 29). They must always assume that they are participating in domains of power and knowledge and are often involved in questions of social control. According to this view, therapists must work to demystify and unmask the hidden power relations implied in their techniques and practices.

Under the second feature, "separating from unitary knowledges," White and Epston (1990) emphasize that "externalizing the problem" is a way of decentering the dominant discourses and "truths" of a spurious "objective" scientific knowledge. Externalizing the problem helps the person to gain a reflexive perspective on life and to challenge the "truths" while exploring new options.

The third feature, "challenging the techniques of power," follows the same line of thinking and practice. It involves challenging the organization of persons in space, the registration and classification of persons, exclusionary practices, ascription of identity, techniques for the isolation of the person, and surveillance and evaluation techniques. Once the techniques and their power effects have been identified and recognized, then unique outcomes of resistance to such techniques can be sought.

Regarding the fourth feature, White and Epston (1990) neglect to mention that resurrecting subjugated knowledges forms part of Foucault's notion of *genealogy* (see chapter 1). A central focus of the therapy harnesses the notion of resurrecting the subjugated knowledges to generate "alternative stories that incorporate vital and previously neglected aspects of lived experience" (White and Epston, 1990: 31).

Narrative therapy is more than just a new set of skills or techniques. It involves the interlocking nature of theory, ethics, and skills, because it is "partly a consistent ethical stance, which in turn embodies a philosophical framework" (Winslade and Monk, 1999: 21). It is not just a therapy but a lifestyle and a political project that involves speaking and listening respectfully and that is concerned with different ways of producing the self that has a Foucauldian basis and orientation.

NARRATIVE THERAPY'S CHALLENGE TO PSYCHOLOGICAL DISCOURSE AND HUMANIST COUNSELING

On the basis of the foregoing concepts taken from Foucault and from a range of other theorists, White and Epston developed a *countertherapy*. In arguing that the link between thought and practice is inseparable, narrative therapy critiques the assumption that few therapies even recognize—namely, that therapy is inherently a political activity, an activity and set of practices inscribed by power relations (White, 1997, 2000). Following the initial model of narrative therapy of the late 1980s, White and Epston and others have continued writing and discussing how narrative ideas present a postmodern and particularly a poststructuralist critique of both humanism and structuralism as applied within the Western "psy" sciences (Monk et al., 1997; Parry and Doan, 1994; Payne, 2000; Rose, 1989, 1998; White, 1991, 1992, 1995, 1997, 2000; Winslade and Monk, 1999). This has resulted in a reevaluation of the pragmatic, empiricist, instrumental therapies that have dominated counseling and psychotherapy recently (McLeod, 2000a). In taking up a Foucauldian poststructuralist position, narrative therapy is arguably part of what Morss (1996) describes as "*critical psychology*"—a movement that parallels similar moves in "critical pedagogy" and is an indicator of a self-reflexive, critical tone of a profession or discipline turning the "gaze" back on itself.

In his later writings, White (1995, 1997, 2000) strongly objects to suggestions that narrative therapy is "a recycled structuralist/humanist psychological practice" that is involved in "discourses of psychological emancipation." He objects to narrative therapy being cast as a "liberatory approach that assists persons to challenge and overturn the forces of repression so they can become free to be 'who they really are'— so that they can identify their 'authenticity' and give true expression to this" (White, 1997, p. 217). He points out that the alternative identity descriptions of self and relationships that arise from narrative therapy practices stand within "the discourses of culture" but are not necessarily culture-bound. When dealing with people who are not from Western cultures, narrative conversations are able to privilege alternative notions of identity such as kinship and spirituality rather than reproducing a Western self. Narrative therapy does not speak of the "truth" of people's identity but consists of "accounts" that reflect who "we are as multi-desired, as multi-motivated, and as multi-intentioned in life as our lives are multi-storied" (White, 1997, p. 231).

In his critique of humanism, White (1997) points out that he does not criticize all aspects of it,and he acknowledges that the humanist tradition has supported people to challenge domination, discrimination, and oppression. It is the essentialism underlying both humanist and structuralist conceptions of the self and identity in therapeutic culture that he considers to be limiting. Traditional assumptions about the subject in humanism have been discussed in the previous chapter. Based on

Foucauldian theories, White (1997) describes a "triumvirate" of interrelated limiting assumptions in humanism and in much of counseling culture: first, "the will to truth," which questions who we are as subjects—our being, essence, or human nature; second, the "repressive hypothesis," which holds that repression conceals or obscures our true or essential nature, inhibiting our growth or self-actualization and so inducing illness because our authentic needs and desires are frustrated; third, the "emancipation narrative," which seeks to liberate the self from repression (Foucault, 1980a,b,c; Payne, 2000; White, 1997;). Humanistic counseling theories—such as person-centered, psychodynamic, and gestalt—tend to operate on the assumption that the discovery of such a hidden knowledge or self will set them free. Traditional humanist assumptions about the subject in psychology and counseling usually position it as a stable, fixed, autonomous being, often characterized as fully transparent to itself and responsible for his or her actions. In contrast, the notion of identity in narrative therapy tends to be replaced with the notion of "subjectivity" because narrative therapy adopts social constructionist viewpoints that do not assume that people's identities are primarily stable and singular—rather, that they change and are contradictory (Gergen, 1990, 1991, 2001; Lifton, 1993).

The "will to truth" is a Nietzschean notion that Foucault derived from the *Genealogy of Morals* (1956, orig. 1887). It comes after Foucault's "will to knowledge," the title of his inaugural course at the Collège de France, and was to undergo changes and some refinements during the course of his career. Foucault (1980a) raises three distinct doubts concerning the Freudian "repressive hypothesis" (as described in chapter 6, p. 170).

He addresses issues of repression and emancipation in his analysis of power relations and its parallel in forms of resistance, in how power operates in a capillary fashion not simply as a binary opposition between rulers and the ruled (Foucault, 1980a,b, 1984e), and he (Foucault, 1997a) also warns that the notion of liberation needs to be scrutinized and treated cautiously otherwise (see chapter 6, p. 170):

White (1997) argues that although humanist-oriented therapies aim to be emancipatory by enabling the "true self" to emerge at some future point, they are, in effect, diminishing and entrapping, preventing people from questioning the possibilities of how their lives are lived in the present. Psychological concepts of personal development do not disturb, challenge, or confront the sociocultural political forces that have influenced the construction of the problem that the person has sought help with. He further argues that therapists who work with an individual, encouraging personal development, become "unwitting accomplices in the reproduction of the dominant and culturally sanctioned versions of identity, of the popular and revered forms of personhood, of the most familiar and mainstream subjectivities" (White, 1997: 227).

White (1997) argues that a further limitation is the operation of deficit theory, which has strongly encouraged people to think that they have to change, grow, develop, or improve, inadvertently reinforcing the power of experts and institutions that aim to help them to achieve this. So, narrative therapy challenges the way Western psychology generally emphasizes the *individual* subject and expert-centered forms of professional knowledge. It especially challenges the areas of mental health where experts often appear to know more about people's lives than the people do themselves, and where the professional focus upon personal deficits emphasizes the person's failures or weaknesses rather than accomplishments and strengths. The "expert knowledge" and the scientific outlook of traditional Western psychology, based, as it is, on the biomedical model of mental illness, "objectifies," "individualizes," and "normalizes" the subject through diagnosis, which has the effect of locating the problem within the person. For the client, the expert's diagnostic label of their self tends to come to be seen as part of their essential nature and of their identity. Gergen (1990, 1991) suggests that diagnostic deficits so totally affect the past, present, and future of a person's life that the self becomes saturated by the pathology. Although the intent is to help the client, treatments or interventions can inadvertently totalize, pathologize, and disempower the client, as well as producing social hierarchies that erode notions of community and interdependence (Winslade and Monk, 1997).

Therefore, to avoid pathologizing people, narrative therapists do not present themselves as objectively neutral experts who diagnose problems and prescribe or provide solutions, interventions, treatments, or answers. Narrative therapy emphasizes that to make sense and meaning of their lives, people frequently work to understand their lives. Therefore narrative therapy does not consider that the counselor's task is to apply "expertise" to make sense of other people's lives. Instead, it adopts an optimistic, respectful, but "not-knowing" or tentative or curious stance, using listening, therapeutic conversations, and questions to help people to find inconsistencies and contradictions and to craft their stories to unmask hidden assumptions and to open up new possibilities. People are encouraged to find alternative narratives that are not just consistent stories, but are stories that are "richer" rather than "thin" and are more meaningful for people because they are closer to their experience (see Geertz, 1983).

Although it is person-centered to the extent that the person is the focus, paradoxically, through its use of questioning techniques, narrative therapy is directive and influential, yet it can also "empower" the person to find their own voice (Drewery and Winslade, 1997; Speedy, 2000; Winslade and Monk, 1999). The form of "empowerment" that narrative therapy provides is not the one that operates in humanist discourse. Instead, it involves a general sense of "teaching" people how to understand the discursive conditions and power relations of their lives, how they might "reauthor" their lives, and how they can find and use their own voice to work on the problem and to find their own solutions (Drewery and Winslade, 1997). Thus, the notion of the narrative self, or the self as the center of narrative gravity, stresses the discursive production and reproduction of the self while at the same time preserving a notion of narrative agency, which embodies some aspects of traditional humanism. This notion of agency is sometimes referred to as the "return of the self" in Foucault's later work, which emphasizes ethical self-constitution (Foucault, 1997a). In his later writings Foucault does not abolish the self, but he questions the essentialism and humanism underlying the Cartesian-Kantian subject. He returns to the historical production and reproduction of subjectivity as an object of discourse actively constituted at the intersections of truth and power (Foucault, 1988a,b). In narrative therapy, "speaking" and "voice" are used as metaphors for the agency of the client (Drewery and Winslade, 1997). Unlike traditional counseling practices, narrative therapy does not privilege the person's voice or the binaries of the dominant versus the marginalized, hidden voices, or local versus expert knowledges (hooks, 1984). While narrative therapy accepts the equal validity of each "knowledge" and "voice," it acknowledges that "some voices have more meaning-making power than others" (Speedy, 2000: 365). This impacts on power relations for the client as well as on counselor practices because it aims to avoid the unintentional objectifying professional gaze that can occur is therapists are unaware of their role as professional experts in constructing a therapeutic dialogue.

Notions of power under humanism tend to emphasize the ideal of the individual being in control of his or her life and exercising conscious "choices" about it. In contrast, narrative therapy uses Foucault's "analytics of power," which involves the notion that power can be positive and productive, not just repressive and negative (Foucault, 1977a). Foucault's concept of power operates discursively at the micro level to position us and our identities (Foucault, 1997). Power is not regarded as being solely possessed or exercised by individuals; it is part of what people negotiate in their everyday lives and social relationships, where power is about "positioning" in relation to discourse. Subject positioning involves power relations in that it operates discursively, determining whether a person can speak, what is sayable and by whom, and whether and whose accounts are listened to. Understanding power in this way helps us to reconstitute the relationship between counselor and client. Each of us stands at multiple positions in relation to discourse, in which we engage or participate on a daily basis. Thus discourse, in the narrative approach, is seen as the organizing and regulating force of social practices and ways of behaving. Discourses offer socially defined ways of positioning the subject (for example, "teacher," "student," "counselor"). Some discourses are prescriptive and constitute dominant cultural stories, yet within these dominant narratives there are different subjective possibilities for constructing our own distinctive narratives of identity. For example, dominant cultural stories about the family may position us as "wife" or "husband," but in different families and even within the same family at different times we may construct very different "subject positions." Each "subject position" shapes us in certain ways and opens up positions in a possible conversation.

The traditional counseling relationship that has become a central and largely unquestioned and unquestionable tenet of most therapies has come under scrutiny more recently (Payne, 2000; White, 1995, 1997). In White's more recent work (White, 1995, 1997), he puts forward the notion of "therapist decentering," with its related, intertwined notions of "re-membering" conversations, transparency, and "taking-it-back" practices that form a critique of the traditional assumptions about the nature of the relationship between therapist and client. In psychodynamic, behaviorist, transactional analysis, gestalt and cogitive therapies.people are not positioned as experts in their own lives, counselors are. In contrast, both Rogerian person-centered and narrative therapies focus on the client having expertise. But, as Payne (2000) points out, Rogerian orientations extend from deficit assumptions that the client needs to grow and that the problem is located within the person. Growth is about developing the person's inner potential and is promoted through a therapeutic relationship that is warm, empathic, accepting, encouraging, and showing positive regard that allows the person the time and space to explore their problems, feelings, and inner self (see Rogers, 1961). Furthermore—not surprisingly, considering the enormous influence of Rogerian thought in the development of counseling from the 1960s onwards—the notion of a "therapeutic relationship" is seen as "all-important," "healthy," and even as "the aim of the counselling process," so that the counseling outcome can be productive (Mearns and Thorne, 1999: 22). The therapeutic relationship has become a central and largely unquestioned and unquestionable tenet of most therapies. But Payne (2000) argues that this excludes and marginalizes the contribution of a person's relationships and life outside the therapy room as factors that contribute to overcoming their problems, because this "puts the therapy room at the center of the process of therapy, and makes the relationship with the therapist the person's primary relationship in overcoming his problems during the often very lengthy period of meetings usually assumed to be necessary" (Payne, 2000: 212).

Furthermore, it means that the counselor is in a very strong position in terms of power relations as a result of their power-knowledge, and the therapeutic relationship develops a mystique whereby it is elevated above other relationships in the person's life (Payne, 2000). In contrast, narrative therapy sees "that the professional's role is more productive and ethical as a facilitator of the therapeutic actuality and potential of real-life relationships rather than as provider of a 'therapeutic' relationship with the counsellor herself" (Payne, 2000: 212). Payne notes that narrative therapy certainly uses core Rogerian qualities of "empathy, congruence and positive self regard" as a way of relating in therapy but avoids setting up a therapeutic relationship that has the centrality of the person-centered counseling manner.

"Re-membering" conversations air techniques that aim to decenter the therapist by inviting the person to look to the past to seek out or remember people who have been significant but are no longer present or available or are deceased, and to reminisce about their relationship. Ways of joining or reenlisting these people into the person's "club of life" (White, 1997) are explored and create a potentially therapeutic plot-line that links the past with the present as a way of sharing experiences and joining for celebrations; yet this technique is not intended as the religious or spiritual one that it could be assumed to be. In reverse it can also be used to separate, dismiss, or remove an abusive or oppressive person from dominating the person's life—an "un-membering" (Payne, 2000). Of course, it is the therapist who uses their expertise to introduce this notion, but in the process and detail it points away from the relationship with the therapist, toward harnessing relationships with others who populate the person's "real" rather than "therapeutic" life.

White (1997) emphasizes "transparency"—a concept similar to the Rogerian "congruence." Both notions define a moral position about the therapist being "genuine" and avoiding a professionally distanced stance. White argues that a culturally neutral position is impossible and so emphasizes that an ethical priority for narrative therapists is transparency and openness about these. This involves an awareness of power relations and the therapist's "location in the social worlds of gender, race, culture, class, sexual identity, and age" (White, 1997: 205) and how the taken-for-granted privileges of these can inadvertently and unthinkingly marginalize others. Narrative counselors are expected to be vigilant about accidentally or dogmatically imposing their own cultural values on people in ways that have the effect of "colonizing" clients. White states that he has "an ethical commitment to bring forth the extent to which therapy is a two-way process, and to try to find ways of identifying, acknowledging, and articulating the extent to which the therapeutic interactions are actually shaping of the work itself, and also shaping of my life more generally in positive ways" (White, 1995: 168).

As a result, White challenges the traditional therapeutic imperative that considers it at least inappropriate and even unethical for the counselor to share anything of his or her own life with the person. The aim is to keep the focus on the person and their problems and not to be diverted to the therapist. But the inadvertent result of this is that therapy becomes a one-way process that reinforces ideas about personal deficits, "thin" identity notions, and marginalizes the person's identity because the person "is defined as the 'other' whose life is changed" (White, 1997: 127). While the person's life is expected to change, the therapist's is expected to remain the same. The therapist's exclusion of their own self "is actually person-limiting and therapist centring" (Payne, 2000: 218). For White, "taking-it-back" practices form an ethical commitment that acknowledge "our common humanity" and the impact of the therapeutic sessions on the therapist's work and in life. They are not about shifting the focus to the therapist's problems but about decentering the therapist and about noting that therapy is inevitably a two-way process that can have valuable byproducts. It aims to avoids positioning the therapeutic milieu as a microcosm that is separate from people's everyday lives (White, 1997).

Narrative therapy not only challenges humanistic approaches by problematizing the subject or essential self and its constitution through power relations, it also made an early attempt to dissociate itself from the concept of therapy itself. "Conversation" is a term that White and Epston (1989, 1990) considered but did not take up in deliberating on what they saw as the inadequacy of the term "therapy"; yet in recent work "therapeutic conversations" has come to be frequently used (White, 1997, 2000). They point out that definitions of therapy focus on the treatment of disease or disorder, but that in their work problems were not constructed in terms of disease, and they did not imagine that anything done related to a "*cure.*" Without discussing it, they in effect position narrative therapy within the antipsychiatry domain, reflecting some of Thomas Szasz's (1973) criticisms about psychiatric power in *The Manufacture of Madness* and of psychotherapy in *The Myth of Psychotherapy: Mental Healing as Religion, Rhetoric and Repression* (1979). Szasz (1973, 1979) not only pointed to the historical continuity between the persecution of witches and heretics in the past and the persecution of the mentally ill in the present day, but also, in Foucault's assessment, he focused on the power of psychiatric institutions and on perceptions of sexuality to shape "madness" and hysteria and the truth about one's self (Foucault, 1965, 1989e):

> Since the Inquisition, through penitence, the examination of conscience, spiritual guidance, education, medicine, hygiene, psychoanalysis and psychiatry, sexuality has always been suspected of holding over us a decisive and profound truth. Tell us what your pleasure is, don't hide anything of what happens between your heart and your sex, and we will know what you are and what you are worth. (Foucault, 1989e: 109)

As a clear rejection of a scientific emphasis on diagnosis of a clinical condition and in its challenge to the traditional humanist "psy" sciences and deficit models, narrative therapy/countertherapy could perhaps be considered to be "*post-psychological*" (McLeod, 2000b: x).

"THE PERSON ISN'T THE PROBLEM; THE PROBLEM IS THE PROBLEM": SOME FEATURES OF NARRATIVE THERAPY

The maxim: "The person isn't the problem; the problem is the problem" (Epston, 1989: 26)[4] is often used to signify one of the main emphases of narrative therapy—that using externalizing language reflects just how and where narrative therapists locate problems, outside the person. As a counseling theory that is closely informed by its practice, narrative therapy has evolved and changed to a certain extent from its early formulation. From the theoretical discussion about narrative therapy and its rationale, and being mindful of Winslade and Monk's (1999) earlier admonition about narrative therapy being a combination of philosophy, skills, theory, and ethics, it seems apposite to now provide a brief overview of some of the main features and terminologies that are used in the practice of narrative therapy. More detailed descriptions of these features, arguments to back up their usage, and practice-related examples are provided elsewhere (Monk et al., 1997; Payne, 2000; White and Epston, 1989, 1990; Winslade and Monk, 1999).

The Dulwich Centre, Adelaide, founded by Michael White, describes narrative therapy as being premised on the idea that the lives and the relationships of persons are shaped by: the knowledges and stories that communities of persons negotiate and engage in to give meaning to their experiences: and certain practices of self and of relationship that make up ways of life associated with these knowledges and stories. A narrative therapy assists persons to resolve problems by: enabling them to separate their lives and relationships from those knowledges and stories that they judge to be impoverishing; assisting them to challenge the ways of life that they find subjugating; and, encouraging persons to re-author their own lives according to alternative and preferred stories of identity, and according to preferred ways of life. Narrative therapy has particular links with Family Therapy and those therapies which have a common ethos of respect for the client, and an acknowledgement of the importance of context, interaction, and the social construction of meaning. (<http:// www.massey.ac.nz/~Alock/virtual/narrativ.htm>)
In a way that clarifies the above premises, Winslade and Monk (1999) discuss nine assumptions on which narrative therapy is based:

- Human beings live their lives according to stories;
- The stories we live are not produced in a vacuum;
- Embedded within stories lie discourses;
- The modern world is characterized by societal norms that are kept in place by surveillance and scrutiny;
- There are always contradictory or alternative discourses with which some align themselves;
- Dominant cultural stories impose severe limits on people seeking to create change within their lives;
- Deconstructing dominant discourses raises new possibilities for living;
- There is always lived experience that does not get encapsulated in stories;
- The task of the counselor is to help the client construct a more satisfying and appealing story line. (Winslade and Monk, 1999: 22–27)

From these premises and assumptions, narrative therapy has developed its own specific "language" or set of terminologies to describe the general sequence of its therapeutic processes. The following list is not exhaustive. Instead, it is indicative of the sorts of processes and terminologies used in narrative therapy and is compiled from several different sources (Monk et al., 1997; Payne, 2000; White, 1995; Winslade and Monk, 1999; White and Epston, 1989, 1990):

- problem-saturated descriptions;
- dominant stories;
- externalizing the problem;
- invitations to name the problem;
- using metaphorical language ('sneaky poo"; "voice of doubt"; "black

thoughts");
- externalizing conversations;
- deconstructing the problem;
- mapping influences;
- relative influence questions;
- externalizing internalizing discourses;
- deconstruction of unique outcomes;
- inviting the person to take a position;
- client and counselor uniting against the problem;
- using therapeutic documents;
- searching for alternative stories;
- constructing a history of the preferred story;
- reauthoring the story by telling and retelling to enrich the self-narrative;
- creating an audience of sympathetic outsider witnesses to revised stories;
- re-membering;
- preparing for the future through possibility questions;
- ending ceremony

The language used in narrative therapy often sees familiar words employed in new and particular ways, with specific meanings. It could even be argued that narrative has developed its own forms of "jargon," just as other therapies and disciplines have. But using precise language is seen as a central task for narrative therapists, because the social constructionist, Wittgensteinian emphasis of narrative therapy is that language can blur, alter, or distort experience as we tell our stories, it can condition how we think, feel, and act, and it can be used purposefully as a therapeutic tool (White, 1995). Both the language used and how it is used are important, so narrative therapy has started to turn the gaze back on itself by paying particular attention to the language its therapists use. The language used is deliberately nonsexist and ethnically neutral, and it avoids the medical model terms that many mental health professionals use that unthinkingly objectify and pathologize people (e.g., referrals, case notes, clinical work). Therefore, White never uses "cases" or "case histories", and he has replaced the term "client" with "person" (Payne, 2000). It is in the spirit of narrative therapy that this book largely follows White's lead and generally uses "person" rather than "client." "S*peaking*" and "*voice*" are used as metaphors for the agency of the client (Drewery and Winslade, 1997: 43). One major syntactical device that implies hope and encouragement and is used throughout therapy is "externalizing" language: the problem is seen as being outside the person, not embodied within as part of their psyche, personality, or being. However, abuse or violence are not addressed in this manner but are named directly. "Externalizing the problem" is now often called "*externalizing conversations*" (Winslade and Monk, 1999: 36–37), because it reflects the idea of fluidity and that there is seldom only one problem. "Unique outcomes" has sometimes become "*sparkling moments*" or "*unique experiences*"

(Bird, 2000). Much of this attention to detail in language usage reflects the notion of "therapist decentering" as a way of enabling the person to be at the center of her/his own therapy.

In the therapeutic conversation, narrative therapy uses a variety of techniques to deconstruct, expose, and subvert the dominant patterns of relating—patterns that the person often finds problematic. This process opens up spaces for possible change. The conversation is based on shared contributions because the narrative therapist respects that the person has personal/local knowledge, skills, and ability that they can tap to solve their problems. Externalizing conversations are aimed at stopping people being disabled by the problem. Naming the problem is something that therapists invite the person to do and negotiate with them, but the actual decision on the name or even to use naming is up to the person, who may then challenge how it has been taking over things in their life. Unlike other therapies that see questions as intrusive and threatening and so avoid them, the narrative therapist asks creative, curious, persistent questions, yet this is nothing like an interrogation but is part of a dialogue. The questions aim to learn about the meanings of the person's world, to examine socio-politico-cultural assumptions in that world, and to find subplots that are richer and closer to actual experience and to facilitate coauthoring the person's unique story. They are also used as a means of checking how the person is finding the direction of the conversation, their comfort with what and how things are proceeding, and to ask their permission about taking notes and about using therapeutic documents. By working out "*sparkling moments*" when the problem wasn't around, people are assisted to find alternative ways in which they prefer to describe themselves.

The earliest forms of narrative therapy discussed and provided examples of the style, intent, and effect of using letters as a form of literate means that can be used in narrative therapy practice (White and Epston, 1989, 1990). They propose possibly using letters of invitation to engage people who are reluctant to participate or attend therapy; "redundancy" letters, which refer to roles people have assumed over some time that have now become redundant, such as, "parent-watcher, parents' marriage counselor, brother's father" (White and Epston, 1990: 90); letters of prediction, of which the client is fully aware, as a form of six-month follow-up; counterreferral letters; letters of reference; letters for special occasions; and brief letters (see White and Epston, 1989, chapt. 2; and White and Epston, 1990, chapt. 3 and 4). More recently, these have been described as "therapeutic documents" that take many forms, including visual elements, "letters, statements, certificates and creative writing" to "encapsulate new knowledges, perspectives and preferred changes which have become part of the person's enriched but still perhaps slightly fragile view of her remembered experience" (Payne, 2000: 127). Engaging an audience that is significant to the person and harnessing the power that is so often assigned to the written word become effective ways of validating the person's alternative story by briefly documenting the changes that he or she has made in their life. A detailed discussion about therapeutic documents and some cautions and reservations about their use are provided in Payne's work and in White's later work (White, 1995, 1997, 2000).

The distinction between oral and literate traditions was discussed by White and Epston (1989, 1990). In Western culture, therapy is generally conducted in the oral mode, but in many other spheres, especially in official aspects of society, the written is often privileged as more prestigious than the oral. Because writing is visible, it can be referred back to and checked for accuracy, and as a result the written has generally achieved a more authoritative status than the oral. A literate tradition that documents different ideas and theories is what White and Epston have tapped into in formulating their theory. Because the literate mode enables the recording of linear time, it maps experience onto the temporal dimension and so is an important mechanism for producing meaning in people's lives. Therefore, the written has much to offer therapy. Writing in therapy can expand the information-processing ability of short-term memory and can enable people to be "more active in determining the arrangement of information and experience, and in the production of different accounts of events and experience" (White and Epston, 1990: 37). But in other cultural milieux the oral takes precedence—as in someone seeing or hearing it for themselves—as witness to something (e.g., in local knowledges and in Maori and Pacific Island cultures), therefore: "With regard to the oral and literate traditions, although David and I do not consciously rank one above the other in status, we do privilege the oral tradition in our work" (White and Epston, 1990: 37). Engaging an audience that is significant to the person and harnessing the power that is so often assigned to the written word become effective ways of validating the person's alternative story by briefly documenting the changes that he/she has made in their life. The dominant discourse had mostly totalized them, positioning them as one sort of person; the redescription, in contrast, positions them in a new and different way.

NARRATIVE THERAPY IN SCHOOLS

Because the dominant discourse of the institution and of pedagogy has been profoundly influenced by psychological discourse, schools tend to use normalized, deficit-based descriptions that totalize students (Gergen, 1990, 1991). Students are commonly described by their academic performance, socioeconomic background, classroom dynamics, subcultural or peer groupings, and in terms of medical/psychological diagnoses and labels, such as: "maladjusted, attention deficit disordered, severely emotionally disturbed, dyslexic, conduct disordered, oppositional–defiant, emotionally handicapped, learning disabled" (Winslade and Monk, 1999: 54). Surveillance, evaluation, and assessment as mechanisms of the "gaze" are at work in these practices. The standards of normality on which these diagnoses and labels are based are usually hidden, so the in-built cultural and social biases of such accepted standards are seldom open to or able to be questioned. Gergen (1990, 1994) argues that the deficit discourse tends to act in a totalizing way that leads to personal self-enfeeblement and, in turn, to a greater reliance on professional authority and expertise, because the local commonsense knowledges of how to handle problems are undermined and eroded (see Winslade and Monk, 1999).

Ways in which psychological discourse has thought of and "produced" current notions of adolescence have been discussed in chapter 3. But probably the predominant form of psychological discourse in schools is that of developmental psychology. It has provided the language to describe and understand the norms that it has established for desirable child/adolescent development and behavior, and it identifies problems and provides the types of expertise to solve them (Rose, 1989, 1998). In doing so, adolescence is often seen as a transitional, biological, natural stage of life, subject to storm and stress, with raging hormones (Hall, 1905; Havighurst, 1972; Piaget, 1954;). The link between psychology and education—especially the dominance of developmental psychology—has been so profound that Valerie Walkerdine (1984: 162) argues that "developmental psychology and the child-centred pedagogy form a couple" that is intertwined. She argues that child-centered or "progressive" education does not just apply the "scientific" findings of child development, but the pedagogy or school itself becomes a site of production of "development as pedagogy." Human or child development courses have become essential components of many teacher education courses, so that the notion of development itself has largely taken on the status of "truth," and pedagogic practices and staged curricula are, in turn, devised to reflect this "truth."

Teaching practice (and many parents) assumes that children naturally develop in certain ways as a result of a series of interactions with the world, and that some individuals progress or develop faster than others. If their progress is not consistent with norms, various forms of intervention and/or therapy are often proposed as a remedy. In the process, schools have readily adopted psychologized notions that label, diagnose, categorize, calculate, normalize, judge, totalize, and even pathologize young people. But these "truths" have now become strongly contested by the work of Michel Foucault and other theorists writing on poststructuralism, feminism, constructionist psychology, and narrative therapy (Foucault, 1977, 1980a, 1985, 1988b, 1990, 1997a; Gergen, 2001; Lesko, 1996; Nava, 1991; Payne, 2000; Rose, 1989, 1998; White, 1989, 1995, 1997; Winslade and Monk, 1999). The poststructuralist argument treats "truth" as a production, not as a discovery, so development comes to be seen as being produced by sociocultural conditions and practices. Walkerdine (1984: 197) argues that by producing or constituting individuals and "children, as objects of its gaze, [psychology] produces them as subjects."

Walkerdine's critique of the use of developmental psychology in education is Foucauldian, where Foucault characterized social control in contemporary society as having shifted from repressive practices to practices of normalization (see chapter 4, p. 124). Progressive education is usually presented as a liberal, humanist project that is more benign than are traditional, authoritarian forms of pedagogy. But Walkerdine's (1984) work points out that surveillance, regulation, and control of students and teachers are still being exercised, albeit in a more subtle manner, when active learning techniques are used and that teachers record the developmental achievements and progress of individual students. The regulatory process is masked by notions of normalization, and the acceptance of the notion of development as "natural" contributes to the suppression (Morss, 1996).

In schools, the use of narrative therapy has some major implications. It can and is being used by school counselors in their therapeutic work, but the principles involved need not be limited to the domain of the counselor. Narrative approaches of engaging in respectful conversations and power-sharing can certainly be used in the wider school context. Rather than provide any sort of prescription for how schools could harness narrative therapy, this section of the book, in the spirit of narrative therapy, sets out to present some examples of what has been done in some schools and to indicate some possibilities of what might be done. It explores the work of John Winslade and Gerald Monk (1999), who, apart from discussing the use of narrative therapy in the school counseling milieu, speculate on extending this beyond counseling. They conclude their book, *Narrative Counseling in Schools: Powerful and Brief* (1999), by providing five points of what the climate in a narrative–oriented school might look like. The last part of this section discusses how narrative therapy's poststructuralist critique can challenge the dominant forms of authoritarian power relations in schools in a respectful manner. It looks at a specific example of how narrative therapy might be used in instances of bullying and harassment. More aspects and examples could be explored, but that is beyond the scope of this book. However, a cautionary note seems appropriate. In the enthusiasm for adopting narrative approaches in schools, there is a danger of positioning narrative therapy and its poststructuralist principles that critique humanism and structuralism as providing a panacea or solution to all school-related issues. This would be to assign far too much to it.

First, Winslade and Monk (1999) suggest avoiding totalizing ways of speaking about students, their families, and teachers. This would mean that official reports, documents, and files would be "circumspect and tentative in their descriptions of people because teachers would be aware of the power of their word to create people's lives, not just describe them;" they would focus "on appreciating talents and competencies, rather than diagnosing deficits" (Winslade and Monk, 1999: 117; see also p. 224). It is argued that the deficit discourse tends to act in a totalizing way that results in personal self-enfeeblement and leads to a greater reliance on professional authority and expertise at the same time as it erodes the local, commonsense knowledge of how to handle problems (Gergen, 1990, 1994; Winslade and Monk, 1999). Surveillance, evaluation, and assessment, as mechanisms of the objectifying "gaze," are at work in these practices. The standards of normality on which these diagnoses and labels are based are usually hidden, so the in-built cultural and social biases of such accepted standards are seldom open to question or able to be questioned. Winslade and Monk (1999) propose turning the gaze back on itself, to challenge these disciplinary technologies by questioning the hidden standards of normality, in terms of both the process and the assigning of descriptions to students.

As part of this agenda, narrative therapy challenges the gaze by providing a nonjudgmental way of talking with students that avoids the all-too-common attitude of blaming and shaming young people that occur in both benign and repressive school disciplinary regimes. As well as psychologized discourses, counselors are encouraged to be aware of the power of discourses about ethnicity, gender, culture, and class to name, shape, and form the way students experience school. However, not only counselors but teachers also need to be aware that discourses are culturally produced and are only partial stories and to challenge the way discourses and their disciplinary practices limit the sense people make of their lives.

The narrative approach challenges existing forms of power relations and the sorts of language and conversations that are used in schools to talk about and to students. The power relations between teacher and student are often one-sided, with what the teacher says about the pupil usually being assigned more credibility and weight than what the student says about the teacher. The authority of the teacher accrues from the history of teacher–student relations, the effects of school descriptions, plus the way the teacher has power over much of the daily lives of students. The sorts of power relations in schools and how many adults deal with young people often pose problems for students, who may have developed a host of self-protective mechanisms as a result. What narrative therapy aims to do is to "gently subvert dominating patterns of relating and open space for things to change through a deconstructive conversation" (Winslade and Monk, 1999: 59). It is not about being disrespectful to other professionals, and in fact is at pains to avoid such disrespect, because it would be unethical.

Rather than authoritarian methods, the narrative approach aims to establish "respectful conversations" in schools and to negotiate power-sharing between student and counselor and between students and teachers. Suggesting that schools would develop an ethic where "no one was spoken about behind his or her back in ways that could not be said respectfully to his or her face" is perhaps overly idealistic and simplistic, because it confuses issues around gossip, information-sharing, information ownership, discussion, privacy, and confidentiality (Winslade and Monk, 1999: 117). While it appears to be a laudable practice, considerations of sensitivity and being diplomatic about information are seldom quite so easily pigeonholed.

Second, Winslade and Monk (1999) focus on changing power relations by suggesting that there would be "a consciousness of power relations and reflexive processes by which those in positions of privilege were constantly held accountable for their power. The voices of children would be taken seriously and their knowledge respected for the expertise it offered. Teachers would be genuinely interested in learning from children, rather than automatically assuming that they knew better" (Winslade and Monk, 1999: 118).

The notions of "power" and "voice" here need some exploration. I would argue that Winslade and Monk's suggestion of a "consciousness of power relations" and of deconstruction are insufficient. Their suggestions do not seem to be either particularly Foucauldian or poststructuralist and provide only a challenge to authoritarian types of power in schools. They do not explore the implications of power-knowledge. While power relations may start to change by using consciousness and narrative processes, changing the administration and structures of schools, classrooms, and the wider community goes much further. Deweyan and Freirean notions provide more detailed ways for schools to practice forms of democracy that respect who speaks, what is sayable, who is heard, and so on. They address issues about minorities being heard and about partnership and point to the more equal distribution of the speaking and acting chances for all voices in the community to be heard and acted upon.

Although narrative therapy is avowedly poststructuralist, respecting and elevating the child's voice harks back to liberal humanist principles that are commonly found in child-centered psychology and pedagogy. It confuses the normative conception of "having a say" that is anchored in democratic theory, which implies the procedural norm of "turn-taking" and the active distribution of speaking and acting chances, with a humanist concept of "voice," as the unique and most immediate form of self-expression. This is the concept of "voice" that is found, for instance, in humanist literary criticism, where a work is considered the unique expression of its author and the game of criticism becomes one of guessing the author's intention. Yet when some one is ascribed a "voice," whose "voice" is it? Is the child the source of its own voice? If we accept the poststructuralist notion that we are not the authors of our own semantic intentions—that we are not necessarily the originator of our own values and that our voice "echoes" the values and ideas of many others, then we need to ask who speaks "through" the child? How is the child's "voice" constituted, and what are its strands? Who speaks through the child—mother, father, church, peers, media, advertising, culture, propaganda? Whose voice is it? What are its multiple sources, and how do they intersect? What are the sources of values that are embodied in the child's voice?

So if we ascribe a "voice," it harks back to liberal ideals of the individual self and positions that present voice as a unique form of self-expression, a mirror to the soul, and a source of truth-telling—an essentialist demand. On the structuralist view, the focus would be to decenter this liberal humanist understanding of the voice and to question who speaks through one's voice. The poststructuralist might argue, in contrast, that rather than one voice, there are many voices—many people and institutions speak through us. If we accept that when someone speaks, there is not one voice originating from the individual as prime actor in their lives—it is more like a chorus speaking with components that include things we echo, imitate, sublimate, construct, synthesize, and perform—then exploring where these voices come from leads to understandings about the self and one's identity and relationship with others.

The narrative-oriented school might consider narrative as a larger metaphor for the thinking and educative process. What is missing from Winslade and Monk's account is an understanding that an educative process is involved. Narrative as a form of consciousness and thinking (after J. Bruner) is also dialogical and a mirror of the larger educative process. We are not born with a voice—it develops over time. For example, a writer or an opera singer may have some "technical" equipment that forms a basis for their voice, but their expression of that voice involves various forms of training or education to develop it beyond its initial state. Similarly, an educative process that encourages questioning the sources of one's own voice is involved in making sense of the world, gaining a sense of self and identity, and understanding why one thinks and acts in the way one does.

Winslade and Monk (1999) seem to confuse the normative "ought" of a moral position about whether or not students should "have a voice" and whether or not giving students "a say" is part of education from the empirical "is"—the actual or empirical constitution of the voice, its multiple strands, and their possible conflicts. With respect to "voice," the narrative approach of Winslade and Monk repeats and endorses the fundamental working propositions of liberal humanism rather than criticizing or problematizing them and taking its own poststructuralist philosophy seriously.

Third, Winslade and Monk (1999) suggest unmasking dominant stories that operate within the school, through encouraging deconstructive conversations and through actively seeking all kinds of minority voices and ensuring that they all have "legitimate status in the politics of the school" (Winslade and Monk, 1999: 118). They do not take this further, but such unmasking could be accomplished by using the techniques of narrative therapy. Most of these techniques were outlined in the previous section, but the next few paragraphs discuss their application in schools very briefly.

Young people seldom have the opportunity or encouragement to explore their own knowledge and ability in making sense of their problems. A narrative counselor establishes a relationship that assumes and respects that students have the knowledge, skills, and ability about their own lives that they can tap into to solve the problem(s) they present. This is quite the reverse of the stance adult/expert-knows-best taken by many other adults and professionals who deal with students' problems. Narrative therapists enter a conversation based on shared contributions, asking creative, curious, persistent questions, but nothing like an interrogation, aiming to "learn about the meanings of the child's world" (Winslade and Monk, 1999: 29). The distinctive conversational style used with students has the advantage of being much more egalitarian in tone and spirit than many other therapies, and it focuses on young people "calling forth their best selves, rather than dwelling on, or disparaging their worst selves" (Winslade and Monk, 1999: 68). Deconstructive conversations challenge the dominant patterns of relating and so open possibilities and space for things to change. The way that narrative therapy involves "tentativeness rather than a knowing," and "seeks to subsume generalized professional knowledge beneath particularized, commonsense, or local knowledge" provides a type of relationship that is often contrary to the usual manner of relationships between adults and youth and between teachers and students (Winslade and Monk, 1999: 30). Rather than having their lives interpreted for them by "experts" or, worse, being told or persuaded what to think, a narrative conversation is based on a process of shared contributions between client and counselor.

Narrative counselors are expected to be vigilant about unthinkingly or dogmatically imposing their own cultural values on people or "colonizing" clients to their point of view. The motto: "The problem is the problem. The person is not the problem" (Winslade and Monk, 1999: 2) separates the person from the problem, freeing them to see things differently, to stop being disabled by the problem, to name it, and maybe to challenge it and how it has been taking over things in their lives. Positioning the problem as the problem rather than the student as the problem is often a quite radical separation for students and adults. It shifts the location of the problem and removes the all-too-common experience for students who, in both schools and in families, are so often blamed and shamed for misdemeanors and shortcomings in behavior, attitude, ability, and emotional maturity. Once students see things differently, they can stop blaming themselves and being disabled by the problem. Students not only find it freeing to name the problem, but they can sometimes even enjoy the process, especially if they find some irreverent name that objectifies and personifies the problem and is not censored by the counselor. By working out "sparkling moments" when the problem was not around, students are assisted to find alternative ways in which they prefer to describe themselves.

Using therapeutic documents such as certificates and letters harnesses the power of the written word and can often be an extremely powerful means of affirming a person's moves to deal with the problems in their lives (Payne, 2000; White, 1997, 2000). If a student gives permission, the narrative counselor might engage an audience that is significant to the student (perhaps sympathetic teachers, the dean, the principal, friends, church minister, priest, parents, etc.). The audience would hear and validate the student's reauthored story and support them in changes they have made and wish to maintain. The combination of these sorts of narrative techniques challenge the dominant discourses that position students as one sort of person, but the redescription positions them in a different way.

Fourth, Winslade and Monk (1999) suggest using social constructionist ways of viewing problems "as a story, or as a construction of reality" (Winslade and Monk, 1999: 118). Stories that have alternatives and unstoried experiences would be sought and highly valued. "Multiple and diverse perspectives would be thought of as enriching a community" (Winslade and Monk, 1999: 118). In supporting social constructionist viewpoints, the narrative approach does not accept that there is only one "true," authoritative account of life, so the type of knowing and expertise that so often characterizes how teachers deal with students is challenged. Teachers cannot be sure about what is in the best interests of students. Therefore they need to understand the various cultural worlds of their students to gain some element of understanding of how students make sense of their relationships with others. This indicates the possibility of acknowledging and addressing not only relationship problems within a school community, but also conflict and issues of diversity in multicultural schools.

Relationship difficulties and conflict often arise between students and between teachers and students. Apart from dealing with students' personal problems, school counselors are often expected to "fix" students who get into trouble in the classroom or the playground at school. Narrative therapy is not concerned with adjusting students to repressive disciplinary regimes that may inadvertently support social control mechanisms and hierarchies that obscure power relations, in turn marginalizing students. Nor does it liberally tolerate misbehavior as simply the result of the power operating. Instead, it engages in a respectful conversation, so the possibility of change is opened up for disruptive or misbehaving students. Winslade and Monk (1999) argue that in challenging students to change, traditional counseling approaches may not treat them respectfully but may, against their will, "colonize" them as "objects" of their punishment or of behavior modification interventions. For example, despite establishing strong, positive relationships with troubled youth, person-centered approaches are unlikely to be sufficient to produce enough leverage for students to change. Psychodynamic approaches are too slow in producing change when the situation is volatile or a crisis exists, and using cathartic methods to express feelings may sometimes unintentionally support abusive behavior (Winslade and Monk, 1999).

To address racism, teasing, bullying, sexist put-downs, violence, sexual harassment, and other abusive behaviors within school, a narrative counselor is likely to do several things (not in priority order). These things would not be limited to the counselor's office but would involve the wider social context of the school and its structures. One strategy would be to initiate conversations that open the possibility of transforming systems and structures so that school-wide policies and procedures prevent the abusive behavior, encouraging the school-wide community to take responsibility for a safe physical and emotional environment. Another would be separate counseling for the victim and for the abuser that would aim to avoid blame and shame. The victim would not be self-blaming nor be charged with the responsibility for developing new personal capacities to overcome the problem that might draw him/her into a vengeful or violent reaction. Instead, they would be assisted to recognize and condemn the injustice and the power issues involved. The abuser would be invited to address and change his or her behavior. Winslade and Monk (1999) argue that narrative therapy does not excuse abusive behavior but provides a way of "exploring and renegotiating a young person's relationship with trouble in a way that allows for the young person's preferences to be expressed (Winslade and Monk, 1999: 94). The narrative therapist, first, declines to attribute the responsibility for violence to factors beyond the person's influence; second, invites the person to challenge whatever restrains his/her ability to accept responsibility for his/her own actions; third, acknowledges and highlight all the evidence of how the person accepts responsibility for his/her own actions (Jenkins, 1990; Lewis and Cheshire, 1998). There might be a place for "narrative mediation" as opposed to a "problem-solving" mediation to occur if both parties agree to this (see Winslade and Monk 2000). There might well be a place for developing a school-wide support system using narrative-oriented forms. Selwyn College in

Auckland has developed a student-driven "antiharassment team" that involves peer mediation and school-wide consciousness-raising to deal with verbal, physical, and sexual harassment (see Lewis and Cheshire, 1998). Schools could also use similar forms of narrative-oriented support groups to help students to overcome various problems—for example, the anti-anorexia and bulimia league (Epston et al., 1995), fear-busters and monster-tamers club, the antisuspension league, and the combating truancy list (Winslade and Monk, 1999).

Fifth, Winslade and Monk (1999) suggest that the curriculum and evaluation processes would involve narrative thinking:

> Knowledge would always be taught as a cultural product rather than as absolute reality. Postmodern questions about the dominance of a particular narrow range of rational thinking as the one way to establish truth would be opened up for young people to think about. Power relations as they are expressed in discourse would become subjects of study. Evaluation methods would not focus in a judgmental way so strenuously on the individual, but would serve purposes of appreciating and elaborating conversations and communities. (Winslade and Monk, 1999: 118)

Narrative principles and techniques and ways of speaking and relating with students can be applied with individuals, with groups, or with classes. They can be used to change people's perceptions about a student or a class that has a negative label assigned to them or is in trouble or has a bad reputation. They can be used to teach and discuss sensitive or controversial topics that might crop up in health or social education lessons (for an example of a lesson plan for drug education, see Winslade and Monk, 1999).

Winslade and Monk acknowledge that they may appear idealistic, and overenthusiastic and may be dismissed as being out of touch with reality or fanciful dreamers. But they refute this in pointing out that they are in fact working to develop an alternative story that elaborates on what is already known. They maintain that narrative counseling is "tempered by, and even founded on, a rigorous analysis of the operation of power in people's lives" and that searching for "the possibilities of what already exists ensures that narrative optimism remains attuned to what is actual and positive" (Winslade and Monk, 1999: 119). In effect, they are applying a key theme of narrative therapy to the discourse of schools.

Narrative therapy in school counseling holds an obvious promise, both theoretically and in practice. First, it can accommodate the insights of Foucault concerning power-knowledge, power relations, and the constitution of the subject. But by drawing on Foucault's early work, the narrative approach fails to take account of its limitations and the importance on the ethical constitution of the self (Foucault, 1997a). Second, narrative therapy provides a theoretical approach that is to the forefront of developments in the social sciences, emphasizing the turn to narrative and the relationship between narrative, meaning, and the social, cultural, and political context. Third, this narrative model is a set of skills, attitudes and understandings that indicates the possibility of a narrative ethics around the central question of "Who speaks?" and highlights the political problem of "speaking for others." Fourth, narrative therapy utilizes a mode of knowledge that children of all ages find accessible, familiar, and easy to assimilate to their own experience. Fifth, narrative, in both its written and oral forms, provides a mode of knowledge that, developed sensitively, can accommodate different cultures. Further work, of course, needs to be done in relation to the conditions of narrative therapy in school counseling in cross-cultural settings, and, indeed, on all the positive features outlined above. It is good to know that we will not run out of work!

NOTES

CHAPTER 2

1. The term "metanarrative" was coined by French poststructuralist Jean-François Lyotard in *The Postmodern Condition* (1984) and means an overarching or grand-scale concept or idea.
2. "Hegemony" is based on Antonio Gramsci's theory about how dominance is maintained in advanced capitalist societies. Hegemony refers to the way certain social groups maintain dominance over other subordinate groups not by coercion as such, but by imposing a set of dominant rules and ideas, so that the power of the dominant ideology, group, or class appears both legitimate and natural. Hegemony is maintained as long as dominant groups succeed in framing all competing definitions within their orbit, controlling or at least containing subcultures within a space that appears permanent and part of the "natural" order of things, lying outside history and particular interests, but a space that is in fact ideological (see Hebdige, 1979).
3. Dr. Robert Havighurst, developmental and social psychologist, University of Chicago, visited the University of Canterbury in 1953 to investigate the ideologies and moral reasoning of New Zealand adolescents (see Havighurst, 1953b). He coproduced, with Athol Congalton, New Zealand's first scale of socioeconomic status (see Small, 2000).
4. "*In loco parentis*" in New Zealand dates from the Neglected and Criminal Children Act, 1873, where the Master of any Industrial School "became *in loco parentis* to children of parents who, because of their criminal and dissolute habits, were unfit to have guardianship of their children" (Mazengarb Report, 1954: 55). This notion implies a duty of care that teachers are considered to have in place of parents while children are at school and while going to/from school. This could potentially be in conflict with counsellor confidentiality, especially if the counsellor is dealing with young children (see chapter 6; see also Hawkins and Monk, 1995; Ludbrook, 1991; Nelson-Agee, 1997).
5. These lectures were from Foucault's seminar, "Discourse and Truth," at the University of California, Berkeley, in the Fall Term of 1983; they were edited by Joseph Pearson in 1985. Foucault did not write, correct, or edit any part of the text, which is primarily a verbatim transcription of the lectures from the notes of one of the attendees (website <www.repb.net>; accessed 25 November, 2001; now published as Foucault, 2001).
6. Pierre Hadot held the chair of the History of Hellenistic Studies and Roman Thought at the Collège de France.

CHAPTER 3

1. The *DSM IV*, published by American Psychiatric Association (APA, 1994), provides an authoritative, comprehensive classification of all recognized mental disorders. More than 1,000 clinicians and researchers contributed to this revision, which followed on from and updated earlier editions. It responded to criticisms of earlier versions by putting more emphasis on cultural influences, development across the life span, and substance abuse disorders.
2. In the nineteenth century, Puritan morality linked with social concerns to create the Poor Laws and campaigns against drunkenness and immorality in the slums of industrial England. Amid a concern for "saving" and correcting children, education came to be seen to play an important part.
3. The *DSM IV* repeated the definition it had provided in the *DSM III* and *DSM III-R*, defining mental disorder as: "a clinically significant behavior or psychological syndrome or pattern that occurs in an individual and that is associated with present distress (e.g., a painful symptom) or disability (i.e., impairment of one or more important areas of functioning) or with a significantly increased risk of suffering death, pain, or disability, or an important loss of freedom. In addition this syndrome or pattern must not be merely an expectable and

culturally sanctioned response to a particular event, for example the death of a loved one. Whatever its original cause, it must currently be considered a manifestation of a behavioral, psychological, or biological dysfunction in the individual. Neither deviant behavior (e.g. political, religious, or sexual) nor conflicts that are primarily between the individual and society are mental disorders unless the deviance or conflict is a symptom of a dysfunction in the individual as described above" (APA, 1994: xxi–xxii).

4. Existential philosophers include Søren Kierkegaard, Edmund Husserl, Jean-Paul Sartre, and Martin Heidegger; other theorists who could be considered to operate from an existential position include R. D. Laing, Martin Buber, and Paul Tillich.
5. "Inscribed" is used in *Discipline and Punish* (Foucault, 1977) when referring to the public torture and execution of Damiens in 1757. Foucault discusses the use of torture as a form of punishment: "the tortured body is first inscribed in the legal ceremonial that must produce, open for all to see, the truth of the crime" (p. 35). The *Concise Oxford Dictionary* refers to *inscribe* as meaning: "write (words etc. *in, on*, stone, metal, paper etc.); enter name of (person) in book (esp. for presentation)."

CHAPTER 4

1. The Mazengarb Report comments on the use of the term "delinquent" and its application in New Zealand as follows: "The idea of treating children who misbehaved as "delinquents" rather than as offenders against the law arose in Illinois in 1899. This experiment in social welfare was followed in other Sates of America, and the principle was introduced into New Zealand in 1925 [The Child Welfare Act, 1925]" (Mazengarb Report, 1954: 55).
2. Foucault consistently rejected being described as "postmodernist" because he tried to avoid the binary oppositions involved in the "modernist–postmodernist" debate, attempting to get beyond this. He often said that he did not even understand the term (Foucault, 1984b).
3. Kahane (1997) argues that young people are able to live in multiple worlds— for example, those of child and adult—thus overcoming their marginal status and exemplifying what he calls "liminality" as a unique postmodern development.

CHAPTER 5

1. The NZAC team that assisted in formulating this consisted of Helen Bowbyes, Ada Crowe, Bryan Lawrence, Jean Martel, and Sue Webb (NZAC, 1997).
2. Wilson's project at the Farmington Trust Unit, Oxford, incorporated "philosophical insights into the nature of morals, psychological evidence related to moral development, and sociological evidence related to the influence of home, peers, church and school in developing moral character" (Wilson, Williams, and Sugarman, cited in Snook, 1972: 71).
3. An example of the connection can be found in Charles K. Clarke [1857–1924], a famous Canadian psychiatrist, medical director of the Canadian National Committee for Mental Hygiene, and a leading proponent of immigration restriction, a eugenic cause. Clarke's personal prejudices, cultural factors, and a shift in psychiatric practice from working with the insane in asylums to the prevention of insanity among the general public led to his support for immigration restriction (see Dowbiggin, 1995).
4. For a discussion of the eugenics movement in New Zealand, see Peddie (1995).
5. Maryland Department of Health and Mental Hygiene; Johns Hopkins University Department of Mental Hygiene; Research Fund for Mental Hygiene, New York; Mental Hygiene Law, 1998, New York, known as the Alcohol and Substance Abuse Act.
6. The author was involved in both the steering and the management committees in Waitakere City that developed this model of "best practice"; it was renamed "effective practice" and was subsequently taken over by Strengthening Families.
7. Volunteer teen actors came from Chicago, where Coronet was based, and from Lawrence, Kansas, where Centron was based (Smith, 1999).
8. For example Dick York, who played the male lead, Darrin Stephens, in the television series *Bewitched* (Smith, 1999).

9. The Committee was: Dr. Oswald Mazengarb Q.C. (Chairman), Mrs. Rhoda Bloodworth, J.P. (Children's Court), Mrs. Lucy O'Brien (vice-president of Women's Auxiliary of Inter-Church Council on Public Affairs; Arch-Diocesan president, Catholic Women's League), Mr. James Leggat (Headmaster, Christchurch Boys' High School), Dr. Gordon McLeod (Director, Division of Child Hygiene, Department of Health), Mr. Nigel Stace (President, NZ Junior Chamber of Commerce), and Rev. John Somerville (Chairman, Inter-Church Council on Public Affairs). According to Yska (1993), Somerville and Stace were the only members under 45 and Stace (age 39) despite being well past what could in any way be considered "youth" had nevertheless been asked to represent youth.
10. Statistics for child offenses (juvenile delinquency) for 20 years, from 1934 to 1954, were provided by the Superintendent of Child Welfare Division and listed in the Mazengarb Report (1954), p. 15. The prewar rate (1934–1938) per 10,000 of population aged 10–17 years was between 73 and 105; in the war years (1940–44) it was 107–113; postwar (1946–1954) it was 83–81, with the lowest figure during this period being 66 in 1950.
11. Bowlby was influenced by the earlier work of his colleague, Donald Winnicott (a student of psychoanalyst, Melanie Klein) that had popularized maternal deprivation theory (Molloy, 1993).

CHAPTER 6

1. ASCA is American School Counseling Association, ACA is American Counseling Association, NZAC is new Zealand Association of Counsellors, BACP is British Association of Counseloors and Psychotherapists, CAC is Canadian Association of Counsellors.
2. Hawaii, Minnesota, Nevada, and New York currently have no licensure statutes. California's licensure law no longer refers to professional counselors but has recently been modified to refer to licensed marriage and family therapists (<http://www.counseling.org/ resources/ licensure_legislation.htm> 2001).
3. Rose and Milton Friedman, James Buchanan, Gordon Tullock, and Gary Becker established the "Chicago School."
4. The numbers of school counselors reached around 400 in 1990. By 1995, overall membership totaled 1,544, with 400 (25%) school counselors, 530 (30%) in private practice (*NZAC Annual Report, 1994–95*). In 2000 there were over 2,000 members, but the number of school counselors remains at around 400 (figures obtained from the NZAC Executive Officer). To date, despite being in the minority, they still play a major role as officers at both branch and national levels and have support groups in several branches. To ensure representation, there is a specific school counseling portfolio on the national executive among other portfolios.
5. Personal communication (1999) with Janet Irwin, former convenor of Ethics Committee.
6. Bob Manthei, Head of Counselling, University of Canterbury, New Zealand, personal communication.

CHAPTER 7

1. Michael White works at the Dulwich Centre, in Adelaide, Australia, and David Epston works at the Family Therapy Centre in Auckland, New Zealand. Their theory is presented in two coauthored books, *Literate Means to Therapeutic Ends* (White and Epston, 1989), repeated in *Narrative Means to Therapeutic Ends* (White and Epston, 1990). Although the first two chapters are clearly written by White, referring in pages 1 and 38 to "I (MW)" and chapters 3 and 4 by Epston, I reference both authors, since the cover of their 1990 book categorically states, "coauthors" and the chapters are not specifically attributed to either one or the other. The Introduction (1990) talks briefly about the collaboration and general agreement between the two, hence the coauthorship of the books.

2. This chapter uses the 1990 text, which does not differ substantially from the 1989 text, apart from a few minor wording changes, some footnotes either deleted or incorporated into the text; the fact that the 1989 text references four of Foucault's texts and the 1990 text eight; and the fact that the 1990 text includes a previously published chapter from *Selected Papers* (White, 1989). David Epston considers it preferable to cite the 1990 text (personal communication, 24 Sept. 2001).
3. Much of the knowledge, understanding, and meanings about the world of Australian Aboriginal people, including ideas about dream-time are sung in song-lines. In New Zealand, the Maori term *korero* means speech-making, *whakatauki* means proverbs, and *whakapapa* means genealogy. These are examples of ways in which these cultures used the skills of oral language to communicate their cultural identity.
4. Ian Hacking (1999) discusses social construction as a code embroiled in "the culture wars" and "the science wars" that dominate intellectual life.
5. David Epston (1989) points out that this is a maxim that Michael White uses and one that he has taken over to describe "externalizing the problem."

REFERENCES AND BIBLIOGRAPHY

Abbott, A. D. (1988). *The System of Professions: An Essay on the Division of Expert Labor*. Chicago, IL: University of Chicago Press.

Allport, G. (1954). The historical background of modern social psychology. In G. Lindzey (Ed.), *Handbook of Social Psychology*. Cambridge, MA: Addison Wesley: 1–80.

APA (1962). American Psychological Association, Committee on Definition, Division of Counseling Psychology: Counseling psychology as a specialty, *American Psychologist*, 11: 282–285; cited in J. F. McGowan and L. D. Schmidt (eds.), *Counseling: Readings in Theory and Practice*. New York: Holt, Rinehart & Winston: 14–19.

APA (1994). *Diagnostic and Statistical Manual of Mental Disorders: DSM-IV* (4th ed.). Washington, DC: American Psychiatric Association.

Ariès, P. (1962). *Centuries of Childhood*. New York: Knopf.

Audi, R. (1995). *The Cambridge Dictionary of Philosophy*. Cambridge: Cambridge University Press.

Ausubel, D. (1954). *Theory and Problems of Adolescent Development*. New York: Grune and Stratton.

Ausubel, D. (1960). *The Fern and the Tiki: An American View of New Zealand National Character, Social Attitudes and Race Relations*. London: Angus & Robertson.

Bakan, D. (1971). Twelve to sixteen: Early adolescence. In R. Grinder (ed.), *Studies in Adolescence: A Book of Readings* (3d ed.). New York: Macmillan: 3–15.

Baker, B. (2001). *In Perpetual Motion: Theories of Power, Educational History, and the Child*. New York: Peter Lang.

Bandura, A. (1977). *Social Learning Theory*. Englewood Cliffs, NJ: Prentice-Hall.

Bandura, A. (1986). *Social Foundations of Thought and Action: A Social Cognitive Theory*. Englewood Cliffs, NJ: Prentice-Hall.

Bandura, A. (1997). *Self-efficacy: The Exercise of Control*. New York: W. H. Freeman.

Bateson, G. (1972). *Steps to an Ecology of Mind*. New York: Ballantine Books.

Bateson, G. (1980). *Mind and Nature: A Necessary Unity*. New York: Bantam Books.

Beautrais, A. L., Coggan, C. A., Fergusson, D. M., and Rivers, L. (1998). *Young People at Risk of Suicide: A Guide for Schools*. Wellington: Ministry of Education & National Advisory Committee on Health and Disability.

Becker, G. (1964). *Human Capital: A Theoretical and Empirical Analysis, with Special Reference to Education*. New York: National Bureau of Economic Research/Columbia University Press.

Benedict, R. (1938). Continuities and discontinuities in cultural conditioning, *Psychiatry*, 1: 161–167.

Benedict, R. (1950). *Patterns of Culture*. New York: New American Library.

Berger, P., and Luckmann, T. (1966). *The Social Construction of Reality*. New York: Doubleday.

Besley, A. C. (2000). *Self, Identity, Adolescence and the Professionalisation of School Counselling in New Zealand: A Foucauldian-inspired Approach*. Ph.D. Thesis, University of Auckland.

Bettelheim, B. (1969). *The Children of the Dream*. London: Macmillan.

Bhabha, H. K. (1990). *Nation and Narration*. London/New York: Routledge.

Bird, J. (2000). *The Heart's Narrative: Therapy and Navigating Life's Contradictions*. Auckland: Edge Press.

Bond, T. (1992). Ethical issues in counselling in education. *British Journal of Guidance and Counselling*, 20 (1): 51–63.

Bond, T. (1993). *Standards and Ethics for Counselling in Action*. London: Sage.

Boston, J. (ed.) (1995). *The State under Contract*. Wellington: Bridget Williams Books.

Boston, J., and Dalziel, P. (eds.) (1992). *The Decent Society? Essays in Response to National's Economic and Social Policies*. Auckland: Oxford University Press.

Boston, J., Martin, J., Pallot, J., and Walsh, P. (1996). *Public Management: The New Zealand Model*. Auckland: Oxford University Press.

Bowlby, J. (1947). *Forty-Four Juvenile Thieves: Their Characters and Home-Life.* London: Baillière.
Bowlby, J. (1953). *Child Care and the Growth of Love.* Abridged and edited by M. Fry. Harmondsworth: Penguin Books.
Bowlby, J. (1969). *Attachment and Loss.* London: Hogarth Press/Institute of Psycho-Analysis.
Bowlby, J. (1979). *The Making and Breaking of Affectional Bonds.* London: Tavistock Publications.
Bronfenbrenner, U. (1979). *The Ecology of Human Development: Experiments by Nature and Design.* Cambridge, MA: Harvard University Press.
Bronfenbrenner, U. (1986). Ecology of the family as a context for human development: research perspectives. *Developmental Psychology,* 22: 723–742.
Brown, J. (1999). Does guidance have a future? Notes towards a distinctive position. *British Journal of Guidance and Counselling,* 17 (2): 275–282.
Brown, J. A. C. (1954). *The Social Psychology of Industry.* Harmondsworth: Penguin.
Brown, L. M., and Gilligan, C. (1992). *Meeting at the Crossroads: Women's Psychology and Girls' Development.* Cambridge, MA: Harvard University Press.
Bruner, E. (1986a). Ethnography as narrative. In V. Turner and E. Bruner, *The Anthropology of Experience.* Chicago, IL: University of Illinois Press.
Bruner, E. (1986b). Experience and its expressions. In V. Turner and E. Bruner, *The Anthropology of Experience.* Chicago, IL: University of Illinois Press.
Bruner, J. (1986). *Actual Minds, Possible Worlds.* Cambridge, MA: Harvard University Press.
Bruner, J. (1990). *Acts of Meaning.* Cambridge, MA: Harvard University Press.
Bryant, P. (1974). *Perception and Understanding in Young Children: An Experimental Approach.* London: Methuen.
Buchanan, J., and Tullock, G. (1962). *The Calculus of Consent: Logical Foundations of Constitutional Democracy.* Ann Arbor, MI: University of Michigan Press.
Butler, J. (1990). *Gender Trouble: Feminism and the Subversion of Identity.* New York: Routledge.
Caplan, P. (1979). Erikson's concept of inner space: a data-based re-evaluation. *American Journal of Orthopsychiatry,* 49: 100–108.
Caplan, P. (1995). *They Say You're Crazy.* Reading, MA: Addison-Wesley.
Caplow, T. (1966). The sequence of professionalization. In H. M. Vollmer and D. L. Mills (eds.), *Professionalization.* Englewood Cliffs, NJ: Prentice-Hall.
Cioffi, F. (ed.) (1973). *Freud: Modern Judgements.* London: Macmillan.
Cohen, P. (1972). Sub-cultural conflict and working class community. *Working Papers in Cultural Studies,* 2 (University of Birmingham, U.K).
Cohen, S. (1980). *Folk Devils and Moral Panics: The Creation of the Mods and Rockers* (2d ed.). New York: St. Martin's Press.
Coleman, J. S. (1960). The adolescent subculture and academic achievement. *American Journal of Sociology,* 65: 337–347.
Coleman, J. S. (1961). *The Adolescent Society.* New York: Free Press.
Coleman, J. S. (1965). *The Adolescent and the Schools.* New York: Basic Books.
Coleman, J. S. Bremner, R. H, Burton, C. R., Davis, J. B., Eichorn, P. H., Grilchos, Z., Kett, J. F., Ryder, N. B., Doering, Z. B., and Mays, J. M. (1974). *Youth: Transition to Adulthood.* Chicago, IL: University of Chicago Press.
Cooper, J. M. (1999). *Reason and Emotion: Essays on Ancient Moral Psychology and Ethical Theory.* Princeton, NJ: Princeton University Press.
Corey, G., Corey, M. S., and Callinan, P. (1993). *Issues and Ethics in the Helping Professions* (4th ed.). Pacific Grove, CA: Brooks/Cole.
Côté, J. E., and Allahar, A. L. (1994). *Generation on Hold: Coming of Age in the Late 20th Century.* New York/London: New York University Press.
Crocket, A. (1992). Complaints: How they are being dealt with now—steps towards evolving a new set of procedures, *NZAC Newsletter,* 13 (3): 38–40.
Davidson, A. I. (1997). Introductory remarks to Pierre Hadot. In A. I. Davidson (ed.), *Foucault and His Interlocutors.* Chicago, IL/London: University of Chicago Press: 195–202.
Davis, A. (1944). Socialization and the adolescent personality. In *Adolescence, Yearbook of the National Society for the Society of Children for the Study of Education,* 43 (Part 1).
de Mause, L. (ed.) (1974). *The History of Childhood.* New York: Knopf.
Dennettt, D. C. (1991). *Consciousness Explained.* Boston, MA: Little, Brown and Co.
Derrida, J. (1982). *Margins of Philosophy.* Chicago, IL: University of Chicago Press.

Descartes, R. ([1642] 1986). *Meditations on First Philosophy. With Selections from the Objections and Replies.* Trans. John Cottingham, Introduction by Bernard Williams. Cambridge/New York: Cambridge University Press.

Donaldson, M. (1978). *Children's Minds.* Glasgow: Fontana Collins.

Donzelot, J. (1980). *The Policing of Families: Welfare versus the State.* Trans. R. Hurley, Foreword by Gilles Deleuze. London: Hutchinson.

Dowbiggin, I. (1995). "Keeping this young country sane": C. K. Clarke, immigration restriction, and Canadian psychiatry, 1890–1925. *Canadian Historical Review,* 76 (4): 598–628.

Drewery, W., and Winslade, J. (1997). The theoretical story of narrative therapy. In G. Monk, J. Winslade, K. Crocket, and D. Epston (eds.), *Narrative Therapy in Practice: The Archaeology of Hope.* San Francisco, CA: Jossey-Bass: 32–52.

Dreyfus, H. L., and Rabinow, P. (1982). *Michel Foucault: Beyond Structuralism and Hermeneutics.* Afterword by Michel Foucault. Brighton: Harvester Press & University of Chicago Press.

Ellis, A. (1971). *Growth Through Reason: Verbatim Cases in Rational-Emotive Therapy.* Palo Alto, CA: Science and Behavior Books.

Epston, D. (1989). *Collected Papers.* Adelaide: Dulwich Centre.

Epston, D., Morris, F, and Maisel, R. (1995). A narrative approach to so-called anorexia/bulimia. In K. Weingarten (ed.), *Cultural Resistance: Challenging Beliefs about Men, Women, and Therapy.* New York: Haworth: 69-96.

Epston, D., & White, M. (eds.) (1992). *Experience, Contradiction, Narrative and Imagination.* Adelaide: Dulwich Centre.

Erikson, E. (1963). *Childhood and Society* (2d ed.). New York: W. W. Norton.

Erikson, E. (1968). *Identity, Youth, and Crisis.* New York: W. W. Norton.

Erikson, E. (1977). *Toys and Reasons: Stages in the Ritualization of Experience.* New York: W. W. Norton.

Erikson, E. (1980). *Identity and Life-cycle.* New York: W. W. Norton.

Etzioni, A. (ed.) (1969). *The Semi-Professions and Their Organization; Teachers, Nurses, Social Workers.* New York: Free Press.

Everts, J. (1987). Professional counselling in New Zealand—the developmental challenge. *New Zealand Counselling and Guidance Journal,* 9 (1): 1–7.

Foucault, M. (1965). *Madness and Civilization: A History of Insanity in the Age of Reason.* Trans. Richard Howard. London: Routledge.

Foucault, M. (1970). *The Order of Things.* New York: Random House.

Foucault, M. (1972). *The Archaeology of Knowledge.* Trans. A. M. Sheridan. London: Tavistock.

Foucault, M. (1973). *The Birth of the Clinic: An Archaeology of Medical Perception.* Trans. A. M. Sheridan. London: Tavistock.

Foucault, M. (1977). *Discipline and Punish: The Birth of the Prison.* London: Penguin.

Foucault, M. (1979a). *Power, Truth, Strategy.* Sydney: Feral Publications.

Foucault, M. (1979b). On governmentality. *Ideology and Consciousness,* 6: 5–21.

Foucault, M. (1980a). *The History of Sexuality, Vol. I.* New York: Vintage.

Foucault, M. (1980b). The confession of the flesh. In C. Gordon (ed.), *Power/ Knowledge: Selected Interviews and Other Writings 1972–1977 by Michel Foucault.* Hemel Hempstead: Harvester Wheatsheaf: 194–228.

Foucault, M. (1980c). Two lectures. In C. Gordon (ed.), *Power/Knowledge: Selected Interviews and Other Writings 1972–1977 by Michel Foucault.* Hemel Hempstead: Harvester Wheatsheaf: 78–108.

Foucault, M. (1980d). *Power/Knowledge: Selected Interviews and Other Writings 1972-1977 by Michel Foucault.* Edited by C. Gordon. Hemel Hempstead: Harvester Wheatsheaf.

Foucault, M. (1982). The subject and power. In H. Dreyfus, and P. Rabinow (eds.), *Michel Foucault: Beyond Structuralism and Hermeneutics.* Brighton: Harvester Press: 208–226.

Foucault, M. (1984a). Polemics, politics and problematisation. In P. Rabinow (ed.), *The Foucault Reader.* New York: Pantheon Books.

Foucault, M. (1984b). Space, knowledge and power. In P. Rabinow (ed.), *The Foucault Reader.* New York: Pantheon Books.

Foucault, M. (1984c). Nietzsche, genealogy, history. In P. Rabinow (ed.), *The Foucault Reader.* New York: Pantheon Books.

Foucault, M. (1984d). What is Enlightenment? In P Rabinow (ed.), *The Foucault Reader*. New York: Pantheon Books.

Foucault, M. (1984e). On the genealogy of ethics: An overview of a work in progress. In P. Rabinow (ed.), *The Foucault Reader*. New York: Pantheon Books.

Foucault, M. (1984f). Truth and power. In P. Rabinow (ed.), *The Foucault Reader*. New York: Pantheon Books. [e changed to f - old msp 218 was 2001]

Foucault, M. (1985). *The Use of Pleasure: The History of Sexuality, Vol. 2*. New York: Vintage.

Foucault, M. (1988a). Truth, power, self: an interview. In L. H. Martin, H. Gutman, and P. H. Hutton (eds.), *Technologies of the Self*. Amherst, MA: University of Massachusetts Press.

Foucault, M. (1988b). Technologies of the self. In L. H. Martin, H. Gutman, and P. H Hutton (eds.), *Technologies of the Self*. Amherst, MA: University of Massachusetts Press.

Foucault, M. (1988c). The political technology of individuals. In L. H. Martin, H. Gutman, and P. H. Hutton (eds.), *Technologies of the Self*. Amherst, MA: University of Massachusetts Press.

Foucault, M. (1989a). An ethics of pleasure. In *Foucault Live (Interviews, 1966– 84)*. Trans J. Johnston, edited by S. Lotringer. Columbia University, NY: Semiotext(e): 257–277.

Foucault, M. (1989b). The concern for truth. In *Foucault Live (Interviews, 1966– 84)*. Trans J. Johnston, edited by S. Lotringer. Columbia University, NY: Semiotext(e): 293–308.

Foucault, M. (1989c). The aesthetics of existence. In *Foucault Live (Interviews, 1966–84)*. Trans J. Johnston, edited by S. Lotringer. Columbia University, NY: Semiotext(e): 309–316.

Foucault, M. (1989d). The Return of Morality. In *Foucault Live (Interviews, 1966–84)*. Trans J. Johnston, edited by S. Lotringer. Columbia University, NY: Semiotext(e): 317–331.

Foucault, M. (1989e). Sorcery and madness. In *Foucault Live (Interviews, 1966– 84)*. Trans J. Johnston, edited by S. Lotringer. Columbia University, NY: Semiotext(e): 107–111.

Foucault, M. (1989f). An historian of culture. In *Foucault Live (Interviews, 1966–84)*. Trans J. Johnston, edited by S. Lotringer. Columbia University, NY: Semiotext(e): 73–88.

Foucault, M. (1989g). The archeology of knowledge. In *Foucault Live (Interviews, 1966-84)*. Trans J. Johnston, edited by S. Lotringer. Columbia University, NY: Semiotext(e): 45-56.

Foucault, M. (1990). *The Care of the Self: The History of Sexuality, Vol. 3*. London: Penguin.

Foucault, M. (1991). Governmentality. In G. Burchell, C. Gordon, and P. Miller (eds.), *The Foucault Effect: Studies in Governmentality—With Two Lectures by and an Interview with Michel Foucault*. Hemel Hempstead: Harvester Wheatsheaf: 87–104.

Foucault, M. (1997a). The ethics of the concern for self as a practice of freedom. Trans. R. Hurley et al. In P. Rabinow (ed.), *Michel Foucault: Ethics, Subjectivity and Truth: The Essential Works of Michel Foucault 1954–1984, Vol. 1*. London: Penguin: 281–301.

Foucault, M. (1997b). Writing the self. In A. Davidson (ed.), *Foucault and His Interlocutors*. Chicago, IL: University of Chicago Press: 234–247.

Foucault, M. (2001). *Fearless Speech*. Edited by J. Pearson. New York: Semiotexte; Los Angeles, CA: Semiotext(e).

Freedman, J., and Combs, G. (1996). *Narrative Therapy: The Social Construction of Preferred Realities*. New York: W. W. Norton.

Freeman, D. (1983). *Margaret Mead and Samoa: The making and Unmaking of an Anthropological Myth*. Canberra: Australian National University Press.

Freud, A. (1946). *The Ego and the Mechanisms of Defense*. Trans. C. Baines. New York: International University Press.

Freud, S. (1953). *A General Introduction to Psychoanalysis*. Trans. W. Riviere. New York: Permabooks.

Friedman, M. (1962). *Capitalism and Freedom*. With the assistance of Rose D. Friedman. Chicago, IL: University of Chicago Press.

Fromm, E. (1982). *Greatness and Limitations of Freud's Thought*. London: Abacus.

Gallup, G., and Rae, S. F. (1940). *The Pulse of Democracy: The Public Opinion Poll and How It Works*. New York: Simon and Schuster.

Geertz, C. (1983). *The Interpretation of Cultures*. New York: Basic Books.

Gergen, K. J (1990). Therapeutic professions and the diffusion of deficit. *Journal of Mind and Behaviour*, 11 (3–4): 353–368.

Gergen, K. J. (1991). *The Saturated Self: Dilemmas of Identity in Contemporary Life*. New York: Basic Books.

Gergen, K. J. (1994). *Realities and Relationships: Soundings in Social Construction.* Cambridge, MA: Harvard University Press.

Gergen, K. J. (1995). The social constructionist movement in modern psychology. *American Psychologist*, 40: 266–275.

Gergen, K. J. (2001). *Social Construction in Context.* London: Sage.

Gergen, M. M., and Gergen, K. J. (1984). The social construction of narrative accounts. In K. J. and M. M. Gergen (eds.), *Historical Social Psychology.* Hillsdale, NJ: Lawrence Erlbaum Associates.

Gesell, A., and Ames, L. B. (1956). *Youth: the Years 10–16.* New York: Harper & Row.

Gilligan, C. (1982). *In a Different Voice: Psychological Theory and Women's Development.* Cambridge, MA: Harvard University Press.

Giroux, H. (1990). *Curriculum Discourse as Postmodern Critical Practice.* Geelong: Deakin University Press.

Glasser, W. (1965). *Reality Therapy.* New York: Harper & Row.

Glasser, W. (1984). *Take Effective Control of Your Life.* New York: Harper & Row.

Glazebrook, S. (1978). *The Mazengarb Report, 1954: Impotent Victorianism.* M.A. Thesis, University of Auckland.

Goffman, E. (1961). *Asylums: Essays in the Social Situation of Mental Patients and Other Inmates.* New York: Doubleday.

Goffman, E. (1969). *The Presentation of Self in Everyday Life.* London: Allen Lane.

Goldson, J. (1978). *The Problem of Meaning at Adolescence.* M.A. Thesis, University of Auckland.

Goode, E., and Ben-Yehuda (1994). *Moral Panics: The Social Construction of Deviance.* Oxford/Cambridge, MA: Blackwell.

Gordon, C. (1991). Governmental rationality: an introduction. In G. Burchell, C. Gordon, and P. Miller (eds.), *The Foucault Effect: Studies in Governmentality.* Hemel Hempstead: Harvester Wheatsheaf.

Hacking, I. (1981). The archaeology of Foucault. *The New York Review*, May 14: 32–36.

Hacking, I. (1999). *The Social Construction of What?* Cambridge, MA: Harvard University Press.

Hadot, P. ([1987] 1995). "Spiritual exercises" and "Reflections on the idea of the 'Cultivation of the self'." In *Philosophy as a Way of Life.* Trans. Michael Chase, edited and Introduction by Arnold Davidson. Oxford: Blackwell: 83–125, 206–213.

Hall, S., and Jefferson, T. (eds.) (1976). *Resistance through Rituals: Youth Subcultures in Post-War Britain.* London: Hutchinson.

Hall, S. G. (1905). *Adolescence: Its Psychology and Its Relations to Physiology, Anthropology, Sociology, Sex, Crime, Religion, and Education.* New York: Appleton.

Harré, R. (1983). *Personal Being.* Oxford: Blackwell.

Harré, R. (1986). The step to social constructionism. In M. Richards and P. Light (eds), *Children of Social Worlds.* Cambridge: Polity Press.

Havighurst, R. J. (1953a). *Human Development and Education.* New York: McKay.

Havighurst, R. J. (ed.) (1953b). *Studies of Children and Society in New Zealand.* Christchurch: Canterbury University College.

Havighurst, R. J. (1972). *Developmental Tasks and Education* (3d ed.). New York: McKay.

Hawkins, H., and Monk, G. (1995) School counselling: An ethical minefield? *NZ Journal of Counselling,* 16 (1): 1–7.

Hayek, F. (1944). *The Road To Serfdom.* London: Routledge & Kegan Paul.

Hebdige, D. (1979). *Subculture: The Meaning of Style.* London: Methuen.

Heidegger, M. ([1927] 1993). *Being and Time.* In D. F. Krell (ed.), *Martin Heidegger: Basic Writings.* London: Routledge.

Hermansson, G. L. (1990). It won't be long: Counselling and guidance poised for the nineties. In J. Small and T. Ambrose (eds.), *Counselling and Guidance towards the Nineties.* Palmerston North: Massey University/ NZAC: 162–173.

Hermansson, G. L. (1999). *Pieces of Silver: 25 Years of the New Zealand Counselling and Guidance Association/New Zealand Association of Counsellors.* Hamilton: New Zealand Association of Counsellors.

Hook, S. (1968). John Dewey: His philosophy of education and its critics. In R. D. Archambault (ed.), *Dewey on Education: Appraisals.* New York: Random House: 127—159. hooks, b. (1984). *Feminist Theory: From Margin to Center.* Cambridge: Polity Press.

Hoyt, K. B. (1991). Concerns about accreditation and credentialing: A personal view. In F. O. Bradley (ed.), *Credentialling in Counselling*. Alexandria, VA: American Association for Counseling and Development.

Hughes, M. (1986). *Children and Number: Difficulties in Learning Mathematics*. Oxford: Blackwell.

Hume, D. ([1739] 1977). *A Treatise of Human Nature*. Introduction by A. D. Lindsay. London: Dent; New York: Dutton.

Hummel, D. L, Talbutt, L. C., and Alexander, M. D. (1985). *Law and Ethics in Counseling*. New York: Van Norstrand Reinhold.

Illich, I (1977). *Disabling Professions*. London/Salem, NH: M. Boyars.

Irigaray, L. (1993). *An Ethic of Sexual Difference*. Trans. C. Burke and G. C. Gill. London: Athlone Press.

Ivey, A. E, Ivey, M. B, and Simek-Downing, L. (1987). *Counseling and Psychotherapy: Integrating Skills, Theory, and Practice* (2d ed.). Englewood Cliffs, NJ: Prentice-Hall.

James, A., Jenks, C., and Prout, A. (1998). *Theorizing Childhood*. Cambridge: Polity Press.

Jameson, F. (1981). *The Political Unconscious: Narrative as a Socially Symbolic Act*. Ithaca, NY: Cornell University Press.

Jameson, F. (1984). Postmodernism, or, The cultural logic of late capitalism, *New Left Review*, 146: 53–92.

Jenkins, A. (1990). *Invitations to Responsibility: The Therapeutic Engagement of Men Who Are Violent and Abusive*. Adelaide: Dulwich Centre.

Johnson, B. (Ed.) (1993). *Freedom and Interpretation*. New York: Basic Books.

Jones, A. (1977). *Counselling Adolescents in School*. London: Kogan Page.

Kahane, R. (1997). *The Origins of Postmodern Youth: Informal Youth Movements in a Comparative Perspective*. In collaboration with T. Rapoport. Berlin/New York: Walter de Gruyter.

Kamenka, E. (1978). The anatomy of an idea. In E. Kamenka and A. Erh-Soon Tay (eds.), *Human Rights*. New York: St. Martin's Press: 1–12.

Kellner, D. (1992). Popular culture and the construction of postmodern identities. In S. Lash and J. Friedman (eds.), *Modernity and Identity*. Oxford/Cambridge, MA: Blackwell.

Kelly, G. (1955). *The Psychology of Personal Constructs, Vols. 1, 2*. New York: W. W. Norton.

Kelsey, J. (1993). *Rolling Back the State: The Privatisation of power in Aotearoa/ New Zealand*. Wellington: Bridget Williams Books.

Kelsey, J. (1995). *The New Zealand Experiment: A World Model for Structural Adjustment?* Auckland: Auckland University Press/Bridget Williams Books.

Kitchener, K. S. (1984). Intuition, critical evaluation and ethical principles: The foundation of ethical decisions in counseling psychology. *Counseling Psychologist*, 12 (3): 43–55.

Kohlberg, L. (1970). Stages of moral development as a basis for moral education. In T. Sizer (ed.), *Moral Education*. Toronto: University of Toronto Press.

Kohlberg, L. (ed.) (1977). *Assessing Moral Development*. Cambridge, MA: Center for Moral Education, Harvard University.

Kroger, J. (1996). *Identity in Adolescence*. London & New York: Routledge.

Kundera, M. (1984). *The Unbearable Lightness of Being*. Trans. from the Czech by M. Henry. London: Faber.

Kundera, M. (1998). *Identity*. Trans. from the French by L. Asher. London: Faber.

Kvale, S. (ed.) (1992). *Psychology and Postmodernism*. London: Sage.

Lasch, C. (1979). The Culture of Narcissism: American Life in an Age of Diminishing Expectations. London: Abacus.

Lasch, C. (1984). *The Minimal Self: Psychic Survival in Troubled Times* (1st ed.). New York: W. W. Norton.

Lavelle, B. M. G. (1990). *Youth without Purpose: Juvenile Delinquency in New Zealand in the late 1950s*. M.A. Thesis, University of Otago.

Lesko, N. (1996). Denaturalizing adolescence: The politics of contemporary representations, *Youth and Society*, 28 (2): 139–161.

Lévi-Strauss, C. (1966). *The Savage Mind*. Chicago, IL: University of Chicago Press.

Lewin, K., Lippitt, R., & White, R. (1939). Patterns of aggressive behaviour in experimentally created "social climates." *Journal of Social Psychology*, 10: 271–299.

Lewis, D., and Cheshire, A. (1998). Taking the hassle out of school: The work of the anti-harassment team of Selwyn College. *Dulwich Centre Journal,* 1998 (2, 3): 4–58.

Lifton, R. J. (1993). *The Protean Self: Human Resilience in an Age of Fragmentation.* New York: Basic Books.

Light, P, and Simmons, B. (1983). The effects of a communication task upon the representation of depth relationships in young children's drawings. *Journal of Experimental Child Psychology,* 35: 81–92.

Lippitt, R. (1939). Field theory and experiment in social psychology: Autocratic and democratic group atmospheres. *American Journal of Sociology*, 45: 26–49.

Lippitt, R. (1940). Studies on experimentally created autocratic and democratic groups. *University of Iowa Studies: Studies in Child Welfare*, 16 (3): 45–198.

Locke, J. (1964). *An Essay Concerning Human Understanding.* Abridged, edited, and introduced by A. D. Woozley. London: Collins.

Ludbrook, R. (1991). *A New Zealand Guide to Children and the Law.* Wellington: Imprint Ltd.

Luke, A. (2000). The jig is up: An alternative history of psychology or why current concepts of identity and development are part of the problem rather than part of the solution, *NZAC Newsletter*, 20 (3): 12–26.

Lyotard, J.-F. (1984). *The Postmodern Condition: A Report on Knowledge.* Trans. G. Bennington and B. Massumi. Manchester: Manchester University Press.

Lyotard, J.-F. (1988). *The Differend: Phrases In Dispute*. Trans. G. Van Den Abbeele, Foreword by W. Godzich. Manchester: Manchester University Press.

Mabe, A. R., and Rollin, S. A. (1986). The role of a code of ethical standards in counseling, *Journal of Counseling and Development,* 64: 294–297.

Macey, D. (1993). *The Lives of Michel Foucault.* London: Hutchinson.

Mandell, W. (n.d.). *The Realization of an Ideal.* Department of Mental Hygiene and Johns Hopkins University. http://mh.jhsph.edu/.

Manthei, R. J. (1989). The certification of professional counsellors recommendation: drop the idea. *NZCGA Journal,* 11 (1): 34–38.

Manthei, R. J. (1997a). NZAC: Setting standards or policing practices? *NZAC Newsletter*, 18 (1): 44–45.

Manthei, R. J. (1997b). NZAC: Renewing membership. Who measures up? *NZAC Newsletter*, 18 (2): 12–13.

Marcia, J. E. (1966). Development and validation of ego identity status. *Journal of Personality and Social Psychology*, 3: 551–558.

Marcia, J. E. (1980). Identity in adolescence. In J. Adelson (ed.), *Handbook of Adolescent Psychology.* New York: Wiley.

Marcia, J. E. (1993). The relational roots of identity. In J. Kroger (ed.), *Discussions on Ego Identity.* Hillsdale, NJ: Lawrence Erlbaum Associates.

Marcia, J. E. (1994). Ego identity and object relations. In J. Masling and R. F. Bornstein (eds.), *Empirical Perspectives on Object Relations Theory.* Washington, DC: American Psychological Association.

Marshall, J. D. (1996). *Michel Foucault: Personal Autonomy and Education.* Dordrecht/Boston: Kluwer Academic Publishers.

Marshall, J. D. (1997). Michel Foucault: Problematising the individual and constituting "the self." *Educational Philosophy and Theory,* 29 (1): 20– 31. Special issue: *Education and the Constitution of Self,* edited by M. Peters, J. Marshall, and P. Fitzsimons.

Marshall, J. D., and Marshall, D. (1997). *Discipline and Punishment in New Zealand Education.* Palmerston North: Dunmore Press.

Maslow, A. (1968). *Toward a Psychology of Being* (2d ed.). New York: Van Nostrand.

Mazengarb Report (1954). *Report of the Special Committee on Moral Delinquency in Children and Adolescents.* Wellington: Government Printer.

McGeorge, P. (1995). *Child, Adolescent and Family Mental Health Services.* Wellington: Ministry of Health.

McGowan, J. F., and Schmidt, L. D. (1962). Counseling: Readings in Theory and Practice. New York: Holt, Rinehart & Winston.

McLaren, P. (1989). Life in Schools: An Introduction to Critical Pedagogy in the Foundations of Education. New York & London: Longman.

McLeod, J. (1997). *Narrative and psychotherapy.* London: Sage.
McLeod, J. (2000a). The development of narrative-informed theory, research and practice in counselling and psychotherapy: European perspectives. *European Journal of Psychotherapy Counselling and Health,* 3 (3): 331–333.
McLeod, J. (2000b). Foreword. In M. Payne (ed.), *Narrative Therapy: An Introduction for Counsellors.* London: Sage.
McMillan, B. W. (1991). All in the mind: Human learning and development from an ecological perspective. In J. Morss and T. Linzey (eds.), *Growing Up: The Politics of Human Learning.* Auckland: Longman Paul: 30–45.
McNay, L. (1992). *Foucault and Feminism: Power, Gender and The Self.* Cambridge: Polity Press.
McRobbie, A. (1980). Settling accounts with subculture: A feminist critique. *Screen Education,* no. 39 (Spring); also in A. McRobbie, *Feminism and Youth Culture: From "Jackie" to "Just Seventeen"* London: Macmillan, 1991: 16–34.
McRobbie, A. (1991). *Feminism and Youth Culture: From "Jackie" to Just seventeen."* London: Macmillan.
McRobbie, A., and Garber, J. (1976). Girls and subcultures: An exploration. In S. Hall and T. Jefferson (eds.), *Resistance through Rituals: Youth Subcultures in Post-War Britain.* London: Hutchinson: 209–222; also in A. McRobbie, *Feminism and Youth Culture: From "Jackie" to "Just Seventeen"* London: Macmillan, 1991: 1–15..
Mead, M. (1928). *Coming of Age in Samoa: A Psychological Study of Primitive Youth for Western Civilisation.* New York: Morrow Quill.
Mearns, D., and Thorne, B. (1999). *Person-Centred Counselling in Action* (2d ed.). London: Sage.

Melucci, A. (1997). Identity and difference in a globalized world. In P. Werbner and T. Modood (eds.), *Debating Cultural Hybridity: Multi-Cultural Identities and the Politics of Anti-Racism.* London: Zed Books: 58–69.
Middleton, S. (1998). *Disciplining Sexuality: Foucault, Life Histories, and Education.* New York: Teachers College Press/Columbia University.
Mill, J. S. (1961). *Essential Works of John Stuart Mill.* Edited by M. Lerner. New York: Bantam.
Miller, J. H. (1994). Professionalisation in counselling: Are we in danger of losing our way? *New Zealand Journal of Counselling,* 16 (2): 7–13.
Miller, J. H. (1996). From unity to diversity: An account of the growth, development, and change in the NZAC as identified through the association newsletters. *New Zealand Journal of Counselling,* 18 (2): 36– 49.
Ministry of Education (1995). *Report of the Career Information and Guidance Review Panel* [Lynch Report]. Wellington: Learning Media.
Ministry of Education (1997). *Performance Management Systems—No 5: Specialist Teachers.* Wellington.
Ministry of Education (1999a). *Professional Standards: Criteria for Quality Teaching—Secondary School Teachers and Unit Holders.* Wellington.
Ministry of Education (1999b). *Health and Physical Education in the New Zealand Curriculum.* Wellington: Learning Media.
Ministry of Education (1999c). Teacher Performance Management: A resource for boards of trustees, principals and teachers. Wellington.
Moi, T. (1986). *The Kristeva Reader.* Oxford: Blackwell.
Molloy, M. (1993). Science, myth and the adolescent female: The Mazengarb Report, the Parker-Hulme trial and the Adoption Act of 1955. *Women's Studies Journal,* 9 (1): 1–25.
Monk, G. & Drewery, W. (1994). The impact of social constructionist thinking on eclecticism in counsellor education: Some personal thoughts. *New Zealand Journal of Counselling,* 16 (1): 5–14.
Monk, G., Winslade, J., Crocket, K., and Epston, D. (eds.) (1997). *Narrative Therapy in Practice: The Archaeology of Hope.* San Francisco, CA: Jossey-Bass.
Morss, J. (1991). After Piaget: Rethinking "Cognitive Development." In J. Morss and T. Linzey (eds.), *Growing Up: The Politics of Human Learning.* Auckland: Longman Paul: 9–29.
Morss, J. (1996). *Growing Critical: Alternatives to Developmental Psychology.* London & New York: Routlege.
Nava, M. (1991). *Changing Cultures: Feminism, Youth and Consumerism.* Newberry Park, CA: Sage.

Nelson-Agee, M. (1997). Privacy and the school counsellor, *Access*, 16 (1): 20– 36.
Niemeyer, R. A. (1993). An appraisal of constructivist therapies, *Journal of Consulting and Clinical Psychology*, 61 (2): 221–234.
Nietzsche, F. ([1887] 1956). *The Genealogy of Morals*. Trans. F. Golffing. New York: Doubleday.
Nietzsche, F. (1961). *Thus Spoke Zarathustra: A Book for Everyone and No One*. Trans. and Introduction by R. J. Hollingdale. Harmondsworth: Penguin.
Nightingale, D. J., and Cromby, J. (eds.) (1999). *Social Constructionist Psychology: A Critical Analysis of Theory and Practice*. Buckingham: Open University Press.
Nilson, H. (1998). *Michel Foucault and the Games of Truth*. Trans. R. Clark. New York: St Martin's Press.
NZAC (1992). *NZAC Newsletter*, 13 (2).
NZAC (1995). *NZAC Handbook*. Hamilton: New Zealand Association of Counsellors.
NZAC (1997). *NZAC Newsletter*, 18 (2).
NZAC (1998). *NZAC Newsletter*, 19 (4).
NZAC (2000). *NZAC Handbook*. Hamilton: New Zealand Association of Counsellors.
NZAC (2001). *NZAC Newsletter*, 22 (1).
O'Loughlin, M. (1997). Corporeal subjectivities: Merleau-Ponty, education and the "postmodern" subject. *Educational Philosophy and Theory*, 29 (1): 32–49. Special issue: *Education and the Constitution of Self*, edited by M. Peters, J. Marshall, and P. Fitzsimons. Olssen, M. (1999). *Michel Foucault: Materialism and Education*. Westport, CT: Bergin & Garvey.
Onega, S., and Landa, J. A. G. (eds.) (1996). *Narratology: An Introduction*. London/New York: Longman. Parry, A., and Doan, R. (1994). *Story Re-Visions: Narrative Therapy in the Postmodern World* New York: Guilford Press.
Parsons, F. (1909). *Choosing a Vocation*. Boston: Houghton Mifflin.
Parsons, T. (1951). *The Social System*. London: Routledge & Kegan Paul.
Payne, M. (2000). *Narrative Therapy: An Introduction for Counsellors*. London: Sage.
Pearson, J. (1985). Discourse and truth: The problematization of parrhesia— lectures by M. Foucault. Edited by Pearson. <http://www.repb.net>.
Peddie, W. S. (1995). *Alienated by Evolution: The Educational Implications of Creationist and Social Darwinist Reactions in New Zealand to the Darwinian Theory of Evolution*. Ph.D. Thesis, University of Auckland.
Peters, M. A. (1996). *Poststructuralism, Politics and Education*. Westport, CT: Bergin & Garvey.
Peters, M. A. (1999). Neo-liberalism. In M. A. Peters and P. Ghiraldelli, Jr. (eds.), *Encyclopedia of Philosophy of Education*. <http:// www.educacao.pro.br>.
Peters, M. A. (2001a). *Poststructuralism, Marxism, and Neoliberalism: Between Theory and Politics*. Lanham, MD: Rowman & Littlefield.
Peters, M. A. (2001b). *Truth-Telling as an Educational Practice of the Self*. Paper presented at University of Bath, 29 November.
Peters, M. A. (2002). Education and the philosophy of the body: Bodies of knowledge and knowledges of the body. In L. Bresler and J. Davidson, (eds.), *Knowing Bodies, Feeling Minds: Embodied Knowledge in Arts Education and Schooling*. Forthcoming.
Peters, M. A., and Marshall, J. D. (1995). Education and empowerment: Postmodernism and the critique of humanism. In P. McLaren (ed.), *Postmodernism, Postcolonialism and Pedagogy*. Albert Park: James Nicholas: 205–225.
Peters, M. A., and Marshall, J. D. (1996). *Individualism and Community: Education and Social Policy in the Postmodern Condition*. London: Falmer Press.
Peters, M. A., and Marshall, J. D. (1999). *Wittgenstein: Philosophy, Postmodernism, Pedagogy*. Westport, CT: Bergin & Garvey.
Peters, R. S. (1967). *Ethics and Education*. Atlanta, GA: Scott, Foresman.
Piaget, J. (1952). *The Origins of Intelligence in Children*. New York: International Universities Press.
Piaget, J. (1954). *The Construction of Reality in the Child*. New York: Basic Books.
Propp, V. (1968). *Morphology of the Folktale*. Trans.L.Scott, Introduction by S.Pirkova-Jakobson. Second ed., revised and edited and with Preface by L.A. Wagner, new Introduction by A. Dundes. Austin, TX: University of Texas Press.
Quine, W. (1963). *From a Logical Point of View*. New York, Harper & Row.
Rabinow, P. (1984). *The Foucault Reader*. New York: Pantheon.
Rabinow, P. (1997). Preface and Afterword. In *Michel Foucault: Ethics, Subjectivity and Truth, The*

Essential Works of Michel Foucault 1954–1984, Vol. 1. Edited by P. Rabinow, trans. R. Hurley et al. London: Penguin.
Ramazanoglu, C. (ed.) (1993). *Up Against Foucault: Explorations of Some Tensions between Foucault and Feminism.* London & New York: Routledge.
Renwick, W. L. (1972). Guidance in secondary schools. Part II. *Education,* 21 (9): 10–17.
Ritchie, J., and Ritchie, J. (1970). *Child Rearing Patterns in New Zealand.* Wellington: A. H. and A. W. Reed.
Ritchie, J., and Ritchie, J. (1981). *Spare the Rod.* Sydney: George Allen & Unwin. Ritchie, J., and Ritchie, J. (1990). *Violence in New Zealand.* Wellington: Allen & Unwin.
Robertson, P. (1974). Home as a nest: Middle class childhood in nineteenth-century Europe. In L. de Mause (ed.), *The History of Childhood.* New York: Knopf: 406–431.
Rogers, C. R. (1942). *Counseling and Psychotherapy.* Boston: Houghton Mifflin.
Rogers, C. R. (1961). *On Becoming a Person.* Boston: Houghton Mifflin.
Rogers, C. R. (1969). *Freedom to Learn.* Columbus, Ohio: Merrill.
Rorty, R. (ed.) (1967). *The Linguistic Turn: Recent Essays in Philosophical Method.* Edited & Introduction by R. Rorty. Chicago, IL: University of Chicago Press.
Rose, N. S. (1989). *Governing the Soul: The Shaping of the Private Self.* London: Routledge.
Rose, N. S. (1998). *Inventing Our Selves: Psychology, Power, and Personhood.* Cambridge: Cambridge University Press.
Rosenberg, S. (1997). Multiplicity of selves. In D. Ashmore and L. Jussim (eds.), *Self and Identity: Fundamental Issues.* New York: Oxford University Press: 23–45.
Rowbotham, S. (1973). *Woman's Consciousness, Man's World.* Harmondsworth: Pelican.
Said, E. W. (1978). *Orientalism* (1st ed.). New York: Pantheon Books.
Said, E. W. (1993). *Culture and Imperialism* (1st ed.). New York: Knopf.
Sartre, J-P. (1948). *Existentialism and Humanism.* London: Methuen.
Sartre, J-P. (1966). *Being and Nothingness.* New York: Pocket Books.
Searle, J. R. (1995). *The Construction of Social Reality.* New York: Free Press.
Sellars, W. (1963). *Science, Perception, Reality.* London: Routledge & Kegan Paul.
Shklovsky, V. (1991). *Theory of Prose.* Trans. B. Sher, Introduction by G. R. Bruns. Elmwood Park, IL: Dalkey Archive Press.
Shotter, J. (1993). *Cultural Politics of Everyday Life.* Hemel Hempstead: Open University Press.
Shuker, R. (1987). Youth culture and youth rhythms. *Sites,* 14: 108–115.
Shuker, R., Openshaw, R., and Soler, J. (1990). *Youth Media and Moral Panic in New Zealand: From Hooligans to Video Nasties.* Delta Research Monograph. Palmerston North: Massey University.
Siegel, H. (1991). Indoctrination and education. In B. Spiecker, and R. Straughan (eds.), *Freedom and Indoctrination in Education: International Perspectives.* London: Cassell.
Skinner, B. F. (1953). *Science and Human Behaviour.* New York: Macmillan.
Skinner, B. F. (1961). *Cumulative Record.* New York: Appleton-Century-Crofts.
Small, J. J. (1981). The function of guidance in education. In G. L. Hermansson (ed.), *Guidance in New Zealand Secondary Schools: Issues and Programmes.* Palmerston North: Massey University/New Zealand Counselling and Guidance Association.
Small, J. J. (2000). *Almost a Century: Educational Studies at the University of Canterbury 1904–1999.* Christchurch: University of Canterbury.
Smart, B. (1985). *Michel Foucault.* London/New York: Tavistock Publications.
Smith, C., and Nylund, D. (1997). *Narrative Therapies with Children and Adolescents.* New York: Guilford Press.
Smith, K. (1999). *Mental Hygiene: Classroom Films 1945–1970.* New York: Blast Books.
Snook, I. A. (1972). *Indoctrination and Education.* London: Routledge & Kegan Paul.
Sökefeld, M. (1999). Debating self, identity, and culture in anthropology. *Current Anthropology,* 40 (4, Aug.–Oct.): 417–447.
Soler, J. (1988). *Drifting Towards Moral Chaos: The 1954 Mazengarb Report. A Moral Panic Over Juvenile Delinquency.* M.Phil. Thesis, University of Waikato.
Soler, J. (1989). That incredible document known as the Mazengarb Report. *Sites,* 19: 22–32.
Speedy, J. (2000). The "storied" helper. *European Journal of Psychotherapy Counselling and Health,* 3 (3): 361–374.

Spiecker, B. (1991). Indoctrination: The suppression of critical dispositions. In B. Spiecker and R. Straughan (eds.), *Freedom and Indoctrination in Education: International Perspectives.* London: Cassell.

Spivak, G. C. (1999). *A Critique of Postcolonial Reason: Toward a History of the Vanishing Present.* Cambridge, MA: Harvard University Press.

Sprinthall, N. A., and Collins, W. A. (1984). *Adolescent Psychology: A Developmental View.* Reading, MA: Addison-Wesley.

Stoler, A. L. (1995). *Race and the Education of Desire: Foucault's History of Sexuality and the Colonial Order of Things.* Durham, NC: Duke University Press.

Stone, L. (2001). *Misunderstanding, Reading and "Misreading": Foucault's Ethics of the Subject, Relational Sex, and Political (and Educational) Possibility.* Paper presented at AERA, SIG Foucault in Education, Seattle, WA.

Strawson, G. (1997). The self. *Journal of Consciousness Studies*, 4 (5/6): 405–428.

Strengthening Families (1999). *Newsletter*, 8 (May).

Strike, K. A., and Ternasky, P. L. (1993). *Ethics for Professionals in Education: Perspectives for Preparation and Practice.* New York: Teachers College Press.

Sweet, G. (1997). Tea party time with an optimist. NZAC Newsletter, 18 (1): 56-57.

Szasz, T. (1973). The Manufacture of Madness: A Comparative Study of the Inquisition and the Mental Health Movement. Frogmore: Paladin.

Szasz, T. (1979). The Myth of Psychotherapy: Mental Healing as Religion, Rhetoric *and Repression.* Oxford: Oxford University Press.

Tait, G. (2000). *Youth, Sex, and Government.* New York: Peter Lang.

Taylor, C. (1985). *Sources of the Self: The Making of Modern Identity.* Cambridge, MA: Harvard University Press.

Taylor, J. M., Gilligan, C., and Sullivan, A. M. (1995). *Between Voice and Silence: Women and Girls, Race and Relationship.* Cambridge, MA: Harvard University Press.

Tennyson, W. M., and Strom, S. M. (1986). Beyond professional standards: Developing responsibleness, *Journal of Counseling and Development*,
64: 294–297. Thompson, K. (1998). *Moral Panics.* London/New York: Routledge. Vollmer,
H. M., and Mills, D. L. (eds.) (1966). *Professionalization.* Englewood
Cliffs, NJ: Prentice-Hall.

Vygotsky, L. S. (1962). *Thought and Language.* Edited and trans. by E. Hanfmann and G. Vakar. Cambridge, MA: MIT Press.

Vygotsky, L. S. (1978). *Mind in Society: The Development of Higher Psychological Processes.* Edited by M. Cole et al. Cambridge, MA: Harvard University Press.

Wadsworth, E. J. (1970). The role of the school counsellor, *New Zealand Social Worker*, 6: 13–21.

Walkerdine, V. (1984). Developmental psychology and the child centred pedagogy. In J. Henriques et al., *Changing the Subject.* London: Methuen: 157–174.

Walkerdine, V. (1986). Post structural theory and everyday social practices: The family and the school. In S. Wilkinson (ed.), *Feminist Social Psychology: Developing Theory and Practice.* Milton Keynes: Open University Press: 51–68.

Walkerdine, V. (1987). Sex, power and pedagogy. In M. Arnot and G. Weiner (eds.), *Gender and the Politics of Schooling.* London: Hutchinson: 166–174.

Walkerdine, V. (1988). *The Mastery of Reason: Cognitive Development and the Production of Rationality.* London: Routledge.

Watson, J. B. (1913). Psychology as the behaviourist views it. *Psychological Review*, 20: 158.

Webb, S. B. (1998). NZAC—Counting for something, *NZAC Newsletter*, 18 (4): 11–16.

White, H. (1987). The Content of Form: Narrative Discourse and Historical Representation. Baltimore, MD: Johns Hopkins University Press.

White, M. (1989). *Selected Papers.* Adelaide: Dulwich Centre.

White, M. (1991). Deconstruction and Therapy, *Dulwich Centre Newsletter, New Zealand Counselling and Guidance Journal,* 3: 21–40.

White, M. (1992). Deconstruction and therapy. In D. Epston and M. White (eds.), , *Contradiction, Narrative and Imagination.* Adelaide: Dulwich Centre Publications.

White, M. (1995). *Re-authoring Lives: Interviews and Essays.* Adelaide: Dulwich Centre.

White, M. (1997). *Narratives of therapists' lives.* Adelaide: Dulwich Centre.

White, M. (2000). *Reflections on narrative practice: essays and interviews.* Adelaide: Dulwich Centre.

White, M., and Epston, D. (1989). *Literate Means to Therapeutic Ends.* Adelaide: Dulwich Centre.
White, M., and Epston, D. (1990). *Narrative Means to Therapeutic Ends.* New York: W. W. Norton.
Wilcoxon, A. S. (1987). Ethical standards: a study of application and utility, *Journal of Counseling and Development*, 65: 510–511.
Willis, P. (1977). *Learning to Labour.* Aldershot: Saxon House.
Willis, P. (1978). *Profane Culture.* London: Routledge & Kegan Paul.
Winnicott, D. W. (1971). Adolescence: struggling through the doldrums, *Adolescent Psychiatry*, 1: 40–51.
Winslade, J. (1997). Worries about increased surveillance of members, *NZAC Newsletter*, 18 (2): 14–17.
Winslade, J. (1998). Ethics Committee. *NZAC Annual Report 1998.*
Winslade, J., and Monk, G. (1999). *Narrative Counseling in Schools: Powerful and Brief.* Thousand Oaks, CA: Corwin Press.
Winslade, J., and Monk, G. (2000). *Narrative Mediation: A New Approach to Conflict Resolution.* San Francisco, CA: Jossey-Bass.
Winterbourn, R. (1974). *Guidance Services in New Zealand Education.* Wellington: New Zealand Council for Educational Research.
Wittgenstein, L. (1953). *Philosophical Investigations.* Oxford: Blackwell.
Wylie, P. (1942). *Generation of Vipers.* New York: Rinehart.
Wyn, J., and White, R. (1997). *Rethinking Youth.* London: Sage.
Yska, R. (1993). *All Shook Up: The Flash Bodgie and the Rise of the New Zealand Teenager in the Fifties.* Auckland: Penguin.

WEBSITES

ACA website: <http://www.counseling.org/>.
ASCA website: <www.schoolcounseling.org>.
CAC website: <www.ccacc.ca/coe.htm>.
Narrative therapy website: <http://www.massey.ac.nz/~Alock/virtual/ narrativ.htm>.
NZAC website: <www.nzac.org.nz/>.
U.S. legislation website (2001): <http://thomas.loc.gov/>.

INDEX